Africa After Gender?

EDITED BY
CATHERINE M. COLE,
TAKYIWAA MANUH,
AND STEPHAN F. MIESCHER

Africa After Gender?

INDIANA UNIVERSITY PRESS

Bloomington and Indianapolis

This book is a publication of

Indiana University Press
601 North Morton Street
Bloomington, IN 47404-3797 USA

http://iupress.indiana.edu

Telephone orders 800-842-6796
Fax orders 812-855-7931
Orders by e-mail iuporder@indiana.edu

Library of Congress Cataloging-in-Publication Data

Africa after gender? / edited by Catherine M. Cole, Takyiwaa Manuh, and Stephan F. Miescher.
    p. cm.
  Includes bibliographical references and index.
  ISBN 0-253-34816-1 (cloth : alk. paper) — ISBN 0-253-21877-2 (pbk. : alk. paper) 1. Sex role—Africa. 2. Sex role—Research—Africa. I. Cole, Catherine M. II. Manuh, Takyiwaa. III. Miescher, Stephan.
  HQ1075.5.A35A35 2007
  305.3096—dc22

                                                                              2006019762

                    1 2 3 4 5   12 11 10 09 08 07

Contents

Acknowledgments

A project of this scope comes to fruition only through the collaborative energies of many dedicated individuals and the financial generosity of institutions. The initial impetus for the book came from a conference entitled "Africa After Gender? An Exploration of New Epistemologies for Africa Studies," hosted by the Interdisciplinary Humanities Center's African Studies Research Focus Group at the University of California, Santa Barbara, in April 2001. Additional conference funding was provided by the University of California Humanities Research Institute in Irvine. Though we have only published here a few of the papers presented at the conference, we are grateful to all those who attended, for their ideas and interest spurred us to pursue the topic further. Support for editing the book was provided by the Academic Senate and the College of Letters and Sciences of UCSB as well as by the Ford Foundation. These institutions enabled the editors to meet in Accra and Santa Barbara. We especially want to thank our fine editorial assistants: first Adrienne MacIain and Teresa Algoso, then Bianca Murillo whose contribution in the final phase of completing this manuscript allowed two of the editors to travel and pursue their research. Thanks also to two anonymous readers. Dee Mortensen at Indiana University Press expressed an interest in this book early on but also asked the hard questions which helped us develop the final shape of this collection; Kate Babbitt has been a model copy editor—we are grateful to both of them.

Africa After Gender?

Introduction: When Was Gender?

Stephan F. Miescher, Takyiwaa Manuh, and
Catherine M. Cole

In scholarship—as in real estate—location matters. This is especially true in the field of African gender studies. During the past two decades, the relationship between gender studies scholars based in Africa and those based in North America and Europe has been strained, even explosive. This is due in part to differences in political environments and experiences of racism, as well as interpretations of feminist ideologies and different political alliances and coalitions. North-South tensions erupted at a historic women's studies conference in Nigeria in 1992, the first international conference on Women in Africa and the African Diaspora (WAAD). Convener Obioma Nnaemeka was driven by a concern about the commodification of African women in women's studies and feminist scholarship and "their marginalization in the process of gathering, articulation, and disseminating knowledge" (1998a, 354). Nnaemeka brought together scholars and activists from inside and outside Africa. On the first day, three unanticipated controversies exploded: 1) a demand for the exclusion of white participants, 2) an objection to the presence of men, and 3) an ideological fight over different currents of feminism, such as (Northern/white) feminism, womanism, and Africana womanism.

This episode serves as a revealing entry point into the themes and objectives of *Africa After Gender?* At the WAAD conference, identity politics drove much of the controversy: African-American and British-African participants first raised the possibility of excluding the handful of whites who attended. Their concerns illustrated, as Nnaemeka describes it, "the complexity and heterogeneity of the category 'woman'/'black woman'" (1998a, 369). Most African participants, especially the Nigerian hosts, as well as some Diaspora Africans rejected the exclusion of whites. Participants from Southern Africa were, as one might expect, divided. The controversy revealed the powerful violence of racism that has affected people of African descent anywhere, from the Western hemisphere to Cape Town. However, as Nnaemeka argues, it also showed that in order for protests to be "strategically relevant," they must be well chosen in terms of location and moment. Dialogues should not be abandoned for insurgency, "unless we have proven the inefficacy of the former" (ibid.). When, in her keynote address, Ama Ata Aidoo embraced the label "feminist," she was urged by an African American to abandon the term and instead endorse "Africana womanism" (Aidoo 1998; Nnaemeka 1998a, 370). Generally, African participants were less interested in semantics, and they prioritized actions over the rhetoric of *naming* their struggles. Some foreign participants objected to the participation of male presenters. However, many African women responded that they had successfully collaborated with male scholars and activists in their joint endeavors for societal change. These divergent views on participation at the conference demonstrated how much location matters in the constitution of women's studies and feminist scholarship. Sex-based and race-based exclusionary practices in the United States and Europe, such as the all-female classroom or the all-black organization, have a different meaning in most African settings. While separate gendered spaces including schools have a long history, political demands focus less on such gender divisions. Rather, activists struggle for improved health and education for African women. These were for many participants the main priority of the conference.[1]

The controversies that emerged at the WAAD conference provide an interesting case study that highlights the difficulty of forming coalitions around women's and gender issues. One can see the artificiality of any blanket statements about "women" in Africa which earlier generations of scholars were tempted to make in the face of an African studies discipline that had been overwhelmingly masculinist.[2] Yet the WAAD conference also showed the strength of these alliances, for activists, bureaucrats, and scholars from all over the continent and, indeed, the world, attended the conference in droves. Their participation, however fraught, provided tangible evidence that something dramatic and palpable was happening with women's and gender issues in Africa.

Gender is one of the most dynamic areas of Africanist research today, as is evident by a host of new journals, articles, and books dedicated to the topic. Interest in gender is not just academic: the subject has gained widespread currency among the general populace in Africa, from taxi drivers and market traders to policymakers. Aided by nongovernmental organizations (NGOs) and foreign assistance programs that claim the concept in their mission statements, gender has come to mean something in Africa, even if there is little agreement about *what* it actually means. Outside Africa—in Europe and North America—the term "gender" gained popularity in the wake of older monikers such as "women's studies" and "feminism" and came to the fore for several reasons: gender allowed for the study of men as well as women and it placed greater emphasis on relational analysis between the sexes. In addition, gender emphasized the difference between biological sex, on the one hand, and performed identities of masculinity and femininity, on the other. Furthermore, gender studies highlighted issues of sexuality, which had always been a theme in women's studies and feminism but were often subordinated to other concerns. Finally, gender was more palatable for the general public, who adopted it as a way to discuss women and equality that was more oblique than the politicized "feminism."

Gender's ascendancy as a discursive term in everyday life in Africa and as a field of study in research shares some features from elsewhere but also follows a distinctive path.[3] Unlike North America and Europe, where gender was introduced as a way to discuss both men and women, gender in Africa usually connotes women. As is true elsewhere, gender has been seen as a relatively nonthreatening concept, and the term became institutionalized within governments, private industry, and the academy to a degree that would have been unimaginable with feminism. Historically, many in Africa have been suspicious of feminism due to its origins in family structures, values, and social conditions that are not indigenous to Africa. Some have asked whether gender is just one more trend to hit the continent, ill suited to local contexts, full of biased assumptions from foreign lands.[4] Yet despite controversies, gender has been widely adopted—and adapted—in Africa.

Our book's title, *Africa After Gender?* poses a provocative question, one that is deliberately ambiguous. It suggests a temporal flow of ideas (a "before" and "after"), a possible teleology of progress (progressing through stages of development), or even the eclipse and demise of a discourse on gender in Africa that, as many know, has barely begun to take root. The interrogatory phrase is heuristic. Rather than suggest that gender has reached its useful shelf life in Africa, we wish to highlight its temporal location. "Gender" arrived in Africa and African studies only recently, and contributors ask us to consider how both the continent and the field have changed as a result of its arrival. The essays in this volume demand that we think critically and analytically about where "gender" came from, what kinds of knowledge it has and has not authorized in Africa, and how expansive or limiting the term might prove in future.

Africa After Gender? is driven by two overarching concerns: Our primary objective is to make a productive intervention in the dynamic of North-South relations, between scholars living and working in Africa and those who reside in Europe and North America. We wish to move the discourse on gender in Africa beyond simple dichotomies, entrenched debates, and the polarizing identity politics that have so paralyzed past discussions. We see transcontinental, multigendered, and multiracial collaboration as a crucial and necessary component in achieving a healthy North-South flow of information. Our editorial team includes an African, an American, and a European. We are gender mixed: two women and one man, of different sexualities. The book's contributors are also diverse: from Southern, East, and West Africa as well as the United Kingdom and the United States. Some contributors reside in their country of birth— whether that is Ghana, Uganda, or the United States—while others are transnational subjects, such as women from Nigeria and Cameroon and a man from Switzerland who all teach in the United States. The views of Africa presented here come from a variety of locations, races, genders, and ethnicities. We believe that this collaboration across identities and locations of knowledge production is a necessary and important intervention in the evolving discourse on gender in Africa.

Our second argument is that gender in Africa requires a genuinely interdisciplinary or, more precisely, transdisciplinary approach. More so than any other analytical social category—be it class, race, seniority, or ethnicity—gender has energized the scholarship about African contexts across the disciplines within the humanities and social sciences over the last twenty years. Yet even as respective disciplines have each contributed to the emerging field of gender studies in Africa, each has biases and omissions that become apparent only when work in one field is juxtaposed with alternate approaches. For example, literary studies usually assume that the relation of words to meaning is rarely transparent and perceive the importance of the author's or speaker's intention with great skepticism ("the intentional fallacy"). Literary scholars are trained to read against the grain of texts, deciphering layers of significance in narrative technique, tone, style, and genre. This appreciation for the expressive capacity and opacity of language is an important corrective to historical and social science scholarship, which often assumes a direct, transparent connection between word and meaning, between signifier and signified. On the other hand, literary scholars are often less sensitive to the specificities of different cultural and historical contexts as well the larger issue of continuities and change within historical transformations. These latter concerns, however, are much in the foreground in anthropological and historical studies. Thus, a transdisciplinary approach promises to overcome biases and omissions inherent within various disciplinary perspectives.

Interdisciplinarity is modeled in the production of *Africa After Gender?* itself: our editorial team includes a historian, a social scientist and legal scholar, and a critic of literature and the arts. Contributors are likewise equally drawn from the social sciences, humanities, and arts. In addition, we commissioned essays from scholars whose individual methodologies, objects of study, and theoretical orientations combine methods from two or more fields. Anthropologist Paulla Ebron, for instance, writes about films and the performance of oral tradition, looking at the ethnographic interview itself as a moment of gender performativity. Similarly, Susan Andrade, who is a literary critic, tackles a subject that is traditionally the domain of historians and political scientists—class formation and the history of protest among women in Africa—yet she uses the perspective of African women novelists as a point of entry into the subject.

Africa After Gender? features a combination of theoretical and empirical pieces. The volume has a particular focus on how gender works on the ground in African contexts and how this relates to or contrasts with theory. Exploring the usefulness and limitations of gender for Africa, contributors ask: How has gender as a research focus and teaching subject evolved in Africa? How has gender as a political agenda acquired new importance as NGOs and policymakers, among others, began using it as a badge and compass for their work? Have gender identities formerly seen as "imported" become indigenized through the processes of colonization and Christianization? How does masculinity studies fit into this emerging field? We focus in particular on alliances that are simultaneously fragile and strong, necessary and problematic: between activists and scholars (as described in Takyiwaa Manuh's essay on the institutionalization of gender in Ghana), between men and women (as Adrienne MacIain observes in her essay on Yorùbá theatre), between people of different sexualities (as seen in Sylvia Tamale's article on her attempts to build coalitions between women's rights and gay rights in Uganda), and between persons based in Africa and those moving between worlds (as seen in Nwando Achebe and Bridget Teboh's auto-biographical piece).

Africa After Gender? is organized around four themes: 1) volatile genders and new African women; 2) activism and public space; 3) gender enactments and gendered perceptions; and 4) masculinity, misogyny, and seniority. Each section reveals how a multidisciplinary approach to gender studies in Africa, a radically collaborative one in terms of the location of knowledge production, moves us far beyond the polarizing impasses of the past.

Volatile Genders and New African Women

Nearly every level of every society in Africa has seen extraordinary tu-mult in the twentieth and early twenty-first centuries, and gender identities have been a particularly vexed area of social transformation. The essays in this section depict the volatility of new gender identities, particularly those that arise from political coalitions and the introduction of formal education. For ex-ample, volatility is evident in public discourse around homosexual rights in Uganda (Tamale), gender coalitions across race and class in the "new" South Af-rica (Seidman), anxieties about pregnant schoolgirls in colonial Kenya (Thomas), and the unique constraints faced by African women who earn postgraduate de-grees abroad and return home to conduct research (Achebe and Teboh). African gender identities are volatile in two senses of the word: they are both precarious and explosive.

The most volatile case is provided by Sylvia Tamale, who documents the re-cent wave of homophobia she triggered in Uganda when she proposed that the Equal Opportunities Commission should address the rights of homosexuals as a marginalized social group. Tamale was personally vilified in local newspapers, and many intimated that her only interest in the issue was as a means to procure funding from the West. Tamale's activism opened the Pandora's box of not just the taboo subject of homosexuality but also the larger issue of sexuality and sexual rights. Tamale sees the state's legislation of heteronormativity as a vehicle for perpetuating patriarchy and enforcing women's subordination.

In a similar vein, a drive to reform the state prompted the creation of the South African Commission on Gender Equality in 1996. Formed in the wake of South Africa's new democracy, the commission embodied the nonracist and nonsexist principles of South Africa's new Constitution. Yet despite its promise and sustained efforts, the Commission on Gender Equality was in crisis only four years after its formation. As Gay Seidman reports, "By mid-2000, South Africa's feminist project was in obvious disarray" (this volume). The larger question that Seidman prompts us to ask is this: How can feminist agendas that used to occupy marginal spaces become successfully woven into democratic institutions? Given gender's ascendancy throughout the African continent, this line of inquiry is of profound significance.

Women in Africa are often seen as the carriers of culture and the procreative link between generations, a link that is both biological and spiritual. Women's access to formal education has been a particularly fraught area of gender transformation, as the social mobility and autonomy that education affords can threaten reproductive expectations and practices. Historian Lynn Thomas notes present-day anxieties about the timing and circumstances surrounding educated girls' conception of children and the way in which formal education has transformed local gender practices. Thomas reminds us of the importance of historicizing contemporary debates, for she demonstrates that present-day concerns over schoolgirl pregnancies derive from a long and sustained history of generational struggles in Kenya over health, wealth, and power. Thus, the "new African woman" is sometimes not as new as she might at first appear, and a historical perspective is essential to a fuller appreciation of present struggles.

Researchers Nwando Achebe and Bridget Teboh are themselves "new African women." Both women were born and raised in Africa, pursued doctoral training at leading U.S. universities, and have conducted research on women in their home communities in Africa. Both identify first as members of their ethnic groups, Igbo and Moghamo, respectively. Yet when situated in the North, they become "Africans" and Nigerian/Cameroonian nationals. Their outside location and training have not only affected their approaches to their research subjects, women in Igbo- and Moghamolands, but also their subjects' perception of them as female researchers. This essay leads one to question the dichotomies and facile identity politics that in the past have disrupted and even arrested discussions about gender in Africa. Identities are complexly constituted, as racial and national identities are enmeshed with ethnicity. North-South divisions are transformed and deeply complicated through the movement of transnational subjects and African women's active role in the production of knowledge about African women. What becomes evident here is that although location does matter, it determines neither who one is nor what and how one thinks.

Activism and Public Space

Discourses on gender in Africa, as elsewhere in the world, are inextricably connected to demands for equal rights and access to resources. Essays by Sylvia Tamale and Gay Seidman in the first section provide a glimpse of the struggles and internal dynamics of such activism, which is riven with fault lines that may come clearly into focus only in the very heat of political action. Literary critic Susan Andrade puts such struggles in a historical context, and she also guides us to see the connection between historical facts of African women's activism and literary representations of that activism. Andrade draws our attention to the gap between African women who wrote novels in English and French and their literary subjects, including plebeian women who engaged in gender-marked rebellion across the continent. Andrade demonstrates the disciplinary particularities of how African women are read and interpreted, given her own perspective on the tendency toward the celebratory within the field of African literary scholarship. We note that this celebratory tendency can also be seen in other disciplines, such as the early work on women in African history.

The link between fiction and fact and women's role in the public sphere can also be seen in the essay by performance scholar Adrienne MacIain, who analyzes gendered conflicts on the public stage of Yorùbá popular theater in Nigeria. This genre is famous for its negative female stereotypes and conservative patriarchal ideologies. Using an invaluable and understudied collection of Yorùbá plays transcribed and translated by Karin Barber and Báyò Ògúndíjo (1994), MacIain draws our attention to the preponderance of negative female stereotypes in the Adéjobì theatre company's repertoire. She identifies one play, *Láníyonu*, as aberrant within the repertoire due to its sympathetic female characters and representation of a marriage based upon an amicable partnership between husband and wife. MacIain speculates about the historical circumstances of this play, which was produced in 1967, a time when Nigeria was destabilized by the outbreak of the Biafran War. MacIain interprets the unusual gender representations in this play as evidence of how gender becomes, through displacement, a vehicle for larger economic and social anxieties. Rather than take aim at women and the threat women represent to male economic power, as Yorùbá plays usually did, *Láníyonu* lambastes authority figures outside the family such as chiefs and places blame on an external malevolent evil spirit. MacIain's use of sources from popular culture is significant, as these plays represent—far more than newspapers and print culture do—the general climate of Nigerian culture, which historically has been predominately nonliterate. MacIain provides a methodological model for interpreting exceptional cases within an overarching pattern in data: exceptions can highlight the underlying function of gender discourse, and sometimes this function is not nearly so much about men and women as one might at first think.

Just as the importance of class and the dynamics of reception in gender activism could be seen in Susan Andrade's essay, the essays by anthropologist Takyiwaa Manuh and sociologist Hussaina Abdullah explore similar issues, but from a different disciplinary perspective. Their writings from Ghana and Nigeria, respectively, allow us to see how class divisions, as well as the transnational pressures NGOs and the United Nations exert, shape the dynamics of gender activism on the ground in Africa. Manuh begins with a story of her frustrations with the feminist knowledge production within the United States. The preeminent feminist journal *Signs* was imported to Ghana and from her perspective was singularly irrelevant to local feminist concerns. The issue of theory, in particular, is a sore point. What kind of theory do African scholars and activists consider useful? This is just one of the many questions Manuh posed to thirty of her colleagues who work on gender in Ghana, both inside and outside the academy. Manuh's ethnographic study illuminates the uneasy relationship between gender theory, which mainly developed outside Africa, and gender research, teaching, and activism in the context of contemporary Ghana. Knowledge about gender in Africa that is also *produced* in Africa provides an essential point of view, a necessary corrective. This perspective troubles and disrupts facile assumptions about the role of theory and empirical data in evaluating the "quality" of research. Manuh's critique has significant implications for the gatekeeping practices of academic publication. What role do gender scholars and activists located *in* Africa have in setting the terms of value for research?

Whereas Manuh's piece illuminates the asymmetry of the North-South flow of ideas about gender within the academy, Hussaina Abdullah gives a richly detailed view of how development agendas set in the North influence and shape activist practices about gender on the ground in Nigeria. Abdullah assesses the development of women's organizations in Nigeria that was triggered by the UN's Decade for Women, 1975–1985. What has this global initiative (which emanated from the North) wrought in one particular African context? How do global and local activist agendas serve to undermine one another? Abdullah traces women's activism of the 1990s to the founding of Women in Nigeria (WIN), the country's first feminist organization, and evaluates feminist organizations in their quest for the advancement of women's rights and participation in the emerging democratic environment. She is particularly interested in how these groups forge alliances among each other and with other organizations that pursue common goals. Abdullah argues that nongovernmental organizations, seeking to transform Nigerian gender inequities, draw their legitimacy from grassroots alignment with poor urban and rural women. One can also see the asymmetries of power within the African continent by comparing Abdullah's essay with Gay Seidman's piece on gender coalitions in South Africa. Whereas the Nigerian gender activism presented by Abdullah is strongly influenced by forces outside the country, the gender activism examined by Seidman in South Africa is far more internally driven.

Gender Enactments, Gendered Perceptions

The essays in this section highlight the way gender is a "doing," as American philosopher Judith Butler (1990) has argued, and also a way of perceiving, which anthropologists, literary critics, and historians approach differently. Gender performance is captured in women's critical agency as represented in African fiction (Julien and Wilson-Tagoe), in the ethnographic interview (Ebron), and in the practice of scholarly work itself (Boris). Such gendered perceptions have been one-sided. An older generation of literary critics and theorists of African liberation ignored gender issues, particularly women's contributions. International feminist theory, derived from northern cultural frameworks, could benefit much by paying closer attention to African gender studies, thereby acknowledging the operation of powerful, asymmetrical global frameworks in the production of knowledge.

For Paulla Ebron, the performance of women's burden and labor in West African documentary films is a commentary on the inequities of the global economy, aspects not developed in northern theories of gender performance. Instead, African pedagogical qualities of gender performance may open new research trajectories in the South *and* in the North. Historian Eileen Boris, offering a perspective from outside Africa, takes the North-South argument a step farther. Her feminist colleagues have much to learn from Africa's gender theorists and practitioners. Boris identifies three crucial African interventions in the larger field of feminist research: a disruption of the relationship between biological and the social, an interrogation of how some studies privilege gender over other social attributes, and the understanding of gender as an expression of power that is inextricably linked to colonization and liberation. African gender scholarship thus might serve as a corrective to international debates in the field of women's and gender studies. In similar fashion, Ebron's examples show that gender performance and performativity are no longer separate analytic categories, as in Western settings. Rather, performance can be both an ethnographic representation and a theoretical commentary.

Literary scholars Eileen Julien and Nana Wilson-Tagoe offer a different kind of analysis about gendered enactments and perceptions. How does gender shape the practices of fiction and perceptions of literary processes in the project of African nation-building? Julien focuses her inquiry on a play by Nigerian playwright Wole Soyinka, the much-anthologized *Death and the King's Horseman*, and two novels by Senegalese author Mariama Bâ, *Un chant écarlate* (*Scarlet Song*) and *Une si longue lettre* (*So Long a Letter*). All of these works depict a man's marriage to an additional wife, one who somehow represents African "tradition." Women serve as signifiers of the past and stabilizing forces in the present. But where Soyinka's play uses the polygynous marriage as a utopic defense of African essence and honor, Bâ's novels deploy an ironic tone that implicitly—though not without ambivalence—criticizes patriarchal privilege in postcolonial Africa. Wilson-Tagoe further pursues the issue of gender performativity and uses it as a way to critique the masculinist assumptions of African literary studies driven by nationalist agendas. She takes issue with the gender representation in the work of two prominent commentators: Frantz Fanon and Amilcar Cabral. Instead, Wilson-Tagoe is interested in the relationship between culture and identity shaped by global forces. This dynamic is viewed through the lens of women's fictional narratives, those of Ghanaian author Ama Ata Aidoo and Zimbabwean novelist Yvonne Vera. Both authors redefine and reimagine the connections between oppressive gender codes and a community's larger anticolonial struggle. Aidoo and Vera confront "contradictions in narratives that not only combine nationalist and gender discourses, but also write distinctive trajectories of women's agency" (Wilson-Tagoe, this volume).

The four chapters here not only situate African gender enactments and gendered perceptions within a global framework but also suggest that a North-South dialogue on gender theory and practices opens ways for a productive and beneficial exchange.

Masculinity, Misogyny, and Seniority

Section four turns our attention to gendered men and masculinity and the issues of misogyny and seniority. Looking at gender as an everyday experience, the contributors show that gender is not just about women but involves relations between *and* among men and women. Yet only over the last decade have Africa's gender scholars begun to unpack the constructions of masculinity and study men as gendered social actors. Historians Lisa Lindsay and Stephan Miescher discuss how notions of masculinity were debated and practiced in twentieth-century West Africa. Whereas Miescher looks at the continuity around ideas of elderhood and subjectivity within a Ghanaian mission church, Lindsay outlines the emergence of the male breadwinner as a gender ideal among railway men in colonial Nigeria. Like the authors in the previous section, Lindsay is interested in the performative aspect of gender. Not only does she examine how trade unions and colonial officials debated the virtues of the male breadwinner ideal but also how male wage laborers, their market women wives, and the colonial state's representatives engaged with this ideal to pursue different objectives. Yorùbá women's historical access to and autonomous control of wealth, especially in food markets, ran counter to British ideas of domesticity inculcated through colonialism, such as the idea that men should be primary family supporters. Lindsay's research demonstrates the value of gender studies' relational analysis as it foregrounds how masculine identities are inextricably linked to female roles. She makes a compelling case for the historical specificity of gender ideals and demonstrates how Nigerian men and women were active agents in the construction of gender norms. In response to colonial officials, trade unionists, and employers, men and women from southwestern Nigeria exploited ambiguous gender identities for their own ends.

While Lindsay highlights the difference between gender discourses and practices, the way in which certain gender ideals were performed, Miescher's chapter takes us to the question of gendered subjectivities: how particular individuals dealt with different and competing forms of masculinity. He focuses on masculine identities in the Kwawu area of southern Ghana during the colonial and postcolonial period, particularly their changing nature in tandem with notions of elderhood. Seniority is, arguably, a category as central to identity in Ghana and indeed throughout Africa, as gender is. Miescher's essay, based upon oral histories and missionary records, illuminates in rich detail the dynamic realm where age and gender status converge. In Akan societies, elderhood could be achieved by both men and women, but female elders wielded a more hidden, indirect form of power. Miescher's work brings into view the historical construction of identities and we see how the adoption of Christianity transformed gender and age ideals that had more indigenous roots.

In her discussion of West African popular theatre, performance scholar and art critic Catherine M. Cole unpacks images of misogyny and violence against women, which are frequently applauded by audiences. She reads these as examples of how gender is a carrier for a range of cultural anxieties, not only those that arise between the sexes. Taking a historical approach, her chapter begins in the early years of Ghana's independence and moves on to recent times as she analyzes plays from the so-called concert party. Identifying the misogynist stereotypes and narratives so prevalent in this theatre form, Cole explores why particular female archetypes—the schoolgirl, the orphan, and the widow—proved so popular and enduring. She looks at evolving gender roles in drama and how these transformed only when real women began acting, writing, and producing in a field that had been exclusively male. As does Miescher, Cole shows how gender as an aspect of personhood is linked with other identities. Like MacIain and Julian, Cole reveals how gender in fictional narrative is a carrier for a wide range of cultural anxieties.

Literary critic Helen Mugambi continues the theme of misogyny. Engaging in an interdisciplinary dialogue about the current epistemological status of gender in African studies, she brings us full circle. Mugambi insists that we must grapple with the gulf between the theoretical concepts of gender and the actual lived experiences of women, in particular the ubiquity of domestic violence at all levels of the socioeconomic spectrum in much of Africa. The most extreme example of such gendered violence has been the 1994 Rwandan genocide, where women became targets for physical and sexual assault. Mugambi's subject is the Ugandan postcolonial state, acclaimed for its policies of affirmative action concerning gender equity. And yet, in 2002, Uganda's female vice president made headlines because she was slapped by her husband. Only after some hesitation did this highest female official publicly acknowledge that she had become a victim of spousal abuse. Finally, Mugambi's piece also frames the "postgender" question in African studies signaled by our volume's title. She pursues both a theoretical inquiry about what the temporality implied in our title might mean and interrogates the distance between theoretical musings about gender and the on-the-ground experiences in Africa that include persistent gender power asymmetries. Thereby Mugambi sums up many of the collection's concerns, such as the pervasiveness of gender hierarchies and the difficulties of navigating gender discourses, North or South.

The contributors of this collection open up new questions within the larger field of African gender studies, past and future, before and "after." Only a decade ago, the WAAD conference was deadlocked by polarizing debates around identity politics, terminology, and conflicted assumptions. There was a demand for the exclusion of white participants, an objection to the presence of men, and an ideological rift over different currents of feminism, such as (Northern/ white) feminism, womanism, and Africana womanism. None of these tensions have dissipated or disappeared, yet the overall discourse on gender in Africa has clearly gestated and matured. Rather than allowing differences to divide us, we see that a rich and nuanced understanding emerges through collaborations across difference. Contributors have come together in this book as scholars and activists, Africans and non-Africans, men and women, humanists and social scientists. As we have seen and argued, alliances across difference are simultaneously fragile and strong, problematic and necessary. While we may disagree profoundly about issues, goals, methodologies, or intellectual agendas, the quality of knowledge we are producing together is far richer than if we worked in isolation.

Notes

1. Nnaemeka published the papers from this pioneering conference in the monumental volume *Sisterhood, Feminisms, and Power: From Africa to the Diaspora* (Trenton, N.J.: Africa World Press, 1998).

2. See pioneering studies that commented on African women's central role in agriculture, deplored their loss of status under colonialism, stated the widespread feminization of poverty, and introduced class analysis, such as Boserup (1970), Hafkin and Bay (1976), and Robertson and Berger (1986); see also the review by Robertson (1987).

3. For gender's ascendancy in African studies, see the important intervention by historian Nancy Rose Hunt (1989), who advocated "en-gendering" African history and urged scholars to examine not only the differences between men and women but the differences among women and among men. Other useful reviews include Potash (1989), Hunt (1997), Mama (1996), and Lewis (2002). For collections featuring social science and historical work, see Iman, Mama, and Sow (1997), Mikell (1997), Grosz-Ngaté and Kokole (1997), Hodgson and McCurdy (2001), and Allman, Geiger, and Musisi (2002); for literary studies, see Ogundipe-Leslie (1994), Nfah-Abbenyi (1997), Nnaemeka (1997), and Harrow (1998); see also Mugambi (this volume). For additional readings, see the resources for further reading at the end of this volume.

4. This argument has been made most prominently by Oyewumi (1997, 2002, 2003) for the Yorùbá people of Nigeria. For a critique that sees Oyewumi's attention to linguistic and ethnographic evidence as selective, see Matory (2003). Others have argued for African gender epistemologies such as the Igbo's dual sex system (Nzegwu 2001) or the Nnobi flexible gender system (Amadiume 1987); see also Nzegwu (2003).

References

Aidoo, Ama Ata. 1998. "The African Woman Today." In *Sisterhood, Feminisms, and Power*, edited by O. Nnaemeka, 39–50. Trenton, N.J.: Africa World Press.

Allman, Jean, Susan Geiger, and Nakanyike Musisi, eds. 2002. *Women in African Colonial Histories.* Bloomington: Indiana University Press.

Amadiume, Ifi. 1987. *Male Daughters, Female Husbands: Gender and Sex in an African Society.* London: Zed Books.

Barber, Karin, and Báyò Ògúndíjo. 1994. *Yorùbá Popular Theatre: Three Plays by the Oyin Adéjobì Company.* African Historical Sources Series 9. Atlanta, Ga.: African Studies Association Press.

Boserup, Ester. 1970. *Women's Role in Economic Development.* London: Allen & Unwin.

Butler, Judith. 1990. *Gender Trouble: Feminism and the Subversion of Identity.* New York: Routledge.

Grosz-Ngaté, Maria, and Omari H. Kokole, eds. 1997. *Gendered Encounters: Challenging Cultural Boundaries and Social Hierarchies in Africa.* New York: Routledge.

Hafkin, Nancy, and Edna Bay, eds. 1976. *Women in Africa: Studies in Social and Economic Change.* Stanford, Calif.: Stanford University Press.

Harrow, Kenneth W. 1998. "'I'm not a Western feminist but . . .': A Review of Recent Critical Writings on African Women's Literature." *Research in African Literatures* 29, no. 4: 171–190.

Hodgson, Dorothy L., and Sheryl A. McCurdy, eds. 2001. *"Wicked" Women and the Reconfiguration of Gender in Africa.* Portsmouth, N.H.: Heinemann.

Hunt, Nancy Rose. 1989. "Placing African Women's History and Locating Gender." *Social History* 14, no. 3: 359–379.

———. 1997. "Introduction." In *Gendered Colonialisms in African History,* edited by N. R. Hunt, Tessie P. Liu, and Jean Quataert, 1–15. Oxford: Blackwell.

Imam, Ayesha M., Amina Mama, and Fatou Sow, eds. 1997. *Engendering African Social Sciences.* Dakar: CODESRIA.

Lewis, Desiree. 2002. "African Feminist Studies: 1980–2002. A Review Essay for the African Gender Institute's 'Strengthening Gender and Women's Studies for Africa's Social Transformation 'Project.'" African Gender Institute, University of Cape Town. Available online at http://www.gwsafrica.org/knowledge/index.html (accessed July 2, 2004).

Mama, Amina. 1996. *Women's Studies and Studies of Women in Africa during the 1990s.* Working Paper Series 5/96. Dakar: CODESRIA.

Matory, J. Lorand. 2003. "Gendered Agendas: The Secrets Scholars Keep about Yorùbá-Atlantic Religion." *Gender & History* 15, no. 3: 409–439.

Mikell, Gwendolyn, ed. 1997. *African Feminisms: The Politics of Survival in Sub-Saharan Africa.* Philadelphia: University of Pennsylvania Press.

Nfah-Abbenyi, Juliana M. 1997. *Gender in African Women's Writing: Identity, Sexuality, and Difference.* Bloomington: Indiana University Press.

Nnaemeka, Obioma, ed. 1997. *The Politics of (M)Othering: Womanhood, Identity, and Resistance in African Literature.* London: Routledge.

———. 1998a. "This Women's Studies Business: Beyond Politics and History (Thoughts on the First WAAD Conference)." In *Sisterhood, Feminisms, and Power,* edited by O. Nnaemeka, 351–386. Trenton, N.J.: Africa World Press.

———. 1998b. *Sisterhood, Feminisms, and Power: From Africa to the Diaspora.* Trenton, N.J.: Africa World Press.

Nzegwu, Nkiru. 2001. "Gender Equality in a Dual-Sex System: The Case of Onitsha." *Jenda: A Journal of Culture and African Women* 1, no.1. Available online at http://www.jendajournal.com/vol1.1/nzegwu.html (accessed July1, 2004).

———. 2003. "O Africa: Gender Imperialism in Academia." In *African Women and Feminism,* edited by Oyeronke Oyewumi, 99–157. Trenton, N.J.: Africa World Press.

Ogundipe-Leslie, Molara. 1994. *Recreating Ourselves: African Women Critical Transformations.* Trenton, N.J.: Africa World Press.

Oyewumi, Oyeronke. 1997. *The Invention of Women: Making an African Sense of Western Gender Discourses.* Minneapolis: University of Minnesota Press.

———. 2002. "Conceptualizing Gender: The Eurocentric Foundations of Feminist Concepts and the Challenge of African Epistemologies." *Jenda: A Jour-*

nal of Culture and African Women Studies 2, no. 1. Available online at http://www.jendajournal.com/vol2.1/oyewumi.html (accessed July 1, 2004).

——, ed. 2003. *African Women and Feminism: Reflecting on the Politics of Sisterhood.* Trenton, N.J.: Africa World Press.

Potash, Betty. 1989. "Gender Relations in Sub-Saharan Africa." In *Gender and Anthropology,* edited by Sandra Morgan. Washington, D.C.: American Anthropological Association.

Robertson, Claire. 1987. "Developing Economic Awareness: Changing Perspectives in Studies of African Women, 1976–1985." *Feminist Studies* 13, no. 1: 97–135.

——, and Iris Berger, eds. 1986. *Women and Class in Africa.* New York: Africana Publishing Co.

Part One *Volatile Genders and
New African Women*

1 Out of the Closet: Unveiling Sexuality Discourses in Uganda

Sylvia Tamale

Introduction: February 2003

The issue of homosexuality took center stage in Uganda during the month of February 2003, with the media being dominated by emotive views and opinions from the public. This wave of homophobia was triggered by a rec-ommendation emanating from a section of the women's movement that urged the proposed Equal Opportunities Commission (EOC) to address the rights of homosexuals as members of the category of marginalized social groups in Uganda.[1] The newspaper report that activated much of the homophobic furor was entitled "Makerere [University] Don Defends Gays."[2] I had come out strongly in support of homosexuals and articulated my position in the national and in-ternational media. For this reason, I was caught in the eye of the homophobic storm and became a punching bag for the public to relieve its pent-up rage.

It is impossible to describe the depth of the ugliness, rage, revulsion, disgust, and malevolence exhibited by the vocal homophobic public. The few voices in support of homosexual rights were drowned out by deafening homophobic out-cries. Through radio, television, newspapers, and the Internet, I endured the most virulent verbal attacks, including calls for the "lynching" and "crucifying" of Tamale.[3] I had previously been aware of the intolerance toward and preju-dice against homosexuals in Uganda. I must confess, however, that the degree and extent of this bias came as a nasty shock to me; such bigotry and injustice I had read about only in history books on slavery and apartheid. That society could vilify the harmless, private, victimless acts of consenting adults defies logic.

Soon after the newspaper report referred to above, I received an SMS message on my cell phone from one of my friends: "Congs Sylvia; on your way to be-coming a millionaire!" She later explained that there was an assumption that my support for the rights of homosexuals meant that money was going to pour in from gay and lesbian organizations in Western Europe and North America to "facilitate" my work. Many more comments along similar lines followed in the electronic and print media. Implicit in these was the supposition that I was in-volved in a campaign that was driven from the West. The public seemed to think that there was a network of homosexual organizations "out there" with an explicit agenda to "recruit" young African men and women into their "decadent, perverted habits." It is of course interesting that the public never seems to consider heteronormativity to be a form of "recruiting" individuals into heterosexuality.

I should have been prepared for the virulent reactions, given my activist experience in the women's movement and the injustice I had seen meted out against Ugandan women over the years. But the February furor acted as an important eye-opener to me in several different respects, leading me to ask whether I had been naïve about my society's sense of fairness and justice and whether my isolation in the "ivory tower" had sheltered me from the reality outside. The homophobic storm engulfed me and presented huge challenges to my legal and feminist scholarship. The study I decided to undertake on the subject is ongoing. What I intend to do here is to reflect on the contestations and discourses around homosexuality in Uganda with reference to questions of gender, power, and identity in the contemporary African setting.

Sexual Politics in Uganda

One of the most efficient ways that patriarchy uses sexuality as a tool to create and sustain gender hierarchy in African societies is by enshrouding it in secrecy and taboos. Another option is to use the law to prohibit all "sex outlaws" in the social ghettoes of society. Prominent among the sex outlaws that have historically resisted and subverted dominant cultures are homosexuals, bisexuals, and transgendered individuals. Punitive laws against prostitution, abortion, adultery, erotica, and prostitutes serve a similar purpose. By maintaining a tight grip on certain activities and silencing the voices of individuals and groups that engage in them, the patriarchal state makes it extremely difficult for these individuals and groups to organize and fight for their human rights. Sociocultural norms and religious beliefs (such as virginity testing, female genital mutilation, female chastity, occult sexuality, taboos around polyandry, and so on) constitute the screws that keep the clamp of sexual repression firmly in place.

I have met many Ugandan gays and lesbians who have never had any form of interaction (direct or indirect) with whites. Some organizations, such as the Gays and Lesbians Alliance (GALA) have members throughout rural Uganda. A good number are nonliterate or semi-literate. It is quite clear that whether they arrived at their homosexuality through "nature" or "nurture" (I personally do not think that it matters either way), outside influence played no part in determining their sexuality. When we turn to the past, we find that, contrary to popular belief, homosexuality in Uganda predates colonialism and other forms of subjugation (Murray and Roscoe 1998). Historically, as was the case elsewhere in the world, homosexual practices were neither fully condoned nor totally suppressed (Feminist Review 1987). Among the Langi of northern Uganda, the *mudoko dako* "males" were treated as women and could marry men (Driberg 1923). Homosexuality was also acknowledged among the Iteso (Laurance 1957), the Bahima (Mushanga 1973), the Banyoro (Needham 1973), and the Baganda (Southwold 1973). Indeed, there is a long history of homosexuality in the Buganda monarchy; it was an open secret, for example, that Kabaka (king) Mwanga was gay (Faupel 1962). Trends in both the present and the past reveal that it is time for Africans to bury the tired myth that homosexuality is "un-African." (Some other myths and reductionist beliefs that I have heard during the course of my research include "homosexuals are naturally violent," "most gay men are pedophiles," "same-sex boarding schools breed homosexuals," and so on.) Ironically, it is the dominant Judeo-Christian and Arabic religions upon which most African anti-homosexuality proponents rely that are foreign imports.

Political, cultural, and religious fundamentalisms have played a crucial role in suppressing and stifling sexual pluralism in Uganda. During the month of February, I appeared on several radio talk shows and gave public lectures on the topic of homosexuality. The level of hypocrisy, the double standards, and the selective sexual morality that such fundamentalists exhibited always took me by surprise. Any variation in sexual activity and sexual partners from heteronormativity is considered "pathological," "deviant," and "unnatural" and is condemned in the strongest possible terms. The gendered politics implicit in these views are crucial, since sexual activities that go against the grain of mainstream ones subvert conventional gendered relations and hierarchies. Sexuality therefore becomes a critical site for maintaining patriarchy and reproducing African women's oppression.

The gendered dimensions of sexuality are very clear when we consider the implicit erasure of lesbian identity in Ugandan society. Even the law seems to be more preoccupied with male-on-male sex when it criminalizes intercourse "against the order of nature."[4] Somehow, the dominant phallocentric culture maintains the stereotype of women as the passive recipients of penetrative male pleasure; sex that is not penetrative does not count as "real" sex. In fact, the sexuality of Ugandan women is often reduced to their conventional mothering role and conflated with their reproductive capacities (Tamale 2001). What is therefore particularly threatening to patriarchy is the idea of intimate same-sex relationships where a dominating male is absent and where women's sexuality can be defined without reference to reproduction. The main factor in the patriarchal equation is missing; that is, power along sex lines and thus the preservation of the gender hierarchy.

The mainstream aversion to same-sex relations reflects a greater fear. Homosexuality threatens to undermine male power bases in the Ugandan "private" sphere (at the level of interpersonal relationships and conventional definitions of the "family") as well as in public discourses (where myths abound about what it means to be a man or a woman). Homosexuality presents a challenge to the deep-seated masculine power within African sexual relations and disrupts the core of the heterosexist social order.

The Complexities of Subversion:
Kuchu Culture in Uganda

There are several stigmatized terms to describe homosexuals in Uganda, but the most common one is *abasiyazi* (others include *kyafoko* and *eyumayuma*). However, Ugandan gays and lesbians identify themselves simply with the term *kuchu* (plural, *kuchus*). (I had never heard this term before undertaking this study and very few in mainstream society know that it exists.) Society considers them a moral outrage, but they have rejected all negative labels and constructed an alternative positive and empowering self-identification. Most of the gays and lesbians I have interviewed have assumed the *kuchu* identity and consider it as the prime factor in their personal identity.[5] "Straight *kuchus*" take a lot of pride in their orientation, and many consider bisexuals as "not real," somewhat akin to "sellouts."[6] They perceive bisexuals as people who wish to have their cake and eat it too.

Under the repressive conditions of state- and religious-inspired homophobia in Uganda, it is not surprising that most homosexuals find it difficult to "come out" of their closeted lives or to be open about their sexual orientation. Most blend within the wider society and even live under the cover of heterosexual relationships while maintaining their homosexual relationships underground. The tendency is to construct "comfort zones" where they complacently live a different and segregated lifestyle. Gay and lesbian clubs in particular offer comfort zones for homosexuals until they are rudely awakened by an incident such as the one in February.

Kuchuism has taken on a particular and vital importance to homosexuals in Uganda. Because homosexuals in Uganda do not feel a sense of belonging in relation to the dominant culture, they have had to reconstruct affirming identities for themselves. Wendy Clark helps to explain this when she shows how the questions of "identity" and "self" gain particular significance when there is a part of oneself that is hidden and in direct and immediate opposition to the social and cultural mores of society (1987, 208).

The recognized forms of self-definition among *kuchus* allow individuals within the *kuchu* subculture to identify one another within the patriarchal heterosexual social system. This identification among gay men often consists of gestures or mannerisms that repudiate conventional masculinity. Lesbians tend to use mode of dress to distinguish themselves from heterosexual women; almost all the female *kuchus* I have met in Kampala routinely wear trousers, shirts, baseball caps, and other forms of "masculine" attire. Many interpret this as lesbians' desire to be "like men" or to adopt the role of "pseudo-men." *Kuchus* themselves find such interpretations laughable and believe they are simply asserting their right to dress styles that are comfortable. The self-definition of lesbians and gays therefore involves their subversive performance and statement-making as gender outlaws in society.

There are several gay and lesbian organizations in Uganda, including Gay and

Lesbian Alliance, Freedom and Roam Uganda, Gay Uganda, Spectrum, Right Companion, Lesgabix, Frank and Candy, and Integrity. Most of these act as support groups and very few are engaged in activist work to improve their status. Moreover, the different groups are only tenuously connected, some sustaining their membership exclusively through cyberspace. In March 2004 an LGBT umbrella organization called Sexual Minorities Uganda (SMUG) was launched in an effort to strengthen the movement for the rights of LGBT people in Uganda. Lesbians are especially active in the leadership of SMUG. However the organization is still riddled with the initial teething problems that all nascent movements face, aggravated in this case by the exceedingly hostile context within which it operates. Member organizations are still reluctant to speak out publicly and to take activist actions that would begin to crack the mold of heteronormativity.

The avoidance of public visibility by gay and lesbian organizations can also be explained by the severity of Ugandan law, which outlaws homosexuality and punishes it with a maximum sentence of life imprisonment. The anonymous involvement and communication that many organizations afford also proves safe when individuals, especially those in socially esteemed professions or high office, need to preserve the mainstream sexual identity that is often assumed to be part of their social status. Overall, the prohibitive sociolegal environment in which lesbians and gays live and work makes it extremely difficult for homosexuals to demand their rights in Uganda with a unified voice.

Sexuality in the Ugandan Women's Movement

The women's movement in Uganda has not yet embraced issues of sexual orientation with any degree of enthusiasm. It is especially significant that the *kuchu* subculture among Ugandan lesbians is entirely disconnected from the women's movement. The cross-section of the women's movement that urged the Equal Opportunities Commission to support the rights of homosexuals was by no means representative of the mainstream women's movement in Uganda. Indeed, the silence of the women's movement was quite conspicuous during the month of February, when I came under virulent attack from a homophobic society.[7] Yet the fact that *some* gender activists recognized the need to support the rights of gays and lesbians is important, especially given the fact that this stand could mean the loss of a job or ambitions for public office.

When we presented our recommendations to the minister of gender, herself a women's rights activist, she advised that we drop "sexual orientation" from our recommendations as it was bound "to erase all the other good things" we had recommended in the report. Minister Zoe Bakoku-Bakoru reasoned that it was not strategic, "not yet time" to bring up such issues before Ugandan lawmakers. The question is: When will it be time? Today, on this continent, we often hear the same excuse in relation to women's rights to participate in decision making, to control resources, to realize their full potential.

The silence around sexual rights within the Ugandan women's movement may be attributed in part to the taboos surrounding all sexual matters in our society. But the HIV/AIDS pandemic has in many ways flung open the doors on sexuality. In particular, it has forced into the open the myths and secrets in relationships and identities that are often silenced or taken for granted. For women's rights activists, the personal has never confronted and intersected with the political in so explicit and bold a fashion as it has with contemporary issues of sex and sexuality. Although many of us in the women's movement still find it difficult to rid our consciousness of the web of taboos that dims our understanding of the intrinsic link between sexuality and women's oppression and subordination, the process of disentanglement has begun.

Homosexuality represents one of the last bastions of legally backed and state-sanctioned oppression and intolerance on the African continent. In Uganda, the controversy over and wide coverage of the issue in February 2003 forced the skeletons of the country's sexuality out of the closet and compelled many Ugandans to rethink their stance on homosexuality. The discussion bulletin on the online edition of the newspaper *New Vision* logged an unprecedented number of postings on this topic. For over six months, a vigorous and continuing debate was sustained among members of the Ugandan educated elite who have access to the Internet. Overall, the prominence of public debate around homosexuality has placed the topic firmly within the wider ambit of democratic practice.

In the context of this wider ambit, homophobia clearly becomes a gendered concern. Institutions such as culture, the law, and religion are vehicles that states use to perpetuate patriarchy and women's subordination. By maintaining a regime of compulsory heterosexuality, the state seeks to enforce conventional gender relationships and identities and keep a stranglehold on public discourse about these topics. We cannot allow the fire that was lit with the activating of public debate in February 2003 to go out.

Postscript
Compiled by Bianca A. Murillo

The following is a copy of the February 5th, 2003, *New Vision* newspaper report that initiated several of the verbal attacks on Sylvia Tamale for supporting homosexual rights. Included directly after are excerpts from the numerous commentaries and letters published in *New Vision* responding to Tamale's position. These materials were collected from *New Vision*'s online archive at http://www.newvision.co.ug (accessed September 1, 2005). Excerpts from the GWS Africa Project's "News Alert" that introduced the case are also provided and available at http://www.gwsafrica.org/news/index.html (accessed September 1, 2005).

"MUK Don Fights For Gay Rights"

A MAKERERE University don has said gays should be recognised as one of the marginalised groups in the country whose rights need to be protected and recognised. Charles Ariko reports that Dr. Sylvia Tamale, who is a senior lecturer at the Faculty of

Law and a human rights activist, said the Constitution recognised other marginalised groups such [as] women and the disabled, and she saw no reason the gays should not be allowed to enjoy their rights

"I know President Yoweri Museveni is against gays but that does not mean they should be denied their rights to a sexual orientation of their choice," Tamale said.

She was yesterday speaking at a consultative workshop on the draft principles for the establishment of the Equal Opportunities Commission (EOC).

The workshop was organised by a local NGO, Action for Development (ACFODE), in conjunction with a German NGO, Konrad Adenauer Foundation.

Tamale said gays were recognised by international bodies as one of the marginalised groups. She said they should be recognised by the EOC which is to be set up under the 1995 Constitution.

The Constitution says the main functions of EOC are to implement affirmative action policies in favour of groups marginalised on the basis of gender, age, disability or any other reason created by history, tradition or custom.

New Vision, February 5, 2003.

"Gay Rights Not a Priority in Uganda"

SIR—As a student of Makerere University, I would like to protest in the strongest terms possible Dr. Sylvia Tamale's so called concern for the gay as a marginalised group in Uganda.

It is no secret that the West and their puppets are doing all they can to train little children to be gays so as to have a following. A number of single-sex boarding schools are known for this (parents, watch out). If being gay is natural, why must innocent children be trained for this purpose? Testimonies have been given of priests using boys, not only in America, but even here, as has been alleged. The Ministry of Education should probe this allegation.

Secondly, to you Dr. Tamale, human rights activist living in Makerere, have you ever sought audience with the marginalised groups such as the disabled? Are you aware that law cases and other materials in your own faculty are not available in Braille and are therefore not easily accessed by those who are blind?

Do you know that some crippled students cannot have easy access to your own lecture rooms? Have you ever studied the plight of female and non-resident students in Makerere? What about those from war-torn areas? What have you, champion of human rights, ·done for such? Let's be serious Tamale. Should we first start fighting for the rights of those who prefer to mount dogs, sheep and hens as their wives? After all, it is their right to preference.

The Minister of Education should intervene in the issue of training gays in schools, seminaries and the like if we are to build for the future.

Geoffrey Walakira
Minister for Affirmative Action
Makerere
New Vision, February 10, 2003.

"Marginalised?"

SIR—I read with shock and sadness about a Makerere University lecturer, Dr Sylvia Tamale, referring to gays as a "marginalised group," categorising them with women and

the disabled. What sin did women and the disabled persons commit? If you were to continue with the same argument, I would like to see you fighting for the rights of those other categories of people that I have mentioned above. They are also marginalised.
Christine Agnes Alamo
Deliverance Church
Kampala
New Vision, February 11, 2003.

"Don Sticks On Gays"

SYLVIA Tamale, the Makerere University senior lecturer who raised a storm last week when she said she supports gay rights, has reiterated her stand saying even Jesus Christ embraced and tolerated those that were considered outsiders.

Tamale said as a human rights activist, it would be hypocritical for her to pick and choose which category of marginalised/oppressed groups to support. "How could I possibly demand for my own right for equality while stifling that of another human being who just happens to be different from me?" Tamale asked.

In a statement sent to The New Vision, Tamale gave eight reasons why she supports the rights of homosexuals in Uganda.

"As a person who strongly believes in justice, I do not feel that the sexual orientation of two consenting adults should be the basis of discrimination. Such people might be different from the majority of Ugandans but certainly do not harm anyone or violate the rights of fellow citizens by being homosexuals," Tamale said.

She said research had revealed that homosexuality is in fact not 'an importation from the West' as many would like to believe.

"Same sex patterns have been found to exist among many indigenous African communities. Several studies point to the evidence that it was practised in pre-colonial Uganda," Tamale said.

"My support of homosexuals is not simply based on the fact that the 'West recognises it' as some people suggest," she said, adding that, "It took decades for homosexuality to be recognised in most western countries but that does not mean that homophobia does not exist in these societies even today."

She added, "In the US, many youth commit suicide simply because they are not free to express their normal human sexuality," Tamale said

She argued that it was pointless for the Penal Code to criminalise a victimless act like homosexuality in the name of morality especially when the same law does not see any immorality in a husband committing adultery.

"For the Penal Code to criminalise a victimless act like homosexuality in the name of morality makes it jurisprudentially suspect in my eyes," she said.
Charles Ariko
New Vision, February 17, 2003.

"Don't politicise every issue!"

SIR—Sometime last week Monitor FM hosted Pastor Martin Sempa and Dr Sylvia Tamale on Andrew Mwenda Live on homosexuals. Whereas Sempa was surely informed about the subject, both Mwenda and Tamale had shockingly little knowledge on the topic. For example, the two were ignorant about bug-chasers; but instead of seeking Sempa's knowledge, they simply disagreed.

The problem here is that Mwenda and Tamale think every issue is political. I expected Tamale as a professional to argue, for example, on how the anus is adopted to its function as a sexual organ so that homosexualism should be promoted. Instead she resorted to politicking, listing the countries legalising the evil. To what purpose? So that we compare their contribution to the economic stability, political stability or what? We don't just copy everything. She went on to make her own version of the Bible. Later, she resorted to personal attacks on Sempa, calling him a liar. Homosexuals need the help of society. Couselling should be made available. Mwenda should also learn to be neutral.

Mark Luswata, Kampala
NewVision, February 18, 2003.

"I disagree with Sylvia Tamale"

SIR—I have been following the recent media debate in which Dr Sylvia Tamale is advocating for homosexuality as a rights [sic]. I think something has terribly gone wrong with our society. The other day a lawyer in Makerere advocated for scanty dressing, and when some members of the public slotted in comments in the media, he wrote back to say the problem with them was lack of understanding of the English language! Since I may lack understanding of the law concerning homosexuals, I will quote the word of God from the Bible since Dr Tamale knows God's laws as she criticised Pastor Sempa for breaking the law of God by not tolerating people who are not like him. Romans 1:27–28 says: "For even their women exchanged the natural use for what is against nature. Likewise also the men, leaving the natural use of the woman, burned in their lust for one another, men with men committing what is shameful, and receiving in themselves the penalty of their error which was due. And even as they did not like to retain God in their knowledge, God gave them over to a debased mind. . . ."

Name withheld on request
New Vision, February 19, 2003.

"Pan-Africanists rap gay sympathizers"

PAN-AFRICANISTS have attacked sympathisers of homosexuality.

They were meeting at their head offices in Kamwokya on Friday to discuss the issue of 'homosexuality as a humanity right'.

Nathan Byamukama from the Uganda Human Rights Commission said homosexuality is not yet a human right in Uganda and it is therefore illegal.

"If homosexuals want their full rights, let them mobilise and demand for them. Before they do that, it will still be regarded illegal according to the governing laws of the country," he said.

David Mafabi, political director of the Global Pan-African Movement, said debates on homosexuality had to be left to the whites who are believed to have started it.

"Whereas Dr. Sylvia Tamale has the right to express herself on homosexuality, the idea that it should be a human right should not even be debated because it is unthinkable," he said.

Sylvia Tamale, a Makerere University lecturer, recently said homosexuality should be regarded a human right.
Fortunate Ahimbisibwe
New Vision, February 25, 2003.

"I say, Three cheers to Sylvia Tamale!"

SIR—Three cheers for Dr Sylvia Tamale for taking a courageous stand to defend the rights of homosexuals.

It seems to me, that in our country today, we have many things to worry about. Who consenting adults choose to sleep with is not one of them. Those who have chosen to equate homosexuality with paedophilia are being totally disingenuous in this debate.

Gay rights and advocates have consistently argued for the recognition of the rights of adults to choose whom they wish to be their sexual partners—adult and consent, being the operative words here. This, in the context of sexual relations between adult men and women, is now widely recognised as a fundamental human rights.

Secondly, we need to take note of the fact that it is men of a heterosexual orientation, who are responsible for the vast majority of cases of sexual abuse against children, especially young girls.

I am convinced that homosexuality is a natural state of human life. Why on earth, anyone would choose to pursue a life in which they will be subject to ridicule, abuse, humiliation and discrimination of the worst kind, defies logic.

And let us think, in practical terms, what this hatred and fear means. Those homosexuals and lesbians amongst us are forced to live in fear of ever being found out. This means in many cases, they were allowed to live their lives openly without fear of persecution?

I remember not so long ago, when the AIDS pandemic first came to light, Uganda was one of the few countries that recognised that the worst enemy of the pandemic was bigotry, fear and discrimination.

Whilst the world looked on, Uganda openly addressed this issue, and years later, this openness and acceptance, has assured Uganda a place at the forefront of the efforts to come to terms with the pandemic.

If it were up to me, Dr. Tamale and others like her, would be up for the highest award of recognition in the land, for their courage, conviction and commitment to the defence of the human rights of all, even when they are swimming against the tide of public opinion. The world would be a much safer and happier place if more of us were ready to stand up and speak out against narrow-mindedness.

For such narrow-mindedness demeans us as a society.
Sarah Mukasa
Kampala
New Vision, March 1, 2003.

"Kasese RDC blasts Dr. Tamale"

The Kasese resident district commissioner, Musa Ecweru, has lashed out at Makerere University lecturer, Dr. Sylvia Tamale, for advocating for homosexuality.

"If her parents had practiced these acts, how would she have been born?" Ecweru asked. He was speaking during the International Women's Day celebrations at Mundongo Primary School, Nyakiyumbu sub-county, on Saturday.

Ecweru said some top people in the district engaged in homosexuality and had abducted a boy who however escaped.

He said the practice was against the rights of women and men to produce and raise children.
John Thawite
New Vision, March 12, 2003.

GWSAfrica: NEWS ALERT!
"Sylvia Tamale attacked for supporting non-discrimination on basis of sexual orientation"

Professor Sylvia Tamale, a committed member of the GWSAfrica network and leading feminist scholar specialising in human rights and politics, has been at the centre of a raging controversy in Uganda for the last two weeks. At the beginning of February, Prof. Tamale spoke out in support of including sexual orientation as one of the grounds for non-discrimination in the proposed Equal Opportunities Commission legislation. Since then, she has been publicly attacked for her "irresponsible defence of homosexuality."

Her key argument, that discrimination on the grounds of sexual orientation is a violation of human rights, has been ignored by the many Ugandans, ranging from academics to politicians, who have condemned her stand. While Prof. Tamale has appeared on numerous talk shows and made many public appearances to explain the relevance of discrimination on grounds of sexual orientation to human rights struggles, the developing debate in Uganda has been heavily biased towards at worst, virulent homophobic attacks as well as attacks on herself, and, at best, naïve perceptions of homosexuality as "illness." Prof. Tamale has therefore been waging an almost single-handed struggle, through making public appearances, issuing statements to newspapers and speaking on radio talk shows, to establish the status of gay rights as a human rights concern.

In terms of Ugandan law, homosexuality is illegal and carries a maximum sentence of life imprisonment, with the Penal Code Act defining it variously as "carnal knowledge against the order of nature" and an "act of gross indecency" whether in public or private. In the early 90s, systematic purges were undertaken in several prestigious Ugandan schools to investigate and systematically root out the young boys and girls who were believed to be guilty of "carnal knowledge against the order of nature." The purges involved severe corporal punishment for those found guilty, the expulsion of many students, and, in all likelihood, a climate of terror for boys and girls regarding their sexual identity, and the instilled need for them to publicly and consistently demonstrate "normal" (i.e. heterosexist and patriarchal sexual roles and behaviour) sexual identities. It also culminated in formal "sex education" programmes at many schools where young people, from early adolescence are brainwashed and bullied by counsellors, teachers and administrators into accepting the moral judgement enshrined by Ugandan Penal Code. It is against this formidable background that a few brave voices like Tamale's speak out against illogical and blind prejudice.

Tamale's stand is indicative of the multi-pronged battles that many feminists on the continent wage in seeking to challenge the entrenched religious and cultural biases that naturalise gendered and other injustices. New Vision, one of the daily online Ugandan newspaper[s], has received numerous homophobic comments on the raging topic, as well as personalised attacks on Tamale, such as the following:

> It is disgusting to hear learned women like Dr. Tamale demand for the rights of homosexuals.
> First of all we have to sympathise with some of these people because sometimes they are guided

by poverty rather than reason. You remember Bishop Senyonjo. It was found out that he was only making noise to get some money from Western donors who are keen on spreading their disease. Tamale has now decided to follow suit. . . . Please Tamale you can do better than that. I think Sylvia Tamale must have been a sissy in her secondary school days or somewhere in University. . . . That woman must be a great sympathiser of sissies!! We have no place for deviants!!!

If the media stories are true in regard to the comments Dr. Sylvia Tamale made in regard to homosexuality, then I am disappointed in some of the so-called elite people of Uganda. How dare a woman of Dr. Tamale's calibre, whom I think is a mother and at all costs regarded as a model, suggest such obnoxious views? I don't know whether she would honestly feel comfortable if her daughter or son (if she has one) were to break the news to her that they are homosexual. If Dr. Tamale is married, I don't know how she would take it if she found out that her husband were homosexual.

Dr. Tamale may be a lesbian herself but I don't think she has any right whatsoever to demand that our government should allow such abnormality to flourish. We shall terribly all have failed in our responsibility towards each other if we just entertain "the I don't care attitude." If we are to care for others, we are responsible to see that they are fully human in all aspects to the best of our ability. Since we can do something against letting people be corrupted with the cancer of homosexuality that is almost eating away the Western culture, we would do well to fight it other than calling it a lifestyle. Fellow Africans, ignore those decadent foreign ideas and concentrate on strengthening our moral fibre.

I am angry at the way the activists for "homosexual rights" have attempted to hijack the consultations for the equal opportunities commission. The commission will assist in the integration of marginalised groups into the wider society and the protection of their rights. . . . I would like to suggest an addition to the commission's mandate, that is: to identify those small/minority social groups that could prove harmful to the Ugandan society and recommend ways to eliminate them. First, of course, it would be the homosexuals.

(N.d., available online at http://www.gwsafrica.org/news/tamale2.html.)

Notes

A version of this essay was previously published in *Feminist Africa* 2 (2003), available online at http://www.feministafrica.org/fa%202/2level.html.

1. The recommendations were reproduced in *New Vision* on February 10, 2003 (see supplement "The Proposed Equal Opportunities Commission of Uganda," 34). There had been several homophobic "waves" prior to this. For example, in September 1999, President Museveni instructed the police to arrest and prosecute all homosexuals after an alleged homosexual "wedding" was reported in the local papers (see *Monitor,* September 28, 1999).

2. *New Vision,* February 5, 2003, 3.

3. See online discussion board of *New Vision* under the topic "To Be or Not to Be Gay (Homosexual)" at http://www.newvision.co.ug/bulletinboard/.

4. See section 145 of the Ugandan Penal Code.

5. So far, I have interviewed approximately sixty male and female *kuchus*. Naturally, the best-suited sampling method for this kind of project has been the snowball method, in which one self-identified *kuchu* introduces me to another.

6. It is interesting to note how *kuchus* subvert the use of the term "straight" (which normally describes heterosexuals) in reference to themselves.

7. A handful of feminists sent me private e-mails in support of my position, but only one wrote to the media in support; see Mukasa (2003).

References

Clark, Wendy. 1987. "The Dyke, the Feminist and the Devil." In *Sexuality: A Reader*, edited by Feminist Review. London: Virago Press.

Driberg, Jack Herbert. 1923. *The Lango*. London: Thorner Coryndon.

Faupel, John Francis. 1962. *African Holocaust: The Story of the Uganda Martyrs*. New York: P. J. Kennedy.

Feminist Review, ed. 1987. *Sexuality: A Reader*. London: Virago Press.

Laurance, Jeremy C. D. 1957. *The Iteso: Fifty Years of Change in a Nilo-Hamitic Tribe of Uganda*. Oxford: Oxford University Press.

Mukasa, Sarah. 2003. "I Say Three Cheers to Sylvia Tamale." *New Vision*, March 1.

Murray, Stephen O., and Will Roscoe, eds. 1998. *Boy-Wives and Female Husbands: Studies of African Homosexualities*. New York: St. Martin's Press.

Mushanga, Musa T. 1973. "The Nkole of Southwestern Uganda." In *Cultural Sources Materials for Population Planning in East Africa: Beliefs and Practices*, edited by A. Molnos, 174–186. Nairobi: East African Publishing House.

Needham, Rodney. 1973. "Right and Left in Nyoro Symbolic Classification." In *Right and Left: Essays on Dual Classification*, 299–341. Chicago: University of Chicago Press.

Southwold, Martin. 1973. "The Baganda of Central Uganda." In *Cultural Source Materials for Population Planning in East Africa: Beliefs and Practices*, edited by A. Molnos, 163–173. Nairobi: East African Publishing House.

Tamale, Sylvia. 2001. "How Old is Old Enough? Defilement Law and the Age of Consent in Uganda." *East African Journal of Peace and Human Rights* 7, no. 1: 82–100.

2　Institutional Dilemmas: Representation versus Mobilization in the South African Gender Commission

Gay W. Seidman

When South Africa's first democratically elected government came to power in 1994, its rhetoric was explicitly feminist. While the country's new leaders promised above all to address the racial inequalities inherited from centuries of white domination, they also viewed gender equality as a key goal. In his inauguration speech—triumphant after a half-century struggle against apartheid, the system under which South Africa's black majority was brutally controlled by a white minority—newly elected president Nelson Mandela called for the construction of a "non-racist, nonsexist" democracy that would give all citizens equal representation in and access to the state. That rhetoric was carried into the design of the new state: new institutions were expected to address issues of gender inequality, and at every level, the new government would examine the impact of policies on gender relations, seeking to address the sources of gender inequality.

The institutional centerpiece of this effort was the South African Commission on Gender Equality. Independent and powerful, staffed by energetic and committed feminists with a strong commitment to challenging the bases of gender inequality, it appeared to offer remarkable promise for feminist intervention at its inception in 1996. Four years later, however, many of the feminists who helped construct the commission were far more pessimistic. Unclear about its goals, immobilized by internal dissent, the commission appeared to have reached a virtual stalemate. By mid-2000, South Africa's feminist project was in obvious disarray. Activists hurled accusations at each other through the national media, and the Gender Commission declared itself unable even to coordinate activities to commemorate South African Women's Day.

What had undermined the feminist possibility embodied in the Gender Commission structure? Why did a project so full of promise lose steam so quickly? Nationalist movements arriving in power have often promised to give women greater access and representation but have repeatedly failed to follow through (Molyneux 1985; Stacey 1983). Does South Africa represent just another case of a nationalist movement subsuming feminist goals to a nation-building project? Does feminist rhetoric simply mask patriarchal intent, where male leaders claim to support gender equality but fail to provide resources or power to attain it?

Based on a participant observation study of the Gender Commission's head office, I argue that in South Africa, at least, the process has been more complicated, involving conflicts among feminists: tensions related to institutional design, conflicts over the definition of a feminist project, disagreements over how state institutions should relate to the nongovernmental women's movement, and concerns about how feminist issues should be integrated into racial and economic concerns. For five months in early 1999, with an additional visit in mid-2000, I worked in the Gender Commission's legal department in Johannesburg, helping with research and attending meetings; I followed up conversations around the office with more structured interviews with commissioners, staff members, and staff from nongovernmental women's organizations and international donor agencies who interacted with the commission.

The experience of the South African Commission on Gender Equality raises questions about feminist institutional design—specifically, about how institutions can represent women's voices within state policy discussions while simultaneously trying to mobilize a constituency to support feminist aspirations. To some commissioners and staff members, the commission offered a channel through which to voice a feminist critique from within government; other commissioners hoped to mobilize support for feminist concerns, a project that seemed to require a more moderate, pragmatic profile. Unresolved and often unarticulated conflicts over feminist strategies—over the relationship between feminist policymakers, the national state, and the women whose lives the new "femocrats" sought to change—created tensions that impeded the day-to-day work of the Gender Commission.

In this chapter, I argue that the commission's innovative institutional form exacerbated these tensions. Commissioners sought to represent women's concerns within the state while simultaneously trying to mobilize and serve women in civil society. These two goals often came into conflict with each other. But there were other questions too. Should feminist policymakers articulate demands for women within existing gender relations or should they try to articulate a challenge to existing inequalities? How should these debates be incorporated into a broader nation-building project, and to what extent should feminist government officials try to represent the nation as a whole?

These tensions were neither abstract nor theoretical: they were built into the very structures of the state. Conflicts over commission priorities were complicated by political concerns about how best to promote feminism within government, while the personal tensions resulting from this structural impasse created a sense of stalemate so severe by mid-2000 that it risked undermining the very women's movement that had inserted feminist concerns into the new democracy's design. Although by early 2001 the Gender Commission had begun to chart a way out, the dilemmas facing South Africa's feminist policymakers underscore important problems facing those who seek to design gendered democratic institutions.

Constructing a Gendered State

Over the past twenty years, feminist scholars have paid increasing attention to issues of institutional design. In practice, "femocrats"—a term coined to describe the feminist bureaucrats who staff many of these new institutions around the world—have struggled to represent women's voices in the state and begin to address gender inequality. But there is little agreement on what these institutions should look like, beyond a basic sense that whatever institutions are built in the present may shape the way gender issues are understood in the future (Pringle and Watson 1992).

Case studies offer two models of feminist institutions. In advanced industrial societies, feminist institutions tend to emphasize representation and voice, giving women new access to policymaking bodies through independent commissions or ombudspersons (Gatens 1998; Stetson and Mazur 1995). In postcolonial settings, on the other hand, feminist organizations and institutions tend to be oriented toward mobilizing women to participate in national development (Molyneux 2000; Staudt 1998; Macaulay 2000). Especially in countries dominated by socialist or statecentric developmentalist ideologies, women's institutions have tended to be described in top-down terms as women policymakers seek to mobilize women to support state efforts, often by creating special programs for women within a national development strategy.

Appropriately for South Africa's diverse society, its new gender institutions were conceptualized in terms of all these processes: access, representation, and mobilization. During the negotiated transition, starting from the 1990 release of political prisoners and unbanning of political parties, feminist activists managed to insert gender concerns into the national political arena, insisting that if these issues were postponed until later, the new state would probably mirror other new democracies, recreating gender inequality by treating women as mothers and wives rather than as full citizens. Through the early 1990s, leading activists strategically promoted feminist issues, claiming that they represented a grassroots constituency in township women's groups (Hassim 2002; Hassim and Gouws 1998; Kaplan 1997; Seidman 1999). Especially because they united women activists across the political spectrum, these activists managed to make gender concerns visible to such an extent that during the 1994 elections all parties made special appeals to women voters. In 1994, the African National Congress (ANC) instituted a 30 percent quota for women on its nominating lists; in a system of proportional representation where the ANC attained almost a two-thirds majority, the ANC quota meant that when South Africa's Constituent Assembly was formed in 1994, the new parliamentary body included one of the highest percentages of women in the world. The country's first democratic constitution, adopted in 1996, called for the elimination of public and private discrimination not only in terms of race but also in terms of "gender, sex, pregnancy and marital status" as well as religion and ethnicity.

By 1998, South Africa had created a series of national institutions designed to "mainstream" gender. In the Office of the President, a national Office on the Status of Women was established to oversee the internal transformation of the civil service as government structures were redesigned to erase the legacies of apartheid. Within each ministry, "gender desks" were supposed to examine all government policies, seeking to ensure that new policies actively addressed sources of gender inequality—including policies that were not explicitly linked to gender, such as land reform programs (Seidman 1999).

To watch over the whole process, the Constitution created the Commission on Gender Equality. One of several horizontal bodies designed to simultaneously monitor and stimulate transformation in South African society, the Gender Commission stands independent of the South African government while remaining part of it. As in many other new democracies, a negotiated transition meant that change would be slow and gradual. Government departments continued as usual, often staffed by apartheid-era civil servants. New ministers had to rely heavily on the civil servants already in place for information and policy implementation. In this context, independent horizontal bodies seemed important innovations, channels through which citizens could appeal as they sought to define their new constitutional rights. An independent Electoral Commission to oversee elections, a Human Rights Commission to address racial discrimination as well as persistent authoritarian practices, the Commission on Truth and Reconciliation to address legacies of violence and authoritarian rule, a Youth Commission, and, of course, the Commission on Gender Equality—these were all designed to give the new government greater flexibility, to challenge past practice, and to create a more democratic polity and culture.

Among these horizontal structures, the Commission on Gender Equality enjoyed remarkable visibility and unusual powers. With a broad mandate, its powers include the right to subpoena witnesses and evidence and the right to intervene in both public and private sites. The South African Commission on Gender Equality is an innovative institution, designed to allow feminist activists simultaneously to represent "women's interests" within state policymaking and to press for new gender relations in society at large. Drawing on feminist scholarship and international experience, South African activists were able to build into the 1996 Constitution an institutional framework that could empower feminist voices in the state. They created an autonomous horizontal body that would monitor new policies, represent women's concerns, and offer alternative understandings of gender in the public arena.

The commission's framework allowed femocrats to take a more active stance in relation to the broader society. While I worked at the Gender Commission, I sometimes observed lower-level bureaucrats such as policemen or election officers dismiss these new femocrats as representing "special interests," explicitly conflating the commission with a relatively powerless nongovernmental organization (NGO), but I also observed that top-level policymakers took the commission very seriously and that commissioners had easy access to national leaders and media outlets. In a context where a new democratically elected government is committed to principles of equality and nondiscrimination, the Gender Commission structure offered real possibilities for addressing the underlying dynamics of gender inequality.

The staffing of the new commission seemed likely to enhance these possibilities. The regulations for the Gender Commission require that Parliament nominate and the president appoint activists with strong records of commitment to gender equity. Although not all commissioners would necessarily use the term "feminist" to describe themselves, all were committed to organizing women and articulated concerns about gender equity; most had long histories of activism within the anti-apartheid movement, both in exile and within South Africa, lending greater credibility to the feminist agenda within the new government. The first chairperson, Thenjiwe Mtintso, was a prominent figure in both the ANC and the South African Communist Party and had a respected record as a leading guerrilla commander as well as diplomat and politician. Although she left the Gender Commission to become the ANC's deputy secretary general in late 1997, Mtintso's vision is clearly reflected in the Gender Commission's original mission statement. The Commission on Gender Equality (CGE) "will strive for the transformation of society through exposing gender discrimination in laws, policies and practices; advocating changes in sexist attitudes and gender stereotypes; instilling respect for women's rights as human rights" through the "transformation of gender relations; redefinition and redistribution of power; and equal access to and enjoyment of economic, social and political opportunities" (1997, 8; see Mtintso 2003).

Of the initial group of appointed commissioners, seven were women with strong backgrounds in political activism; the eighth, a man, was a progressive Muslim theologian explicitly committed to feminist activism. Several commissioners had strong ties to the South African women's movement as academics and activists; several commissioners had been active in social movements linked to the anti-apartheid movement, including the trade unions and the disabled people's movement. When Mtintso left the commission, she was replaced by Joyce Piliso-Seroke, who was appointed chairperson in 1999. With a long career in both the ANC and the Young Women's Christian Association, Piliso-Seroke has enormous experience in organizing women. In interviews, however, Piliso-Seroke was careful to distinguish her current work from her earlier role, insisting that the Gender Commission must address broader issues than just organizing women. Stressing the need to redefine masculinity and examine issues of reproductive rights and sexuality as well as the need to empower women economically and socially, she clearly viewed the Gender Commission's task in terms of what she called "strategic" feminist interventions that would challenge gender hierarchies instead of making efforts to simply help women survive within the existing gender framework.[1]

The first eight commissioners were appointed for terms up to five years and were generally expected to work full time on commission business. By mid-

1999, the Gender Commission had also hired thirty-eight staff people who worked in the national office or in one of three provincial offices. Recognizing uneven levels of background in feminist thought among commissioners and staff members, the commission required attendance at a three-week course in gender issues, with topics ranging from reproductive rights and sexuality to the construction of masculinity. The course syllabi suggest that the Gender Commission considered itself an explicitly feminist project—although, like endless internal discussions about how to organize the main office or how to regulate relationships between head office and provincial offices or how to negotiate with parliamentary committees and the president's office, the course also demonstrated commission staffers' sense that they were designing that project on the run.

From the ministerial gender desks to the independent Gender Commission, South Africa's "national machinery for women" was staffed by people committed to redefining gender who had a broad and thoughtful approach to what that project would entail. While the staff and commissioners continued to debate the outlines of the project—including some basic issues, such as whether the commission should be primarily a monitoring body or whether it would also engage directly in more programmatic activities or what the relationship should be between politically appointed commissioners and the staff people who worked under them—the commissioners and staff recognized that they were engaged in a remarkable experiment in strategic feminist intervention.

But by the end of the commission's first term in mid-2000, that promise appeared badly tarnished. A series of internal conflicts had left the commission in disarray. By mid-2000, more than half of the staff and several commissioners had resigned or been fired under circumstances that clearly intensified divisions within the broader South African women's movement. The commission's announcement that it could not coordinate activities for South African Women's Day in August 2000 seemed to reflect a loss of capacity and confidence that would be hard to repair.[2]

Outsiders often attributed conflicts in the commission to debate over whether the commission should provide practical services to women in South Africa: Should it just be a gendered development agency, providing help such as job training or income-generating schemes for women in rural communities, or should it see itself as a gender watchdog over the national development project? Although the Gender Commission did not generally conceive itself as a service-providing agency—and thus it avoided programmatic interventions that would attempt to offer women services—the line between policy discussion and service provision was sometimes blurred in reality, as women in specific communities sometimes approached the Gender Commission for help in resolving practical concerns, especially in relation to other, more service-oriented ministries. Yet although finding an appropriate balance between service provision and strategic intervention was often discussed, the question rarely caused internal conflict: most commissioners and staff members considered the commission's structure inappropriate for service provision. Indeed, the entire thrust of the new design was to create a site for policy discussion, mainstreaming gender issues into all government projects rather than creating a "women's ministry." Another common misunderstanding of the commission's internal conflicts emphasized personality strife between prominent individuals, a view given force when the conflicts degenerated into a handful of lawsuits over labor law problems by late 2001.

But as I hope to demonstrate, the stalemate that plagued the commission at the end of its first five years were created as much by underlying structural dynamics, legacies of unresolved tensions in the commission's initial design, as by debates over how to use resources or personality conflicts. Two different visions of the commission's role—which coincided with two different visions of how feminist activists should relate to a broader nation-building project—were in constant tension with each other, creating ongoing disagreements about goals, strategies, and resources.

Representing Women

The challenge facing the Gender Commission was from its inception two-sided. The Gender Commission was designed to represent women's interests, but its incumbents generally believed that their first project needed to be the mobilization of a popular constituency. These tasks involve two very different dynamics: defining and representing women's interests within the state, on the one hand, and mobilizing support for a feminist project, on the other. Balancing them, as the Gender Commission discovered, is considerably more difficult than fulfilling either one would be alone. The Gender Commission first had to decide which "women's interests" should be given priority; but aside from that problem, commissioners sought to offer a feminist critique within state policymaking debates while simultaneously building a constituency that would give that critique weight within the state.

The commission's goals were ambitious. In contrast to programs designed to "uplift" women through development programs, South African institutions were explicitly designed to address more complex issues, ranging from redefining masculinity to recalibrating underlying economic patterns that recreate gender inequality. In explicit contrast to the many new democracies that effectively marginalize women's issues to underfunded, understaffed women's ministries, South African policymakers hoped to empower feminist voices within the state, creating a gendered link between civil society and government officials (Albertyn 1992; Mabandla 1994). But in practice, the various projects embodied in the commission structure often came into conflict in ways that undermined the commission's ability to achieve any one of those aims.

In order to represent women's interests, the Gender Commission first had to define them. Having abandoned a biological, essentialist understanding of gender, how should "women's interests" be defined—especially in a society as divided as South Africa's, where differences of race, class, culture, and politics are magnified by the legacies of apartheid (Sapiro 1998)? Women's interests are always diverse and multifaceted, especially, perhaps, in postcolonial societies such as South Africa, where differences of class, race, and urban/rural location mean that women face very different challenges. Most South African feminists acknowledged the challenge of defining "women's interests," an especially complicated task for the urban middle-class women—white and black—who tend to staff feminist institutions and organizations and who are profoundly aware that they face very different challenges from those that rural black women contend with. Where should the Gender Commission begin the proactive task of constructing a positively gendered citizenship, and where—given the way gender dynamics are interwoven into all social relations—should it step aside to allow other government agencies to address citizens' concerns?

But beyond the problem of interest definition lurked another issue: How should commissioners "represent" women? The problem was magnified by the independence inherent in the commission's horizontal structure. Because commissioners are not elected, there is little direct accountability to a broader constituency. How should commissioners decide what issues to "represent" and which issues to raise in public? Once appointments are approved, the commission has little control over commissioners' public behavior. The Gender Commission lacked control over basic aspects of commissioners' days, including how they spent their working hours, what they chose to say as public representatives of the commission, or whether and when they had to report back to other commissioners. No obvious structural mechanisms existed through which the commission could debate positions before they were taken publicly by any appointed commissioners. Similarly, the commission had no mechanisms through which to respond to commissioners' public statements once they had been made. Commissioners and staff members seemed to voice issues of importance to them as individuals, either because of their personal experience or because of their theoretical understanding of the bases of gender inequality. Commissioners invited to speak in public could do so without first vetting their discussion with the rest of the commission, yet public statements by individuals were often treated as commission interventions (Alexander and Mohanty 1997, xxxix; Seidman 2001). Thus, for example, a commissioner who believed firmly that domestic violence is more common among poorer, less-educated groups suggested that the commission should support educational programs in squatter areas; another commissioner was concerned that the commission monitor public employment programs to make sure women were included; another drew on her experience in adult education to discuss the need to make adult education available to women. In each case, the individual commissioners' public statements were treated in media discussions as if they reflected a broader commission consensus. But in general, commissioners seemed reluctant to ask their fellow commissioners about the underlying justification for public statements.

Commissioners faced a further problem: however defined, the feminist ideology espoused by most commissioners is far from widespread in South African society. The commission was designed to allow democratic input through individual complaints and through provincial workshops. Under this model, commissioners would serve as independent monitors and ombudspersons to ensure that government programs do not persistently reproduce gender inequality. When asked how the commission sets its goals, many staff members referred to input from "the public" as a key stimulus. But when the commission tried to create channels through which ordinary women could articulate their concerns—through individual complaints and through regional workshops—the concerns that were expressed were often far removed from a broader feminist project. Sometimes suggestions simply asked the commission to intervene to help women within an existing set of gender relations; sometimes they took the commission far from what might normally be considered a central concern for feminist policymakers.

Suggestions stemming from individual complaints or local workshops often directed the commission's attention away from programs that could be considered feminist by almost any definition. Individual complaints tended to remain completely within an existing framework of gender relations instead of raising concerns that feminists had not already considered.[3] Nearly two-thirds of individual complaints focused on fathers' failure to pay child support—a systemic problem in South Africa, where high rates of family disintegration are combined with high rates of poverty, unemployment, and migration, producing one of the highest percentages of female-headed households in the world. Gender Commission staff found themselves at a loss. Although they were painfully aware of the deficiencies of the maintenance system—of women's inability to negotiate the court system; of unequal resources that allow men to hire lawyers, postpone hearings, delay payments; of the inaccurate information court clerks sometimes provide; of fathers who simply disappear from the scene, leaving the court unable to enforce maintenance orders—the Gender Commission could not force fathers to perform any better than the court system already did. While the commission supported efforts to propose reforms in the maintenance system, activists in the social welfare ministry and NGOs focusing on child support issues were clearly better equipped for dealing with the intricacies of reform proposals.

Although staff people took individual complaints very seriously, trying to suggest avenues where complainants might get help, they increasingly began to view complaints as a potential source of test cases. This meant, in practice, that there was active searching for potential cases on issues for which the commission sought to mobilize support and promote reforms. For example, staff members were aware that under apartheid, official refusal to recognize customary marriages had created nightmares around inheritance for polygamous households. One morning, the commission's janitor reported that when her friend's husband had died recently, his family refused to recognize the unregistered polygamous marriage. The deceased husband's family removed all his property, leaving his two widows and children destitute. Commission staff members sought out the widows, hoping to use the case to test legislation regarding inheritance in customary marriages, seeking to create more safeguards for the millions of African women in unregistered polygamous households. Thus, the individual complaint provided the basis for a test case, but along reformist lines that the commission had already envisaged.

Similarly, irregularly scheduled provincial workshops were meant to provide channels for public access. Discussions at such workshops prompted the commission to consider the feminist importance of demands for better water supplies, more equitable household arrangements, or the gendered impact of South Africa's HIV epidemic. But sometimes projects designed through processes intended to increase representation came into direct conflict with the commission's efforts to mobilize a feminist constituency, and after the commission had been in existence for several years, it was widely agreed that provincial debates had not stimulated new directions. Sometimes workshops directed the commission's resources toward projects that sat less comfortably with an informed feminist perspective. In 1998, the commission spent an inordinate amount of resources and energy organizing programs in the Northwest Province, responding to frenzied attacks on people whom villagers believed were involved in black magic. Helping the victims of witchcraft violence was certainly a worthwhile effort, but more than half of the victims of the attacks were male. Most analyses of the witchcraft violence of the Northwest Province point to tensions arising from rapid economic dislocation, not gender transgressions (Comaroff and Comaroff 1999a, 1999b). By mid-1999, many staff members argued that other branches of government were better suited for intervening on behalf of the victims than the relatively small Gender Commission, whose resources might be better spent on programs more directly related to gender equity.

By mid-1999, commission staff members had come to view provincial workshops strategically as a site where they could mobilize support and justification for feminist interventions instead of a place where new issues would be articulated by outsiders. Thus, probably the most interesting suggestion to arise from a provincial workshop in the commission's first four years—a proposal to monitor local job-creation programs, to ensure that women also gained employment from state-sponsored public works—turned out to have been initiated within the commission. Although the commission greeted the suggestion with excitement, as if it were a spontaneous suggestion, in fact, the idea was generated within the commission. When a local politician asked the commission to write his speech opening the workshop, a commission staff member inserted the proposal that the Gender Commission should monitor a new job creation program in the province.[4]

The horizontal, independent structure of the commission, then, gave it enormous latitude in deciding which issues it would prioritize. But although this structure increased the autonomy of feminist voices within the state, it sometimes came into conflict with the commission's desire to represent women's concerns: exactly which voices should be represented, and how commissioners would represent those voices, was not explicit in the institutional design. Individual commissioners were rarely held accountable to the commission, while the failure of public channels to point the commission in directions that might be consistent with feminist theoretical concerns led commissioners and staff members increasingly to view their role as stimulating feminist discussions and raising feminist concerns rather than representing or reflecting public debates. As I suggest in the next section, however, this shift created its own problems, as some commissioners began to worry that controversial stances might undermine the commission's credibility.

Mobilizing a Constituency

Although the Gender Commission was initially conceived as a monitoring body, after four years of service, most commissioners discussed their project as much in terms of mobilizing support for a feminist agenda as in terms of monitoring government policies and representing women's interests. Their reasoning explicitly reflected their own background as activists with feminist sympathies. In conversations and interviews, commissioners and staff people acknowledged that public support for feminism is far weaker in South Africa than public statements imply, and they viewed mobilizing support for a new understanding of gender relations as a primary goal. For many commissioners and staff members, a first priority had to be raising feminist concerns in public, creating a greater awareness of gender inequality as a first step toward ending it.

But this emphasis on mobilizing support for feminism often created internal tensions. While some commissioners and staff members argued that the commission should be a voice for theoretically informed feminism, others worried that if the commission took controversial positions, it might be marginalized in the public eye. Repeatedly, commissioners suggested that the broad gap between the commission's stated goals and the public's attitudes required the commission to move carefully: controversy could provoke resistance. Some disillusioned staff members suggested that commissioners who sought to avoid controversy were hoping to advance their individual careers within the government, viewing a noncontroversial term as a Gender Commissioner as a stepping-stone to further government appointments. In contrast, several commissioners saw avoiding controversy as a principled stance, an effort to ensure that the feminist project retained political support within the ANC and the government. Because public support for feminist goals was shallow, several commissioners suggested, the Gender Commission would be wise to demonstrate that strategic feminist interventions could improve the lives of all South Africans instead of pursuing goals that might divide women from men or older women from younger ones. Sustaining popular support in the present would be a critical step in giving popular legitimacy to feminist policies in the future.

Given South Africa's demographic structure, this search for an acceptable face to feminist intervention took a very specific form. Repeatedly, commissioners and staff members insisted that the Gender Commission had no choice but to concentrate on issues relevant to South Africa's majority; that is, issues relevant to the lives of women who are poor and black. The commission's mission statement reflects this concern: although the commission defined its constituency as "all the people of South Africa," it asserts that "its target group is people living on the periphery, especially women in rural areas, on farms, in peri-urban areas, and in domestic employment"—meaning, in the South African context, poor African women rather than the urban middle-class women, white and black. The Gender Commission described its goal as the effort to "bring to the center the voices and experiences of the marginalized, to become part of, and to inform, the nation building and transformation agenda of South African society" (Commission on Gender Equality 1997).

In practice, this vision was quickly redefined away from an initial emphasis on class to a geographic targeting of rural African women (CGE 1997; for more on this position, see Mtintso 2003). In general, consensus could only be reached in relation to issues directly relevant to African women living in rural areas. This target group was regularly invoked in discussions about priorities or when defining how commission resources should be used. For example, the commission was far more active in public debates about how to reform the laws governing customary marriages, under which most African women are married, and in ensuring that job creation and economic development programs include women than it was in challenging the corporate glass ceiling. Staff members were concerned to ensure that commission resources should be concentrated on improving the lives of women outside the main urban centers, to demonstrate that feminist projects were relevant to South Africa's larger nation-building project.

In the day-to-day working of the office, however, this effort had negative consequences for some issues that might have seemed important to a theoretical feminist agenda. Commissioners or staff members invoked the commission's target group—or, as it was sometimes self-consciously referred to, "our constituency"—to block discussion of issues that might provoke controversy. When some staff members proposed a campaign to decriminalize sex work, several commissioners objected strenuously. The debate over sex work seems to have marked the limits of internal tolerance. Opponents of decriminalization clearly viewed sex workers in strongly moralistic terms, rejecting efforts to describe sex work in terms of gendered poverty and vulnerability rather than individual choice. Indeed, when proponents of decriminalization suggested that decriminalization might well help poor rural women because they might turn to sex work for lack of alternatives, an angry commissioner responded that such a stance implied that all African women were prostitutes.[5] Although the plenary session's minutes reflect a decision to address sex work, the commission appeared to have dropped the issue completely, and the staff members and commissioner who initially proposed this direction refused to raise it again. Like many other issues involving sexuality, including reproductive rights and HIV prevention, the decriminalization debate appears to have been too uncomfortable for the commission to pursue it.[6]

The debate over decriminalization of sex work demonstrated the limits of the Gender Commission's feminist interventions. Controversial challenges to standard understandings of "appropriate" behavior apparently posed a threat to the commission's other project, that of mobilizing public support for its goals. Representing the concerns of women involved in sex work might fit a theoretical feminist agenda, but many commissioners apparently feared that such positions would undermine the commission's efforts to mobilize support for feminist perspectives more generally.

The structural tension between trying to pursue feminist interventions while mobilizing a broad constituency—all while trying to privilege the concerns of a target group of poor women in rural areas—contributed in large measure to the stalemate that plagued the Gender Commission in mid-2000. When commissioners invoked "the rural poor" to block potentially controversial programs, they risked undermining the commission's ability to draw on the skills and energy of already mobilized feminist activists. The academics and NGO professionals, black and white, who have generally articulated feminist issues are almost entirely urban and middle class. Although women's groups are spread throughout the country and although rural South African women are often able to describe their concerns in ways consistent with "strategic" feminist agendas, the South African women's movement has been best organized and most visible in urban areas, including poor black townships as well as middle-class sites. In its decision to avoid the activist women's groups in urban areas—especially groups that include middle-class Africans and white feminists—the commission turned away from precisely those groups most likely to support a feminist approach and toward groups of women much less likely to support controversial challenges to existing gender relations.

There are concrete indications that the decision to concentrate on representing "the rural poor" undermined links between the commission and urban feminist activists. In some of its first meetings, the commissioners decided to create a series of consultative workshops around specific areas of concern, hoping to embed the commission's discussions within a broader network of feminist activists and academics. During the commission's first year, many feminist activists were asked to serve on the commission's advisory bodies to ensure that the new structure drew on existing feminist expertise and activism as it developed strategies for intervention. Similarly, in its annual reports, the commission stressed its efforts to build partnerships with women's groups and feminist academics. But the commission never apparently activated these feminist networks of "consultative groups," much to the disappointment of many activists, who increasingly viewed the commission as unhelpful.

Further, the commission had difficulty creating formal links to urban-based women's organizations, including groups that represented poor women in townships and squatter areas. Although the commission sustained strong links to gay and lesbian activist groups, the distance between organized urban women's groups and the commission was perplexing. In mid-1999, a legal NGO called a meeting to discuss child welfare reform proposals. At the meeting, township women's groups' representatives were openly puzzled by the commission, asking who it represented, what it could do for their groups, what its role would be in representing their voices. Commission staff members attended the meeting, but they told participants they were there to listen and learn. An energetic Gender Commission staffer offered to photocopy materials, but the activists were clearly dismayed by the commission's failure either to help shape a feminist response to the proposed legislation or provide concrete resources for their efforts.

Conversely, several commissioners and staff members expressed frustration with the inability of feminist activists outside the government to understand the importance of the commission's other tasks; specifically, the task of mobilizing broad political support for feminist projects. They frequently found fault with individual activists in feminist NGOs, viewing specific individuals as competitive, difficult, or, in the case of some white feminist activists, inadequately sensitive to issues of race and culture.

Over time, tensions over how the commission should define its projects— tensions linked to its efforts to simultaneously represent feminist voices and mobilize support for a feminist vision—undermined the commission's efficacy. By mid-2000, many feminist scholars and NGO activists, black and white, openly expressed a sense of alienation from the very institution they had helped design, criticizing the commission publicly to journalists and even going so far in private conversations as to suggest that the government should consider cutting its funding.[7] Some commissioners, including several with strong links to international feminist networks, resigned their positions, returning to academe or to nongovernmental work, and the commission forced the resignation of its visible chief staffperson. Through the first half of 2000, nineteen staff members resigned or were fired, including several with strong backgrounds in feminist activism or scholarship. Although most of the individuals involved perceived the conflicts in terms of personalities and individual loyalties, underlying the surface tensions were competing visions of feminism. The institutionalized understanding of the Gender Commission's project increasingly stressed a more pragmatic, safer understanding of feminist intervention, emphasizing service to women within an existing framework of gender relations rather than promoting direct challenges to persistent gender inequality.

In the fraught relationship between the Gender Commission and South African feminist activists, the structural tension between representation and mobilization was almost tangible. Gender Commissioners—themselves educated, urban, and middle class—hoped to represent the majority of South African women, but even if most poor rural women are willing to define their interests in terms of challenging gender hierarchies, they rarely articulated their interests in broader feminist terms or sought to challenge the hierarchies of power that sustain gender inequality. Unwilling to pursue issues that might be specific to urban middle-class women or those that might provoke controversy among core political supporters, the Gender Commissioners and staff tended to neglect the more sophisticated—and more urban, more middle-class—women who had already been mobilized in support of feminist goals.

By mid-2000, the Gender Commission's exclusion of already mobilized feminists had produced an ironic result: the commission was far more likely to target an audience that would act like dependents needing assistance than as a constituency the commission represents, effectively recreating the institutional patterns of countless women's ministries across Africa, who have sought to provide services that will help women survive within an existing set of gender relations and undermining the very constituency on whom the commission would have to rely if it wished to promote feminist concerns.

During the first five years of South Africa's democratic experience, gender policymakers appeared so insistent on representing the concerns of poor women that they seemed to undermine the likelihood that already mobilized feminists could participate at all—perhaps replacing the risk that democratization would undermine links between grassroots women's groups and the professional feminists who staff new state institutions with a different problem. Instead, it seemed likely that privileging grassroots and popular gender concerns would undermine the state's ability to take up more controversial or complicated feminist issues. As committed feminists turned away from new state structures in frustration, the Gender Commission became increasingly isolated and embattled.

Conclusion

By mid-2001, the South African Gender Commission seemed to be moving out of its impasse. New appointments to the commission, combined with renewed efforts by feminist activists to reengage with the commission, seemed to reinfuse energy into gender policy discussions. Several strong feminist activists were appointed to the commission, giving it greater credibility within activist feminist circles and helping rebuild its links to already mobilized feminists. The commission also seemed to be taking stronger stances on more controversial issues, even challenging government policy in key areas such as South Africa's HIV epidemic. By rebuilding links with feminist activists, reconstructing working relationships within the commission and between the commission and non-state feminists, the commission seemed to be seeking new directions.

But the lessons of the commission's first few years, as it struggled to design a workable structure for feminist intervention, demand reflection. In the construction of the Gender Commission, feminist activists sought to create an independent body that would have the power to intervene in basic gender relations, an institution that would simultaneously monitor new government policies, provide feminists access to government policymaking processes, and ensure that gender issues could be raised throughout South African society. But in its early years, feminist policymakers confronted institutional dilemmas that resonate beyond South Africa's borders.

Having created an independent body that could move freely—representing feminist voices within the state while maintaining close ties to a nongovernmental women's movement—South African femocrats found nonetheless that political pressures quickly complicated their efforts. Although the commission's designers clearly privileged issues of feminist representation in and feminist access to policymaking discussions, the commission shifted increasingly toward mobilization, orienting the commission's energy and resources toward women less likely to be part of the women's movement. As part of the effort to mobilize support, commissioners avoided controversy—a strategy that created conflict between those femocrats who sought to construct a feminist project within the state and those whose goals involved mobilizing a constituency for women's issues within a broader national development project.

South Africa is perhaps an unusually complicated society, where ordinary disagreements between feminist activists are quickly intensified by differences of racial identity, cultural traditions, and political perspectives. But the experiences of the Gender Commission underscore the institutional challenges facing feminist policymakers, as they feel themselves forced to choose between representation, mobilization, or both.

Of course, that choice may ultimately prove to be a false one. The stalemate at the Gender Commission in mid-2000 may demonstrate that it is not entirely possible to distinguish the task of feminist representation within the state from the effort to mobilize popular support. Perhaps feminist interventions are by nature controversial: inevitably, they challenge basic gender relations, inequality, and power. In the absence of broad support for feminist goals, feminist policymakers who want to represent women's interests within the state in feminist terms will also have to strengthen feminist support outside the state. In seeking a way out of its stalemate, perhaps the Gender Commission will be able to forge a third path, mobilizing support not for a socialist or developmentalist state but for feminist interventions, creating a popular constituency that will provide a base of support for feminist policymakers as they represent women's interests within the state in the future.

Notes

This essay benefited from helpful comments from many people, but I would like especially to thank Shireen Hassim for her theoretical insights and the commissioners and staff members of the South African Commission on Gender Equality for permission to conduct this research. The University of Wisconsin, Madison Graduate School generously provided research support. A longer version of this essay was originally published in *Feminist Studies* 29, no. 3 (Fall 2003): 541–563.

1. Interview with Joyce Piliso-Seroke, June 1999.
2. Turner (2000); interviews by author, 2000.
3. There are, of course, some exceptions. In 1998, the complaints of a young man who had been raped in prison prompted commission efforts to get legislative wording changed to make male as well as female rape a legal offense.
4. Interviews with author, 1999.
5. The racial tensions that emerged during the sex work debate threatened to make visible the racial undertones that often infuse debates about the definition of feminism, like all else, in South Africa. Although commissioners and staff members—who are nearly all black—rejected any racial distinction between "white" and "black" feminisms, some black commissioners insisted that if the commission's public profile became too

"white," opponents could easily dismiss gender equality as a form of cultural imperialism. Similarly, some white commissioners and staff members expressed concern that feminism should be defined in a way that would make it central to South Africa's "nonracial" democratic project, rather than separated out. See Seidman (2001).

6. In mid-2000, almost two years after decriminalization was discussed in a commission plenary, South Africa's Law Commission (a body charged with revisiting existing legislation in order to renew and reform South Africa's legal framework) proposed to consider decriminalizing sex work; but although several women's NGOs and a former commissioner were actively involved in Law Commission discussions, the Gender Commission itself remained silent.

7. Turner (2000); interviews with author, 2000.

References

Albertyn, Catherine. 1992. "Women and Politics: Choices in Structural Mechanisms to Empower Women in a Democratic Government." Paper presented at the workshop on Structural Mechanisms to Empower Women in a Democratic Government, Durban, South Africa, December 4–6.

Alexander, M. Jacqui, and Chandra Talpade Mohanty. 1997. "Introduction: Genealogies, Legacies, Movements." In Feminist Genealogies, Colonial Legacies, Democratic Futures, edited by M. Jacqui Alexander and Chandra Talpade Mohanty. London: Routledge.

Comaroff, Jean, and John Comaroff. 1999a. "Alien-Nation, Zombies, Immigrants, and Millennial Capitalism." American Bar Foundation Working Paper 9901.

———. 1999b. "Cultural Policing in Postcolonial South Africa." American Bar Foundation Working Paper 9902.

Commission on Gender Equality. 1997. Mission Statement. In author's possession.

Gatens, Moira. 1998. "Institutions, Embodiment, and Sexual Difference." In Gender and Institutions: Welfare, Work, and Citizenship, edited by Moira Gatens and Alison McKinnon, 1–15. Cambridge: Cambridge University Press.

Hassim, Shireen. 2002. "Identities, Interests, and Constituencies: The Politics of the Women's Movement in South Africa, 1980–1999." Ph.D. diss., York University.

———, and Amanda Gouws. 1998. "Redefining the Public Space: Women's Organizations, Gender Consciousness, and Civil Society in South Africa." Politikon: South African Journal of Political Studies 25: 53–76.

Kaplan, Temma. 1997. Crazy for Democracy: Women in Grassroots Movements. New York: Routledge.

Mabandla, Brigitte. 1994. "Choices for South African Women." Agenda 20: 22–29.

Macaulay, Fiona. 2000. "Getting Gender on the Policy Agenda: A Study of a Brazilian Feminist Lobby Group." In Hidden Histories of Gender and the State in Latin America, edited by Elizabeth Dore and Maxine Molyneux, 346–367. Durham, N.C.: Duke University Press.

Molyneux, Maxine. 1985. "Mobilization without Emancipation? Women's Interests, the State, and Revolution in Nicaragua." Feminist Studies 11, no. 2: 227–254.

———. 2000. "State, Gender, and Institutional Change: The Federacion de Mujeres Cubanas." In Hidden Histories of Gender and the State in Latin America, edited by Elizabeth Dore and Maxine Molyneux, 291–321. Durham, N.C.: Duke University Press.

Mtintso, Thenjiwe. 2003. "Representativity: False Sisterhood or Universal Women's Interests? The South African Experience." *Feminist Studies* 29, no. 3: 569–579.

Pringle, Rosemary, and Sophie Watson. 1992. "'Women's Interests' and the Post-Structuralist State." In *De-Stabilizing Theory: Contemporary Feminist Debate,* edited by Michele Barrett and Anne Phillips, 53–73. Stanford, Calif.: Stanford University Press.

Sapiro, Virginia. 1998. "When Are Interests Interesting? The Problem of Political Representation of Women." In *Feminism and Politics,* edited by Anne Phillips, 161–192. Oxford: Oxford University Press.

Seidman, Gay W. 1999. "Gendered Citizenship: South Africa's Democratic Transition and the Construction of a Gendered State." *Gender & Society* 13, no. 3: 287–307.

———. 2001. "'Strategic' Challenges to Gender Inequality: The South African Gender Commission." *Ethnography* 2, no. 2: 219–241.

Stacey, Judith. 1983. *Patriarchy and Socialist Revolution in China.* Berkeley: University of California Press.

Staudt, Kathleen. 1998. *Policy, Politics, and Gender: Women Gaining Ground.* West Hartford, Conn.: Kumarian Press.

Stetson, Dorothy, and Amy Mazur, eds. 1995. *Comparative State Feminism.* Thousand Oaks, Calif.: Sage Publications.

Turner, Nicole. 2000. "Disputes Still Rack Gender Commission: Infighting Has Discredited the Commission as an Agent for Change." *The Sunday Independent/ Reconstruct,* July 9, 1.

3 Gendered Reproduction: Placing Schoolgirl Pregnancies in African History

Lynn M. Thomas

More than fifteen years ago, Nancy Rose Hunt (1989) noted the profound irony that while much scholarship on women and gender in African history has been framed through the Marxist-feminist analytics of production and reproduction, historians have left the conventional meaning of reproduction—procreation—largely unexplored. The first generation of women's historians, largely Europeans and Americans, focused their attention on documenting the centrality of women's labor to African economies. As second-wave feminists, they sought to challenge sexist ideologies that situated women exclusively in the domestic realm and reduced their social roles to their biological capacities. For these reasons and for fear of contributing to racist stereotypes dating back to the era of the slave trade that depicted African women as oversexed and exceptionally fertile, they avoided examining the more intimate aspects of reproduction. In identifying feminist historians' reluctance to study procreation, Hunt argued that this scholarship had left an important part of African social and symbolic life unexamined.[1]

Others also noticed the gap. In books published in 1987 and 1997, Ifi Amadiume and Oyeronke Oyewumi pointed to Western feminists' refusal to examine the centrality of fertility and maternity in African women's lives as an example of how exogenous rather than indigenous categories and concerns continued to inform scholarship on Africa. These books contributed to broader debates, discussed in this volume's introduction, over who could and should interpret African women's experiences. Amadiume and Oyewumi argued that Western feminists had fundamentally misunderstood African societies. According to Amadiume (1987, 185), precolonial Igboland was characterized not by men's domination of women but by a "flexible gender system" in which women "could play roles usually monopolized by men, or be classified as 'males' in terms of power and authority over others." Oyewumi (1997, 34–36, 156) went further to argue that gender did not exist in precolonial Yorùbá society, only the reproductive distinction between anafemales (anatomical females, *obìnrin*) and ana-males (anatomical males, *okùnrin*). Gender difference and its accompanying notion that women are of "no account," Oyewumi explained, came with European colonialism. Amadiume and Oyewumi also argued that the most important divisions within precolonial Igbo and Yorùbá societies were constituted through age and seniority, constructs that Western feminists had generally ignored. Together, their arguments about the importance of reproduction and age hierarchies suggested that what women/anafemales have shared is not a common subordination to men but the potential to claim power through procreation. Gwendolyn Mikell (1997, 4) too has emphasized the centrality of fertility and maternity within African women's lives in the postcolonial period by identifying pronatalism as a key tenet of "emerging African feminism."

My research has engaged such insights by exploring the history of reproductive politics in twentieth-century central Kenya. In *Politics of the Womb: Women, Reproduction, and the State in Kenya* (2003), I examine colonial and postcolonial debates and interventions surrounding abortion, female initiation and excision, premarital pregnancy, childbirth, and paternity support. These are important historical episodes because they reveal how various people—including colonial and postcolonial officials, politicians, missionaries and local church leaders, parents, elders, and youth—have viewed the regulation of fertility and sexuality as fundamental to the construction of proper gender and generational relations and political and moral order. While reproduction has been a central political and moral concern in twentieth-century central Kenya, its meanings have continually been contested and consistently linked to both gender and generational relations. The questions of who is fit to conceive and who is fit to give birth have never simply been answered by anatomy, as Oyewumi argues for precolonial Yorùbá society. Rather, these questions have been part of broader debates over how to prepare female bodies and minds for procreation and how to ensure that their fertility contributes to the composition of wealth, not immiseration and misfortune.

In contrast to Oyewumi's argument that reproduction was a socially decisive but ungendered process, my research in another part of the continent suggests reproduction as a crucial site through which distinctions of maleness and femaleness as well as distinctions of age and wealth have been elaborated. Admittedly, my material does not directly address the precolonial period. Yet the range and intensity of debates over abortion, female initiation, bridewealth, childbirth, premarital pregnancy, courtship, and marriage in colonial and postcolonial Africa suggest to me that the intimate relationship between gender ideologies and procreative processes—what I would call gendered reproduction—has deep historical roots in this part of the world, as it does in others. Colonialism, through its racist and sexist ideologies and institutions, no doubt, challenged and ultimately transformed the politics of reproduction within Africa. But to cast gendered reproduction as simply a colonial invention is to grant Euro-American colonizers enormous agency and to deny the efficacy of African reproductive ideas and practices.

The Modern Girl as Pregnant Schoolgirl

This chapter seeks to elaborate the close associations between gender ideologies and procreative processes in a number of different African contexts by examining the figure of the pregnant schoolgirl. This figure is particularly illustrative of how reproduction in twentieth-century Africa was not simply a matter of anatomy but rather was linked to wide-ranging efforts to define proper gender and generational relations and secure wealth. My interest in schoolgirl pregnancy stems from my previous work on the history of reproductive politics in Kenya and a new project on the history of the Modern Girl in a number of different sub-Saharan African contexts. Whereas my earlier research engaged key concerns in Africanist scholarship on gender and women, concerns that have been articulated by the likes of Hunt, Amadiume, Oyewumi, and Mikell, my new project seeks to bring these concerns into conversation with those generated through my participation in the Modern Girl Research Group. This group consists of six faculty members at the University of Washington with regional expertise in Africa, Asia, Europe, and the United States who work in the fields of English, History, International Studies, and Women's Studies. Together, we have developed the Modern Girl as a heuristic category to explore the global emergence during the 1920s and 1930s of female figures who appeared to reject the roles of dutiful daughter, wife, and mother through their engagement of international commodity cultures, mass media, and political discourses (Modern Girl Research Group 2005a, 2005b).[2] Working in close collaboration with non-Africanist colleagues has encouraged me to think more broadly about what distinguishes academic and popular discussions of gender in Africa.

My initial investigations suggest that for much of sub-Saharan Africa, the Modern Girl has been synonymous with the schoolgirl and graduate. And within popular discourse, schoolgirls and graduates have just as often been defined by their reproductive predicaments as by their educational achievements. The figure of the pregnant schoolgirl has become the subject of broad public debate in recent decades. By prompting expulsion from school or temporarily disrupting attendance, schoolgirl pregnancies can ruin reputations, spoil parents' investment in school fees, and dim their and their daughters' hopes that schooling will lead to lucrative employment and/or marriage to a wealthy man. African novelists from Meja Mwangi in *Striving for the Wind* (1990/1992) to Sindiwe Magona in *Mother to Mother* (1998) have powerfully explored the intimate, and often imbalanced, gender relations that give rise to the pregnant schoolgirl. They have also highlighted the dashed dreams, stymied investments, and unanticipated dilemmas embodied in her being.

This chapter seeks to place these contemporary concerns in historical perspective by suggesting how the timing and social circumstances surrounding conception and birth have long been a concern to parents and young people and the communities in which they live. Present-day concerns over schoolgirl pregnancies belong to a long and broad history of gendered and generational struggles over health, wealth, and power. I will focus on two aspects of this longer and broader history. The first involves the relationship between schoolgirl pregnancies and pre-initiation pregnancies; the second centers on the relationship between the figures of the schoolgirl, the prostitute, and the pregnant fiancée. Keeping with the transdisciplinary spirit of this volume, I use historical evidence to make arguments that share the concern of structuralist anthropology with persistent social forms and the attention of literary studies to archetypes.

Schoolgirl Pregnancies and Pre-Initiation Pregnancies

Many of the reproductive debates and interventions I have examined took place in Meru, a rural area encompassing the northeastern slopes of Mt. Kenya and the surrounding plains.[3] During the 1910s and 1920s—the first decades of colonial rule in Meru—female initiation was an elaborate prenuptial process extending from several months to a couple of years. Initiation began only after a girl had passed puberty and, ideally, had become betrothed. It entailed three separate physical procedures—ear piercing, abdominal scarification, and female genital cutting—each of which was surrounded by dances, celebrations, and teachings. Excision was followed by a seclusion of three or more months during which older women cared for initiates, feeding them large amounts of food and instructing them about how to behave in their future roles as wives and daughters-in-law. Female initiation required parents, neighbors, and kin to pool enormous amounts of material resources so initiates and others who participated in the celebrations could feast on meat, porridge, and beer.[4]

Within this context of female initiation as a highly valued and much-anticipated process, one of the greatest breaches of morality and respectful behavior (*nthoni*) was for an uninitiated girl to become pregnant. As women interviewed in the 1990s explained, a being conceived under such circumstances was not a proper person. If born and allowed to live, it would endanger the lives of kin and neighbors, bringing misfortune and even death.[5] Pre-initiation pregnancies violated morality because they occurred within bodies that had not been prepared for procreation. Pregnancy and birth did not belong to girls but to those who had become women through initiation. In discussing this belief, one Methodist missionary, who worked in Meru during the 1930s, explained that people viewed children as a link between themselves and their ancestors; ancestors cursed children conceived by uninitiated girls in order to express their anger at those girls for becoming pregnant before they had been consecrated to do so (Holding 1942). The most common remedies for curbing the destructive potential of pre-initiation pregnancies were abortion and, when that failed, infanticide.[6] The stigma of such pregnancies, however, clung to the girls even after the fetus was aborted or the newborn killed. Those whose boyfriends refused to marry them often married older men as second or third wives.[7]

Merus were not alone in these beliefs and practices. Nandi who lived in the Rift Valley area of colonial Kenya also believed that pregnancies conceived by uninitiated girls posed grave moral dangers.[8] According to one colonial officer, it was fear of such pregnancies that motivated others in Kenya, including Kikuyus, to initiate girls prior to puberty rather than prior to marriage.[9] Farther afield, in central and southern Africa, where female initiation did not usually include genital cutting, people also believed that pre-initiation pregnancies threatened the living. As Audrey Richards wrote in her classic study of Bemba female initiation, children born to uninitiated girls were "creature[s] of ill-omen" who brought misfortune to their home villages by stopping rainfall, making granaries empty quickly, and compelling their parents and themselves to be driven into the bush (1956/1982, 33–34).[10] Similarly, in his 1933 study of premarital pregnancy among the Tswana, Isaac Schapera explained that previously, a girl who became pregnant prior to initiation and marriage was "subjected to every possible humiliation"; she was called "whore" and "publicly mocked by the other girls and women, who would . . . sing obscene songs reviling her and her people." Schapera noted that such pregnancies ended in abortion or infanticide (Schapera 1933, 59–89, esp. 67). These accounts of severe condemnation of pre-initiation pregnancies suggest how in late precolonial and early colonial contexts, if not earlier, many Africans viewed initiation as an indispensable process for readying girls for conception and childbirth. In their survey of adolescent fertility, Caroline Bledsoe and Barney Cohen (1993, chapter 4) provide further examples of how girls have secured reproductive entitlement through initiation processes that usually require the investment of significant resources by parents.

Such insights raise a number of important issues about the relationships between initiation, schooling, and pregnancy. To a certain extent, schooling appears to have inherited from initiation the role of pooling parents' resources in order to prepare girls for reproduction and marriage. In 1990s Meru, I found that older women who had rejected female initiation for their daughters often explained their decision by stating that while in their youth they had eagerly anticipated the celebrations that initiation entailed and the status it conferred, girls today rightly direct their attention and enthusiasm toward schooling.[11] Similarly, Pamela Feldman-Savelsberg (1989, 216) has noted that older women in postcolonial Cameroon equate schooling with previous practices of seclusion and fattening of adolescent girls. They observe that "girls [are] sitting in school doing no physical labor, eating up household resources, and preparing themselves for marriage." Schooling also appears to have inherited from initiation the ability to define some pregnancies as unacceptable. Accounts from contemporary African newspapers, novels, and medical journals of schoolgirls procuring backstreet abortions or dumping newborns in pit latrines resonate quite strongly with older remedies for limiting the dangers of pre-initiation pregnancies (Amelsvoort 1976, 42–44; "Tough Choices" 2000).[12]

Yet it is not possible to see schooling as simply replacing initiation. Today, many girls attend school and undergo initiation.[13] In such contexts, it is important to consider the different and perhaps overlapping ways people view these two forms of education as preparing girls for their future roles as mothers and wives. Schooling also departs from initiation in appearing to offer more room for negotiating which pregnancies are socially viable. With pre-initiation pregnancies in Meru, at least, the fact of whether one was initiated or not determined whether a pregnancy was acceptable or problematic. Schooling, on the other hand, is not such an easily defined process. It can span many years and conclude at various points. Moreover, not all schoolgirl pregnancies end in abortion or infanticide. To better understand the possible continuities and disjunctures between social condemnation of pre-initiation and schoolgirl pregnancies, we need to know more about why some schoolgirls have accepted motherhood while others have not.[14] To what extent have religious beliefs, material concerns (variously linked to bridewealth, school fees, and marriage), and considerations of reputation informed their decisions, and how have these considerations shifted over the twentieth century?

To understand the relationship between pre-initiation and schoolgirl pregnancies, we must also identify the disparities obscured by analogies drawn between the two processes. In her ethnography of schooling, Amy Stambach (2000) considers why so many people in 1990s northern Tanzania talked about initiation as a form of schooling. Why, Stambach asks, did they describe initiation by using the Swahili and English terms for "schoolteachers" (*walimu*), "school lessons" (*mafundisho*), and "graduation ceremonies?" She concludes that such comparisons have been influenced by colonial ethnographies and schooling itself, both of which have "objectified" initiation, representing it as discrete "educational" process (77–89). In other words, analogies drawn between initiation and schooling are just as much a testimony to the power of ethnographic texts and schooling to frame people's view of the world as they are a reflection of any observed similarities between the two social processes. This point is important because it focuses attention on what such analogies obscure. Initiation has sought to ground people in local hierarchies rooted in maturity, bravery, wealth, and seniority. By contrast, school education has sought to draw people into broader worlds structured by differential notions of "civilization," "race," and "modernity" and by hierarchies rooted in Christianity, Islam, and colonialism. It is crucial to explore how these more recent notions and hierarchies have reframed how people interpret ongoing processes of initiation and how they have altered young women's understandings of sexuality and reproduction. For instance, in my current research, I plan to explore how mid-twentieth-century colonial and commodity regimes that often valorized youth and whiteness challenged the seniority-based logic of initiation and possibly reshaped young women's assessment of the most attractive sexual and reproductive partners. Such examination should further elucidate the material concerns and moral ambitions that both link and differentiate pre-initiation and schoolgirl pregnancies.

The Schoolgirl, the Prostitute, and the Pregnant Fiancée

In addition to examining the relationship between schoolgirl and pre-initiation pregnancies, historicizing schoolgirl pregnancies means comparing the figure of the schoolgirl to two other sexualized female figures: the prostitute and the pregnant fiancée. As Luise White's work has demonstrated (1990), prostitution flourished in colonial Nairobi, playing a crucial role in the development of the African areas of the city. But despite the economic success that such work could bring, rural Kenyan morality vilified prostitutes as the worst kind of women. When schools for girls were first founded in central Kenya during the early 1900s, parents worried that by sending their daughters to school, they might turn them into prostitutes. As John Lonsdale has argued, parents were nervous about "their daughters' adolescent transition to full sexuality occur-r[ing] in the ritual seclusion of school, subject to foreigners" (1990, 392). Such fears were only heightened in the late 1920s when Protestant missionaries, who ran the majority of girls' schools in central Kenya, sought to end female genital cutting, a practice believed by many locals to discipline excessive sexual desire. My research on the history of colonial maternity services in Meru reveals that the greatest obstacle to recruiting schoolgirls for midwifery work was parents' fear that a training stint in Nairobi would render their daughters prostitutes (Thomas 2003, chapter 2). Over time, central Kenyan parents certainly became more accustomed to the idea of sending their daughters to school and to Nairobi for training. Yet I would argue that the widespread stories of "sugar daddies" who provide schoolgirls with gifts of cash, food, and clothing in exchange for sex suggest how the taint of prostitution still clings to the figure of the schoolgirl. Animating these stories is an anxiety that by leaving home and attending schools, girls become open to wealthy men's predations and vulnerable to being bought.[15]

Recent research on the HIV/AIDS epidemic in Eastern and Southern Africa has revealed the analytic pitfalls of branding all sexual relations that involve the exchange of material things as prostitution. In his study of AIDS in northern Tanzania, Philip W. Setel (1999, chapter 4) elucidates fourteen Swahili- and English-language terms used to differentiate between male-female relationships, most of which involve some exchange of food, gifts, and/or money. Similarly, in an article examining the close association between sex and gifts in the spread of HIV infection in KwaZulu-Natal, Mark Hunter persuasively argues for the need to move beyond the category of prostitution to recognize "the vital role that gifts play in fuelling everyday sexual relations between men and women" (2002, 100). Such insights are crucial to understanding why HIV infection is disproportionately high among girls and young women. In many parts of Eastern and Southern Africa, females between the ages of 15 and 24 are more than twice or even three times as likely as their male counterparts to be infected.[16] This disparity reflects the facts that the sexual organs of girls and young women are more vulnerable to the virus and that girls and young women are more inclined to have older sexual partners who are better able to provide them with food, clothes, and cash to pay school fees and support their families.[17] Regarding all such relationships as "prostitution" certainly obscures the complexity and variety of sexual relations and thus makes for bad social analysis. Nonetheless, at a discursive level in twentieth-century Kenya, at least, people frequently wielded the figure of the prostitute to denounce unruly women and demarcate the boundaries of female respectability.

Within the history of early postcolonial Kenya, one of the most illuminating discussions of the relationship between the figures of the prostitute and the schoolgirl took place during the repeal of the Affiliation Act in 1969. The Affiliation Act, passed a few years prior to political independence, granted all single women the right to sue the fathers of their children for paternity support. The act proved extremely controversial. While welfare and women's organizations hailed it as a crucial step toward providing for "illegitimate" children and protecting women from irresponsible men, many male politicians and members of the public complained that it was a colonial imposition that made men the "slaves" of women and encouraged female promiscuity and prostitution.[18] Yet during the parliamentary debates over the act's repeal, even the most ardent critics of the law argued that some sort of protection needed to be maintained for schoolgirls. They claimed that they would enact a new law to provide for schoolgirls who commit their "first mistake" or who were lured by presents and false promises offered by government ministers, members of Parliament (MPs), and others with "fat salaries" and "big positions and cars."[19] While schoolgirls might engage in activities that looked a lot like prostitution, MPs insisted that they were different. As one MP put it:

> We are all fathers and we have daughters. In the rural areas, Mr. Speaker, we have case after case where a school master has made a school girl pregnant, we have heard of these cases. We have heard of cases where a county council clerk, or a district commissioner himself, have made school girls pregnant. I think we have a big danger there because without some form of protection we might regret this later on.[20]

As this quote makes plain, MPs' empathy for pregnant schoolgirls stemmed from their own positions as fathers of schoolgoing daughters. Understanding that such pregnancies sullied reputations and disrupted parents' investment in school fees, they argued for a special law to protect schoolgirls.[21] Interestingly, Grace Khwaya Puja and Tuli Kassimoto (1994, 54–75, esp. 71) found in their research on schoolgirl pregnancies in Tanzania during the 1980s that parents, teachers, and education officials also favored the introduction of a law that would severely punish men who impregnated secondary schoolgirls. Yet as far as I know, neither the Kenyan nor the Tanzanian government has ever introduced such a law.[22]

The fact that such laws have been proposed but never instituted speaks to the ambiguity schoolgirls embody. On the one hand, politicians and parents recognize schoolgirls as a uniquely valued group of females requiring special protections. On the other, some schoolgirls engage in activities that place them dangerously close to that group of females deemed most undeserving, prostitutes. After all, one man's schoolgirl daughter can be another's mistress just as one girl's father can be another's sugar daddy. To understand why schoolgirls are uniquely valued but ultimately not accorded special protections, we need to know more about how schoolgirls and prostitutes have been conflated and differentiated across the twentieth century. How have changes and continuities in gender and generational relations informed parents' assessment of the rewards and risks of sending girls to school? How has schoolgirls' simultaneous embodiment of promise and promiscuity been variously manifested over the past century and from one context to another? And in what ways has the distinction between the schoolgirl temporarily led astray and the prostitute been defined by class divisions and aspirations?

The relationship between the schoolgirl and the prostitute is further complicated by the figure of the pregnant fiancée. In central Kenya, since the middle of the twentieth century, at least, pregnancies have often encouraged couples to marry. Based on his work in and around the Methodist hospital at Maua (Meru) during the 1940s, Dr. Stanley Bell observed that among initiates it was fairly common to become pregnant and then to quickly marry. He added, "Indeed, it seems as though her value as a wife and potential mother is verified should she be pregnant." Rather than being a problem, an initiate's pregnancy provided a positive impetus toward marriage.[23] While Bell described such arrangements without condemning them, Dr. Clive Irvine of the Presbyterian mission station at Chogoria repeatedly railed against them as "trial marriage." Irvine claimed that young people used premarital sexual relations to test whether their union would be fertile and, hence, avoid childlessness—"the supreme tragedy to an African."[24] Although Irvine denounced this approach that placed reproduction before marriage as "immoral," it became a fairly routine practice among the young women and men who attended the schools on his mission station and others in central Kenya.

Marriage promises could quickly turn a schoolgirl pregnancy or the pregnancy of an unmarried school graduate from a disturbing predicament to the beginning of new and valued familial relations. In 1990s Meru, it was rare to attend a wedding between a school-educated bride and groom at which the bride was not visibly pregnant or the couple did not already have a child together. Examination of pregnancy compensation law suits from 1950s and 1960s in central Kenya similarly revealed how out-of-wedlock pregnancies could prompt couples to marry. Under the customary law of pregnancy compensation, fathers had the right to sue men responsible for their unmarried daughters' pregnancies. Court records suggest that such suits often represented one phase in a protracted set of social negotiations aimed at transforming a reproductive quandary into marriage (Thomas 2003, chapter 4). Thus, some premarital pregnancies—if appropriately timed and well received by all parties—have embodied nuptial promise rather than sexual promiscuity.

Conclusion

In this chapter, I have sought to historicize schoolgirl pregnancies in order to demonstrate that in many parts of sub-Saharan Africa, issues of who is fit to conceive and who is fit to give birth have long been a matter of more than anatomy. By exploring the links and disjunctures between pre-initiation and school pregnancies and by relating the figure of the schoolgirl to that of the prostitute and the pregnant fiancée, I have examined the close connections between procreative processes and gender ideologies—what I defined at the start as gendered reproduction. Ideologies of who and what is male and female have also been intimately linked to efforts to ensure proper generational relations and secure material wealth. Concerns over schoolgirl pregnancies, like those over pre-initiation pregnancies, have stemmed from the principle that reproductive entitlement is achieved through educating minds, disciplining bodies, and repaying parental investments. The pregnancies of young unmarried women who have ignored this principle have often resulted in abortion or infanticide. But schoolgirl pregnancies appear to have embodied greater ambiguity than pre-initiation ones. The very fact of moving outside their homes and attending schools, often staffed by men, has offered girls and young women the possibility of joining broader and, in many cases, more promising and permissive social worlds. At the same time, such possibilities could leave them vulnerable to sexual predation and endanger familial reputations and investments.

Through this analysis of the pregnant schoolgirl, I have also sought to demonstrate the continued efficacy of African reproductive ideas and practices in the wake of colonialism. In *The Invention of Women* (1997), Oyewumi ultimately grants Euro-American colonizers tremendous agency by arguing that they introduced gender difference in a place where it was previously unknown. Whereas Oyewumi convincingly argues that "the fundamental category 'woman'" did not exist in the Yorùbá language prior to "sustained contact with the West," she does not demonstrate that the anatomic distinction between bodies that are capable and incapable of reproducing—a distinction that Oyewumi insists was socially decisive—was free of gender associations (ix). The existence of processes of male and female initiation in so many parts of the continent suggests to me that anatomic distinctions have often been a basis for generating elaborate and complex ideologies of gender difference. Historians and social scientists need to elucidate how gender concerns in contemporary Africa derive from previous centuries of both African and European history.

Political projects of colonization, modernization, and, more recently, globalization have wrought profound changes in gender categories and hierarchies across sub-Saharan Africa. Although these political projects have been enormously influential, they have never been all-encompassing. The gender and reproductive concerns they have introduced have vied and combined with those that already existed on the continent. Schoolgirl pregnancies, I would argue, generate so much controversy in the contemporary period precisely because they resonate with long-standing notions about the dangers of reproduction gone awry at the same time that they can be easily evoked to epitomize all that is wrong with the modern day.

Notes

1. Hunt (1999) goes a long way toward correcting this silence. Of course, other fields within African studies explored procreation. Social anthropology came of age in Africa through studies of kinship and marriage.

2. Our group is indebted to the generous support we have received from various sources at the University of Washington, most notably the Walter Chapin Simpson Center for the Humanities and the Graduate School.

3. The colonial government designated the territory northeast of Mt. Kenya as Meru District in 1910, three years after the installation of the first colonial officer. Because of its great distance from Nairobi and the railway lines, Meru was the last section of the central highlands to come under a colonial authority.

4. Interviews with Martha Roben, Rebecca M'Mwendwa, Tabitha M'Angaine, and Isabella M'Arimba by G. Kirimi and Thomas, September 15, 1990, Kathera, South Imenti, tape 1, transcript page 7; interview with Veronica Mpindi by Nduru and Thomas, October 25, 1990, Kinoru, North Imenti, tape 7, transcript page 13. The following are the earliest documentary accounts of female initiation in Meru: Meru District, *Annual Report, 1910,* PC/CP/1/9/1, Kenya National Archives (hereafter KNA); Orde Browne (1913, 137–140; 1915); Clive Irvine, "Yaws in East Kenya: A Description of the Disease as Found in the Mountainous Districts to the East of Mount Kenya, with some Unusual Forms, and Suggestions for Eradication," unpublished manuscript, 1925, Clive Irvine papers, Chogoria Mission Archives (hereafter CMA); M'Inoti (ca. 1930); Laughton (1938); and E. Mary Holding, "The Understanding of Indigenous Sex Relationships as Assisting Toward the Solution of Some Problems which Confront the Christian Church in Meru," essay submitted as part of final exam, 1940, Methodist Offices, near St. Paul's Church in Meru town (hereafter MOM), 17.

5. Interview with Tabitha Maigene by Nduru and Thomas, October 17, 1990, Kionyo, South Imenti, notebook 17; interview with Maliceral Igoki by Nduru and Thomas, October 18, 1990, Kionyo, South Imenti, tape 5, transcript page 5.

6. Interview with Sara Ayub and Esther Evangeline, September 6, 1990, notebook 17; interview with Margaret Ncence, September 12, 1990, notebook 17; interview with Tabitha Maigene, October 17, 1990, notebook 17; interview with Esther M'Ithinji and Julia Kiruja, October 14, 1990, Kathera, South Imenti, notebook 17; interview with Maliceral Igoki, October 18, 1990, tape 5, transcript page 5; interview with Isabella M'Arimba and Isabella John, October 13, 1990, Kathera, South Imenti, tape 1, transcript page 26; interview with Zipporah Kagugira by Jackson, Gatwiri, and Thomas, December 28, 1994, Mulathankari, North Imenti, tape 2, transcript page 21; interview with Rebecca Ncoro by Rigiri and Thomas, February 8, 1995, Mwichiune, South Imenti, tape 20, transcript page 35; interview with Jennifer Karea, March 24, 1995, notebook 27; interview with Beatrice Tiira, March 30, 1995, tape 22, transcript page 29; interview with Margaret Karoki, April 5, 1995, tape 29, transcript page 10–12; interview with Justus

M'Ikiao by Kithiira and Thomas, May 1, 1995, Mpuri, North Imenti, tape 35, transcript page 24; interview with Elizabeth Kabita by Mworoa and Thomas, May 3, 1995, Kangeta, Igembe, tape 37, transcript page 28; interview with Veronica Ciothirangi, June 6, 1995, tape 50, transcript page 29–30. Also see M'Inoti (ca. 1930, 4–5); and Laughton (1938, 59–60).

7. Interview with Sara Ayub and Esther Evangeline, September 6, 1990, notebook 17; interview with Margaret Ncence, September 12, 1990, notebook 17; interview with Esther M'Ithinji and Julia Kiruja, October 14, 1990, notebook 17; interview with Tabitha Maigene, October 17, 1990, notebook 17; interview with Maliceral Igoki, October 18, 1990, tape 5, transcript page 6; interview with Zipporah Kagugira by Jackson, Gatwiri, and Thomas, December 28, 1994, Mulathankari, North Imenti, tape 2, transcript page 21; interview with Elizabeth Kabita, May 3, 1995, tape 37, transcript page 31. For an account of colonial efforts to prevent pre-initiation pregnancies and stop abortion, see Thomas (1998, 121–145, and 2003, chapter 1).

8. C. M. Dobbs, Ag. Chief Native Commissioner, "Memorandum on Infanticide," January 12, 1930, Rhodes House, MSS/Afr/s/665/1.

9. H. E. Lambert, "Notes on Difference between Kikuyu and Meru Tribe and Its Result," January 1, 1934, Jomo Kenyatta Memorial Library, Lambert papers 1/7/1; Lambert, "The Meru Yet to Come," December 25, 1941, PC/CP/4/4/7, KNA.

10. Also see McKittrick (1999, 265–283, esp. 268).

11. For instance, see interview with Sara Ayub by Nduru and Thomas, August 27, 1990, notebook 17.

12. For a review of the relevant medical literature for Kenya, see Lema and Kabeberi-Macharia (1992) and Rogo, Bohmer, and Ombaka (1999).

13. For instance, see Nypan (1991, 39–65); Shuma (1994, 120–132); Walley (1997, 405–438); and Stambach (2000, 76–79).

14. For anthropological studies that have explored such decision making during the 1990s, see Johnson-Hanks (2002, 1337–1349) and Stambach (2003).

15. For a quick overview of scholarship on "sugar daddies," see Bledsoe and Cohen (1993, 108–109).

16. United States Agency for International Development, AIDSCAP, and Family Health International (1996, 18); Baltzaar et al. (1988, 4–7); Joint United Nations Programme on HIV/AIDS (2005).

17. Ogden (1996); Kielmann (1997); Schoepf (1997, 310–332); Setel (1999).

18. For a more extended analysis of this law, see Thomas (2003, 135–172).

19. Kenya, *National Assembly Debates,* June 10–17, 1969, 979–80, 985, 1050, and 1114.

20. Ibid., 981.

21. Ibid., 1054.

22. While I have yet to come across laws specifically focused on schoolgirls, in many African countries, customary and statutory litigation related to seduction damages, pregnancy compensation, and maintenance payments has most often involved schoolgirls. For instance, see Vellenga (1974, 77–101); and Thomas (2003, 103–171). Also see Rwebangira (1994, 87–210); and Rwebangira (1998, 165–202).

23. Bell (1955, 233); also see Dr. Clive Irvine, Church of Scotland Mission, Chogoria, to H. E. Lambert, District Commissioner, Meru, October 10, 1939, quoted in Meru District, AR, 1939, DC/MRU/4/5, KNA.

24. Dr. Clive Irvine, Church of Scotland Mission, Chogoria, to Foreign Mission Committee, Church of Scotland, Edinburgh, "Let's Be Honest," November 1, 1944,

Acc/7584/B275; Dr. Clive Irvine, Church of Scotland Mission, Chogoria, to Foreign Mission Committee, Church of Scotland, Edinburgh, Annual Report, 1944, Acc/7548/C1. Both in National Library of Scotland in Edinburgh.

References

Amadiume, Ifi. 1987. *Male Daughters, Female Husbands: Gender and Sex in an African Society.* London: Zed Books.

Amelsvoort, Vincent van, comp. 1976. *Medical Anthropology in African Newspapers.* Oosterhout, Netherlands: Anthropological Publications.

Baltzaar, G. M., J. Stover, T. M. Okeyo, B. O. N. Hagembe, R. Mutemi, and C. H. O. Olola, eds. 1988. *AIDS in Kenya: Background, Projections, Impact and Interventions.* 5th ed. Nairobi: National AIDS/STDs Control Programme, Ministry of Health.

Bell, Stanley. 1955. "The Ameru People of Kenya: A Medical and Social Study. Part 1. Geographical and Ethnological Background." *Journal of Tropical Medicine and Hygiene* 58, no. 10: 223–239.

Bledsoe, Caroline, and Barney Cohen.1993. *Social Dynamics of Adolescent Fertility in Sub-Saharan Africa.* Washington, D.C.: National Academy Press.

Feldman-Savelsberg, Pamela. 1989. "'Then we were many': Bangangte Women's Conceptions of Health, Fertility and Social Change in a Bamileke Chiefdom, Cameroon." Ph.D. diss., Johns Hopkins University.

Holding, Mary E. 1942. "Women's Institutions and the African Church." *International Review of Missions* 31: 291–300.

Hunt, Nancy Rose. 1989. "Placing African Women's History and Locating Gender." *Social History* 14, no. 3: 359–362.

———. 1999. *A Colonial Lexicon: Of Birth Ritual, Medicalization, and Mobility in the Congo.* Durham, N. C.: Duke University Press.

Hunter, Mark. 2002. "The Materiality of Everyday Sex: Thinking beyond Prostitution." *African Studies* 61, no. 1: 99–120.

Johnson-Hanks, Jennifer. 2002. "The Lesser Shame: Adolescent Abortion in Cameroon." *Social Science and Medicine* 55, no. 8: 1337–1349.

Joint United Nations Programme on HIV/AIDS. 2005. "UNAIDS." United Nations. Available online at http://www.unaids.org/en/default.asp (accessed on July 19, 2005).

Kielmann, Karina. 1997. "'Prostitution,' 'Risk,' and 'Responsibility': Paradigms of AIDS Prevention and Women's Identities in Thika, Kenya." In *The Anthropology of Infectious Disease: International Health Perspectives,* edited by Marcia C. Inhorn and Peter J. Brown, 375–411. Amsterdam: Gordon and Breach Publishers.

Laughton, W. H. 1938. "An Introductory Study of the Meru People." MA thesis, Cambridge University.

Lema, Valentino M., and Janet Kabeberi-Macharia. 1992. *A Review of Abortion in Kenya.* Nairobi: The Centre for the Study of Adolescence.

Lonsdale, John. 1990. "The Moral Economy of Mau Mau: Wealth, Poverty, and Civic Virtue in Kikuyu Political Thought." In *Unhappy Valley: Conflict in Kenya and Africa*, vol. 2, *Violence and Ethnicity*, edited by Bruce Berman and John Lonsdale, 265–504. Nairobi: Heinemann.

M'Inoti, Philip. ca. 1930. "Asili ya Wameru na Tabia Zao" (The Origin of the Meru and Their Customs). Unpublished manuscript, Boston University Library.

Magona, Sindiwe. 1998. *Mother to Mother*. Boston: Beacon Press.

McKittrick, Meredith. 1999. "Faithful Daughter, Murdering Mother: Transgression and Social Control in Colonial Namibia." *Journal of African History* 40, no. 2: 265–283.

Mikell, Gwendolyn. 1997. "Introduction." In *African Feminism: The Politics of Survival in Sub-Saharan Africa,* edited by Gwendolyn Mikell, 1–50. Philadelphia: University of Pennsylvania Press.

Modern Girl Research Group (Tani E. Barlow, Madeleine Yue Dong, Uta G. Poiger, Priti Ramamurthy, Lynn M. Thomas, and Alys Eve Weinbaum). 2005a. "Modern Girl around the World." *Gender & History* 17, no. 2: 245–294.

———. 2005b. "The Modern Girl Around the World Project at the University of Washington." Institute of Transnational Studies, University of Washington. Available online at http://depts.washington.edu/its/moderngirl.htm (accessed July 19, 2005).

Mwangi, Meja. 1990/1992. *Striving for the Wind*. Portsmouth, N.H.: Heinemann.

Nypan, Astrid. 1991. "Revival of Female Circumcision: A Case of Neo-Traditionalism." In *Gender and Change in Developing Countries,* edited by K. A. Stolen and M. Vaa, 39–65. Oslo: Norwegian University Press.

Ogden, Jessica. 1996. "Producing Respect: The 'Proper Woman' in Postcolonial Kampala." In *Postcolonial Identities in Africa,* edited by Richard Werbner and Terence Ranger, 165–192. London: Zed Books.

Orde Browne, G. St. J. 1913. "Circumcision Ceremonies among the Amwimbe." *Man* 13: 137–140.

———. 1915. "Circumcision Ceremony in Chuka." *Man* 15: 65–68.

Oyewumi, Oyeronke. 1997. *The Invention of Women: Making an African Sense of Western Gender Discourses*. Minneapolis: University of Minnesota Press.

Puja, Grace Khwaya, and Tuli Kassimoto. 1994. "Girls in Education and Pregnancy at School." In *Chelewa, Chelewa: The Dilemma of Teenage Girls,* edited by Zubeida Tumbo-Masabo and Rita Liljeström, 54–75. Östersund, Sweden: Nordiska Afrikainstitutet.

Richards, Audrey. 1956/1982. *Chisungu: A Girl's Initiation Ceremony among the Bemba of Zambia*. New York: Routledge.

Rogo, K. O., L. Bohmer, and C. Ombaka. 1999. "Developing Community-Based Strategies to Decrease Maternal Morbidity and Mortality Due to Unsafe Abortion: Pre-Intervention Research Report." *East African Medical Journal* 76, no. 1: S1–S71.

Rwebangira, Magdalena Kamugisha. 1994. "What Has the Law Got to Do with It?" In *Chelewa, Chelewa: The Dilemma of Teenage Girls,* edited by Zubeida Tumbo-Masabo and Rita Liljeström, 187–210. Östersund, Sweden: Nordiska Afrikainstitutet.

———. 1998. "Maintenance and Care in Law and Practice." In *Haraka, Haraka . . . Look before You Leap: Youth at the Crossroad of Custom and Modernity,* edited by Magdalena K. Rwebangira and Rita Liljeström, 165–202. Stockholm: Nordiska Afrikainstitutet.

Schapera, Isaac. 1933. "Premarital Pregnancy and Native Opinion: A Note on Social Change." *Africa* 6, no. 1: 59–89.

Schoepf, Brooke Grundfest. 1997. "AIDS, Gender, and Sexuality during Africa's Economic Crisis." In *African Feminism: The Politics of Survival in Sub-Saharan Africa*, edited by Gwendolyn Mikell, 310–332. Philadelphia: University of Pennsylvania Press.

Setel, Philip W. 1999. *A Plague of Paradoxes: AIDS, Culture, and Demography in Northern Tanzania*. Chicago: University of Chicago Press.

Shuma, Mary. 1994. "The Case of the Matrilineal Mwera of Lindi." In *Chelewa, Chelewa: The Dilemma of Teenage Girls*, edited by Zubeida Tumbo-Masabo and Rita Liljeström, 120–132. Östersund, Sweden: Nordiska Afrikainstitutet.

Stambach, Amy. 2000. *Lessons from Mount Kilimanjaro: Schooling, Community, and Gender in East Africa*. London: Routledge.

———. 2003. "*Kutoa Mimba:* Debates about Schoolgirl Abortion in Northern Tanzania." In *The Sociocultural and Political Context of Abortion from an Anthropological Perspective*, edited by Alaka Basu, 79–102. Oxford: Clarendon.

Thomas, Lynn M. 1998. "Imperial Concerns and 'Women's Affairs': State Efforts to Regulate Clitoridectomy and Eradicate Abortion in Meru, Kenya, c. 1910–1950." *Journal of African History* 39, no. 1: 121–145.

———. 2003. *Politics of the Womb: Women, Reproduction, and the State in Twentieth-Century Kenya*. Berkeley: University of California Press.

"Tough Choices: How Six Young Women Dealt with Unplanned Pregnancies." 2000. *Daily Nation* (Kenya), October 28.

United States Agency for International Development, AIDSCAP, and Family Health International. 1996. *AIDS in Kenya: Socioeconomic Impact and Policy Implications*. Arlington, Va.: AIDSCAP, Family Health International.

Vellenga, D. D. 1974. "Arenas of Judgement." In *Domestic Rights and Duties in Southern Ghana*, edited by Christine Oppong, 77–101. Legon, Ghana: Institute of African Studies, University of Ghana.

Walley, Christine. 1997. "Searching for 'Voices': Feminism, Anthropology, and the Global Debate over Female Genital Operations." *Cultural Anthropology* 12, no. 3: 405–438.

White, Luise. 1990. *The Comforts of Home: Prostitution in Colonial Nairobi*. Chicago: University of Chicago Press.

4 Dialoguing Women

Nwando Achebe and Bridget Teboh

What does it mean to be an African and female? What are the highlights, the joys, and the tribulations of conducting research on our own people?[1] How do we see and interpret the African world around us as well as the stories that have been entrusted to us? Who owns African knowledge and, most important, how have we as African gender historians navigated our various research environments?

On Being African

Nwando Achebe

When I think of my identity, a number of questions immediately come to mind. First, what does it means to be African? Second, what does Africa (and especially Nigeria) mean to me? And third, how do I choose to locate and name myself?[2] The issue of how I choose to name myself informs my very identity. I am first and foremost Igbo, then I am a woman, and third I am African. Only last do I name myself Nigerian. Being black does not even enter into the equation, since race has never been a distinguishing category in Africa.[3] We are simply people, nations of different ethnicities, language groups, and cultures.

Therefore, Igbo is who I am, it is my culture, it is my worldview, it is the way I think, the way I speak, the way I write, and the way I dream. But a big part of my Igbo identity is also shaped by being a woman. For an Igbo woman's world is vastly different from an Igbo man's—her mannerisms, the way she carries herself, the expectations society has of her and she of herself, the way in which she is socialized—all make her uniquely female. Being African, on the other hand, represents my connectedness with all African peoples, my rejection of the colonial boundaries that divide us, my embracing of the various sisterhoods and brotherhoods that I find so African and so very appealing (hence my conviction that even though my colleague Bridget Teboh is from Cameroon, she is truly my sister). This African identity of mine is certainly more pronounced than my Nigerian identity—a feeling that is reinforced every day as a somewhat displaced person who has lived most of her life in the United States.[4]

Nigeria holds a sweet yet oftentimes bitter place in my heart. Nigerian nationalism for me has thus evolved into an acquired taste—something like the bittersweet taste of an *udala* fruit—initially overwhelming your taste buds with a sweetness as pure as honey and then just as quickly slapping you with a bitterness that extends almost to the pit of your stomach. My relationship with Nigeria has been much like that *udala* fruit. As many times as Nigeria has made me proud, she has just as surely made me want to dig the ground and bury myself in shame. But I have also come to appreciate something else—that each time I overcome that incredible shock to my senses, that lingering assault in my mouth occasioned by a second bite into the juicy flesh of the *udala* fruit— the lasting taste in my mouth is almost always much sweeter than it is bitter. Through thick and thin, Nigeria has remained a country that I identify with and one that has most surely shaped my identity—the who and what I am.

So why are these reflections important? Certainly because my relationship with Africa and Nigeria and the fact that I am Igbo shapes in a profound way what I am willing to do or not do when it comes to research. It shapes, rightly or wrongly, how I identify with my research collaborators—a fact that has a direct effect on what I choose to write about and my interpretation of data—as well as my notions of accountability. And as an Igbo woman conducting research on Igbo women and gender, I feel accountable to my research collaborators because not only do I identify myself with Igboland, my home community, I also recognize that no matter what, I will return home!

Bridget Teboh

When I think of my Africanness as an identity, several questions come up. For example, what is Africa? Is it merely a geographic location or also a construct of varying images and impressions and contested meanings? What does it mean to be African? What does Africa mean to me? Who am I, and how do I position myself within this construct? Since the late 1880s, when those arbitrary boundaries were imposed on various ethnic, cultural, and language groups in Africa, Africa has witnessed a creation of new labels. These new labels and forms of individual and shared selfhood triggered new identities, which have been shaped by inter-, intra- and trans-African transformations of gender, class, religion, language, ethnicity, culture, race, and country/nation. As a result, alternative ways of answering old questions such as "Who are Africans?" "Who am I?" have emerged. Additionally, these transformations created a close bond, a connection with all sons and daughters of Africa—a connection that is even more binding for Africans living outside continental Africa as we become sisters and brothers in struggle or in self-exile.

There is an assumption that all black people in and outside continental Africa have accepted their Africanness and thus are happy to be called Africans. Most of us indeed know that we are Africans and have acknowledged it as an identity. Some have adopted African names and names of African countries as proof of their Africanness, but others have not. "Africa is too chaotic" or "Africa has too many problems," they say. What region of the world has no problems? I suggest that Africa should be seen not only as an identity but as a critical perspective, one that allows us to raise questions such as Whose Africa? Who named Africa and why?[5]

Africa now exists in specific disadvantaged and nervous conditions[6] within a complex cultural blend and global context (Williams and Chrisman 1994). My own Africanness is a huge part of who I am: one among many daughters and sons of Mother Africa. When I stand in front of a mirror, I see first a Moghamo, second a woman, third an African, fourth an Anglophone, and, last but not least, a Cameroonian.

I am first and foremost Moghamo. My belief system, my culture, my world-view is Moghamo. It determines the way that I speak, write, eat, and dress. Similarly, my Moghamo identity is shaped by the fact that I am a woman. My world as a Moghamo woman is different from that of a Moghamo man—my expectations and the expectations that Moghamoland has of me, my stance, my behavior and mannerisms as well as the way in which I am socialized all make me especially female.

My Cameroonian identity is often challenged by existing Anglophone-Francophone problems. Despite economic decline in recent years and extreme dissatisfaction with the current Biya administration,[7] Cameroon still holds a special place in my heart. Cameroon is home to me and is where the rest of my family lives. Cameroon represents the one place I can always return to whenever I want, no questions asked. She is an important place especially now for all of us Cameroonians living abroad in times of such uncertainty and fast-changing immigration policies in the United States and elsewhere. For instance, what if U.S. Homeland Security agents decided to send away all "aliens"? Then at least we will have a home to return to.

On Being an African Woman Researcher

Bridget Teboh

I feel both pride and anxiety as I ponder my role as an African and as a woman researcher. My anxiety stems from the following questions that nag continuously at me: What am I supposed to do? What do people expect of me? Do I have to "fix" all the (mis)representations that surround African women—conceptualizations of them as victims, marginalized, oppressed, unimportant? My pride, on the other hand, stems from the realization that I occupy a privileged position and that I can do something to make possible change in the way African women have been represented. This privileged position is enabled by the hybridity of my circumstance (as an African woman scholar born and raised in Africa and now living abroad). That hybridity connects me to Mother Africa and yet sets me apart.

My interest in writing Moghamo[8] history developed out of a need to uncover the other "truth" about women in Moghamoland, to tell the story that European and North American scholars deliberately chose to leave out.[9] And more important, to capture the reality of elite women's stories as a key factor in African history.[10] My research on the Moghamo suggests that while giant steps have been made to bring women's issues to the forefront in African historiography, the precolonial and colonial period has remained neglected. Additionally, previous research on African women has almost all been carried out within the "women and development" framework, thereby limiting the scope or full potential of women's contributions. Some exceptions are Musisi (2003), Kanogo (1987), Hunt (1999), Thomas (2003), and Byfield (2002).

In my work, I set out to examine how women in Moghamoland reacted to and coped with the radical changes that they and their community underwent from around 1889 to 1960 (Teboh 2002). This period was characterized by significant changes in the local economy and social life as a consequence of the colonial regime. I argue that these changes not only affected women's lives at individual and collective levels but, more important, also shifted the traditional balance of power between genders and the complementarity upon which Moghamo political, economical, and social life rested.

Nwando Achebe

Elsewhere I have taken myself through an honest process of self-naming (Achebe 2002). I described my positionality as one of a relative insider—relative to the men and women who entrusted me with their stories. My village of origin is situated in southern Igboland, while my research area is located in northern Igboland, a fact that might not at first sight seem like much of a distinction. However, Nigeria is made up of over 350 different ethnic groups whose members speak different languages and have different cultures. Of those groups, the Igbo, Yorùbá, and Hausa are the most populous. The Igbos number over 28 million and are divided into eastern, northern, southern, and western geographical and political enclaves, each speaking a distinct dialect. I would estimate that there are over 50 different Igbo dialects in all.

Ogidi and Akwa—the natal towns of my father and mother, for instance—are both important towns in southern Igboland that occupy a land mass that is separated by thirty kilometers at best. The difference in dialects between people who originate from these areas is, however, quite remarkable. For example, my father's people would say *bia eba* for "come here," but my mother's people would say *bia ika*—a change in the second word from an *eba* to *ika*. For the word "no," Ogidi people would say *mba*, while Awka people would say *waa*. Here the difference in dialects between these two groups is more pronounced. However because these groups live in such close proximity to one another, comprehension between both groups remains relatively easy.

The same is not true with regard to southern and northern Igbos, however. For the universal greeting "welcome," it is common to hear southern Igbos say *nno* or *ndewo*. Northern Igbos, on the other hand, repeat the phrase *ala, deje . . . ala, deje . . . ala, deje* numerous times to ensure that the fact that their visitor is most welcome is not lost on the newcomer. For the phrase "that is not okay," southern Igbos would say *odiro mma*, whereas northern Igbos would say *odugu oyi*. Now even an untrained eye can see quite clearly that these two Igbo dialects have little in common.

So why this mini exercise in linguistics? It was important to bolster my belief that far from being a mere insider, my positionality in relation to my research environment is much more problematic. I am certainly, linguistically speaking, an outsider to some extent,[11] but alas, dialect is not all that sets me apart from my research collaborators. There has been a good share of resentment and distrust among the two groups that dates back to the colonial times and continues unabated today; a number of southern Igbos feel that they have been unjustly forced out of their northern Igbo homes by the "true" indigenes. My insider/outsider positionality is further complicated by the fact that I was actually born and raised in northern Igboland and have made an effort to learn and speak the northern Igbo dialect—a gesture that was not left unnoticed by my Nsukka[12] collaborators, who were quick to proclaim me a Nsukka daughter on many occasions during my fieldwork. Therefore, in many ways my relative insider status has placed me in a rather precarious position of having to constantly negotiate my positionality within the field setting.

But that is not all. Being female also shapes my field experience in both enriching and not-so-enriching ways. One major issue women researchers face and, indeed, I faced was the issue of how to establish my credibility as a woman researcher in the field. This is especially important in an area where men for the most part have been the "traditional" documenters of history in the written form.[13] Interestingly enough, during my own fieldwork I did not encounter the "in your face" kind of sexual discrimination one might be inclined to believe would exist in such research settings. In fact, the only times that I encountered gender discrimination were not in the traditional setting of collecting oral histories in the villages but in a formal research setting of the Nigerian National Archives and a faculty seminar at the University of Nigeria, Nsukka. I will not talk about the second instance in detail here because I have discussed this experience in an earlier article (Achebe 2002). When I first arrived at the National Archives in Enugu to do my research, I noticed that the clerk was nowhere to be found and therefore there was no one to collect documents on my behalf. The next couple of days, I experienced much of the same. He would retrieve one or two documents for me after I had badgered the receptionist and then would disappear. I would be informed at closing that "he [was] no longer on seat." What upset me most was the fact that all the other researchers, who were male, had constant stacks of documents before them! I decided to take matters into my own hands and up I went to the chief archivist's office. Once there I stated my case and my utter dissatisfaction with the way I was being treated. No sooner had I finished then the chief archivist assured me that everything would change. And change it did! From that day on, the clerk not only secured all the documents that I requested but also would on occasion stop by my table to see if I needed some more! In going over the clerk's head, I had demonstrated in no uncertain terms that I was no pushover.

Another issue of concern is the dearth of viable sources of information for researchers conducting work on women and gender in Igboland. Written sources are practically nonexistent, and archival sources—both in Europe and Nigeria— are few and far between. The Nigerian National Archives in Enugu, for instance, suffered greatly from almost total destruction of its materials during the Nigerian/Biafra Civil War (1967–1970). What is more, the little that was salvaged after the war has fallen into disrepair due to the undesirable conditions under which these documents are housed. Conditions there have been exacerbated by a lack of funding for the general upkeep of the facility and for computers and software and the fact that the electricity supply is sporadic. In addition, employees sometimes are not paid for months. The ongoing challenge for male and female scholars conducting research in Nigeria is to continue to produce good work under deplorable conditions.

Research on African Women and Gender in Moghamo and Igbolands

We have both found that as women/gender historians, sometimes the only way to produce complete histories of women and gender in our various regions is to use the oral resources that are available still in the rural and urban areas. We will consider some of the challenges we have faced in our attempt to document the oral histories of women and gender in Moghamo and Igbolands, respectively. Specifically, we will address issues of method, historical approach, and writing—issues of accessibility and whether or not to theorize, whose writing to use and from whose point of view, and access to publishing.

Bridget Teboh

Research on African women and gender demands an interdisciplinary methodology. Despite the expansion of the print and mass media, loyalty to the spoken word has not diminished in African societies. Thus, during my 1998–1999 fieldwork in Cameroon, I spent the bulk of my time in Moghamoland collecting oral histories. The very first challenge I encountered was related to my interview technique. I was firmly told by an elderly woman that "We will not allow you to interview us. Sorry." Confused at this turn of events, especially given that we had become good friends, I asked around for explanations. And I got an earful. In Moghamo, the expression used for this type of dialogue that I wished to do is "to interview," as in "to interrogate," like the Germans and British did. It is *ni muugh*.[14] That was a valuable lesson my research collaborators taught me, and I took to heart. Accordingly, from then on I planned my oral history collection around these conversations. These women and men were entrusting me with their personal narratives and life histories. I owed it to them (as any good researcher of Africa/women should) to really listen to them and represent them and their histories as they represent themselves. For who is more knowledgeable or who knows better what happened to them than the research subjects (Appiah 1992; Ashcroft, Griffiths, and Tiffin 1989)?

As a Moghamo woman, my knowledge of the people, region, and language provided me with invaluable preparation for historical research. I am proficient in Pidgin English, fluent in French and three other Cameroon languages, acquainted intimately with Batibo Sub-Division, and had privileged access to elders of Moghamo society. I am a native speaker of the language (Moghamo) and therefore an insider. I thought I would encounter few problems with regard to language use in the field. These qualifications were not, of course, by themselves sufficient to the task, and challenges of a different kind arose. I had to use common sense and adopt flexibility, as I wrote in my report of my experience in 1996 (Teboh 1996).

As an insider, I was expected to participate in and respect the customs of my people and their "tradition."[15] All these activities took a lot of time. Yet these were the best sources of information on Moghamo's norms, gender relations, belief system, and etiquette. I also became an unwitting and unauthorized U.S. ambassador to Cameroon and Cameroon ambassador to the U.S., answering all kinds of questions from everyone on every U.S. topic imaginable![16] This role helped with my interviews.

In a family, one really becomes conversant with those intimate details of daily life about which we cannot politely inquire. I made friendly visits to many homes and families. Most women opened up to me and talked about everything once they recognized me as one of theirs. Men also recognized and respected my accomplishments and came to talk to me, a woman, and be interviewed willingly. In the reciprocal give and take of daily life, details emerged about family life, education, poverty, and government that would have been impossible to grasp if I had lived alone in the name of focusing on my research.

This research was not mine alone, it was that of the Moghamo people also, thus making it our collaborative effort, our research. Flexibility on my part as the researcher was a key technique I often used to accomplish my task. It became important to care for and tend to the needs of informants, to work around their schedules, and to nudge them into a better mood.

Nwando Achebe

I write African history from within, on its own terms. To this end, I have consciously centered northern Igbo constructions of their own stories, so that in the final analysis my own interpretation of the evidence gathered becomes less important. I define myself as a people's historian, an imagined term on my part that elucidates the fact that I serve as the medium that transfers the spoken word entrusted me into the permanent medium of writing in as close a form as possible as the original articulation. In this positioning, therefore, the very interaction between collaborator and researcher—the words spoken, the songs sung, the proverbs related—all combine to become the crust of the interpretive text. What exactly is this interpretive text and how does it emerge? Through a time-consuming interactive process in which I seek the advice and expertise of a collaborator in the interpretation of events shared by asking pertinent questions such as: "What exactly does that mean?" and "Why did women react in that way?" Their shared oral elaborations are then transcribed into a written form that privileges the people's interpretations of their own histories rather than my own.

My collaborators were able to teach me and I was willing to listen, hear, and absorb indigenous explanations of what it means to be a woman,[17] what it means to be female,[18] and how northern Igbos conceptualize gender. By privileging northern Igbo perceptions of their own history—this all-inclusive and -accommodating history that celebrates the connection between the spiritual and physical worlds—the above-enumerated interpretative categories assumed new and added meaning. Take the term gender, for instance. In addition to its conventional definition, which centers almost exclusively on its human quality as a social construct—northern Igbo sensibilities ascribe nonhuman/spiritual qualities to this concept as well. In my own writing, therefore, gender becomes not merely a viable interpretative category for human phenomena but one that I have also used to embrace and explain female manifestations of power in the spiritual realm, especially the orientation of female forces such as medicines, goddesses, and oracles.

In a related article (Achebe 2002), I consider the turbulent character of northern Igboland during and after the Atlantic slave trade that led in part to the creation and shaping of a new indigenous "slave" system of deity wives or dedicatees.[19] During the last decade of the nineteenth century, the northern Igbo village of Alor-Uno was sacked as a result of the slaving activities of the Aro and Nike; as a result, it broke up and its people scattered in various directions. The people of Alor-Uno subsequently concocted a powerful protective *female* medicine called Adoro to safeguard the remaining Alor-Uno citizens from further devastation and appeal to the exiled Alor-Uno populace "to return home"—*ka fa we donata*. I therefore explore the place and evolution of this female protective medicine, Adoro, who at various times in the life of her community assumed the role of protector and warrior medicine, court, and, thereafter, a full-blown universally respected and worshipped female deity who married wives (in a process called *igo mma ogo*) and thus fulfilled the birthing responsibilities of mother goddess.

The evolution of this deified female medicine becomes a viable and important topic for African women's/gender history because the northern Igbo world privileges as relevant the interconnections between spiritual forces and the human world as determinants of the course of major events. To ignore Adoro's story would therefore amount to telling only part of Alor-Uno (her)story. Herein lies that which separates a history that has been visualized in African terms from one that has not. For Western[20] sentiment does not allow medicines, which are in essence gendered forces, a place in its history. It is only when research-ers position themselves on the inside, ask the right questions, and then listen and hear the stories shared with them that they begin to retell the history of the African peoples that they study in its entirety. I have listened very closely and heard the stories, the whispers, and the silences from within, and these communications have shaped my own production of northern Igbo (her)stories as well as the terminology and/or theory I have adopted in the writing of these stories.

How was I able to decenter myself, my agenda, and whatever interpretative biases that I may have come into the field with while centering the actual stories entrusted me? During my fieldwork, I had the privilege of interviewing and col-lecting the life histories of numerous women in Nsukka Division, northern Ig-boland. As a rather unseasoned historian conducting predissertation fieldwork for the first time in September of 1996, I was privy to a situation that shaped my research methods. I walked into the home of Lady Obayi to collect her life history. During the interview she explained to me in painstaking detail the role the Christian church played in shaping her very identity, her womanhood. She also elaborated on the power she felt had accrued to her as a result of that rela-tionship with the Catholic Church. I remember sitting there stunned and dazed, stunned because her life history would certainly not fit into my neatly imagined thesis of the total loss of female power that visited Igbo women as a result of their relationship with the Christian church. But just as I was about to compart-mentalize this information as being "unimportant," Lady Obayi drew me back to the present by insisting that I explain to her what it was that she had just shared with me. She maintained that this process of speaking back that which had been spoken to me was particularly important to her because she "[did] not trust all of [us] book people." Because Lady Obayi was not literate, she wanted to make sure that I would represent her in my writings the way she represented herself. This is the same understanding that King Agonglo, the eighth king of Dahomey, had over 200 years earlier when he bemoaned the ability and thus power of the written word to either represent peoples fairly or completely de-stroy them![21] Therefore as Lady Obayi held my hands in hers, I heard myself repeating to her exactly what it was she had said—what I had only a few mo-ments earlier dismissed as "untrue." That meeting was the beginning of a learn-ing and maturing journey—a journey that made me soon realize that there was no one "truth," no one thesis or analysis. Instead, there were multiple "truths," multiple analyses of those "truths," and it was more important to represent Nsukka women the way that they represented themselves and by so doing reap the benefits of that representation—namely, a much richer history that chal-lenged its readers to dare to imagine, to hear the whispers and shouts of the rightful owners of knowledge. Lady Obayi had taught me that the relationship between the researcher and "the researched" should be interactive and collabo-rative rather than exclusively one-sided. She taught me that researchers owe it to their collaborators to listen carefully, to leave preconceived ideas and agendas out of the research environment, and represent "the researched" the way they represent themselves. This lesson captures the unarticulated duty of any researcher of Africa to present African lives the way Africans present themselves so that those collaborators might in fact one day relish the thought of seeing themselves in the histories that emerge.

Writing and Publishing

Nwando Achebe

As a student of history, I always balked at having to read yet another boring history text. I found that I thoroughly enjoyed texts that were written with very little jargon and remained accessible to its readers. This ideal has not only influenced me but has in fact become the driving force in my own writing. I am a firm believer that a writer or historian must define and situate her audience because once it is defined, that audience does in fact influence the way the scholar writes. This audience will also influence decisions about whether or not to use theory and if so, what kind of theory one should use.

I write for two distinct audiences. My primary audience is African—specifically the northern Igbo people who granted me entry into their lives and on whom my study is based. My second audience is students of African thought and history the world over. As soon as I identified my intended readership (especially the makeup of my primary audience), it became imperative that my writing be accessible. When I talk about my writing being accessible, I speak not only about the readability of the written word but also about the availability and affordability of the published document. My choice of publisher was shaped primarily by considerations about making my book accessible to my primary audience. I reached the decision to publish with Heinemann for two main reasons: first, because Heinemann has a long-standing history and reputation of publishing and distribution in Africa, and second, because they understand the need to keep books cheap, hence their commitment to reissuing Heinemann books using cheaper materials for their African markets.

Because I have identified my primary audience as being African, one of my most primary motivations is that my writing remain accessible and straightforward—that it is almost entirely devoid of the jargon that many of my colleagues privilege sometimes above comprehension in their writings and in so doing alienate general audiences and encourage unnecessary dialogue with one another. If I, a Ph.D., pick up a text and have to consult my dictionary over and over again, then surely that writing is not accessible. I want my audience to be able to read what I have written, understand it, and see themselves in the emergent history. When they do not, I want them to critique it. It is this possibility of meaningful back-and-forth dialogue between the researched and the researcher that I am most interested in. And I am not merely paying lip service to this identified ideal. During my Fulbright-Hays dissertation research I was privileged with the opportunity to present my work to a knowledgeable group of Nsukka indigenes and students of Igbo studies in a seminar co-sponsored by the History and African Studies departments at the University of Nigeria, Nsukka, where I was affiliated. The occasion allowed for this back-and-forth collaboration of informed minds I have spoken of—an interaction that served variously to critique and uphold my thesis.

On the rare occasion when it may be necessary to use a theory to explain and expand upon knowledge, I draw on interpretative categories determined by northern Igbos—those concepts that allow indigenous peoples to explain society to itself—to fashion insider theoretical models or explanations that have everything to do with the thought processes of the people who evoke them. Listen now to a theory I evolved out of indigenous explanations and have used to elaborate northern Igbo (her)stories.

In my book *Farmers, Traders, Warriors and Kings: Female Power and Authority in Northern Igboland, 1900–1960* (Achebe 2005), I use the concept of a seasonality of women's power and authority to describe how women manipulated certain periods of time in their lives, otherwise referred to as seasons, to their advantage. I suggest that over an Igbo woman's lifetime, specific seasons can be identified in which female power is elevated. I have categorized these into chronological, positional/locational, and reproductive seasons, as well as planting and harvesting seasons of power.

An Igbo woman's life can be divided into the following chronological seasons: the *nwata* (childhood) season, the *nwa agboho* (adolescence) season, the *okenye* (adult) season, and the *agadi* (postmenopausal) "season." I suggest that with each passing season of time, an Igbo girl (who possesses little or no power and authority) journeys from childhood to adolescence and later becomes an adult woman (a season in which her power is somewhat elevated). But it is only when this woman becomes an elder or passes menopause that she is elevated to the position of "honorary man"[22] and receives all the rights and honors that go with that station.

The season of time when a woman is either defined as *nwada* (daughter) or *omu-ala* (wife) is what I have called a positional/locational season of time and power. This category of power is solely contingent on a woman's geographical location or position. In other words, every Igbo woman is at one time or season a *nwada* and at another an *omu-ala*. As a daughter, she assumes the supreme position of power of chief arbitrator and high court as well as "husband" to all the women married into her natal village. During the season of time that a daughter visits her mother's lineage, she is accorded the special place of honor as *nwadiana*[23] but will be forced into the diminished position as an *omu-ala*, or wife, during the season of time that she lives in her husband's village. Married Igbo daughters have therefore learned how best to navigate their variable locational/positional seasons of power to their advantage.

Igbo women often manipulate the nine-month reproductive season of pregnancy to their advantage. This is typically a time when husbands make sure that all their wives' needs are met. The act of reproduction that advances a wife, *omu-ala,* into a mother, *nne,* also ushers in a prolonged season of enhanced power, for once a woman becomes a mother she remains forever more powerful than a wife. Additionally, more power and prestige is conferred on a mother of a son than on a mother of a daughter. This elevation of power is manifest in the reproductive imperative of bearing a male child and has its origins in the patrilineal nature of Igbo society, where inheritance is passed down from the male line.

Finally, let us turn to the gendered division of crops and cropping. In northern Igboland, as elsewhere in Igboland, crops are gendered; they are considered either "male" or "female." Men principally farmed the "male" yam crop[24] while women cultivated "female" crops such as cocoyam, beans, vegetables, maize, and cassava. These "female" crops, incidentally, made up the staple diet and supported the subsistence needs of families. It is my contention that the planting and harvesting season of women's crops was a more advantageous season for women's power and authority than the two-month reign of the so-called king of crops, the yam. What was more, yam was only eaten once a day, in the afternoon, while women's crops were eaten in the morning and evenings. In my writings I have incorporated some of these theories to explain happenings in society.

A word on writing African worlds and ownership of knowledge: not too long ago a piece that I had worked extremely hard on emerged in published form. However, my excitement at seeing my effort in print was squashed almost immediately as I began to read what supposedly were my own words. Before me, I read word after word "reworked" in vital places to promote an argument that I had in fact not made. The chapter that stared back at me, in many places, did not read as mine. Could I, Nwando Achebe, Igbo woman, Nigerian woman, be the one writing that Nigerian women earned 40 percent of what Nigerian men did, when women earned exactly what men did? Was I also the one evoking "female genital cutting" as an interpretive model when I had explicitly stated in e-mail correspondence to the editors that it was my belief that that term was politically loaded and did not in fact describe the reality in Nigeria? In my version of the chapter—the version that they assured me would stand as was written—I had used the term clitoridectomy, which is what is practiced in areas of Nigeria where women are circumcised. Women in Nigeria do not cut anything off; the foreskin on the clitoris is merely scraped, much like the foreskin on the penis would be during male circumcision. And these are but a few examples of the problematic "rewrites" that assaulted my senses as I read my so-called chapter. I mention this situation here not because I am looking for an opportunity to rant and rave but because it does speak to the power of certain individuals who own knowledge about Africa and women and who have the ability to squash opposing points of view when they do not neatly fit into their perceived worldviews. And unfortunately these owners of knowledge—the owners of publishing houses, the editors of compilations and journals—are for the most part not African (Achebe 2003).

Who are the authors, painters, filmmakers, or owners of publishing companies? How is their knowledge of Africa and women distributed (Edwards 1993; Lutz and Collins 1993)? Additionally, who are the "experts" on Africa who have claimed "authorship" on Africa and continue to perpetuate these unchanging negative images of Africa? For a long time, "experts" have been white men and women from western Europe and North America. What this means for me as an African woman researcher is that I can go to the heart of issues of race, class, and gender by critiquing the mental processes we all go through and the assumptions we make about the subject, Africa(n) woman.

One of the impediments in attempting to provide answers for Africa is a tendency toward generalizations, for one can never hope to fully analyze the realities of Africans and women from over fifty different countries and numerous cultures. How do we avoid emphasizing existing divides and dichotomies (Carby 1987; Woodhull 1993)? Any cultural feminist vision of a unified female sphere would not come close to describing the complex relations among African women and between women, men and the state, or African women researchers and men. Such an attempt would obscure the important ways in which women have constituted themselves in arenas of power. One option is to resort to the politics of difference to create a legitimate public persona for African women researchers and African women "subjects," thereby generating new possibilities for women in a rapidly changing (sociocultural, economical, political, and global) landscape.

Who has the authority to speak for the other? Who is other? To go beyond superficial answers, it became necessary for me to use unconventional research methods and tools, especially those that enabled women to tell their stories in their own words. What Edward Said pointed out years ago still holds true today: "The act of representing (and hence reducing) others almost always involves violence of some sort to the subject of the representation."[25]

As Africans we should and must speak in order to get out of the web of colonial subjugation and subjectivity that is evident everywhere, especially in academia. How can Africans speak? So far, there seems to be a secret or unwritten consensus among Westerners and Western publishing houses that Africans can only speak in certain situations, in certain privileged languages and given certain conditions approved by Western standards. The assumption is that Africans do not have the necessary conditions and resources to enable them to speak. When will Africa/ns rise up and take control? When will African governments recognize the importance of publishing companies and actually set funds aside to improve existing publishing houses and start new ones that will take care of their specific interests?[26]

In case African governments need reminding, language is power. That is why we talk of the imperial language when discussing all those foreign languages— now official languages—brought to and imposed on Africans by colonialists.[27]

Every author is aware of his/her audience, and to effectively communicate with that audience, the author must use a language that the audience can understand. The fact that the imperial language is seen as literary in Africa creates problems for Africans and for women in particular because it implies that anyone who does not have access to or use the imperial language is left out, is powerless, and is considered the other (Césaire 1946, 1972). Consequently, they cannot control the distribution of knowledge via books, journals, art, and films. The exclusive use of techniques and languages that are borrowed from the West limit the writer or researcher who uses them. Little wonder, therefore, that years ago Frantz Fanon (1967) called for the "community's engagement in combative social action," a new theory about the use of foreign languages by Africans.

In my research, I used Pidgin English, paid attention to idioms and proverbs that shed more light on the role of Moghamo women, and allowed them to represent themselves. Gayatri Chakravorty Spivak (1990) once asked, "Can a Subaltern speak?" Like Spivak, I ask, Can Africans speak? And add, When they speak, is anyone listening to what they have to say? Let us examine for a moment this telling passage in Pidgin English:

> Mami tok say meeting dey here tomorrow. E say all woman dem go first waka
> for group go for chief E tong. wey dem go sing then dance make chief know sey
> woman dem get tory for tok. Afta na im wey meeting proper go start for mami
> house. Dat ting wey man dem di shidong do all time wey dem di decide palava
> for market place, plus how much we go pay for new shade, wey dem no even ask
> we sef must to end. All girl pikin, nyong girl, woman witi big mami wey im get
> bisnez for market must to forget tomorrow wok for sika sey dem must joon witi
> we for tok dat big big tory ana for see wetin next we go do. No bi so? Na so! Wana
> gree? Yes! We gree![28]

This passage contains important information regarding a protest movement in the making. Mami normally means mother, but here Mami means more than mother. She has another role: Mami emerges as a leader of her community as well as a powerful articulate figure to be reckoned with as she mobilizes women to go make their grievances known to the local and government authorities (before taking action if need be!).

Pidgin English is the most popular, most understood, and most spoken language in all of English-speaking West Africa. Yet because this language is unknown and therefore unacceptable in academia and to the West, users of Pidgin English, no matter how brilliant their ideas are, seem doomed to remain unheard, to be (re)presented wrongly, or to have their voices muted. Such violence should be unacceptable. Speakers lack the publishing houses and technology to produce and publish their own works. As African women researchers, we can deconstruct the imperial language by subverting authority of language, ownership, and the subject and making it ours, at least within Africa. Let others try for a change to figure out what we are saying when we speak in Pidgin English! Pidgin can thus be seen as a form of resistance, a way to free us from the imperial language and critique traditional ways of writing. Moreover, incorporating Pidgin English in our research gives those who speak it more access to oral sources, since most Anglophone West Africans and women speak it.

Final Thoughts

Our contribution to this volume is a dialogue in which we confront issues of method, epistemology, interpretative categories, and theory. The premise of our chapter has been that as African female researchers, our location in relation to our work does in fact shape and inform the quality of research/analysis that emerges. During our respective fieldwork in Cameroon and Nigeria, we collaborated with indigenous historians and consciously placed ourselves on the inside. This assumed positionality allowed us to privilege Moghamo and northern Igbo constructions of their own histories. In our role as documenters, we have become intermediaries through which Moghamo and northern Igbo (her)stories are realized in written form, and the ensuing narrative has been consciously shaped and structured from within. The end product of this process, our books, will be firmly rooted in the realization of the representations and conclusions about female power and authority that have been enabled by Moghamo- and Igbo-inspired interpretative categories and analytical frameworks. We began this dialogue with our lives, since our understanding of the importance of gender politics in Africa and academia profoundly shaped our own social and professional locations and identity. We are confident that we have raised consciousness and created awareness with regard to some of these challenges.

Notes

1. We will problematize this term "our own people" within the body of this chapter.
2. For more on this process of self-naming and -locating, see Achebe (2002).
3. The only departure from this rule in Africa would be Africans who have been forced to confront their blackness as a result of living with Europeans who have settled in Africa.
4. As an Igbo woman living in the United States, oftentimes the most obvious and therefore distinguishing part of my identity is the fact that I am African. This is because Africa (the idea, the imagined, the land mass) is what most Americans can relate to.
5. For more information on the subject, see Mudimbe (1988, 1994) and Mbembe (1992).
6. I borrow this term from Tsitsi Dangarembga's *Nervous Conditions* (1988), a novel that best captures some of the conditions that produce Southern Africans' nervousness.
7. Paul Biya, the current president of the Republic of Cameroon, took power in 1983, following the resignation of the former (now deceased) president, Ahmadou Ahidjo. In the early 1980s, Biya was regarded as the educated president who would take the nation to a higher level of prosperity and progress. Today, following failed dreams, he is

critiqued for condoning corruption and inappropriate policies and for being a puppet working for the French government instead of taking care of his people and country.

8. Moghamoland is made up of twenty-two villages. The people who inhabit the Batibo and Momo divisions of the Northwest Province of Cameroon form the southeast portion of the (Bamenda) Grassfields of Cameroon.

9. Recent studies and novels on Africa have also sought to paint a different picture. See Emecheta (1979) and Ogundipe-Leslie (1985) as well as studies edited by Allen Isaacman and Jean Allman in the Heinemann Social History of Africa Series, for example Penvenne (1995), Byfield (2002), Grier (2005), and Peterson (2004).

10. For an excellent overview, see Johnson-Odim and Mba (1997), Kuzwayo (1985), and Personal Narratives Group (1989). See also Berger and White (1999).

11. In fact, in certain northern Igbo village groups, I had to use a linguist to translate some intricate words from my field tapes.

12. Nsukka is my research area and a town in northern Igboland.

13. We must make the distinction between those who have documented and reproduced histories in written form and those who embody these histories, for Igbo women have always been and continue to be the repositories of many of these histories.

14. *Ni muugh* in Moghamo means literally "to tell a story or to carry on a conversation." It is also the terminology that I adopted and used for my previous interviews.

15. For example, birth celebrations (*ibu'uh* or "born-house"), death ceremonies/funeral rites (*ideik* or "cry-die"), marriages/weddings (*enami*), church fund-raisers (regardless of religious beliefs), the annual traditional dance (*abin*), social and financial network groups (*njanggis*), and development plans.

16. The difficulty of getting information from women, especially about secret societies, was greatly reduced once I decided to take questions that were not related to my dissertation and tried to provide answers that helped many families in the management of their and their children's daily lives.

17. The category "woman" is used in the culture to describe the biological and physical characteristics that determine femaleness.

18. The word "female," or "male," for that matter, is used in this culture to describe one's gender—the beliefs, attitudes, behavior, and actions that differentiate women from men.

19. I use the terms "deity wives" and "dedicatees" interchangeably to define a specific category of *ohu mma* (literally, "spiritual 'slaves'") who came into being in northern Igboland after the abolition of the Atlantic slave trade.

20. "Western" here is used specify the dominant Judeo-Christian point of view.

21. King Agonglo of Dahomey was said to have expressed his great upset at the maligning of his people in "books that never die" to Governor Abson of the African Company's fort at Whydah. See Dalzel (1793).

22. I use "man" here to describe a gendered reclassification that is not sexual. A similar point is made by Akyeampong and Obeng (1995) for Asante postmenopausal women.

23. The *nwadiana*'s role, like that of the *nwada*, is primarily one of peacemaker and arbitrator. As *nwadiana,* the daughter, however, fulfills these services in her mother's lineage rather than in her own natal lineage.

24. It is important to note that in Igboland there were no absolutes; therefore, women could also and often did farm and own yams as well.

25. For more discussion on this violence, see Said (1985). See also Chakrabarty (1992).

26. There are a handful of publishing companies that publish works by African writ-

ers and works on Africa: Heinemann, Africa World Press; and a few university presses that publish books in African studies: Ohio University Press, University of Wisconsin Press, University of Chicago Press, Indiana University Press, and Cambridge University Press.

27. Almost all African nation-states now use the term "official languages" to mean European or colonial languages such as English, French, German, Portuguese, Spanish, which at independence became the language of instruction in all schools and the language of government and the workplace.

28. Mother said that there shall be a meeting here tomorrow. She said all women must first march as a group to the *fon*'s [chief's] palace, where they will sing and dance in protest/ demonstration to let the *fon* know that women have a grievance/complaint to make. Only following that will the actual meeting start at the Women's House. That unacceptable behavior of men which allows them to always sit and make decisions regarding the marketplace [women's domain/space] as well as how much we women have to pay for market stalls/sheds without even asking/consulting us must end! All girls, young women, wives, mothers, and grandmothers who conduct business at the marketplace or have related business at the marketplace or are relatives of market women (and that means all of us here today) must forget about all work tomorrow in order to join forces with us to present a united front as we present our case and see where the debate takes us [or see what next step we must take]. Isn't it? It is! Do you all agree [with Mother]? Yes, we all agree!

Excerpt from a Pidgin English call to rally, Batibo, Cameroon, 1998.

References

Achebe, Nwando. 2002. "Nwando Achebe—Daughter, Wife and Guest—A Researcher at the Crossroads." *Journal of Women's History* 14, no. 3: 9–31.
———. 2003. "Nigeria." In *Sub-Saharan Africa: The Greenwood Encyclopedia of Women's Issues Worldwide,* edited by Aili Mari Tripp, 311–337. Westport, Conn.: Greenwood Press.
———. 2005. *Farmers, Traders, Warriors, and Kings: Female Power and Authority in Northern Igboland,* 1900–1960. Portsmouth, N.H.: Heinemann.
Akeampong, Emmanuel, and Pashington Obeng. 1995. "Spirituality, Gender, and Power in Asante History." *International Journal of African Historical Studies* 28, no. 3: 481–508.
Appiah, Kwame Anthony. 1992. *In My Father's House: Africa in the Philosophy of Culture.* New York: Oxford University Press.
Ashcroft, Bill, Gareth Griffiths, and Helen Tiffin. 1989. *The Empire Writes Back: Theory and Practice in Post-Colonial Literature.* London and New York: Routledge.
Berger, Iris, and E. Frances White, eds. 1999. *Women in Sub-Saharan Africa: Restoring Women to History.* Bloomington: Indiana University Press.
Byfield, Judith. 2002. *The Bluest Hands: A Social and Economic History of Women Indigo Dyers in Western Nigeria, 1890–1940.* Portsmouth, N.H.: Heinemann.
Césaire, Aimé. 1946. "Et les chiens se Taisent." In *Les Armes Miraculeuses.* Paris: Gallimard.

———. 1972. *Discourse on Colonialism.* Translated by Joan Pinkham. New York: Monthly Review.

Carby, Hazel. 1987. *Reconstructing Womanhood: The Emergence of the Afro-American Woman Novelist.* Oxford: Oxford University Press.

Chakrabarty, Dipesh. 1992. "Postcoloniality and the Artifice of History: Who Speaks for 'Indian' Pasts?" *Representations* 37: 1–26.

Dalzel, Archibald. 1793. *The History of Dahomey: An Inland Kingdom of Africa.* London: The Author.

Dangarembga, Tsitsi. 1988. *Nervous Conditions.* London: Women's Press.

Edwards, Elizabeth, ed. 1993. *Anthropology and Photography, 1860–1920.* New Haven, Conn.: Yale University Press in association with the Royal Anthropological Institute, London.

Emecheta, Buchi. 1979. *The Joys of Motherhood.* New York: George Braziller.

Fanon, Frantz. 1967. *Black Skin, White Masks.* New York: Grove Press.

Grier, Beverly. 2005. *Invisible Hands: Child Labor and State in Colonial Zimbabwe.* Portsmouth, N.H.: Heinemann.

Hunt, Nancy Rose. 1999. *A Colonial Lexicon: Of Birth Ritual, Medicalization, and Mobility in the Congo.* Durham, N.C.: Duke University Press.

Johnson-Odim, Cheryl, and Nina Emma Mba. 1997. *For Women and the Nation: Funmilayo Ransome-Kuti of Nigeria.* Urbana: University of Illinois Press.

Kanogo, Tabitha. 1987. *Squatters and the Roots of Mau Mau, 1905–1963.* Oxford: James Currey.

Kuzwayo, Ellen. 1985. *Call Me Woman.* San Francisco: Spinsters Ink.

Lutz, Catherine A., and Jane L. Collins, eds. 1993. *Reading National Geographic.* Chicago: University of Chicago Press.

Mbembe, Achille. 1992. "Prosaics of Servitude and Authoritarian Civilities." *Public Culture* 5, no. 1: 123–145.

Mudimbe, V. Y. 1988. *Invention of Africa: Gnosis, Philosophy, and the Order of Knowledge.* Bloomington: Indiana University Press.

———. 1994. *The Idea of Africa.* Bloomington: Indiana University Press.

Musisi, Nakanyinke. 2003. *Makerere University in Transition, 1993–2000.* Oxford: James Currey; Kampala: Fountain Publishers.

Ogundipe-Leslie, Molara. 1985. "Women in Nigeria." In *Women in Nigeria Today,* edited by D. L. Badejo, 119–137. London: Zed Books.

Penvenne, Jeanne. 1995. *African Workers and Colonial Racism: Mozambican Strategies and Struggles in Laurenço Marques, 1877–1962.* Portsmouth, N.H.: Heinemann.

Peterson, Derek. 2004. *Creative Writing: Translation, Bookkeeping, and the Work of Imagination in Colonial Kenya.* Portsmouth, N.H.: Heinemann.

The Personal Narratives Group, eds. 1989. *Interpreting Women's Lives: Feminist Theory and Personal Narratives.* Bloomington: Indiana University Press.

Said, Edward. 1985. "An Ideology of Difference." *Critical Inquiry* 12, no. 1: 38–58.

Spivak, Gayatri Chakravorty. 1990. "The Problem of Cultural Self-Representation." In *The Post-Colonial Critic: Interviews, Strategies, Dialogues,* edited by Gayatri Chakravorty Spivak and Sarah Harasym, 138–151. New York: Routledge.

Teboh, Bridget. 1996. *The Role of Women as Entrepreneurs in Batibo, Moghamoland: A Case Study.* Bamenda, Cameroon: A*WICO/HELVETAS, Swiss Embassy.

———. 2002. "Women and Change in the Cameroon Grassfields: A Social and Economic History of Moghamoland c. 1889–1960." Ph.D. diss., University of California Los Angeles.

Thomas, Lynn. 2003. *Politics of the Womb: Women, Reproduction, and the State in Twentieth-Century Kenya.* Berkeley: University of California Press.

Williams, Patrick, and Laura Chrisman, eds. 1994. *Colonial Discourse and Post-Colonial Theory: A Reader.* New York: Columbia University Press.

Woodhull, Winifred. 1993. *Transfigurations of the Maghreb: Feminism, Decolonization, and Literatures.* Minneapolis: University of Minnesota Press.

Part Two

Activism and
Public Space

5 Rioting Women and Writing Women: Gender, Class, and the Public Sphere in Africa

Susan Z. Andrade

This chapter examines the value, both formal and received, of literary writing by women, specifically of novels in English and French. I investigate the relation of class and gender to the emerging public civil sphere as colonialism in Africa gave way to independent nation-states. At a time when the cultural production and political agitation of African men were easily assimilated to a nationalist paradigm, the culture and politics of women were often understood as not engaged with nationalism and therefore as not really interested in politics as such. Nationalism, the most visible macropolitical discourse of the continent at the moment of decolonization, appears to be absent from women's literary writings. By shifting the terms of feminist inquiry to place women's writing in relation to that of men and by broadening the scope of women's political actions beyond the realm of the literary, I am able not only to make visible a larger field of politics but also to speak to the interrelation of different registers and various categories of identity—such as class, gender, and ethnicity—as well as to what it means to participate in "public activity." I focus my concerns through a reading of two distinct groups of women: "writing women"—middle-class educated women who wrote novels, and "rioting women"—plebeian and peasant women who engaged in gender-marked rebellions and uprisings. Juxtaposing these two different groups in relation to each other makes visible a reconception, first, of the complex and cross-classed configuration of the public sphere. Second, this juxtaposition allows me to reexamine women's relation to decolonizing nationalism as well as to the question of civil society.

Just as the domestic is related to the national, so, too, is literature as a mode of political expression related to nonliterary modes of political expression. On the one hand, broadly following a model proposed by Jürgen Habermas (1962/1991), for whom the public sphere was constituted for Western Europe during its Enlightenment era, I trace the emergence of mid-twentieth-century middle-class African women who entered the sphere of literary writing, particularly novel writing. On the other hand, I explore how plebeian and petit bourgeois African women negotiated civil society at around the time of decolonization.

The public sphere concept of civil society is a valuable analytic and historical development which must be acknowledged; for Africa, it offers an index by which to understand a form of political participation that was embraced by politicians and men of letters at the moment of decolonization. This sphere, however, does not and cannot encompass the breadth of political processes and political expression, except those of the local elite, who would soon become what Fanon would disparagingly call "the national bourgeoisie." The result of my analysis illustrates the usefulness of Habermas's category of the public sphere and is supported by Nancy Fraser's revision of it on behalf of subaltern counterpublics. The end of this chapter turns to the ways in which ethnicity rather than gender is more productive as a category of analysis and as a mode by which to imagine social change, as it offers a better way to understand grass-roots political organization.

African Novels and Gender

The novel as a form does not have as a long history in Africa as, for example, do lyric and narrative poetry and drama. Africans took the form from their colonizers and by the late 1950s and 1960s period of transition to independence had begun producing a wealth of novelistic writing that was fully engaged with the topic of anticolonial nationalism. Some works depicted an idealized African past, others dwelled on the vicious dehumanization of the colonial system. Whatever their perspective or ideological position, the literary works were understood to be hopeful gestures whereby Africans educated in European languages sought to "imagine communities" (Anderson 1990) and "invent traditions" (Hobsbawm and Ranger 1983).

The Guinean Camara Laye's autobiographical and nostalgic novel *L'Enfant noir* (1953) participates in tradition-inventing by evoking a rural and as-yet-unspoiled African past in its bildungsroman of a village boy. Colonialism as such does not enter the picture; instead of what Gerald Moore has called "orthodox postures of protest" (1980, 89), we are offered a luminous picture of a village life about to vanish with the incursion of colonial modernity. Orthodox postures of protest, each differently configured, do nevertheless describe the two other francophone novelists whose works have come to stand for anticolonial nationalist writing. Both novels were published shortly before Chinua Achebe's more famous *Things Fall Apart* (1958), and both novelists come from the francophone side of the dual-language state of Cameroun. *Une vie de boy* (1956) is Ferdinand Oyono's first novel, and *Le pauvre Christ de Bomba* (1956) is Mongo Beti's second. Oyono's project illustrates a fundamental shared humanity that the systems of racism and imperialism deny. Through the diary of a servant (one who is supposed to obey), it depicts an individual who, through knowledge of the truth of infidelity, also knows, by synechdochal logic, the workings of the larger lies of colonialism. In *Le pauvre Christ*, Beti deploys savage irony to skewer both the Catholic Church and its sexual taboos and local hierarchies by making visible various forms of perversion engendered by colonialism.

"Imagining communities" offers an important way to understand why, for example, the Nigerian Chinua Achebe's first novel, *Things Fall Apart*, is almost universally felt to be the first African novel, despite the fact that it was published after other well-known Nigerian novels, namely *The Palm-Wine Drinkard* (1952) by Amos Tutuola and *People of the City* (1954) by Cyprian Ekwensi. Achebe's oeuvre as a whole and *Things Fall Apart* in particular has generated a flood of critical commentary because, according to Simon Gikandi, Achebe's novels conjoin "the social and historical conditions of African societies before and during colonization . . . with the utopian impulse that underlies the novel as a genre" (1991, 4). Just one of many examples is Barbara Harlow's *Resistance Literature* (1997), a path-breaking book on writings from Latin America, the Arab world, and Africa that opens by engaging *Things Fall Apart*.[1] Considered to be both self-critical and anti-colonial, *Things Fall Apart* not only became incorporated into but has since been understood to shape and symbolize African nationalist literary discourse. However one feels about cultural nationalism, any discussion of literature and politics in mid-twentieth-century Africa must involve some discussion of the importance of it as well as of the relation of novel writing to it and to decolonization.

Close attention to the relation between nationalism and African literature reveals two things: one, the obvious fact that African novelistic literature consists of many more male than female writers, and two, something less obvious about the reception of female writers. At a time when literature by most men was in some way engaged with the category of the national, novels by women were understood to be uninterested in politics. Put another way, I have found that especially in the beginning, women writers rarely used explicitly nationalist themes in their novels. On the few occasions they did include them, those themes diminished or displaced the telling of tales about the female characters. Here, I think especially of Aminata Sow Fall, a Senegalese writer of the same generation as Mariama Bâ and, within Senegal, of a comparable level of prominence. Sow Fall's novels have not been particularly invested in the "feminine" but are rather pointedly invested in the "political." The very title of one of her later novels, *L'Ex-père de la nation* (1987), specifically addresses nationalism; it illustrates the naturalized nexus of family, gender, and nation into a single figure by pointing precisely to its undoing: the ex-father and the expert, a pun in French.[2] Through an awkward syntax, Sow Fall's title and novel foreground the linguistic turn, the relation between biology or parenting, on the one hand, and national politics, on the other. And the novel unstitches a metonymy that is seamlessly rendered in masculine nationalist iconography, but it does so without foregrounding a woman's agency or coming to consciousness, two hallmarks of novels received as "feminist."[3] Likewise, in Lauretta Ngcobo's *Cross of Gold* (1981), a novel about the South African anti-apartheid struggle written during and about some of the bleakest moments, the female character with whom the novel opens dies within the first two chapters. The character who takes up her mantle and continues the struggle is her son, the hero of the nation. At an initial level of reading, then, these two novels would seem to depict a nationalist politics that subsumes what even a feminist-sympathetic woman might say about women in her writing. The very entrance of female authors into the literary public sphere is itself a political success; women had been educated at a significantly lower rate than men and their writing was published at a later moment and in smaller quantities. The content of that writing is another story, as women's novelistic writing has been historically understood to be apolitical; that is to say, not interested in nationalist themes.

This section seeks to explain the reception of African women's writing and suggest new interpretative frames. First of all, until quite recently, it was impossible to even pose political questions about female-authored novels within a frame of feminist inquiry because in African literary studies, feminism was dismissed as a European import. Feminism is the only theory that has been given the nativist or cultural nationalist burden of producing ideas that are "authentic" to Africa. Marxism, originating in Germany and England and reaching its height of influence in the former Soviet Union, has rarely, if ever, been subjected to a comparable scrutiny. Literary critics are less openly dismissive of feminism now than they were twenty years ago, but their history of dismissal has left a certain defensive legacy: feminist critics of African literature have tended to celebrate female-authored texts simply for giving voice to a feminine subjectivity.[4] I do not disparage this earlier feminist scholarship; indeed, I could not have made this intervention without its path-breaking work. But by historicizing and thematizing such scholarship and placing it in a larger context, I hope to explore why it is that feminists, with the exception of some working out of South Africa, have not subjected women's writing to much rigorous cross-class and public political scrutiny. I will also suggest what such scrutiny would mean.

My conceptual apparatus, which departs from the celebrationist posture of much feminist scholarship of African literature, exposes a structure of national politics that women's fiction is not usually understood to represent. In brief, my first point has to do with reading practices: the tendency of early female African novelists to tell family stories has historically gone hand in hand with nationalism's confirmation of the domestic sphere as separate from the public, "political" one.[5] As a result of the dominance of nationalist reading paradigms, readers have been unaware of the literal or allegorical relations between private and public structures and forms of power in the fiction of these writers. I suggest that one should come to these novels by African women with an understanding of the necessary implication of the domestic in the public and with an understanding that national allegories informed the reading of the male-authored novels that dominated the literary tradition into and out of which these women wrote. This perspective puts the reader in a better position to perceive how domestic life functions both materially and allegorically in relation to nationalism.

My second point has to do with literary history: the earliest female-authored novelists seemed less "political," less interested in relations of public social power, than were their literary successors. I suggest that in the face of the bewildering job of being the first to inhabit and claim their place in the sphere of letters (that is to say, to engage in nontraditional behavior), early African women novelists told stories whose settings were themselves removed from the modern and urban world. We see this in the work of two of the first Anglophone female novelists, Nigerian Flora Nwapa and Kenyan Grace Ogot. The earliest examples of this kind of novelistic writing—*Efuru* and *The Promised Land,* respectively, both of which were published in 1966—appear parochial and insular and seem to be manifestly excluded from the narrative of nationalism. I say manifestly because deploying "tradition" (Igbo-inflected linguistic structures for Nwapa, Luo folk tales for Ogot, and uncontaminated-by-Westernization rural settings for both) served as a vehicle by which to claim moral authority and more comfortably enter the very modern world of letters and publication.

A related literary historical point is that the passage of time changes things noticeably. Novels authored thirteen years after Nwapa's and Ogot's, as in the case of Senegalese author Mariama Bâ's *Une si longue lettre* (1979/1981), or eighteen years after, as in the case of Zimbabwean author Tsitsi Dangarembga's *Nervous Conditions* (1988), more openly yoke public politics and female subjectivity to their narrative. What remains the same is that the female-authored novels continue to engage macropolitics more obliquely than their male contemporaries. In Senegal, this can be seen in Ousmane Sembène in relation to Bâ; in Zimbabwe, Chenjerai Hove and Shimmer Chinodya in relation to Dangarembga. All of the male authors have published novels that openly represent and engage the nation. I suggest that the Bâ's and Dangarembga's indirect references to national symbology might be characterized as "strategic covertness."[6]

Not being the very first writer appears to be correlated with the ability of women writers to explicitly depict things national. For example, two of the most acclaimed female novelists from Africa position themselves as participants in the nationalist narrative in part because their entrance into writing inscribes them into a novelistic genealogy; that is to say, each responds through the novel to an earlier writer of her own national-ethnic literary tradition. Buchi Emecheta's famously combative *The Joys of Motherhood* (1979) and, to a lesser extent, Bâ's *Une si longue lettre* both owe the force of their social commentary to their positions as literary successors to works by authors who had already thematized gender and sexuality. The very title, *The Joys of Motherhood,* constitutes an ironic rewriting of *Efuru*'s uncertainty about the chances of a childless woman for happiness. Emecheta's comment on *Efuru* consists of giving her protagonist, Nnu Ego, so many children that all her resources, and indeed her entire life, are consumed by their care. Bâ's less polemical novella is a rewriting of Ousmane Sembène's *Xala* (1973); the intertextual relation is visible primarily through thematic resonances rather than formal similarities.[7] Writing a successor-novel is directly related to a certain boldness of expression of female subjectivity articulated within a national frame. That is to say, there is a direct relationship between women writers' self-conscious understanding of themselves as part of a literary tradition and their willingness to engage openly both private- and public-sphere discourses—in other words, those of family and nation. Even Ogot, whose earlier fiction was the most quiescent, published *The Graduate* (1980) less than two decades later, a novel that opens with the death of a male character, a cabinet minister. This fortunate circumstance clears the way for a woman to take his place. However, having begun by thematizing female ambition and naming it as requiring male death, the novel then devotes itself to retreating from its bald claim.

My third and most important point is that as critics become more adept at shifting their interpretive lenses, macropolitical themes such as nationalism become more legible and will reveal themselves to be part and parcel of women's micropolitical or domestic spheres. A reading strategy more attentive to the relation between the domestic and national spheres can more productively address the relation of women's writing to a larger literary history. Attentive reading of the macro and the micro makes visible a set of plots in dialogue with nationalism and anticolonialism as well as with domestic issues.

Habermas, the Public Sphere, and Some Reconceptions

The African women writers discussed above were in the process of entering a mid-twentieth-century, post-independence literary market—a public sphere in the sense Habermas describes in his influential book, *The Structural Transformation of the Public Sphere* (1962/1991). Although Habermas generates his specifically European model out of culturally and historically derived materials, he offers much to those interested in the development of civil society at the moment colonization turns into decolonization. *The Structural Transformation* remains a careful exploration of a particular moment when certain possibilities for human emancipation were unlocked, something with which the decolonizing moment has much in common. Moreover, because Habermas ties the development of the bourgeois public sphere and a nascent civil society to the development of print culture and, in particular, the development of the novel, he is useful in understanding the larger cultural and political context into which the women writers launched their earliest efforts. For Habermas, the public sphere is marked by the valuing of rationality over authority; it is a "sphere which mediates between society and state, in which the public organizes itself as the bearer of public opinion" (1974, 49).

Nancy Fraser (1997) recognizes that even at its very best and most inclusive, the Habermasian concept of the public sphere was inadequate to full cross-class participation and, in historical terms, was one in which the bourgeoisie's gains came at the expense of the proletariat. Her notion of competing public spheres points to the variety of means of accessing public life and to a multiplicity of public arenas in which to deliberate. She foregrounds the fact that Habermas idealizes the bourgeois public sphere to such an extent that he appears to believe that differences of status and identity might actually be bracketed in the act of dialogue. Fraser's bold stroke is to destabilize the liberal conception of the public sphere, while remaining a theorist. She argues that where Habermas saw one sphere, there are many:

I contend that, in stratified societies, arrangements that accommodate contestation among a plurality of competing publics better promote the ideal of participatory parity than does a single, comprehensive, overarching public. . . . Members of subordinated social groups—women, workers, peoples of color, and gays and lesbians—have repeatedly found it advantageous to constitute alternative publics. I propose to call these [groups] subaltern counterpublics in order to signal that they are parallel discursive arenas where members of subordinated social groups invent and circulate counterdiscourses, which in turn permit them to formulate oppositional interpretations of their identities, interests and needs. (81)

Habermas's idealized, unattained, and possibly unattainable notion of critical liberalism can be reinvigorated for a broader notion of democracy and political participation when fertilized by the identitarian notion of collectivity that Fraser advances. Rejecting a purely meritocratic claim in favor of greater participation on the part of the entire polity, Fraser shifts the original argument so that it is precisely identity or need—when acted on collectively—that enables otherwise disempowered individuals to participate in shaping the common good. Such an argument offers the possibility of reading identitarian and rationalist notions of democracy in productive dialectical relationship. Fraser argues that participation in the public sphere ought to be so important, so valued, as to permit every potential interlocutor to speak in his or her own voice, thereby simultaneously constructing and expressing her or his own identity through idiom and style. Fraser calls the "idea of the 'public sphere' in Habermas's sense"

a conceptual resource. . . . It is the space in which citizens deliberate about their common affairs, hence, an institutionalized arena of discursive interaction. The arena is conceptually distinct from the state; it [is] a site for the production and circulation of discourses that can in principle be critical of the state. The public sphere in Habermas's sense is also conceptually distinct from the official economy; it is not an arena of market relations but rather one of discursive relations, a theater for debating and deliberating rather than for buying and selling. (70)

I will suggest that both market relations and other forms of identitarian beliefs might be progressively mobilized in this age of globalism.

It might be argued that African women who demanded equal participation in the masculine domain of public literary activity were fundamentally and radically transgressive. They challenged the norms of some of the most restrictive strata of society, those of novel writing and novel publishing, and they gradually succeeded in reconfiguring those norms in order to be able to gain access. On the other hand, one might point out that the quiescence of these elite women with regard to the content of their entrance to this modernity (the seemingly apolitical or non-nationalist content of their novels, their writing of novels that overwhelmingly celebrated "tradition") was not particularly transgressive. In this respect, they stand in sharp contrast to the bellicosity and loud grumblings of the plebeian and working-class women who took to the streets before novel writing became a significant feature of public life.

These peasant and plebeian women, who would not figure at all in Habermas's conception of the public sphere, in fact participated in a mode of public political activity through uprisings, strikes, and other types of actions, some of which, as part of larger and more concerted efforts by male anticolonialists, helped foster the progression toward independence. While the rebellion of these women has been given some scholarly attention, until recently these actions have not been seen as directly related to nationalist activities, and never have they been considered in relation to the liberal democracy vaunted by Habermas and others. Fraser's more inclusive conception considers multiple groups and modes of political expression in relation to each other, thereby stretching the original conception of the public sphere.

Rioting Women

Unlike their "Western"—or "Northern"—sisters, peasant and plebeian African women have always had access to public space, although this space would not be understood as the public sphere of civil society. Separate and powerful women's organizations, both social and economic in nature, have always existed in West, East, and Central Africa. Men and women had their own societies and made separate decisions. Women's organizations almost never had the same status as those of men, but they were integral to the social structure. West African women in particular are famous as traders, and they have had enormous influence over the domestic economy by setting prices and controlling the availability of goods.

In marked contrast to the writing women, peasant and market women were (and have historically been) visibly engaged in public behavior. Indeed, a significant portion of the historiography of African women is devoted to the many examples of women's riots and rebellions as well as to the women's organizations that gave rise to them. A few of the earliest documented anticolonial rebellions include the 1929 Igbo Women's War in Nigeria, the Anlu uprising undertaken by Kom women in the former British Cameroons in 1959, and the tax riots by Pare women in Tanzania in 1946. All of these rebellions had in common the spectacular use of the female body and female reproductive sexuality in order to shock, and especially to shame, the onlookers into granting the women their rights as women within a largely gender-segregated world.

The most famous of these rebellions, the 1929 Igbo Women's War, or Ogu Umunwaanyi, may be read as one violent culmination of traditional manifestations of Igbo women's power.[8] The British system of indirect rule in Nigeria under which these women lived had established a system of Native Courts presided over by designated Africans, or warrant chiefs. These men rarely held customary positions of respect, were ultimately beholden only to the British, and, because of their bilingualism, served as powerful intermediaries between colonizer and colonized. The fact that the British relied on these intermediaries was compounded by their general ignorance of the Igbo language. Under these conditions, the colonial juridical system soon became hopelessly corrupt.

Add to this drama the onset of the 1929 world economic depression and the plummeting price of palm oil, a crucial resource in the women's economy. When the British indicated that they would extend direct taxation to the eastern provinces, the women took collective action. In November and December of 1929, tens of thousands of Igbo and Ibibio women from Calabar and Owerri provinces "made war on" the warrant chiefs and the British overlords. They originally mobilized around the issue of women's taxation, but their demands soon included abolishing the Native Courts (or including women on them) and the return of all white men to their own country. Information about and money for the uprising was conveyed through the system of women's market networks. Not knowing how to respond to half-naked, palm-frond-waving women, the British and their subsidiaries shot at them. Approximately fifty women were killed and another fifty were wounded. Despite the casualties, the uprisings can be read as one blow dealt the colonial state by the natives. The women succeeded in toppling the corrupt system of the warrant chiefs. As a result of their efforts, the British attempted to emulate the precolonial Igbo model in a new system of administration. One might read this particular movement as a forerunner to one that would take place some seventy years later.

Rebellion Studies

A serious consideration of the meaning of these women's uprisings should address the critical scholarship of Nancy Rose Hunt, who has published two essays outlining the range of feminist historiography of sub-Saharan Africa. In her first essay, Hunt (1989) asserts that social scientific feminism of Africa has been overly invested in a simple recovery of agency and mere recovery of buried narratives. Influenced by Joan Scott (1988), Hunt insists on gender as a category of analysis, refusing what she considers to be the ahistorical celebrationism of female subjects of earlier scholarship.[9]

Hunt's developmental hierarchy of historiography is in strong dialogic tension with the work of preceding generations of historians who sought to represent African women as more than simply subjugated by their gender or colonial status. She objects to the scholarly freight rebellion carries, framing her objections in terms of the essentialism and economism that drives that earlier scholarship. Her critique has an intention (if not an effect) that is similar to my own in literary studies. That is to say, like Hunt, I understand my work to be simultaneously feminist and antipathetic toward the celebrationist model of feminist criticism.

The first sentence of Hunt's essay signals a polemical intervention. "African women," she claims, "whether as subjects or objects (and to a lesser extent as authors) of history, are no longer invisible in African historiography" (1989, 359). She objects to the determined rather than overdetermined feminist scholarship that reads women only in relation to the economic sphere, which, she believes, locks the scholar into imagining women's escape from patriarchy or colonialism. These models, she suggests, are romantic by virtue of the emphasis on change or, even worse, obsessive in their minute detailing of the grimness of women's daily condition. Reading this critique in reverse order is far less persuasive; the logic of that process suggests that vulgar economism produces vulgar liberation. While liberation like the liberation that accompanied national independence may prove to be seriously limited in what it can actually deliver, the wholesale dismissal of freedom or liberation because it is excessively teleological as a category seems wrongheaded indeed. Hunt lays out, in chronological order, three increasingly sophisticated tendencies by which scholarship on African women may be categorized: the first, "an interest in forms of female resistance"; the second, "the use of life histories as a way of approaching women's agency and subjectivity"; and the third, "a rethinking of the dynamics involved within competing gender constructs during the colonial period" (362). Hunt's argument against economistic Marxism was a theoretically bold move at the time. Curiously, however, few of those who engage Hunt seem to have noticed that in 1989, when her essay appeared, a revolution was already under way in the field of peasant studies.[10] In her second review essay, Hunt (1996) returns to the above themes with an even sharper critique.

I admire Hunt's desire to produce knowledge about Africa and simultaneously inquire into the conditions and effects of knowledge production: in short, to read cultural artifacts as not simply passive reflectors of their time but also as active producers of it. And I am in agreement with her wish to bring together feminism and a sophisticated conceptual apparatus. Her critique is made on the grounds that she wants to avoid the approach of earlier feminists who themselves so fear "a passive victims approach" and who are so committed to making women the subjects of their own history that they diminish engagement with the historical and structural constraints of African women even if "the structural constraints on women's lives and female agency are not always reduced to the categories of 'male manipulations and fate determiners'" (1989, 362).

Although Hunt does not make this point, I am also deeply mindful of cautions against reading African women as rebellious subjects in a world context where the actions and agency of most are profoundly shaped (and sometimes undermined) by global forces entirely out of their control. Hunt does caution about the ways in which our intellectual work as scholars is mediated, for all such work—indeed, all representation—is mediated. However, I differ from her—and differ strongly—in my reading of the way this mediation works. Hunt's mediation critique is made primarily at the level of biography: she claims that the attention to African women's uprisings involves a psychological projection of agency on the part of white female academics in the United States who were living out a different relation to gendered power through the subjects of their study. I intend to argue that this critique is not so devastating, for indeed, at some level, all of us may be said to work out through our teaching and research what Bruce Robbins (1999) has called "allegories of vocation"—critical works that, while doing whatever other interpretive tasks they set themselves, also perform a second, more implicit function of inventing and arranging their concepts and characters so as to narrativize and argue for the general value and significance of the intellectual vocation they exemplify. Robbins says: "Examples include Raymond Williams' *Culture and Society,* which tells the story of how leftist critics like Williams himself arose from romanticism to write *Culture and Society,* and Gilbert and Gubar's *The Madwoman in the Attic,* which turns *Jane Eyre* into a paradigm for the rise of the twentieth-century feminist critic."[11] Robbins's figuration, or allegorization, of vocation offers a more nuanced, yet astutely critical model of what Hunt attempts. Understanding that a particular intellectual paradigm might have a secondary interpretive (and biographical) value is itself worthwhile. Dismissing it merely because one has "discovered" its secret or its anxiety or because one has performed a deconstructive reading of it, however, is inadequate to the intellectual task at hand. Robbins continues in his comments about Williams and Gilbert and Gubar: "But I have not *criticized* any of these works by identifying the genre to which they belong. If we accept the premise that we *want* to do significant work—that we want the privilege, if you like, of doing work that is more significant than earning a living—then we must desire and value texts that help explain, to ourselves and to others, why a particular sort of work is meaningful and valuable" (255, Robbins's italics).

Within feminist discourse theory on the representation of Third World women—at least regarding those Third World women living outside the United States and Europe—we might situate Hunt's position as one side of what I will call the problematic of how to depict the Third World and feminine Other. The other side of this dichotomy might best be represented by a famous essay by Chandra Mohanty. In "Under Western Eyes" (1991), Mohanty persuasively argues that Zed Press's tendency to represent Third World women as the passive victims of native male and colonial oppression stands for white feminism's valorization of its own political and theoretical efficacy at the expense of the agency of the subjects of their discourse.[12] Mohanty also suggests that there is a biographical element to this particular feminism, that the positioning of Third World women as subjugated permits a certain celebration of the liberatory potential of feminism, understood and narrated as (always already) white. Taken together, Hunt's and Mohanty's versions of the critique of gender and colonialism may be said to exemplify the two sides of the same coin of mediation involved in representing Third World women; each focuses on representation through an excess, one of agency (Hunt) and the other of passivity (Mohanty). Unlike Hunt, Mohanty neither gives up on the narrative of liberation that drives Marxism nor, and perhaps more important, does she find earlier, less theoretically sophisticated scholarship entirely unproductive.

Hunt never offers a connection between the feminist overinvestment in African agency—a politics that contains the intellectual disadvantage of teleology and identity politics—and the commitment to study riots, rebellions, and uprisings, particularly among the rural peasantry as it exists in Marxist histories and historiographies of Europe. One thinks not only of the writings of E. P.

Thompson and Christopher Hill on England, but also Eric Hobsbawm's writing on various parts of Europe and Natalie Zemon Davis's work on France. By addressing women's rebellions without reference to the larger tradition of men's (or mixed-gender) rebellions, Hunt participates in an old-fashioned gesture: that of reading women's traditions as entirely separately from those of men instead of seeing them as overlapping with or informing an understanding of men's traditions because they are more subaltern.[13] Hunt's critique of the feminism of Africanist scholars is made at the level of identity: she argues that the identities of the early Africanist feminists themselves offer a reason to critically examine their work. My critique of Hunt's work is also made on the grounds of identity, but for the sake of the difference, in this case, of class. Following and extending Nancy Fraser, I am in sympathy with the notion that an identity-based politics might advance the cause of liberal democracy with rationality as its foundation. I hope to sort out various concepts of identity for my idealized notion of a multiclassed public sphere.

I would like now to return to Fraser's assertion that the Habermasian public sphere is "conceptually distinct from the official-economy." She claims that "it is not an arena of market relations but rather one of discursive relations, a theater for debating and deliberating rather than for buying and selling." I wish to disagree and, in disagreeing, to extend her model slightly, for in the African context, understanding the ability of groups that are defined in economistic and identitarian terms to both articulate self-interest and move beyond it permits the widening of the public sphere that Fraser wants to see. Fraser's notion effects a bridge between the coherence of identitarian women's organizations such as lineage groups (matrilineally and patrilineally traced associations of women), on the one hand, and voluntary congeries such as market women's organizations, on the other. This coherence could and often did ultimately allow these groups to speak toward the "common good" and not simply toward their own narrow interests, a point to which I will return at the end. Though these African women's groups are not defined by their members' literacy and by a bracketing of status, as in the Habermasian model, the public sphere I discuss is, despite its identitarian foundation, legible as a vehicle for the improvement of more than just those who assert themselves in it, since the actions undertaken often go beyond women's interests in the narrow sense to encompass interests of the group at large, whether defined in terms of ethnicity, class, or nation. Moreover, I will argue that understanding subaltern counterpublics as more flexible and inclusive than "a theater of talk" allows one to include otherwise excluded political activity.

Conclusion, or More Rebellion?

The earlier portions of my chapter, then, sought to claim several things. With regard to women's political action, we in African literary studies have not always imagined women's writing to involve a complex, potentially ambivalent set of politics that is simultaneously legible in both microdiscursive and macro-discursive registers. Scholars of literature have not known how to make sense out of the relation of women writers to nationalism because of our inadequate reading practices; in other words, our inability to decipher or read the unsaid. Turning to the political expression of rioting women, I juxtaposed the noisiness of plebeian market women with the putative silences of elite literary women with regard to the content of their novels. Although they have not necessarily written in open support of decolonizing nationalism, it is the writers and other educated women who have benefited the most from independence and the consolidation of the nation-state. With this realization, I came up against the historical fact that the realm in which liberal constitutional democracy has been most powerfully articulated and the realm that continues to be the most celebrated in political theory—that is, the public sphere—remains a bourgeois one.[14] Moreover, even modifications of that sphere, such as those proposed by Fraser, do not, or perhaps cannot, fundamentally challenge the class-bound notion of such democracy.

Hard on the heels of that understanding came my suspicion that as time passes, these older forms of women's organizations, feminine solidarity, and political expression have been surpassed and eclipsed by the emergence into print of an increasingly educated African middle class. In tracing the effects of women's uprisings and in looking at Hunt's critique of their representation, I have come to wonder whether this mode has become outdated—whether the exercise of feminine power in the form of the female riot or strike has a place anymore in contemporary Africa. One reason one might think not is because of the destruction of the female-dominated Makola market in Accra. In 1982, Accra market women went on strike until their control over pricing within the market was reinstated. They were scapegoated by the "revolutionary" Rawlings regime as symbols of wealth, and Accra's largest market was burned down (Bryce 1992; see also Robertson 1983).

Recently, however, a historical event germane to these questions took place, one that, in relation to the other materials presented thus far, suggests that "traditional" African feminine modes of rebellion are not simply residual in relation to the emerging writing women but perhaps are also emergent with regard to new formations with which to engage global capitalism.[15] Since some of these events and political actions are still in the process of playing themselves out, and because the past ones are still very recent, I must emphasize that even more than usual, my comments here are contingent, sometimes even speculative.[16]

In July 2002, a group of women in the Delta region of Nigeria challenged some multinational oil companies in nonviolent confrontations that powerfully resembled the Igbo women's 1929 anticolonial Ogu Umunwaanyi, or "sitting on a man." A group of about 150 local women took over a ChevronTexaco oil platform in a nonviolent action that made a brief splash in headlines around the world but whose waves continue to be felt in the oil-rich and economically impoverished riverine communities of Nigeria. Moreover, as in the 1929 event, the women threatened to disrobe before ChevronTexaco's mostly male staff when negotiations faltered. Remarkably for confrontations between locals and outsiders, there was no shooting.

Though the Delta region is the site of the vast majority of Nigerian oil production and Nigeria is Africa's biggest oil producer, Delta State is home to some of Nigeria's poorest inhabitants. The oil professionals are mostly Euro-Americans or, less commonly, Nigerians from elsewhere. On July 8, 2002, several hundred ChevronTexaco workers changing shifts at the crude-oil tank farm in Escavros (Urhobo) found their work interrupted by the surreptitious arrival of about 150 mostly middle-aged or elderly women, some with babies strapped to their backs, all carrying bundles of food, sleeping mats, cooking pots, and other household items.[17] Most of the women were Itsekiri, one of Nigeria's many ethnic minorities, though the Itsekiri form the majority of residents in the communities around the oil facility.[18] Without using violence, the women disembarked and overran the dock, helipad, offices, and common areas of the tank farm. They issued a set of some forty demands that were relayed to ChevronTexaco's headquarters in Warri, Lagos, and San Francisco. Some had to do with the oil company's greater and better employment of more local men, particularly the sons of local women. The women asked the company to honor past promises, notably that Chevron help develop a better local infrastructure.[19] Many of the demands involved addressing and providing retribution for the environmental degradation produced by the extraction of oil. Many of the protestors had made their living as fisherwomen, and all were mothers of children perceived to be at risk from ChevronTexaco's terrible record of oil spills and gas flaring in this part of the Niger Delta.[20] Since fishing was no longer possible in most of the ruined creeks and rivers around their homes, the women also demanded that Chevron build fish and chicken farms for their own future employment, the understanding being that food from these enterprises might be sold to the petroleum workers. The women also complained that the corporation's own hired security forces and Nigerian mobile police and military personnel (whose weapons and living expenses were rumored to be paid for by the oil companies in the Delta) had targeted women for violence when moving through the villages or patrolling the perimeters of petroleum facilities, even using rape as a weapon of terror.[21] Some were concerned about the increase of sex work in and around petroleum facilities, seeing open prostitution around their villages as an incitement to foreign men to display a lack of respect for all women.

The occupation itself seems to have been a relatively peaceful affair. Neither oil workers nor protestors behaved violently toward each other, and after a thwarted attempt on the part of some of the permanent staff to leave the compound, most of the oil workers went about their business on the tank farm, freely answering the telephone and talking with members of the international press (Agence France-Presse 2002a). Pumping of oil into tankers was suspended throughout the occupation, however, which put economic pressure on representatives of ChevronTexaco to resolve the situation as rapidly as possible.[22] As word about the women's action spread by "bush radio" and local media, more women arrived to supplement the original 150. The *Oread Daily* suggests that as many as 2,000 women occupied the compound by the fourth day, although this number seems exaggerated. The size of the original protest group did swell significantly, eventually growing beyond the control of the original women's leadership.[23]

The protestors offered a media spectacle almost from the beginning, both within and outside Nigeria. Large mixed-gender protests against the petroleum corporations had taken place in this region of Nigeria since the 1980s; some had turned violent and several others included hundreds and even thousands of women. Nevertheless, there had been little coverage of these events outside the international human rights and environmentalist media. The only exception to this low level of coverage took place in 1995 with the trial and execution of Ken Saro-Wiwa, writer and indigenous rights activist, and other members of the Ogoni Nine. After about a week of occupation of Escavros, some women became unsure that the corporation was bargaining in good faith, in part because about 100 military and police officers had surrounded the terminal compound during the week of negotiation—the same police associated with anti-female violence who were reportedly funded by the oil multinationals. Some protestors at the Escavros facility felt compelled to invoke their "weapon of nakedness" out of frustration with ChevronTexaco, which, though it had agreed to negotiate, had, by day six of the standoff, not responded to the women's demands in any substantive way. The perceived physical threat from the militia groups and the company's ability to stonewall—to use its size and staying power against the protestors who had not come prepared for weeks of occupation—provoked the women to invoke their moral stature as female elders, as women who had reproduced and nurtured the social group, and as individuals who therefore had special claim not only to the group's well-being but also to individual signs of respect.

That the protest against giant ChevronTexaco began with 150 unknown, unarmed, middle-aged women who somehow managed to bring oil production to a halt at Escavros offered locally based journalists an interesting spin, enabling them to write reports about indigenous environmental and human rights protests that would ordinarily have been ignored by larger media outlets. The BBC, Agence France-Presse, and the Associated Press's stringer, D'arcy Doran, were particularly effective in publicizing the story of the protests to an international audience.[24] Apparently, what first attracted press attention was the sheer novelty of a mass female-only nonviolent demonstration against a multinational oil company. So when after a week of occupation the David of the noisy Itsekiri village women challenged the faceless Goliath of ChevronTexaco with the incongruous threat of taking off the "bright printed dresses" (Doran 2002a) that had given some of the original local color to the story, news outlets from the BBC and CNN to the *Baltimore Sun* and the *Financial Times* suddenly moved the story from the back international pages to prime-time coverage and high-profile editorials. Most of the global coverage of the threat of women protestors' collective nudity was couched in a light and somewhat patronizing tone; even otherwise respectful reportage, like that of Branigan and Vidal (2002) in the British daily *The Guardian,* was saddled at the editorial level with sensationalist headlines ("Hands Up or We Strip!").[25] Some local journalists did recognize the seriousness of what was taking place in the Escavros facility. Doran (2002d, 2002e) reported soberly that this was a "traditional and powerful shaming gesture." Curiously, neither global nor local media described this sanction as one with a history; local media did not even recall that female nudity had had success in previous women's campaigns against corporations and colonial regimes in southeastern Nigeria.[26] Some of the most thoughtful journalistic analysis involving the threat of elder female undress came from Doran, who nevertheless wrote in terms of "tradition" or "custom"—terms that evoke in media discourse small-scale groups outside the reach of global modernity, a notion that in the face of their objection to oil pumping is wrong indeed.

Although Fraser's conception of subaltern counterpublics is an inadequate accounting of all of the nuances of women's participation in politics, it offers me the best way I currently have to understand the women's protests as activities of a category of people who are simultaneously *gendered* and *ethnic* as well as class-identified. Here one might see ethnicity, just as much as gender, as a category of analysis and as a mode by which to imagine social change. Ethnicity, after all, was what had allowed the women to call upon the resources of the Itsekeri youth to join together in a particular gender cluster.[27] Fraser's formulation appears to me to offer the fullest articulation of gender in relation to other categories because it explicitly assumes a high level of social stratification and because it responds by conceptually and politically imagining "subaltern counterpublics" to speak to the dominant power in their own style or idiom and to do so in a shared discursive arena. Subaltern counterpublics of the sort engaged in by the protesting women at Escavros provide "parallel discursive arenas where members of subordinated social groups invent and circulate counter-discourses, which in turn permit them to formulate oppositional interpretations of their identities, interests and needs." I find it laudable that while Fraser allows for an identitarian politics, she does not base her notion of public discourse on sheer identitarianism. Rather, "needs" and "interests" are given as much pride of place as identity. Moreover, speaking in the protesting women's own idiom of morality involves a high degree of differentiation between viewing female nakedness for pleasurable stimulation and understanding it as shameful. A reproductive or maternal body that should command great respect produces shame in the viewer, especially when flashed to a man; the viewer/interlocutor is forced to know this before discourse can proceed. This is but one form of moral leverage that women were able to use against the oil companies at their critical moment of insecurity. More to the point, the working men at Escavros accepted this distinction and deferred to it. Even at a moment when globalization and the transfer of financial capital across the boundaries of nation-states and continents appears to make human-scale resistance futile, a group of mostly uneducated and poor women were able to interrupt the work, and especially the earnings, of several multinational oil companies. Whether they can do much to effect long-term transformation of the actually existing conditions under which they live is, unfortunately, another story whose end we do not yet know.

Notes

1. See Simon Gikandi's lengthy introduction to Heinemann's latest edition of *Things Fall Apart* (1996) for this argument in its most succinctly articulated form. He develops it most fully in *Reading Chinua Achebe* (1991).

2. I am indebted to Odile Cazenave for this insight.

3. One result of not being understood as a feminist author is that with the notable exception of single chapters in books by Irene d'Almeida (1994), Nicki Hitchcott (2003), and Mary Kay Miller (1996), Sow Fall's work has received scant feminist critical attention.

4. Feminist critics guilty of this celebratory mode include myself, Carole Boyce Davies (1986), Francoise Lionnet (1989), Florence Stratton (1994), Chikwenye Ogunyemi (1996), and Irene d'Almeida (1994), Odile Cazenave (1986/1993), and others. This tendency is due to more than an ideological and critical defensiveness; it is also, in some sense, historically explicable. It was only in 1986 that Davies and Anne Adams Graves's *Ngambika*, the first collection of feminist criticism, was published. *Research in African Literatures* first devoted an issue to women's texts and feminist criticism only in 1988, under the special editorship of Rhonda Cobham and Chikwenye Ogunyemi (1988). Feminist criticism published on the African continent made its appearance even later. See *Nigerian Female Writers: A Critical Perspective*, edited by Otokunefor and Nwodo (1989) and the special issue of the South African journal *Current Writing* devoted to feminist scholarship, edited by Cecily Lockett (1990).

5. In the Indian context, one now-well-known example of how the public/private divide served gender-conservative decolonizing nationalism has been examined by Partha Chatterjee in the two gender-focused chapters of *The Nation and Its Fragments* (1993). The symbolic value of middle-class women in nineteenth-century century Bengal helped consolidate (middle-class and nationalist) Bengali men's self-definition against (as well as their appropriation of) the discourse of English nationalism in the interest of establishing an intellectual and ideological position for decolonizing Indian nationalism.

6. I have developed a reading of *Nervous Conditions* as a novel that speaks both a domestic and a national politics in "Tradition, Modernity and the Family as Nation" (Andrade 2002).

7. Whereas Sembène satirizes a bourgeoisie so corrupt that it lays waste to the national coffers with which it has been entrusted, the protagonist of *Une si longue lettre* laments the personal betrayal of one woman by one man, a betrayal parallel to, and almost obscured by, the betrayal by the individual man of the nation, of which the couple forms a part.

8. I have developed my argument about the 1929 Igbo Women's War and its relation to African women's literary writing at some length in "The Joys of Daughterhood," in *Cultural Institutions of the Novel* (Andrade 1996). For further discussion, see especially Bastian (2001, 2002), also Ifeka-Moller (1975) and Van Allen (1972, 1976).

9. The two essays I examine here do not constitute the focus of Hunt's area of specialization, which concerns birth and medicalization in Zaire/Congo and from which I have learned much.

10. I refer here to the work of the Indianist historians who published over eight volumes of field-shifting history and historiography. The collective went by the name of their journal, *Subaltern Studies,* and the scholars were critical of a simple nationalism. Influenced by Gramsci, they saw this as serving bourgeois interests and yet were unwilling to dismiss entirely the value of Marxist teleology, the interest in the relation of decolonization to the present moment, or even the notion of a "usable past." Some of Terence Ranger's work has been written in dialogue with the subalternists. More intellectually comprehensive work is being done by a younger generation of Africanist historians such as Frederick Cooper, who has produced at least one essay in dialogue with the subaltern studies corpus (1994). Note also that for about a decade a Latin American subaltern studies group existed that attempted to use similar configurations of peasant studies to rethink that configuration of area studies.

11. I would add to Robbins's model the historical writings of C. L. R. James, who, in his magnum opus, *The Black Jacobins* (1938), illustrates the intellectual and political relation between the violent overthrow of a plantocracy in Haiti and the bourgeois uprising that constituted the French Revolution. In so doing, James narrates his own vocation as a radical historian who bridges the gap between the insurgent tradition of Pan-Africanism and the intellectual tradition of European Communist Party thought.

12. I thank Stephanie Newell for suggesting the comparison between Mohanty and Hunt to me.

13. See E. P. Thompson's historical classic (1963) and Eric Hobsbawm's scholarship on banditry (1959) and Hill (1975). Natalie Zemon Davis's work on *chiarivari* (1975) is quoted approvingly by Hunt in her first essay.

14. In many postcolonial African nations today, Habermas's idealized public sphere is nonexistent even for those with secondary or tertiary educations, let alone the uneducated —a historical fact of particular importance to any hopes of cross-class public discourse. The concept continues to motivate those committed to notions of democracy and open conversation. For a deeply thoughtful accounting of the question of democracy as it bears both on ethnicity and race in Africa, see Mahmood Mamdani (1996).

15. See Raymond Williams's (1977) discussion of dominant, residual, and emergent phenomena. For Williams, residual phenomena would appear to be incommensurate with the dominant culture, whereas emergent ones would involve "new meanings and values, significances" in the face of dominant cultural formations. The thing to underscore is that these are distinctions that illustrate the relation of the dominant to people's lives within it—as well as being a way of potentially harnessing an aspect of culture for instrumental or political use.

16. The following section was drafted in dialogue with Misty Bastian, an anthropologist and Africanist whose particular area of expertise in southeastern Nigeria includes evangelical Christianity and women's rituals. I thank her for permission to use this work here, and I thank Saleh Waziruddin for forwarding me much electronic information from Agence France-Press on the women's riots.

17. Escavros, a relatively remote storage facility, traces its origins to the Portuguese word for "slave" and serves as a reminder of earlier forms of commerce in the region.

18. Itsekiri youth groups may have assisted the protestors in gaining control of the canoes that took them to the platform. Such young men have been instrumental in most protests against the oil multinationals over the past decade. It is significant that a sex-

segregated group, or group of locals perceived to be especially powerless or peaceful, made greater inroads with the oil companies than have others before.

19. ChevronTexaco's past agreements with Itsekiri elders included promises that the corporation would support local schools, pay for university scholarships, wire villages for electricity, install running water, and construct roads and proper houses for the towns close to the multinational's petroleum facilities. It is unclear how much money Chevron-Texaco has actually given over the years, and, of that, how much actually made its way past local chiefs and bureaucrats to the mostly poor local inhabitants.

20. Chevron's environmental problems in Nigeria are a recent extension of the multi-national's checkered history in the United States and around the globe.

21. Terisa Turner and M. O. Oshare (1993) and Turner (2001) suggest that rape and other violence against women have become endemic in the Delta and other coastal areas since the arrival of the petroleum companies in the mid-1950s. The protesting women's claims about ChevronTexaco's involvement in these systematic campaigns of terror have been investigated by outside agencies like Human Rights Watch (1999) and are widely accepted as fact among Nigerian Delta activists.

22. Oduniyi and Nzeshi (2002) claim that the protests caused a loss in production of around 110,000 barrels of oil per day, costing the multinational millions for each day of occupation.

23. As time passed and negotiations continued with ChevronTexaco, some of those leaders complained to reporters that the newer protestors exhibited a more confronta-tional spirit than that expressed by the first women to occupy the facility.

24. A relatively full accounting of the international press stories from the BBC, Agence France-Presse, and D'arcy Doran can be found in the list of media sources at the end of this chapter.

25. Other such headlines include AfricaOnline's "Nigeria: Dare to Go Bare?" (Africa-Online 2002) and the *Baltimore Sun's* "Barefoot and Powerful" (Baltimore Sun 2002).

26. See Ifeka-Moller (1975), Turner and Oshare (1993), and Bastian (2001, 2002).

27. Note that Ibibio women held a similar, some have said copycat, female uprising nearby. However, it did not have the same scope or force.

References

Achebe, Chinua. 1958. *Things Fall Apart.* London: Heinemann.

Anderson, Benedict. 1990. *Imagined Communities.* Rev. ed. New York: Verso.

Andrade, Susan Z. 1996. "The Joys of Daughterhood: Gender, Nationalism and the Making of Literary Tradition(s)." In *Cultural Institutions of the Novel,* edited by Deidre Lynch and William B. Warner, 249–75. Durham, N.C.: Duke University Press.

———. 2002. "Tradition, Modernity and the Family as Nation: Reading *Chimurenga* into and out of *Nervous Conditions.*" In *Emerging Perspectives on Tsitsi Dangarembga,* edited by Ann Elizabeth Willey and Jeanette Treiber. Trenton, N.J.: Africa World Press.

Bâ, Mariama. 1979/1981. *Une si longue lettre.* Dakar: Les nouvelles éditions africaines. Translated by Modupé Bodé-Thomas as *So Long a Letter.* London: Heinemann.

Bastian, Misty L. 2001. "Dancing Women and Colonial Men: The *Nwaobiala* of 1925."

In *"Wicked" Women and the Reconfiguration of Gender in Africa*, edited by Dorothy L. Hodgson and Sheryl A. McCurdy, 109–129. Portsmouth, N.H.: Heinemann.

———. 2002. "'Vultures of the Marketplace': Southeastern Nigerian Women and Discourses of the *Ogu Umunwaanyi* (Women's War) of 1929." In *Women in African Colonial Histories*, edited by Jean Allman, Susan Geiger, and Nakanyike Musisi, 260–281. Bloomington: Indiana University Press.

Beti, Mongo. 1956. *Le pauvre Christ de Bomba*. Paris: R. Laffont.

Bryce, Jane. 1992. "West Africa." In *The Bloomsbury Guide to Women's Literature*, edited by Claire Buck. New York: Prentice Hall.

Cazenave, Odile. 1986/1993. *Femmes Rebelles: Naissance d'un nouveau roman africain au féminin*. Paris: L'Harmattan.

Chatterjee, Partha. 1993. *The Nation and Its Fragments: Colonial and Postcolonial Histories*. Princeton, N.J.: Princeton University Press.

Cobham, Rhonda and Chikwenye Ogunyemi. 1988. "Introduction." In special issue, "Women's Writing." *Research in African Literatures* 19, no. 2: 137–142.

Cooper, Frederick. 1994. "Conflict and Connection: Rethinking Colonial African History." *American Historical Review* 99, no. 5: 1516–1545.

d'Almeida, Irene Assiba. 1994. *Francophone African Writers: Destroying the Emptiness of Silence*. Gainesville: University Press of Florida.

Dangarembga, Tsitsi. 1988. *Nervous Conditions*. Seattle: The Seal Press.

Davies, Carole Boyce. 1986. "Feminist Consciousness and African Literary Criticism." In *Ngambika: Studies of Women in African Literature*, edited by Carole Boyce Davies and Anne Adams Graves. Trenton. N.J.: Africa World Press.

Davis, Natalie Zemon. 1975. *Society and Culture in Early Modern France*. Stanford, Calif.: Stanford University Press.

Ekwensi, Cyprian. 1954. *People of the City*. London: Heinemann.

Emecheta, Buchi. 1979. *The Joys of Motherhood: A Novel*. London: George Braziller.

Fall, Aminata Sow. 1987. *L'Ex-père de la nation*. Paris : L'Harmattan.

Fraser, Nancy. 1997. "Rethinking the Public Sphere: A Contribution to the Critique of Actually Existing Democracy." In *Justice Interruptus: Critical Reflections on the "Postsocialist" Condition*. New York: Routledge.

Gikandi, Simon. 1991. *Reading Chinua Achebe*. Portsmouth, N.H.: Heinemann.

———. 1996. "Introduction to Chinua Achebe, *Things Fall Apart*." Oxford: Heinemann.

Gilbert, Sandra M., and Susan Gubar. 1979. *The Madwoman in the Attic: The Woman Writer and the Nineteenth-Century Literary Imagination*. New Haven, Conn.: Yale University Press.

Habermas, Jürgen. 1962/1991. *The Structural Transformation of the Public Sphere: An Inquiry into a Category of Bourgeois Society*. Translated by Thomas Burger, with the assistance of Frederick Lawrence. Cambridge, Mass.: MIT Press.

———. 1974. "The Public Sphere: An Encyclopedia Article." *New German Critique* 3.

Harlow, Barbara. 1987. *Resistance Literature*. New York: Methuen.

Hill, Christopher. 1975. *The World Turned Upside Down: Radical Ideas during the English Revolution*. Harmondsworth, England.

Hitchcott, Nicki. 2003. *Women Writers in Francophone Africa*. Oxford: Berg.

Hobsbawm, Eric. 1959. *Primitive Rebels: Studies in Archaic Forms of Social Movement in the 19th and 20th Centuries*. New York: W. W. Norton.

———, and Terence Ranger, eds. 1983. *The Invention of Tradition*. Cambridge: Cambridge University Press.

Human Rights Watch. 1999. *The Price of Oil: Corporate Responsibility and Human Rights Violations in Nigeria's Oil Producing Communities*. New York: Human Rights Watch.

Hunt, Nancy Rose. 1989. "Placing African Women's History and Locating Gender." *Social History* 14, no. 3: 359–379.

———. 1996. "Introduction." *Gender & History* 8, no. 3: 323–337.

———, Tessie P. Liu, and Jean Quataert, ed. 1997. *Gendered Colonialisms in African History*. Malden, Mass.: Blackwell.

Ifeka-Moller, Caroline. 1975. "Female Militancy and Colonial Revolt: The Women's War of 1929, Eastern Nigeria." In *Perceiving Women*, edited by Shirley Ardener, 127–157. London: Malaby Press.

James, C. L. R. 1938. *The Black Jacobins: Toussaint L'Ouverture and the San Domingo Revolution*. London: Secker and Warburg.

Laye, Camara. 1953. *L'Enfant noir*. Paris: Plon.

Lionnet, Françoise. 1989. *Autobiographical Voices: Race, Gender and Self-Portraiture*. Ithaca, N.Y.: Cornell University Press.

Lockett, Cecily, ed. 1990. Special issue, "Women's Writing." *Current Writing* 2, no. 1.

Mamdani, Mahmood. 1996. *Citizen and Subject: Contemporary Africa and the Legacy of Late Colonialism*. Princeton, N.J.: Princeton University Press.

Miller, Mary Kay. 1996. "Aminata Sow Fall's *L'Ex-père de la nation:* Subversive Subtexts and the Return of the Maternal." In *Postcolonial Subjects: Francophone Women Writers*, edited by Mary Jean Green et al. Minneapolis: University of Minnesota Press.

Mohanty, Chandra. 1991. "Under Western Eyes: Feminist Scholarship and Colonial Discourses." In *Third World Women and the Politics of Feminism*, edited by Chandra Mohanty, Ann Russo, and Lourdes Torres, 51–80. Bloomington: Indiana University Press.

Moore, Gerald. 1980. *Twelve African Writers*. Bloomington: Indiana University Press.

Ngcobo, Lauretta. 1981. *Cross of Gold*. London: Longman.

Nwapa, Flora. 1966. *Efuru*. London: Heinemann.

Ogot, Grace. 1966. *The Promised Land*. Nairobi: East Africa Publishing House.

———. 1980. *The Graduate*. Nairobi: Uzima.

Ogunyemi, Chikwenye. 1996. *African Wo/Man Palava: The Nigerian Novel by Women*. Chicago: University of Chicago Press.

Otokunefor, Henrietta, and Obiageli Nwodo, eds. 1989. *Nigerian Female Writers: A Critical Perspective*. Lagos: Malthouse.

Oyono, Ferdinand. 1956. *Une vie de boy*. Paris: René Julliard.

Ranger, Terence. 1992. "Power, Religion and Community: The Matobo Case." In *Subaltern Studies VII: Writing on South Asian History and Society*, edited by Partha Chatterjee and Gyanendra Pandey. New Delhi: Oxford University Press.

Robbins, Bruce. 1999. *Feeling Global: Internationalism in Distress*. New York: New York University Press.

Robertson, Claire. 1983. "The Death of Makola and Other Tragedies." *Canadian Journal of African Studies* 17, no. 3: 469–495.

Scott, Joan Wallach. 1988. *Gender and the Politics of History*. New York: Columbia University Press.

Sembène, Ousmane. 1973. *Xala.* Paris: Présence africaine.
Stratton, Florence. 1994. *Contemporary African Literature and the Politics of Gender.* New York: Routledge.
Thompson, E. P. 1963. *The Making of the English Working Class.* London: Victor Gollanz.
Tutuola, Amos. 1952. *The Palm-Wine Drinkard.* London: Faber and Faber.
Turner, Terisa E. 2001. "'The Land Is Dead': Women's Rights as Human Rights: The Case of the Ogbodo Shell Petroleum Spill in Rivers State, Nigeria." E-mail to Africa Policy Electronic Distribution List (APIC), July 29.
——, and M. O. Oshare. 1993. "Women's Uprisings against the Nigerian Oil Industry in the 1980s." *Canadian Journal of Development Studies* 14, no. 3: 329–357.
Van Allen, Judith. 1972. "'Sitting on a Man': Colonialism and the Lost Political Institutions of Igbo Women." *Canadian Journal of African Studies* 4, no. 2: 165–181.
——. 1976. "Aba Riots' or Igbo 'Women's War'? Ideology, Stratification, and the Invisibility of Women." In *Women in Africa,* edited by Nancy J. Hafkin and Edna G. Bay, 59–85. Stanford, Calif.: Stanford University Press.
Williams, Raymond. 1977. *Marxism and Literature.* Oxford: Oxford University Press.

Media Sources

AfricaOnline. 2002. "Nigeria: Dare to Go Bare?" July 26. Available online at http://www.africaonline.com/site/Articles/1,3,48754.jsp (accessed July 29, 2002).
Agence France-Presse. 2002a. "Nigerian Women Occupy Oil Facilities to Get Jobs for Sons." July 9.
——. 2002b. "Negotiations to End Mothers' Siege of Nigerian Oil Plant." July 10.
——. 2002c. "Nigerian Women Demand Talks with Chevron Boss." July 11.
——. 2002d. "Nigerian Mothers, Oil Company in Talks to End Terminal Siege." July 12.
——. 2002e. "No Progress in Talks on Women's Siege of Nigerian Oil Terminal." July 14.
——. 2002f. "Nigerian Women Release 300 of Their Chevron Hostages." July 15.
——. 2002g. "Contract Workers Picket Shell Operation in Nigeria." July 16.
——. 2002h. "Nigerian Women Seize Four More Oil Facilities." July 17.
——. 2002i. "Chevron Signs Deal to End Nigerian Oil Siege." July 17.
——. 2002j. "Women Protesters Leaving Nigerian Terminal." July 18.
——. 2002k. "No End to Women's Occupation of Nigerian Oil Stations." July 19.
——. 2002l. "Chevron Halts Nigerian Oil Production after Fire." July 21.
——. 2002m. "Protesters Claim Chevron Fire Caused Oil Spill in Swamp." July 22.
Agoi, Joel Olatunde. 2002a. "Protesters Demand Talks with Chevron, Allege New Oil Spill." Agence France-Presse, July 22.
——. 2002b. "Nigerian Villagers Brand Oil Industry a Curse." Agence France-Presse, July 22.
Associated Press. 2002. "Nigerian Villagers Agree to End Siege." July 15.
Baltimore Sun. 2002. "Barefoot and Powerful." July 21. Available online at http://www.baltimoresun.com/news/opinion/bal-ed.women21jul.story (accessed July 29, 2002).
Branigan, Tania, and John Vidal. 2002. "Hands Up or We Strip!" *Guardian Unlimited,*

July 22. Available online at http://www.guardian.co.uk/Archive/Article/ 0,4273.4466062,00.html (accessed July 29, 2002).

Clark, Dave. 2002a. "Deal to End Nigerian Oil Terminal Siege Imminent." Agence France-Presse, July 16.

———. 2002b. "Nigerian Oil Protests Spread as Terminal Siege Continues." Agence France-Presse, July 17.

———. 2002c. "Oil Giants Strike Deal with Protesting Women Amid Second Protest." Agence France-Presse, July 17.

———. 2002d. "Women Leave Terminal but Nigerian Oil Protest Spreads." Agence France-Presse, July 18.

Doran, D'arcy. 2002a. "Nigerians Protest at ChevronTexaco." Associated Press, July 11.

———. 2002b. "Oil Execs Meet Nigerian Occupiers." Associated Press, July 12.

———. 2002c. "Nigerian Women Stick to Oil Demands." Associated Press, July 13.

———. 2002d. "Oil Standoff Women Threaten Nudity." Associated Press, July 14.

———. 2002e. "Women Storm Nigeria Pipeline Stations." *Washington Post,* July 17, 2002. Available online at http://www.washingtonpost.com (accessed July 17, 2002).

———. 2002f. "Poverty Spurs Nigeria Oil Standoff." Common Dreams Newscenter, July 17. Available online at http://www.commondreams.org/headlines02/ 0117-03.htm.

———. 2002g. "Nigerian Women Take Two Hostages." Associated Press, July 19.

———. 2002h. "Fire Starts at Nigerian Oil Terminal." Associated Press, July 20.

Ikhariale, Mike. 2002. "The Niger-Delta Struggle and the 'Weapon Nakedness.'" *Gamji.* Available online at http://www.gamji.com/NEWS1526.htm (accessed August 7, 2002).

Independent Media Center. 2002. "Nigerian Women Take on Oil Giant." July 11. Available online at http://nigeria.indymedia.org/article_id=744 (accessed July 29, 2002).

Marshall, Andrew. 2002. "Oil Deal 'Off,' Nigerian Women Say". Common Dreams Newscenter, July 17. Available online at http://www.commondreams.org/ headlines02/0717-07.htm.

Oduniyi, Mike, and Onwuka Nzeshi. 2002. "Chevron, Ijaw Women Reach Accord." *This Day* (Lagos), July 26. Available online at http://www.allafrica.com (accessed July 26, 2002).

6 Let Us Be United in Purpose: Variations on Gender Relations in the Yorùbá Popular Theatre

Adrienne MacIain

May God give us good husbands. May God give us good wives. Amen. You know that whatever a man becomes in life, it's partly due to his wife. And whatever a woman becomes in life, it's partly due to her husband . . . so anyone who likes can say amen to this prayer that I want to make.

Oyin Adéjobí, *Kúyè*

Strange Bedfellows; Powerful Progeny

The marriage of gender and African studies—a shotgun wedding of sorts, greeted with as much controversy as celebration—has encouraged a large-scale reexamination of both disciplines and has initiated long-overdue dialogue among peripheral disciplines. The resulting liaisons have frequently been passionate and contentious power struggles, each discipline grappling for top billing and/or final analysis. Yet these heated struggles have ironically underlined the need for, and indeed paved the way for, an interdisciplinary dialogic approach to gender studies within African contexts. Thus, however quarrelsome a couple African and gender studies may seem, their alliance and its quickly proliferating progeny have indubitably enriched the larger scholastic community.

This embracing of interdisciplinarity has not only influenced the direction of current scholarship but has invited a reexamination of previously studied material from alternate disciplinary angles. My intention in this chapter is to bring to the scholarly community's attention a rich and heretofore largely neglected resource for culturally specific material that is pertinent to scholars in multiple disciplines: the Yorùbá popular theatre. Popular performance makes evident many of the assumptions that remain implicit and invisible in the written press and the recorded observations of outsiders; popular theatre therefore offers invaluable insight into that which is all too often left unsaid within and about the culture of which it is a product and a reflection. Karin Barber has undeniably proven this to be the case with Nigeria's Yorùbá popular theatre, a genre she has deftly used to shed light on historical shifts in Nigeria's socioeconomic landscape.

Barber's introduction to *Yorùbá Popular Theatre* (Barber and Ògúndíjo 1994), a collection of three plays that she and Báyò Ògúndíjo co-translated from the Yorùbá, seeks to contextualize *Kúyè, Lániyonu,* and *The Road to Riches* (*Ònà Òlà*) within Yorùbá society, a project that reflects Barber's commitment to anchoring her research within specific cultural contexts during particular historical periods instead of making sweeping claims about an imagined monolithic ahistorical "African culture." However, while Barber raises extremely useful questions about the money-related anxieties within the three plays, she does not address other anxieties that are implicitly, if not always explicitly, present within all three: anxieties over gender relations and the institution of marriage.[1] My aim in this chapter is to recuperate some of the still-buried treasure within these texts by applying Barber's own arguments to the three plays she helped to translate. More specifically, I explore the range of female characters and male-female relationships offered within these three plays and contextualize these shifting portrayals within the Nigerian social and political landscape during the specific historical moments in which these plays were written and performed. This is not intended to be an exhaustive study of the wealth of material available within this rare collection of translated plays. Rather, it is a relatively brief example of the uses to which popular performance archives like those collected by Barber may—and by all rights *ought to*—be put by scholars across the disciplinary spectrum.

Exploring gender relations within an African context is always a challenging endeavor. It cannot be assumed that notions about the construction and application of gender categories are necessarily cross-culturally relevant. For example, Oyeronke Oyewumi argues in *The Invention of Women: Making an African Sense of Western Gender Discourses* that

> the concentration of feminist scholars on the status of women—an emphasis that presupposes the existence of "woman" as a social category always understood to be powerless, disadvantaged, and controlled and defined by men—can lead to serious misconceptions when applied to Òyó-Yorùbá society. (1997, xiii)

Oyewumi and fellow Nigerian scholar Ifi Amadiume, who claims that the gender system in precolonial Igboland was flexible and separate from biological sex (1987, 185), argue that the concept of gender difference has emerged in Africa only as a result of European colonialism.[2] I am certainly sensitive to warnings against projecting Euro-American notions of gender onto African contexts and must agree that it seems inappropriate to discuss the ways that "men" and "women" were constructed in relation to one another in precolonial Òyó-Yorùbá society. Nonetheless, I find that it is both pertinent and important to understand the role of gender in post-independence Nigeria, the period during which the popular plays in question were written and performed. This is why I insist that the Yorùbá plays translated by Barber are valuable historical documents and why I have chosen to further Barber's analysis of them with regard to gender roles and relations.

The Opening Glees: Overcoming Delilah

Barber's introduction to *Yorùbá Popular Theatre* seeks to illustrate how within the realm of Yorùbá popular theatre "the same material" may be used "to say different things" (1994, 43). As Barber explains in her conclusion to *The Generation of Plays,* it is only through specific examples that a general concept can be comprehended; furthermore, it is in the discrepancies between the examples given that one finds enlightenment (2000, 428). Thus, it is in the differences between these three plays that we are to gain an understanding of Yorùbá popular theatre as well as the larger cultural framework of Yorùbá society within the given time frame (late 1960s to early 1980s).

Both in the critical introduction to *Yorùbá Popular Theatre* and in *The Generation of Plays* (372–398), Barber has analyzed the differing messages proffered by these plays in terms of the following issues: "the reasons for people's good and bad fortune, the basis and nature of wealth, how and why some people do better than others, and the appropriate attitudes to be taken up by both the fortunate and the unfortunate" (Barber and Ògúndíjo 1994, 23). Issues of wealth and fortune are certainly central to the plays in question, but they are by no means the *only* issues shared among the three. Barber explains her decision to concentrate on these particular issues by underscoring their prominence within the "opening glee," a selection of songs that serves as a kind of introduction or prelude to each performance and that reflects the larger moral paradigm from which the individual plays are derived. Indeed, the opening glee of each one of these plays features a song that begins: "Open your hands with joy to receive good things / The child of Awúrelà is asking for blessings." This song quotes heavily from Ifá divination verses and is apparently intended to invoke blessings of wealth and longevity.

However, the opening glee of each play also offers a second and often a third song, some of which appear markedly less concerned with individual wealth and more concerned with relationships, community, and the health and prosperity of the Nigerian nation. One of the major preoccupations of the other songs is the centrality of a successful marriage. "I want a wife," begins one such song:

> Make me meet a wife that suits me . . .
> A wife of noble character. . . .
> Oh my Destiny . . .
> Don't let me fall into the hands of a wife
> Who has loose morals and mean manners
> A tell-tale of a wife who betrays her husband to the world . . .
> I want a wife who's worth much money
> A sympathetic woman

One who is calm and gentle as a dove . . .
A wife that makes life restful
Knowing that we will never betray each other . . .
My Destiny, my Creator . . .
Please make me overcome
A wife like Delilah. (453–455)

Although this song is still somewhat preoccupied with matters of destiny and wealth, a new issue has been added to the mix: the centrality of the husband-wife relationship as a source of success or failure in life. The biblical reference to Samson and Delilah is intended to remind audiences of the extent to which a bad marriage can affect a man's fortune: "Samson was a strong man / He was a warrior / It was his wife / Who enabled his enemies to overcome him" (455). The song lyrics extend Adéjobí's statement that "whatever a man becomes in life is partly due to his wife," implying that the wrong wife has the power to destroy a man utterly (453). Conversely, it can also be assumed from the opening glees that a loving loyal wife of "noble character" is considered an essential key to a man's good fortune.

The assignation of marriage to such a central position in a man's fortune is certainly worthy of note within a Yorùbá context. As Barber points out in *The Generation of Plays*, classical Yorùbá society holds friendship between men to be the most sacred and significant relationship (2000, 285), whereas marriages are seen as peripheral and important only insomuch as they extend the man's lineage through the bearing of sons. The notion that a single wife could make or break a man's fortune would seem to be linked to the shift from the polygynist family structure of precolonial Yorùbá society to the modern nuclear family of one man, one woman, and their children.[3] As Andrea Cornwall wrote of marriage in post-independence southwestern Nigeria, "The meaning of marriage was changing. Once a functional bond wrought through links between families, marriage in the 1960s had become more of a relationship between individuals" (2001, 77).[4] The range of perspectives on marriage reflected in both the opening glees and the three plays themselves suggest that although performers and audience members alike were ready to embrace the idea of marriage as a relationship between individuals, the question of how that relationship was supposed to function exactly was still very much up for debate.

Although some of the songs in the opening glees appeal to a higher power to provide an ideal mate who will secure the singer's wealth and status, others portray a successful marriage as one in which two ordinary people are able to establish mutual trust and unity of purpose and are therefore to secure their own fortune through mutual hard work and thrift. "People are my cloth," begins such a song, found in the opening glee of both *Kúyè* and *The Road to Riches*. This Yorùbá proverb indicates that it is the people in one's life who actually confer wealth and status rather than the "voluminous, sumptuous robes" that have come to be associated with success (Barber and Ògúndíjo 1994, 73, 260n9). The song then launches into a plea to friends and family: "Tell me / That you will not betray me / Even if the world so changes / That I am left without even a sleeping-cloth"; in other words, please stick by me even if I am completely destitute (73). This indicates anxiety over relationships that are based only on financial alliance and a desire for a connection that will transcend the unpredictable fluctuations of material wealth and social status. Next comes a long series of repetitions of the phrase "Ah, my wife," echoed by a chorus of "Over there is my husband," followed by the following statement:

> Let us be united in purpose
> So that good may seek us out
> It is divided minds
> That are losers in life. (75)

The message here is that instead of relying on the blessings of a higher power, one's success is assured through unity of purpose with one's spouse—a fairly radical statement in the context of a society that generally views partnership as something existing between two men rather than between a man and a woman, let alone husband and wife (Barber 2000, 285).

The plays themselves also present a range of models, some positive, some negative, of contemporary marriage relationships. And although there appears to be fairly universal agreement as to what constitutes an *un*successful marriage— a deceitful, manipulative wife and a weak-willed, subservient husband—the Adéjobí repertoire presents a larger range of possibilities of what the converse might look like. As readers will see in the following sections, two of the three plays (*Kúyè* and *The Road to Riches*) present an androcentric formulation in which the husband is in charge and the wife is subservient and essentially voiceless. Yet one of the three, *Láníyonu*, presents an altogether different vision of women and of the relationship of marriage: here women are presented as wise and courageous and an emphasis is placed on partnership in marriage.

Kúyè and *The Road to Riches:* Wayward Women and Useless Men on Parade

In her introduction to the first and oldest play in the collection, *Kúyè*, Barber explains that the characters and basic storyline were adapted from a novel of the same name, written by J. F. Odúnjo, published in 1964 (Barber and Ògúndíjo 1994, 47). A deaf and mute boy named Kúyè is abused and abandoned by his relatives, then stumbles into good fortune and the love of a princess. Chased into the forest by a jealous rival, he discovers a magical plant that restores his hearing and power of speech. Years later, his cruel relatives are brought before the king on the charge of an unpaid debt and he is offered a chance at revenge. But he refuses to punish them, insisting that if they had not chased him away, he would not have attained his current social status.

In outlining a few of the differences between the novel and the play, Barber quickly notes that "both Odúnjo and Adéjobí show Kúyè's worst tormentors as women; but while Odúnjo's women are just bad-tempered, selfish people, Adéjobí's display the great female faults of popular stereotype: greed, unfaithfulness, duplicity" (51). Barber's article on "Radical Conservatism" explains that Yorùbá popular plays were products for sale and were therefore obliged to conform to the tastes of the buyers. "It has to sell," she writes, "with the result that it is both conservative and gimmicky" (1986, 5). The characterization of women as treacherous, cruel, and self-centered is one in which the buying public—which, as Barber points out, consisted mainly of young men from the lower layers of urban entrepreneurial society—was heavily invested (24). The onstage scapegoating of women provided an outlet for the frustrations of the predominantly male audience, reinforcing their position as morally superior to women and thereby justifying their retention of their privileged status as "breadwinner," or head of household. By the time of *Kúyè*'s revival in 1981, that status was rapidly slipping through the fingers of lower-class working men. Andrea Cornwall explains that "expectations of what a 'husband' or 'wife' should do or be have their own historicity, bound up in complex ways with changing notions of responsibility and of agency" (Cornwall 2001, 70). In 1980s Nigeria, due to shifting ideas about masculinity and male responsibility, gender roles could not be taken as a given but rather had to be actively defined and defended.[5] Cornwall argues that in fact male privilege—at least with regard to marriage—had begun to erode as early as the 1960s, when *Kúyè* was originally staged.

> Rather than marrying just to have children and enduring whatever came along as their mothers did, this generation of women had, and made, choices. They were also beginning to be able to exercise their rights: demanding that their husbands "provide proper care" [i.e. pay for their children's upkeep] and "packing out" [i.e. leaving] if husbands turned out to be "useless." (77)

Indeed, if women had not had the option of leaving "useless" (i.e. lazy, poor, or simply weak-willed) husbands or of demanding what they believe to be their rightful share of the marital wealth, there would have been no need to remind women of their moral responsibility to stick by their husbands, nor would there have been any need to warn men against exploitative wives. As it stands, however, the perceived need for such lessons appears to be significant, in that the prime satirical targets within the Adéjobí repertoire appear to be the same "useless men" and "wayward women" Cornwall discussed in her essay (2001). In the following passage, she emphasizes that these figures are intrinsically tied to changing social conditions:

> Wayward women and useless men populate discourses on the present, but are completely absent from narratives about the past. *N'igba atijo*[,] "in the olden days[,]" . . . order prevailed. These days there is no such certainty. The changes that people pinpoint in intimate relationships between men and women parallel other changes, in other relationships: those between men and their mothers, between co-wives, between parents and their children. (68)

This idea is equally present in Barber's argument that the prevalence of selfish, deceitful women in the popular theatre stems from a common fear among working-class men that women's opportunities for financial independence are expanding as their own opportunities shrink. The creation of the villainous female stereotype thus coincides with the reality of an increasingly disempowered generation of men. As Barber explains, the apparent misogyny in many Yorùbá popular plays must be understood as a defensive reaction to power shifts that were taking place in contemporary society.

> The effect is not of the reiteration of received ideas. It is more like a shrill cry of protest from the class of men who lose most by women's changing opportunities: an attempt, not so much to preserve a valued traditional order as to put the brakes on social change at all costs. (1986, 23)

In other words, if men are invested in protecting themselves from the power of women to destroy them, it is because women are beginning to be seen as powerful.

Female scapegoats abound in the world of *Kúyè*. In fact, the first character to walk onstage is the shrewish, greedy aunt of Kúyè, who sells pepper for a living. Not only is the Pepper Seller determined to sell off the only inheritance Kúyè has received from his deceased father, but she viciously turns on him when he refuses to allow her to so dispossess him. First she insults him and mocks his "huge" mouth that cannot speak. Then she falsely accuses him, beats him, and curses him mercilessly (99, 105, 111). The excessiveness of her cruelty becomes even more pronounced when contrasted with the moderate behavior and kind intervention on the part of Àlàbí, a male relative who agrees to take Kúyè into his home. However, this is no exaggerated fairy-tale harpy: the Pepper Seller is an ordinary woman presented in a realistic playing mode, implicating all women as possible sources of such behavior.[6]

At first, it appears that only women are being targeted as recipients of the moral lesson at hand. This sense is compounded when we are introduced to Sègi, wife of Àlàbí, who turns out to be even more treacherous than the Pepper Seller. First, she echoes the Pepper Seller's insults, calling him a "pathetic wretch" and mocking his "great gaping mouth" (157).[7] Later, she neglects to make Kúyè something to eat but instead puts him to work polishing shoes. Much more serious than her treatment of Kúyè, however, is her blatant adultery, which Kúyè cannot help but witness.

Again, at this point, Àlàbí's good character stands in stark contrast to his wife's antics. After a while, however, what appeared to be an innocent gullibility is exposed as a stubborn refusal to recognize the reality in front of him. It is not until debt collectors arrive at his home that Àlàbí's denial finally disperses. He then vehemently denounces Sègi's behavior, particularly her disobedience to him as her husband. "This is what happens when a woman doesn't obey her husband in the house," he declares. Later he repeats this and adds: "What we men pray for is that God will send us wives who obey us" (221, 223). This sentiment, which we must assume is one that the primarily young male audience is eager to hear, is nonetheless undermined by Àlàbí's earlier willingness to turn a blind eye to Ségi's bad behavior. Though he tells the debt collectors to take her away, she is once again able to turn the tables, insisting that he should be held equally responsible. Thus, however much the audience may sympathize with Àlàbí's plight, they cannot hold him entirely blameless: in allowing Ségi to manipulate him, he has let down the whole of the male community by allowing a bad woman to get the better of him. Thus when he is brought before the transformed Kúyè for judgment, the audience is able to view him as deserving of whatever punishment Kúyè may decide to lay upon him. And so it is revealed, upon closer inspection, that women are not the only, nor even necessarily the prime, targets of this satire: men are equally indicted.

The sense that a husband should be held responsible for his wife's behavior is even more prominent in *The Road to Riches*. The third play in the collection, written in 1981, *The Road to Riches* recounts the tale of a self-made man, Oláòsebìkan, whose longtime friend, Tàfá, at the insistent urging of his domineering wife, Ìyáa Sèyí, begs Oláòsebìkan to pass on the secret of his wealth. Oláòsebìkan insists repeatedly that his fortune was made through hard work and perseverance, but Tàfá and Ìyáa Sèyí refuse to believe him. Finally, out of frustration, and in order to teach the greedy couple a lesson, Oláòsebìkan agrees to initiate them into his fictitious money-making cult and puts them through a humiliating and painful ordeal, at the end of which they (and the audience) receive the following moral lessons: people do not want to accept the truth, and wealth requires hard work and sacrifice. There is, however, another message that comes across just as clearly in the course of *The Road to Riches:* a husband who allows his wife to dominate him deserves whatever misfortune she brings upon their household. From the beginning, Ìyáa Sèyí is portrayed as a temperamental manipulator with no regard for social convention. When Tàfá attempts to show off his rather crude dancing skills at a party thrown by Oláòsebìkan, Ìyáa Sèyí tries to physically pull him away and then storms out angrily when he refuses to comply. When next we see her, she releases a torrent of insults upon her husband. "Useless wretch," she begins, "wouldn't anyone who heard me talking to him like a baby say that I was the master in the house?" (479). It becomes quite clear that she is, in fact, master of the house. Although Tàfá is equally liberal with his insults, he ultimately does everything Ìyáa Sèyí tells him to do and even tells Oláòsebìkan that "she's the husband in the house, I'm her wife" (533). Thus, although Tàfá is also shown to be greedy, lazy, and deceitful,[8] Ìyáa Sèyí comes across as being considerably worse, and Tàfá is condemned not so much for his own shortcomings but for succumbing to the will of his self-centered wife.

Thus, the main moral message regarding marriage provided in these two plays appears to be that wives must obey their husbands and that husbands must not tolerate disobedience from their wives. Interestingly, though, the ultimate message, at least in the case of *Kúyè*, is not that one must find an already-ideal mate but that one must play well the role of wife or husband to the person one's Destiny has chosen. This becomes particularly clear in the case of Kúyè and Princess Mojísólá. Mojí is a beautiful girl, but she immediately defies the audience's expectations of a quiet, humble, and well-behaved princess. Instead, she is outspoken, impulsive, and impertinent with her father. Their unlikely coupling presents a perfect parody of the classic folkloric ending: instead of the strong, brave hero marrying the quiet and beautiful princess, we have a strong, brave princess marrying a quiet and handsome hero. Miraculously, though, when we meet the couple again, they appear to have traded places: Mojísólá has morphed into an ideal wife and daughter: quiet, respectful, and obedient.[9] Likewise, Kúyè has undergone a transformation: no longer the tongue-tied innocent from a few scenes back, he has grown into an eloquent man of regal bearing and powerful presence. In short, they have assumed their respective roles as husband and wife. In this way, the transgressive comedy of the earlier role reversal is "corrected" and the desired social order reinforced.

Through their reliance on a negative stereotype of the modern Nigerian woman, their merciless mocking of subservient husbands, and their fervent support of a male-centered household, *Kúyè* and *The Road to Riches* serve as prime examples of the defensive tone described by Barber in "Radical Conservatism." The men in these two plays, protagonists aside, are continually shown to be "useless," while their wives are cast as "*ilemosu*," or "wayward women."[10] Writes Cornwall: "Those women who do make it on their own represent more than simply a threat to conventional morality. They are able to occupy the space left empty by 'useless men' and provide for themselves, literally displacing their husbands" (Cornwall 2001, 80). For men who had married at a time when traces of the old ways persisted, argues Cornwall, "the 'new women' were almost by definition 'wayward,' simply for asserting their right to make any kinds of choices for themselves" (77). The fear that women will begin displacing their husbands is palpable within both *Kúyè* and *The Road to Riches,* as illustrated by the array of "useless men" and "wayward women" populating the worlds of these two plays.

Láníyonu: What "We" Want

The play that, chronologically, resides between the two plays discussed above, provides a sharply contrasting view of women, gender relations, and marriage. *Láníyonu* recounts the story of the title character, another self-made man, whose jealous friends conspire to steal from him the "money machine" they are sure he is hiding from them. They kill his wife, Àdùké, and drive him out of his home into the forest. There he is attacked by a group of evil spirits and subsequently resurrected by a female deity, Omídiyùn, who gives him a staff that will kill any creature it touches. He then comes across a princess, Adéìfé who has been left as a sacrifice to a voracious evil spirit, and saves her life by slaying said spirit with a touch of his magical staff. The chiefs of the town, a bumbling and cowardly crew, at first refuse to believe Láníyonu and Adéìfé's tale, but eventually they offer Láníyonu kingship of the town as well as Adéìfé's hand in marriage.

Remarkably, nearly all the female characters inhabiting *Láníyonu*'s landscape are positive role models. Àdùké, the protagonist's first wife, is shown to be an agreeable woman of good humor and considerable intelligence. Likewise, Princess Adéìfé is shown to be courageous and wise beyond her years: although the inept council of chiefs tries to trick the princess into believing she is only going to carry the sacrifice to the shrine, Adéìfé is well aware that she herself will be sacrificed and is prepared to face her fate as her father the late king would have wanted her to. The princess sings:

> When all the town chiefs assemble and debate
> And give me messages to deliver before I go—
> They can only mean to offer me in sacrifice.
> I hear
> I accept.
> We resemble those who begot us. (377)

Her bravery becomes all the more astonishing in contrast to the craven, deceitful behavior of the council of chiefs. Omídiyùn, the hero's savior, is presented as an idealized mother figure: powerful, endlessly generous, but stern when necessary. Interestingly, the only negative female model comes in the form of an *iyálóde*, the most powerful female figure in the Yorùbá social hierarchy, acting on behalf of the town's women within the council of chiefs. She is shown to be hot-headed, foolish, and ultimately a coward, though she is certainly not made to look any worse than her cohorts within the council of chiefs. The council members are shown to be uniformly selfish and slow-witted regardless of gender.[11] This suggests that it is political corruption rather than inappropriate gendered behavior that is being lampooned in *Láníyonu*.

The first marriage relationship presented in *Láníyonu* is that of the protagonist and Àdùké. Their interactions are noticeably different than those of the married couples represented in the other two plays: although Àdùké is clearly expected to perform her role as domestic worker by serving food to her husband and his friends, Láníyonu appears to treat her as an equal in other areas of their relationship. He consults her on financial matters, such as his decision to lend money to his two friends so they can open their own business rather than continually relying on his handouts. She responds to his idea, which she thinks is a good one, by saying "as long as they understand what we want."[12] The fact that she uses "we" rather than "you" is quite significant, in that it suggests partnership, that elusive unity of purpose evoked in the opening glees.

The second marriage relationship is that of Láníyonu and Princess Adéìfé. Láníyonu addresses her as an equal from the moment they meet, despite her helpless position and semi-hysterical state.[13] When the two return to the town to confront the council of chiefs, he continually addresses her rather than speaking directly to the chiefs, although they clearly outrank her. The chiefs are noticeably vexed by this, telling Adéìfé, "You talk too much, explaining everything to him!" (401). Weary of the chiefs' antics, Láníyonu repeatedly threatens that "if it weren't for this young lady," he would use his staff to smite the lot of them, impressing upon the chiefs, and the audience, how much worthier Adéìfé is of respect and deference than these so-called leaders (405). Likewise, Adéìfé treats Láníyonu with due respect and gratitude, addressing and referring to him as *babaà mi,* literally "my father," a term that implies high status and praise (447n33). Their mutual respect and admiration culminates in Láníyonu's reaction to being offered Adéìfé's hand in marriage:

Àràbà: So we all agree that when you ascend the throne, you should take her as your wife.
Láníyonu: Who? Who? Who? Who? Who should I take as my wife? When she says she's marrying a blacksmith![14] *(To Adéìfé)* Well, do you agree to this idea?
Adéìfé: Yes, I do.
Láníyonu: You do? O.K., then I don't mind. (431)

By refusing to accept Adéìfé's hand without her consent, Láníyonu is not only showing remarkable respect for Adéìfé's opinion but is offering up an ethical lesson to the chiefs about the proper way to treat a woman. Moreover, the play is offering in this moment an alternative model for marriage, one based on mutual consent and partnership rather than coercion and hierarchy. Instead of concentrating on what he stands to gain through the alliance, Láníyonu's primary concern is that this should be a mutually beneficial endeavor and that he and his betrothed should be "united in purpose."

Thus, through its markedly more positive portrayals of women, particularly its alternative conception of the institution of marriage, *Láníyonu* provides audiences with a vastly different view of Yorùbá gender relations than that propounded by *Kúyè* and *The Road to Riches*. Not only does *Láníyonu's* portrayal of behavior among and interactions between men and women not conform to the standard set by the other two plays, it goes farther than simply reversing negative stereotypes of women and turning gendered hierarchy on its head. Rather, it presents a world in which the imperative to perform one's gender (or one's role as husband or wife) well is secondary only to the imperative of acting with good will and noble character toward all members of the community.

Conclusions: United against a Common Enemy?

At this point, the question of what the variations in female representation and gender relations presented in *Kúyè, Láníyonu,* and *The Road to Riches* might signify poses itself. One important detail that should be noted is that both of the negatively stereotyped wives (Sègi and Ìyáa Séyí) were played by the same actress, "Deborah," known for her improvisational comic bravura (Barber and Ògúndíjo 1994, 54; Barber 2000, 152). This is significant because, as Barber explains in *The Generation of Plays,* "Dramatic plots were constructed to match the composition of the company" (2000, 131). Thus, the two domineering wives may have been included largely to show off Deborah's talent for playing them. The real mystery, though, is not the presence of negative female stereotypes, since Barber describes the company's repertoire as being fairly well saturated with them, but the marked absence of such a role in *Láníyonu.* Barber points out that although strong, positive roles for women could often be found within the Adéjobí repertoire, they were usually paired with a negatively stereotyped, "opposite" female role. She writes: "*Láníyonu* is unusual in that it is the only one that combines an all-good female presence (apart from the Iyalode, who is just comical) with not one but two respectful, cooperative partnerships." She adds, however, that the positive elements in *Láníyonu* are to be found elsewhere in the company's repertoire and that the women, though portrayed in a positive light, are still "very much ancillary to the central narrative of the male hero's fall, rise, and eventual triumph."[15] To clarify: my argument is not that *Láníyonu* is the company's most progressive play but that its lack of a stereotypically negative female character and its focus on partnership in marriage are worth closer consideration.

Barber offers an explanation in terms of how such a play could appear within this particular company's repertoire when she explains that the "more liberal model for conjugal relations" discernable in *Láníyonu* and other plays may be the effect of the peculiar situation in which the company members, particularly Adéjobí and his wives, found themselves. Barber argues that the conditions of the work, in which division of labor and responsibility is fairly evenly distributed among company members, created a relatively gender-neutral hierarchy and encouraged an unusual level of equality and cooperation among husbands and wives. This experience among the actors, she proposes, may have allowed the Oyin Adéjobí company's plays to go beyond the stereotypes of women normally found in Yorùbá popular theatre. And though Barber does not explicitly say so, her argument would seem to extend to the company's portrayal not only of female characters but also of their interactions with the male characters, particularly their husbands or future husbands.

While this theory provides a reasonable explanation for the more partnership-oriented view of marriage found in *Láníyonu*, it offers no suggestions as to why this particular perspective might have appeared more attractive or important at the particular historical moment in which it was crafted. Furthermore, considering the emphasis Barber herself puts on the supply-and-demand nature of the Yorùbá popular theatre, it seems short-sighted to exclude the impact of the audience's attitudes and input. She explains in *The Generation of Plays* that plays could become drastically altered over time due to audience reactions. Scenes that received the most enthusiastic response were expanded; scenes that did not appeal to audiences were reduced in length or cut altogether (2000, 170). Clearly, *Láníyonu*, along with every play performed by the Oyin Adéjobí company, is thus a reflection not only of the attitudes of the performers but also of the social milieu in which it was performed.

So the question narrows: Why should this apparently anomalous treatment of marriage and gender relations materialize at this particular moment; that is, in between the other two plays chronologically? One possibility is that the difference may be tied to a momentary shift in the anxieties of the young male audience away from the supposed threat posed by women and toward the common enemy of civil war. *Láníyonu* was composed in 1967, the year that marks the outbreak of the Nigerian civil war, also known as "the Biafran War."[16] Essentially a conflict between those who wanted to keep Nigeria unified and separatists who had declared the eastern Biafra region an independent state, the war did not remain on battlefields alone but disrupted the daily lives of Nigerians on both sides of the conflict. Although politics are not implicitly discussed in the plays,[17] the opening glees of all three certainly highlight a preoccupation with political events, asking God to protect Nigeria from war and to "improve our country for us" (Barber and Ògúndíjo 1994, 77–81, 277–279, 451–453). Barber is quite right to warn that the plays' narratives should not be viewed as allegorical tales offering encoded commentary about Nigerian politics (2000, 303). However, that should not be taken to mean that the plays are not reflections of popular political attitudes and anxieties or that the plays could not have been read by audiences, particularly during politically charged moments of Nigerian history, as offering useful insight on current events. *Láníyonu*'s marked preoccupation with partnership and unity of purpose may in fact be an indication that audiences in 1967 were anxious about the separatist movement and the destructive potential of interethnic conflict more generally. It may, moreover, suggest that the war, which posed an equal threat to all sectors of society, provided a common enemy for men and women and shifted the focus of intergender animosities toward those forces that threaten the most basic community unit: the family.

Although it is admittedly a questionable endeavor to tie this play, which was still seen as relevant to the lives of audiences in the 1980s, to a single historical event such as the Nigerian civil war, I argue that it is nonetheless a useful one. Reading the world of *Láníyonu* as a creation and a reflection of a people on the brink of civil war may help illuminate the unusual attitudes about gender roles and domestic life espoused therein. I argue that faced with the specter of civil war, there was more at stake for these performers and audience members than bloodshed or the possible dissolution of Nigerian national unity. More than merely an abstract threat to the national economy, war meant restrictions in wage increases, a ban on labor strikes, and a dramatic increase in inflation, all of which can be translated as a threat to job security and income (Adamson 1989, 8). This would put the young working-class men in the audience in the defensive position described by Barber in "Radical Conservatism": preoccupied with a purported threat to their ability to be economic providers, they are eager to watch plays that condemn the forces they feel themselves to be pitted against. In the case of *Láníyonu*, rather than viewing the primary threat as wives who are voracious and competition from "wayward" working women, the young men on and off stage appear to be more focused on the political enemies of corruption, war, treachery, and disunity. This is evidenced by the hostile lampooning of authority figures (the greedy and ineffective council of chiefs), the palpable terror inspired by an insatiably violent and uncontrollably destructive outside force (the evil spirit to which Adéìfé has been sacrificed), and the overall moral message regarding loyalty and unity of purpose.

Within this context, the moment in *Lániyonu* when the hero pointedly asks for Adéifé's consent before agreeing to marry her becomes even more significant. Not only does it suggest that women should have a say in whether and whom they choose to marry, it offers the larger lesson that without consent, there can be no true unity. In the given political climate, it is reasonable to assume that audiences would interpret that lesson in terms of national unity. In other words, the play was likely to be read as making the following political statement: unless the various ethnic groups within the European-constructed borders of Nigeria consciously agree to come together as a nation, to be, as it were, "united in purpose," there can be little hope for a peaceful, long-lasting union.

There are, of course, many other possible interpretations that could be proposed and explored.[18] What should by now be clear, however, is that the issues of gender and gender-related anxieties present in these texts have implications reaching far beyond the Oyin Adéjobí troupe and even their immediate audience. The rich ideological information found within the three plays can provide valuable insight regarding the interactions between theatre, gender relations, economy, and politics during a specific period of Nigerian history.

As alliances among disciplines continue to mature, we scholars could do well to hang on to the volatile attraction and precarious suspicion of the newlywed couple. Much like domestic partnership, interdisciplinary scholarship can be extremely rewarding but is often by no means easy. For example, it has become amply apparent that gender constructions cannot simply be lifted out of one sociohistorical context and uncritically applied to another. Nor can studies focused on specific periods, spaces, and places afford to ignore the impact of gender relations and the (im)balance of power undergirding them. As research encompassing issues of gender within African contexts expands and solidifies, continual efforts must be made to contextualize findings and rely as much as possible on primary sources. It was my intent in this chapter to remind readers of one source of primary material that remains chronically underexplored: popular theatrical performance. Let us, too, be united in purpose— literary theorists, historians, performance scholars, sociologists, and others—so that good (research) may seek us out also.

Notes

The epigraph that opens this chapter is from the opening glee of *The Road to Riches* (Barber and Agúndíjo 1994, 453).

1. Note also that issues of economy and gender are considerably intertwined in Yorùbáland, as the work of Lisa Lindsay attests (1999, 2003).

2. Within the past twenty years, the scholarship on gender in Africa has expanded considerably (Lindsay and Miescher 2003; Hodgson and McCurdy 2001), as has the de-

bate over the relevance of Western feminist political agendas to the lives of women in Africa (Steady 1987; Gaidzanwa 1992; Okeke 1996; Nnaemeka 1998).

3. For a more in-depth account of precolonial Yorùbá marriage practices and the changes wrought by colonialism, see Denzer (1994).

4. Ironically, the troupe members themselves do not conform to this modern monogamous model: despite director Oyin Adéjobí's staunchly Christian convictions, he found himself in a position of needing to marry additional wives in order to have a steady supply of actresses on hand. The stigma attached to performance as a livelihood was difficult for all actors, but it became particularly problematic in the case of women, for whom reputation is often a matter of survival. "If it was undesirable for a son to be an actor, it was disastrous for a daughter," explains Barber (2000, 282). Because parents and (especially) husbands were unwilling to allow their daughters and wives to participate in such a disreputable pursuit, theatre "bosses" were obliged to provide actresses with domestic respectability by marrying them themselves or cajoling their own wives into performing with the company (65, 283). Thus, Adéjobí and his wives have found themselves in the awkwardly hypocritical position of preaching monogamy while practicing polygamy. This tension may also play into the company's preoccupation with marriage- and gender-related issues.

5. Lisa A. Lindsay (1999) tracks the historical trajectory of some of these shifts.

6. As Barber points out, the Pepper Seller's entrance immediately establishes a realistic convention that suggests that we have joined a life that was already in progress before the curtain rose (Barber 2000, 353). She speaks as though she were in mid-conversation, although she is apparently speaking alone, since Kúyè, who follows behind her, is deaf and mute: "What a bloody fool I am, what on earth am I thinking of? I've gone and forgotten the very thing I was supposed to be bringing along with me" (Barber and Ògúndíjo 1994, 81).

7. She does add one insult of her own when she refers to Kúyè as a sacrificial offering, a reference to his shabby appearance; slaves and destitute or abnormal people were the most common victims of sacrifice in ancient times (263n40).

8. In Scene 8, a female laborer comes to complain that Tàfá, who was overseeing a project in order to get the money for his "initiation," has cheated her out of a portion of her pay.

9. In fact, Mojí has only two lines in the whole of the final scene and does not talk back to her father when he gives her advice on how to treat her in-laws. Instead, she simply replies, "That's true" and says no more (257).

10. It should be noted that the term *ilemosu* is not reserved for women who have actually committed adultery; it can be applied to any woman living alone, regardless of whether she went astray or left for some other reason (mistreatment, for example).

11. The only exception to this rule is Àràbà the diviner, who is portrayed in a relatively positive light.

12. "*Kí wón ó sá ti mò ón fún a ni*" (301).

13. It stands to reason that Lániyonu would be kind to someone who has been victimized by those she trusted, since he has just come through a similar ordeal himself, as he points out by saying "The world is hard. It was some people I did a kindness to that drove me all this way from home" (385).

14. It has just come to the council's attention that Adéifé was betrothed to a blacksmith in the compound of Chief Jagun.

15. Personal correspondence with Karin Barber, April 16, 2004.

16. Although tensions had been high for quite some time, war was declared on July 6, 1967.

17. Barber explains in "The World of the Work" that the company's reticence to directly tackle Nigerian political events is not merely due to fear of censorship: rather, it reflects a philosophical stance that "politics . . . is a subcategory of ordinary morality" (2000, 304).

18. Another possibility—one that is by no means mutually exclusive to the one outlined above—is that the positive female characters and more respectful treatment of women in *Lániyonu* may have been the result of pressures from the women in the company and/or the audience. This seems unlikely, however, given the apparent enthusiasm with which the actresses played shrewish characters (perhaps as a momentary escape from the obedience imperative of their everyday lives) and the eagerness with which women in the audience accepted the lesson provided by these negative stereotypes (Barber 2000, 217–220).

References

Adamson, Yahya K. 1989. "Structural Disequilibrium and Inflation in Nigeria: A Theoretical and Empirical Analysis." Montclair, N.J.: Center for Economic Research on Africa.

Amadiume, Ifi. 1987. *Male Daughters, Female Husbands: Gender and Sex in an African Society.* London: Zed Books.

Barber, Karin. 1986. "Radical Conservatism in Yorùbá Popular Plays." In *Drama and Theatre in Africa,* edited by Eckhard Breitinger and Reinhard Sander, 5–32. Bayreuth African Studies Series 7. Bayreuth, Germany: Bayreuth African Studies Series.

———. 1991. *I Could Speak Until Tomorrow: Oriki, Women, and the Past in a Yorùbá Town.* Edinburgh: Edinburgh University Press for the International Africa Institute of London.

———. 2000. *The Generation of Plays: Yorùbá Popular Life in Theatre.* Bloomington: Indiana University Press.

———. 2004. Personal communication.

———, and Báyò Ògúndíjo. 1994. *Yorùbá Popular Theatre: Three Plays by the Oyin Adéjobì Company.* African Historical Sources Series no. 9. Atlanta, Ga.: African Studies Association Press.

Cornwall, Andrea. 2001. "Wayward Women and Useless Men: Contest and Change in Gender Relations in Ado-Odo, S.W. Nigeria." In *"Wicked" Women and the Reconfiguration of Gender in Africa,* edited by Dorothy L. Hodgson and Sheryl A. McCurdy, 67–84. Portsmouth, N.H.: Heinemann.

Denzer, LaRay. 1994. "Yorùbá Women: A Historiographical Study." *The International Journal of Africa Historical Studies* 27, no. 1:1–39.

Gaidzanwa, Rudo. 1992. "Bourgeois Theories of Gender and Feminism and Their Shortcomings with Reference to Southern African Countries." In *Gender in Southern Africa: Conceptual and Theoretical Issues,* edited by Ruth Meena, 92–125. Harare, Zimbabwe: SAPES Books.

Hodgson, Dorothy L., and Sheryl A. McCurdy, eds. 2001. *"Wicked" Women and the Reconfiguration of Gender in Africa*. Portsmouth, N.H.: Heinemann.

Lindsay, Lisa A. 1999. "Domesticity and Difference: Male Breadwinners, Working Women, and Colonial Citizenship in the 1945 Nigerian General Strike." *American Historical Review* 104, no. 3: 783–812.

———. 2003. *Working with Gender: Wage Labor and Social Change in Southwestern Nigeria*. Portsmouth, N.H.: Heinemann.

———, and Stephan F. Miescher, eds. 2003. *Men and Masculinities in Modern Africa*. Portsmouth, N.H.: Heinemann.

Nnaemeka, Obioma, ed. 1998. *Sisterhood : Feminisms and Power from Africa to the Diaspora*. Trenton, N.J.: Africa World Press.

Okeke, Philomena E. 1996. "Postmodern Feminism and Knowledge Production: The African Context." *Africa Today* 43, no. 3: 223–243.

Oyewumi, Oyeronke. 1997. *The Invention of Women: Making an African Sense of Western Gender Discourses*. Minneapolis: University of Minnesota Press.

Steady, Filomena. 1987. "African Feminism: A Worldwide Perspective." In *Women in Africa and the African Diaspora*, edited by Rosalyn Terborg-Penn, Sharon Harley, and Andrea Benton Rushing, 3–24. Washington, D.C.: Howard University Press.

7   Doing Gender Work in Ghana

Takyiwaa Manuh

"What can we do for African women?" "What about micro-credit?"[1] my new friends asked, as we sat sipping wine in the lounge of a beautiful residence hall of a small American college in mid-2005. As the interrogation progressed, I was amazed at the almost absolute lack of knowledge about Africa and its people in the twenty-first century by these well-meaning, well-educated senior women college professors attending a women's studies conference. The exception was one person who had her own West African ties and whose son or daughter had almost been caught in the cross-fighting in la Côte d'Ivoire.

Where and how was I expected to start off as I was inundated by the barrage of questions and liberal good feeling? How much of Africa was I expected to cover, and which African women would be the object of our concern that evening? I had escaped from the dance and was making my way to my dorm room, when I was hailed to join the group. I had accepted but had not bargained for the "African Women 101" course I was being called upon to deliver. The old weariness set in as I watched these specialists of Latin America and Asia attempt to explain their lack of specific or even general knowledge of African issues in our highly interconnected globalized world where CNN beams news of happenings even as they occur.

What indeed can any woman anywhere do for African women that they cannot do for themselves? How did this thinly disguised unconcern, shallowness, and ignorance repackaged as mild interest intersect with the almost frenzied activities and contestations around gender in several African countries by women who might claim kinship at a certain level with some of my new friends?

The disconnect I was experiencing sent me back many years in recollection of another event. It was the early 1980s and this was an arid time in Ghana. Books and reading material were, like soap and sugar, considered "essential commodities."[2] In response to this scarcity, the Cultural Affairs Officer at the United States Information Service provided some academics in the arts and social sciences at my university access to articles in two or three journals they considered valuable for their work. Typically, one selected a few articles from the table of contents of the chosen journals, and copies of these articles arrived free of charge. *Signs: The Journal of Women in Society and Culture* had been one of my selections, and through this facility, I was able to share in a larger intellectual community located elsewhere. However, it became increasingly difficult for me to make any selections when the *Signs* table of contents arrived because I found it harder and harder to relate to what I considered to be abstract, surreal, and narcissistic theorizings on dreams, bodies, and other individualistic projects that increasingly suffused the pages of the journal. This was especially so as I compared these writings with the very real issues of lack of rights and democratic space, Structural Adjustment Programs (SAPs) and their privations, the increasing dictate of the international financial institutions in Ghana and several African countries, and the responsibilities and possibilities that faced me as a woman and scholar. My opinion of *Signs* persisted for much of the early to mid-1990s when I lived in the United States, and my disaffection was reinforced by what I experienced in women's studies programs at the university where I was located. For someone who had been a scholar and an activist, these were very lonely times, as I found little to relate to in what was offered as women's studies.

Returning to Ghana in 1998, I was struck by the pace of work around democratization and political space, trade, economic policymaking, and gender, mostly by civil society activists. While both women and men worked on all the other issues, gender work was almost exclusively "women's work," even as it encompassed and extended beyond the issues civil society activists were engaged in. Thus, antiviolence projects and activities around women's economic rights and political participation were mainly the domain of female gender activists, with the exception of a gender development "institute" whose executive director was male.

How has gender become institutionalized around Africa and in Ghana? What issues have animated gender activism in Ghana? What forms have gender debates in Ghana taken and how do they relate to larger concerns of the women's movement in Ghana, Africa, and globally? What has been the place of theory in gender work in Ghana? I argue that whatever its source, gender has become indigenized around Africa and Ghana and is being used to chart an agenda for social and political transformation, as African women and some men do for themselves, in light of realities on the ground in Africa. There is growing autonomy for gender work even as there are divergent motivations and understandings of gender work. This chapter argues that rather than being indifferent to theory, gender workers in Africa actively reflect on the conditions for theory production and create theory in their everyday highly empirical work and emphasize the need to redress the balance between theoretical and empirical dimensions in knowledge production.

This chapter addresses the first set of issues through a broad overview of gender work in Africa and Ghana to bring out what African/Ghanaian women and some men who are located in the academy and/or civil society are doing to deal with pressing problems in Africa and their views on some of the continuing contestations over the relevance of gender in/to Africa.

In the second section of the chapter, I draw on a survey conducted among academic and activist colleagues to explore their understandings of and motivations for gender work, the links between activism and teaching and research on gender, the place of theory in gender work in Ghana, and the potential of teaching and research work on gender for national development and transformation in the area of gender equality and social justice.

Institutionalizing Gender in Africa

Ghana's contemporary gender activists are part of a larger continental movement that was set in motion from the mid-1970s, particularly with the onset of the United Nations Decade for Women (1975–1985), when the development industry began sponsoring research on and projects with African women in response to growing poverty and the perceived failure of development programs around Africa (Mama 2001). Much of the scholarly work on women, and later on gender, were rooted within a WID (women in development) paradigm (Rathgeber 1990) that was removed from feminist theories and activism and suspicious of them as well. As Amina Mama (1996) notes, gender studies on the African continent have proven to be less controversial than "women's studies" or any kind of explicit feminist scholarship because they can and have been adapted to state and donor projects that are not aimed at transformation of gender relations and the position of women within African nations.

The founding of AAWORD (the Association of African Women for Research and Development) in Dakar, Senegal, in 1977 by scholars "with distinct feminist proclivities" (Mama 1997, 417; see Arnfred 2003; Pereira 2003) marked a crucial turning point in the decolonization of research on African women. AAWORD's membership was made up of scholars, activists, and practitioners from around Africa who were committed to undertaking research, training, and advocacy from an African and gender perspective. AAWORD also provided a forum for African women based outside the continent to participate in and help shape its direction (AAWORD 1985). The anniversary volume *AAWORD/AFARD 1977–1999: Deconstructing Research and Development for Gender Equality* (AAWORD 1999) documents the association's evolution and achievements over twenty years. Unfortunately, institutional weaknesses coupled with the increasing exodus of senior female scholars in response to national crises and personal agendas deprived AAWORD of much-needed leadership for its continued growth and vibrancy. While AAWORD still operates, its influence is limited and its vanguard role has devolved to newer national and regional organizations.[3]

In 1991, CODESRIA (Council for the Development of Social Science Research in Africa), also based in Dakar, Senegal, within which many AAWORD members have worked,[4] hosted an influential seminar entitled "Gender Analysis and African Social Science." The seminar brought together mainly African-born scholars working on gender issues at institutions across the continent and in the African Diaspora and resulted in the publication of the pioneering collection *Engendering African Social Sciences,* edited by Ayesha Imam, Amina Mama, and Fatou Sow (1997). Although Imam (1997) in her introduction acknowledged the need to broaden the focus of gender analysis to incorporate masculinities as well as femininities, the contributors tended to focus on women. Still, the volume testifies to the richness of the emerging gender research on the

African continent. Charmaine Pereira (2002, 6) has criticized much gender research in Africa for too frequently running parallel to the "malestream" work of scholars and research institutions such as CODESRIA, in which "gender blindness" remains the "accepted norm." Analyzing two CODESRIA studies edited by Mkandawire and Olukoshi (1995) and Hutchful and Bathily (1998) on structural adjustment programs and militarism, respectively, both deeply gendered processes with impacts on women's lives, Pereira demonstrates how even progressive African male researchers fail to use gender as an analytical tool (2002).

In addition to these two organizations, gender scholars and activists around Africa have organized several national, regional, and continental groups and networks on women's rights and access to resources, political voice, participation and power, gender violence, HIV/AIDS, and new technologies such as ICTs (information and communications technologies) and have been concerned with issues of policy as well as practical actions to improve the conditions of women.[5] Over the last decade, attempts have been made to strengthen these ties and provide a support network for institutionalizing gender and women's studies on the African continent. The African Gender Institute (AGI), which was established at the University of Cape Town in 1996, has played a crucial role and has become the most important site for coordinating, stimulating, and disseminating feminist research and teaching in gender studies in Africa.

The AGI, established "with a continental mandate," seeks "to develop intellectual capacity for equality in African contexts" (Mama 2002a, 5). In 2001, the AGI started the ambitious initiative called the Gender and Women's Studies for Africa's Transformation Project (GWS Africa Project), which focused on "strengthening and building gender teaching and research capacity through a series of training, research, and publishing activities" across the African continent to end the isolation and fragmentation of feminist teachers and scholars located at African universities (Boswell 2003, 1). In response to this problem, the GWS Africa Project conducted a survey "to locate gender teaching and research sites on the continent for pushing the boundaries of knowledge production" (ibid.). A questionnaire was circulated to over 300 African universities, and this generated, by 2003, thirty responses from mainly Anglophone institutions.[6] The survey determined that South Africa has the greatest number of gender and women's studies programs; nine out of its twenty-seven universities offer such teaching. Seven out of forty Nigerian universities offer courses in women's and gender studies. Ghana and Cameroon each have two universities offering such teaching. The other nine countries included in the survey each have one institution with gender and women's studies teaching. Across Africa, four gender studies programs have full departmental status: Makerere University's Department of Women and Gender Studies (Uganda)—the largest on the continent[7], the University of Buea's Department of Women's Studies (Cameroon), the University of Cape Town's AGI, and the University of Zambia's Gender Studies Department. At other institutions, gender studies courses are located within existing departments or units such as the Development and

Women's Studies program (DAWS) at the University of Ghana.[8] Throughout Africa, gender and women's studies are taught at both the undergraduate and graduate levels.[9]

The AGI has worked to expand the curriculum in gender and women's studies courses at African universities. AGI's first curriculum meeting, hosted by the Institute of African Studies at the University of Ghana in 2003, focused on sexuality, culture, and identity. Participants discussed such topics as heterosexual marriage and motherhood, monogamy, polygamy, birth control, and men's use of ideological perceptions of womanhood to control women. They also addressed sensitive issues such as age differences in sexual relations, homosexuality and bisexuality, sexual violence and women's sexual desires, governmental control of sexuality, sexuality and religion, pornography and consumerism, the sexual abuse of children, and trafficking in women. Finally, participants talked about the development of curricula and supporting resources for teaching.[10] AGI research and activities have provided ample evidence of the growing field of women's and gender studies at African universities.[11] Yet the small number of Ph.D. programs in gender studies (three) is cause for concern. This not only limits the production of locally grounded knowledge but it also restricts the impact of African feminist works on mainstream scholarship (Mama 2002a).

Institutionalizing Gender in Ghana

Gender work as self-aware institutional practice in Ghana can be traced to the immediate post-independence period when the new nation sought to project women onto the political and social scene in the interest of the nation-building project (Manuh 1991; McClintock 1995), despite important precolonial and colonial antecedents.[12] In what would be one of the first uses of affirmative action, the Convention People's Party government passed the Representation of the People (Women Members') Act of 1960 to allow for the election of ten women members to the National Assembly. It used a top-down approach, and some measurable progress occurred in women's education, employment, and social life, albeit harnessed to the interests of the ruling regime. But no autonomous women's movement was permitted, a legacy that dogged the Ghanaian state until the end of the 1990s (Manuh 1991; Tsikata 1989).

With the proclamation of International Women's Year in 1975 and the subsequent decade for women, the state-sponsored project to "integrate women into development" under the auspices of the United Nations and its agencies came into its own with efforts to address deepening poverty and underdevelopment. National machineries for the advancement of women were set up with the aim of achieving equality in all spheres for life for both women and men (United Nations Commission on the Status of Women 1991). Their institutional forms, locations, and performance in different African countries have been the subject of a series of case studies (Third World Network 2000; Mama 1995a).

In Ghana, the National Council on Women and Development (NCWD) was established in 1975 to promote gender equality in general and to monitor the implementation of international commitments entered into by government, such as the Nairobi Forward-looking Strategies of 1985, the Convention on the Elimination of all Forms of Discrimination against Women (CEDAW), and the Beijing Platform for Action.[13]

Ghana under the P/NDC[14] governments (1982–2000) presented itself to Africa and the world as a progressive state, committed to African affairs and new international relations based on equity and social justice. Through its ratification of several international conventions and legal instruments on women and children, the Ghanaian state projected a commitment to gender issues and gender equity and a redefined place and role for women. Within Ghana, laws were promulgated to deal with long-standing traditional practices such as widowhood rites and ritual servitude (*trokosi*) as well the registration of customary marriages and divorce (PNDCL 112), fixed age for marriage, and intestate succession (PNDCL 111). The 1992 Constitution guaranteed women's rights, and the law establishing the district assemblies, the decentralized units of local government that provided that a certain percentage of the members should be women, also reinforced the state's progressive image.

Equally, if not more, important was the high profile of First Lady Nana Konadu Agyeman-Rawlings and her movement, the 31st December Women's Movement (DWM), which presented itself variously as the "women's wing of the revolution" and an NGO.[15] With the support of the state as well as bilateral and multilateral donors, it commanded vast resources and initiated nationwide projects for women and children and had undisputed control of the space for gender work for nearly two decades. However, studies such as Manuh (1991, 1993) and Tsikata (1989, 1997) have questioned the limits of state and state-sponsored policies, actions, and practices toward women, arguing that the state in Ghana, as elsewhere, is highly gendered and has promoted policies that do not question the status quo but reinforce the superordination of men over women in society and interpersonal relations. As the report *Women in Ghanaian Public Life* (ISSER 1998) clearly pointed out, institutions of public life in Ghana are generally male dominated, and despite some efforts at various levels, the male gender profile of public office in Ghana has remained unchanged.

Gender work in Ghana has developed under conditions of a weak political and policy advocacy culture following more than two decades of authoritarian, masculinist military rule generally unfriendly to women, economic austerity, and the adoption of economic policies and programs such as the SAPs and their adverse effects on women and the poor.[16] While the return to constitutional rule in 1992 theoretically opened up the political space, this continued to be occupied until 2001 by Nana Konadu Agyeman-Rawlings and her 31st December Women's Movement. A review of the NCWD conducted in 1999–2000 noted that it was characterized by many institutional weaknesses and was still stuck in a WID paradigm even though it couched its discourses in the language of gender (Mensah-Kutin et al. 2000). Since 2001, the national machinery in Ghana has taken the form of the Ministry of Women's and Children's Affairs, headed by a minister with cabinet status, ostensibly a demonstration of the government's commitment to gender issues.[17]

In Ghana, as elsewhere in Africa, the long period of militarization and non-representative government and increasing disenchantment with the state contributed to the spread of NGOs and their occupation of the space for independent action. Many NGOs have been concerned with service provision and are not membership organizations that are accountable to domestic constituencies. They have also tended to focus on single issues or themes and do not often develop holistic frameworks for their work or link up with broader concerns or developments. For example, work on trafficking of persons does not often connect with work around economic justice and the poverty that drives the trafficking. The dependence of many NGOs on international funding sources has also meant that they have tended to couch their activities and have highlighted local concerns within universalistic claims and discourses to secure funding. That notwithstanding, some NGOs have evolved from a service provision background to step into gaps created by the pulling back of the state from many sectors and are broadening their focus and concerns as well as attempting to develop alternative discourses and funding sources.

Gender Activism in Ghana

The late 1990s coincided with a new era of democratization around Africa, and gender work in Ghana begun to assert some autonomy from the state and donor agencies, albeit with an overwhelming focus on women. In the process, gender activists have begun to cast a critical look at their practices and politics (cf. Tsikata 2001 and contributors). Particularly over the past two decades, when gender activism was harnessed to the needs of ruling regimes around West Africa to maintain themselves in power, gender has become a highly invested and evocative concept and has developed a prominence in public discourse and action.

For many people in Ghana, it does not matter that gender is a concept of relatively recent origin, has a Western provenance, and has no easily translated equivalent in local languages (Oyewumi 1997). As many activists note, there are no local words for many other concepts that we use, but this does not seem to invalidate such concepts. What has mattered is that using gender as a badge and compass, activist women and a few men have attempted to deal with a multiplicity of issues facing women and men in society and the economy in ways that seem to have the potential to transform society and politics. It can also be argued that the language of gender serves to address some of the imbalances that have come in with or have been accentuated by imported economic and political structures.

While the NCWD and later the 31st December Women's Movement dominated gender work for more than a decade and a half, working mostly to promote income-generating activities for rural and urban women[18] as well as legal reform in family law and property rights, various NGOs began to assert them-selves beginning in the late 1990s. They also broadened the range of concerns and issues and challenged the status quo in profound ways, often focusing on customary or traditional practices deemed harmful to women or taking up the state and economic policymaking processes that affect the livelihoods and con-ditions of millions of women and poor people generally. The Ghana Association for the Welfare of Women and FIDA, the Ghanaian branch of the International Federation of Women Lawyers, were influential in initiating amendments to the Criminal Code that abolished dehumanizing customary practices such as cruel widowhood rites and female circumcision and the practice of ritual servitude, or *trokosi*. NGOs such as International Needs have worked on *trokosi,* the prac-tice of ritual servitude, under which females are sent to live and work at shrines for life to atone for crimes committed by other members of their families.

Major ongoing work for gender activists is occurring around gender-based violence. This was initiated by the Gender Studies and Human Rights Docu-mentation Centre (Gender Centre), an NGO in partnership with the Trades Union Congress and various nongovernmental and community-based organi-zations, in response to the findings of a nationally representative survey, focus-group discussions, and review of agency records in 1998 (Coker-Appiah and Cusack 1999). The study showed that one in three women had experienced some form of violence in intimate relationships. This led the Gender Centre to undertake a series of awareness-raising activities to increase the visibility of gender-based violence as a gender equality issue of national proportion. The result was the setting up by the state of a Women and Juvenile Unit (WAJU) within the Police Service in the three major cities, first in Accra, the capital city, then in Tema and Kumasi. Currently there are units in all ten regions of Ghana. The Gender Centre has worked with WAJU, the Police Service, health work-ers, and the Department of Social Welfare to develop capacity and improve the response of state agencies to reported cases of violence. It has also explored community-based approaches to dealing with perpetrators of violence. Several other NGOs have contributed to work on violence against women in relation to policy and legislative advocacy, training for law enforcement and other relevant authorities, research, the provision of services and public awareness-raising. These include FIDA-Ghana, The Ark Foundation, Women's Initiative for Self-Empowerment (WISE), and Leadership and Advocacy for Women in Africa (LAWA-Ghana Incorp.).

In addition to the work of these NGOs, a number of coalitions and net-works have been formed around specific issues over the past five years. Activ-ists have used the common platform provided to urge government officials and policymakers to strengthen their political will and take action to address women's rights and concerns or to improve services for women. They include Sisters' Keepers, NETRIGHT, the Gender Violence Survivors' Support Network (GVSSN), the Coalition on Domestic Violence Legislation, and the Coalition on the Women's Manifesto for Ghana.

Sisters' Keepers

Between 1998 and 2001, over thirty women were murdered in and around Accra in what became known as the serial killings of women. Following the inability of the government and police to stop the murders and arrest the perpetrators and their seeming indifference to those tasks, the Sisters' Keepers coalition was formed in 2000 by individual women and men, NGOs, and other groups as an activist, issue-based coalition committed to resisting all forms of violence against women. It mobilized the public and held press conferences, issued press statements, organized sit-down strikes and demonstrations, petitioned Parliament and the Executive to draw attention to the fear and insecurity women were experiencing, and pressured the government to urgently mobilize the necessary resources to investigate these cases, arrest the perpetrators, and bring them to trial. In 2001, the coalition disbanded after the arrest, trial, and conviction of a self-confessed perpetrator and when it became apparent that the serial killings had stopped.

NETRIGHT

The Network for Women's Rights (NETRIGHT) is a coalition of groups and individuals formed in 1999 to promote women's rights and gender equality in Ghana by providing a common platform for NGOs to respond collectively to issues of national importance and bring a gender perspective to national processes in ways that address the gaps in individual organizational actions.[19] It has provided a base for more effective lobbying, advocacy, and campaigning on different issues as and when the need arises. NETRIGHT has worked on several issues such as the Ghana Poverty Reduction Strategy and economic justice issues generally and has added its collective voice to many campaigns of other organizations, including Sisters' Keepers, the Coalition on Domestic Violence Legislation, the Coalition on the Women's Manifesto.

Gender Violence Survivors' Support Network (GVSSN)

The GVSSN was formed in 2001 as a network of organizations dedicated to providing improved and integrated community support services to survivors of violence. Its strength derives from its members' commitment to enhancing existing services through collaboration and through educating its members and the community. Activities of the GVSSN have included public awareness campaigns, the launch of a Resource Directory with a list of member organizations committed to providing support services to survivors, and the organization of a Domestic Violence Bill Strategy Workshop that kick-started advocacy to garner support for the passage of the draft bill into law. This led to the establishment of a national coalition to press forward the demands for the passage of specific domestic violence legislation. Other activities include setting up the GVSSN/WAJU Trust Fund to pay for the costs of medical examination of women and children survivors of sexual assault (rape, incest, defilement) who have been referred to hospitals by WAJU to enable it provide evidence to prosecute. It has also organized training workshops to build the capacity of member organizations to respond to survivors of violence.

National Coalition on Domestic Violence Legislation

The National Coalition on Domestic Violence Legislation is an umbrella organization of over 100 human rights groups and individuals formed in 2003 with the singular aim of ensuring the passage into law of the draft Domestic Violence Bill prepared by the Attorney General's Department in 2002. What has stymied the passage of the law is the demand for the repeal of Section 42g, the marital rape exemption, of Ghana's Criminal Code (Act 29), which prevents a wife from bringing charges against her husband for rape in marriage. The Coalition has sought to achieve its goals through public discussion and education and through lobbying opinion leaders and influential groups within the Ghanaian community and relevant government officials. The draft Domestic Violence Bill has generated intense discussion and scrutiny in face of the direct hostility and opposition of some government officials charged with ensuring its passage.[20] The work of the coalition was given a major boost in 2004 when the Ghana Medical Association expressed its support for the passage of the bill at its annual conference. However, it still has not been passed into law, and the coalition continues in its efforts to ensure its passage (for a discussion group on this issue, see http://www.groups.yahoo.com/group/dvbillcoalition/).

The Coalition on the Women's Manifesto for Ghana

The Coalition on the Women's Manifesto is a broad coalition of NGOs, individuals, and other civil society organizations formed out of the processes involved in the production and dissemination of the Women's Manifesto for Ghana in 2003 and 2004. The manifesto was produced out of a concern for the insufficient attention paid to gender issues, the limited presence of women in public life, and the poor participation rates of women in politics and decision making in Ghana. The process of drawing it up built on the experiences of women in Uganda, Botswana, Tanzania, South Africa, and Zambia who have undergone a similar experience and where the adoption of manifestos in tandem with measures by the state have led to increases in women's representation in politics and decision making and put women's issues on the political agenda.

The manifesto is a political document that provides a platform for making a common set of demands for the achievement of gender equality and equity and sustainable national development in Ghana. It is framed around ten themes: women's economic empowerment; women, social policy, and social development; women in politics, decision making, and public life; women, human rights, and the law; discriminatory cultural practices; women and land; women and media; women, conflict, and peace; women with special needs; and institutions with the mandate to promote human rights. Each section begins with a gender analysis of the nature of the problem and follows up with concrete demands that the government, political parties, ministries, departments and agencies, and civil society address the situation within specific time lines.

This overview of gender activism has brought out the issues and strategies of the organizations involved. Much of this activity occurs in large urban centers, but activists also work at regional and district levels and in rural communities as well as at subregional, continental, and global levels. Gender activists have translated some of their documents into Ghanaian languages and have links with community, occupational, and faith-based organizations. They have used the media, including the popular TV program *Mmaa Nkomo* (Women's Conversation/Talk) which is presented in Twi, the most widely spoken language in Ghana, to communicate and disseminate information. Gender activists have not hesitated to take on government and powerful individuals to register their dissent or to make specific demands, and many have become well known on the national scene. Through their online discussion groups and other fora, they debate issues and strategies and display their understandings of gender issues and varying attitudes toward the state and other power structures. Outwardly they often present a united front in the face of media and other commentators who would be more than eager to seize on perceived differences and antagonisms between groups and individuals. Yet such differences do exist. Some of them are highlighted in the findings from the survey I conducted of academic and activist colleagues presented below.

Survey on Gender Work

I sent out thirty questionnaires to academic and activist colleagues to explore their understandings of and motivations for gender work. I received responses from fourteen women and one man; two of the respondents were non-Ghanaian Africans and the rest are Ghanaian. Six respondents are university teachers/researchers and also gender activists, another is an independent researcher, and the remaining eight are gender activists working in NGOs. Most of the respondents have a university education and some also have advanced degrees from Ghanaian and/or foreign universities. All the respondents have been active in gender work for periods ranging between five to twenty years. While all respondents attempted to answer all the questions posed, the responses to the questions on theory tended to be briefer, even from some of the academics.

Five major themes emerged from the responses I received: the need for autonomy for gender work; individual understandings of "gender" and "gender work"; links among activism, teaching, and research on gender; opinions about the place of theory in gender work in Ghana; and views on theory produced from Western-dominant discourses.

Autonomy for Gender Work

According to some scholar-activists, autonomy for gender work has been affected by the national context outlined above and the weakness of Ghana's political economy, the lack of a policy framework on gender, and dependence on donors to sustain gender work and programs, all of which act as inhibiting factors for individuals and organizations. But international developments were not just seen as constraining. According to one scholar, "We have moved from various shades of authoritarian, masculinist military rule, generally unfriendly to women, to varieties of 'democratic' rule. But at the same time, gender work in Ghana has been informed by international developments and shifts in ideas about gender. I think international developments have contributed towards acceptance and the recognition that gender matters."

Other respondents stressed that organizational cultures and individual personalities also affect the scope for autonomy but believed that motivated individuals have often brought about change.

In contrast, two NGO activists thought there was "in fact too much autonomy," with some individuals and organizations focusing on areas "which may not necessarily help to transform society." They implied that it was the possibility of attracting donor funding that motivated the choice of areas of work, rather than its utility to the community or the state, and that too much autonomy affected the coordination of activities and networking among organizations.

Universities were generally perceived as offering the space for autonomous gender work. Interestingly, scholar-activists differed among themselves on how they rated particular universities. Two respondents from the University of Cape Coast said the University of Ghana has offered a more favorable space for women and men to "flourish and make change" than their own university, where there are fewer female activists.

Understandings of Gender and Motivations for Gender Work

Responses highlighted differences in understandings of the concept of gender among both scholars and activists. Many scholar-respondents understood gender in its relational aspects, which tend to be unequal and discriminatory in systemic ways. Gender is also seen as complex in its manifestations because of its intersections with class, location, and age. On the other hand, many activist respondents in NGOs understood gender as the process whereby people are socially processed into becoming men or women in society, while gender work was understood as any activities done with the objective of "understanding gender," "bridging the gender gap," "repairing/resolving problems arising out of the social processing," and sensitizing people about issues related to gender. Respondents noted that while gender "includes both sexes, men and women," popular understandings simply equate gender with women.

Scholars and some NGO activists defined gender work as work done to create understanding about gender issues and their deconstruction in order to dismantle gender inequities and inequalities in whatever form or sphere they appear and at different levels: family, community, national, regional, and international. Some scholars and activists laid stress on the scrutiny of power in institutions and relationships and the different impacts these make on different categories of persons. They were also aware of the intersections of this power with other axes of inequalities such as race, class, or ethnicity to inform processes and interventions.

While all respondents understood gender as implying a quest for equality between women and men and gender work as bringing about changes so that women receive the same access and justice as men, some respondents did not always link this to power and politics. According to one NGO activist, "I think a main challenge is the lack of understanding about gender—not necessarily a political unfriendliness for its own sake. So if you can bring people closer to being on the same page half the battle is won."

Motivations for gender work are varied and draw on personal values and principles—such as "justice"—and/or more political and strategic considerations. For some of the scholar-activists there was "outrage" at what they saw as the "pervasive gender discrimination in Ghanaian society and the complacency that exists about it." Gender work, then, is a political issue linked to the need for change in the gender status quo. Their motivation is to help both men and women understand these inequalities and their origins, to understand the ways and forms in which they are constructed and perpetuated, and to work with them to formulate strategies to address these inequalities. The ultimate aim is to attain a society that is equitable and free of social injustice and that recognizes the worth of both men and women.

Other respondents wanted to transform gender relations in Ghana to ensure that women's lives are not constrained by gender inequalities as manifested in domestic violence, sexual abuse, and discrimination in many areas of life, including women's representation in leadership, and they blamed "culture" directly for this. Said one NGO activist, "I have met several women in my family and elsewhere who were denied the opportunity to utilize their talents for the benefit of society because of cultural prescriptions."

For other NGO activists, gender inequalities are inefficient or fetter development. The goal of their involvement in gender work is therefore to sensitize and highlight inequalities in social relations and their consequences for development.

Links among Activism, Teaching, and Research on Gender

Both activist and scholar respondents charged that the links among activism, teaching, and research on gender are weak and unidirectional because teachers and researchers do not often learn from activists or solicit their support. They asserted that much gender work did not use local case studies or situational analysis but relied on resources from elsewhere. "There is too much reliance on foreign material," they said.

Some respondents felt that the isolation of gender teaching and research from activism had contributed to the gender-blindness of policy in the larger society, as they did not trust policymakers to be able to do the necessary analysis and incorporate gender issues and concerns into policy. At the same time, the respondents urged advocates and activists to acquire knowledge in gender and research to inform their work and activism. But a few individuals were seen to straddle all three areas of activism, teaching, and research, as many of those who teach and research gender are also activists in their own right.

According to one respondent,

> I think that in Ghana and the Third World generally, researchers do not have the luxury to cleanly demarcate the separations. If the person is genuinely concerned about justice and change then s/he will, whether activist or researcher, merge the two. Because there is so little data, even the activists have been compelled to become "researchers," and because of the inaction and slow pace of change, researchers are activists. Also because Third World intellectuals are still very much free to confront and struggle for all other kinds of democratic and political changes, they/we are compelled to act.

Given the lack of information and knowledge that characterizes many advocacy efforts and public policymaking in Ghana, teaching and research to serve governance and policymaking agendas was seen as strategic, a way to provide powerful knowledge and tools to inform policymaking and in turn enrich and open up political spaces to women. However, other respondents question the ability of gender researchers and teachers to influence policy.

Three scholar respondents viewed the potential of teaching and research on gender for national development and transformation as generally poor at the moment, even though useful research was being produced and students were learning gender analysis skills. How this translated into national development and transformation depended not only on researchers and teachers but also on the environment in which they operate as well as their ability to form strategic alliances. Respondents also viewed the absence of gender perspectives in major national documents as a constraint on their ability to influence national processes.

Other scholar respondents were more hopeful and saw enormous potential once avenues were created to channel research findings into national policy and more holistic and strategic framing occurred. They advocated more planning, mobilization of resources and implementation, and lobbying of institutions.

Some NGO activists saw the challenge as that of teaching gender in "interesting, but not so theoretical ways" so that gender theory and learning could be "reduced" or made "understandable, practical, and 'do-able.'" According to them, most participants in training sessions they conducted found gender teaching or training (particularly gender analysis) "abstract and uninteresting," directly raising the role of theory in gender work in Ghana.

The Place of Theory in Gender Work in Ghana

> As the theories we subscribe to also shape our sense of what needs to change in order to work towards a particular vision of society, so theory provides a framework for reflecting on and analysing experience, to show how experiences are structured and indicate ways of arriving at a particular goal, in terms of change.
>
> Independent African scholar

The place of theory in gender work refers first to theory as it is currently produced and/or used and second to the place theory ought to occupy in work on gender. In relation to the first, the notion that theory is "abstract" or "uninteresting" appears to be shared not only by participants at training sessions but also by many NGO activists in the survey who do not see its significance in their everyday lives or work. As "practical" persons seeking to deal with life-threatening problems of gender-based violence or other deprivations of rights, many activists find theory "remote" or not readily usable in their situations. While they employ frameworks and concepts in their work, many do not see these as arising from any coherent body of theory or knowledge. Rather, they see them as techniques or practical guides for their work. In addition, while some NGO activists often conduct research or use findings from research as "data" or resources for their work, many tend to see research as a neutral tool with no particular assumptions or biases and do not foreground its explicit theoretical orientations. Many activists were unsure about the kind of theory that would be useful or relevant in their work because they had not posed the issue in that way or had not had sufficient time to reflect on it.

On the other hand, five scholar respondents saw the place of theory in gender work as crucial and likened it to a "road map" or a framework for reflection, explanation, and analysis that functioned to explain the assumptions that guide their work and chart the way forward. But even they conceded that theory occupied a restricted space in current gender work in Ghana and was not as well developed as it could be, largely because of the conditions for its production.

As some scholar respondents noted, theory can be seriously developed only in contexts where institutions such as universities function as sites for knowledge production. In countries such as Ghana, this would entail the provision of services and infrastructure and sufficient remuneration for and a lessening of enormous teaching loads for scholars. Households should also not constitute a significant drain on the time and labor of women scholars. These conditions are necessary to shape the possibility that women as well as men scholars will have enough time and energy to develop theory within their own locations. Currently, African scholars who remain within their own countries rarely have enough time to develop theory around the issues or content areas that are of concern to them. If they move out of their location, they are likely to have more time, but they become less connected to the relevant content areas, which are likely to get displaced by other issues and concerns in terms of priorities for theorizing. This applies to African scholars generally, whether they are working on gender or not.

In addition, those engaged in work on gender are going against the grain in a number of ways, particularly if they are women scholars and especially if they are feminist women scholars. This is because they face additional constraints/restrictions/burdens that shape the possibility of having enough time and energy to develop theory. In many universities, women end up doing a lot of counseling and welfare-type work with students and staff. Gender-based family and household demands on their time and labor and, in some cases, constraints on their mobility also mean less time to do research. If they are feminists, they may face hostility from other academic staff. Even if they do not, they may have their work ridiculed, dismissed, or not recognized as valid academic research. Since there are relatively few African feminist scholars in universities, the pool of scholarly work to which they might refer and use to develop their own work is also small. The end result is that many women end up at the lower end of the academic hierarchy and get paid less so they are also less able to afford the books and materials that are necessary to nurture theory-building. In contexts where the state does not work effectively, as in most postcolonial states, women scholars, like men, take on other assignments to earn enough money to survive, which again makes it harder for them to have enough time and energy to develop theory.

The question about the place theory ought to occupy in gender work was answered by five of the scholar respondents, the independent scholar, and activist, who saw theory as critical to clarifying understanding of the origins of social relations and institutions. As the theories we subscribe to also shape our sense of what needs to change in order to work toward a particular vision of society, so theory provides a framework for reflecting on and analyzing experience (Taiwo 2004). Theory shows how experiences are structured and indicates ways of arriving at a particular goal in terms of social change. Thus, theory is critical for sharpening our arguments for change as well as shaping our sense of strategy. But theory must be rooted in the concerns of African-based women and men in order to make the theoretical contributions correspond to our experience. But this also requires strong theoretical methodological grounding and the development of appropriate theory in order to get our ideas across effectively and ensure that the actions that are predicated on these ideas are translated into policy and are implemented so the goals of gender justice, gender equality, and social justice can be realized.

Examples of theory that were considered useful by these respondents included socialist feminist theorizing within the political economy traditions that take account of Africa's colonial history and current place in the world, theory that pays attention to context and history, theory that is process oriented, theory on content areas similar to or relevant to their own areas of interest, or theory that opens up the theory-building process (see Mama 1995b on race and subjectivity). Respondents also considered language to be pivotal, and they reported that inaccessible language was a definite "turnoff."

Ghanaian and African Scholars and Theory Produced in the North

African-based gender scholars take different positions in relation to theory produced from the global North as well as other corpuses of theory. In general, the responses vary according to the scholars concerned and their perspectives on theory-building as well as the texture and content of the Northern theories being referred to. Respondents' positions ranged from eclectic and selective incorporation of theory to the adoption of concepts without their whole baggage to more systematic approaches. Others use such theory as a guide to test their reality as they develop their own approaches, while a few others reject a theory simply because it is "Western." Thus, while some argue that such theory is foreign and has no relevance, others think that externally produced theories provide a useful guide as we develop our own theory within Africa. Even if externally generated theories are based on the particular experience of those who produce them, these ideas are seen as having relevance as a way of explaining social reality and serving as useful guides for social change. This accords with the viewpoint Imam urges (1997, 17) that African scholars be "less concerned with the source of analysis than its nature and implications" and that they criticize theories "not because they are Western, but to the extent that, having developed in cultural, historical, class, racial and gender realities in the West, they misrepresent African realities and obscure analysis" (see also Bunwaree 2004).

In general, scholars stated that they paid attention to *how* the theory is described as having been generated, the context in which it takes place, and whether or not the content seems relevant to the issue they are addressing. Respondents ask, "Will this theory improve our own understanding or our methods of enquiry and analyses?" In general, "how" questions were seen as more important than "what" questions: "How are processes described? How are arguments put together? How does the theory derive its explanatory force?" These questions were seen as equally, if not more, important than "what" questions alone such as "What does the theory say? What arguments are being made?" Respondents seem to have a process of paying attention to the combination of different elements and do not isolate any particular dimension a priori.

In terms of how African-based scholars are positioned in relation to Northern-based theory by Northern scholars, respondents saw themselves generally at a disadvantage. Many scholars see their own work as subordinated to that of Northern scholars, who rarely refer to the work of African scholars, while they have to refer to the work of Northern scholars to show their awareness and familiarity with debates elsewhere and to stand the chance of getting their work published in international journals. They explain this as the result of several factors, including a) neoimperialism and the global economic order, which renders Northern countries more affluent/overdeveloped; b) the privileged status of Northern universities and their access to resources as well as epistemological dominance over what counts as knowledge; and c) the functioning of the state in Europe and North America, which has to varying extents been able to maintain infrastructure and basic services. All of these combine to make it more possible for Northern scholars to have time to theorize in areas they have constructed as appropriate for knowledge-building and to get their work published and thereby recognized as theory. This is undoubtedly made easier by Euro-American control of structures that validate theory-building, such as academic journals and book publishing.

Do African Women Scholars Have Theory?

Whose theory and whose empiricism? What they mean is that our work sometimes does not enter some of their heavy theoretical debates or academic fads such as postmodernism. Have they considered that some of the theories are not relevant to our situation and if there are enough opportunities for debates and writing, we will find our own voice? As it is, we are stifled by having to respond to their theorization while they continue to ignore our critique and our attempts at theorizing unless it is sensational or making claims about African matriarchy or polygyny. We should be interested in contributions to knowledge in general rather than just contributions to theories.

Scholar-activist at the University of Ghana

The systems of binary thought and dualisms that pervade and sustain academia and scholarship speak to a hierarchy of knowledge production and power the North possesses. In these dualisms, empirical data or fieldwork are often juxtaposed with theory, which is unquestionably accorded higher value. Many African women academics, who have generally entered academia only in the past few decades under constrained, overworked, and disempowered conditions, struggle to maintain a foothold on many fronts. They must battle their isolation in underresourced and crowded departments and institutions that do not nurture women as scholars and where the demands on their time pull them in many directions in neocolonial African states. Acquiring the necessary books and tools and being part of a community of scholars who affirm each other is often not the norm. While history, popular traditions, and women's multiple roles and activities in their communities and the state attest to their worth and contributions over the *longue durée,* they have been largely absent in the construction of knowledge about their societies. Many scholars also function as activists as they seek to ensure the conditions for the respect of women's citizenship rights and measures to promote and enhance their livelihoods. In these conditions, the space and time for reflection, for consolidation and theory-building has been insufficient.

Nevertheless, many African-based scholars reject charges and sweeping generalizations that they lack theory. Others, such as the author of the quote cited above, equate these criticisms with an "imperialist gaze" that prescribes adherence to prevailing fads or an "othering" through the discovery of distinctive African forms to gain attention. Indeed, an interesting response from one scholar-activist called for the unpacking of the notion of "undertheorized" and the treatment of this independently of the question of the degree of empirical detail present in the work in question. Other respondents, both scholars and NGO activists, agreed with the view that the work of African women scholars may often be undertheorized but probably for different reasons from those given by editors of Northern-based journals. They contend that "undertheorized" does not mean a generalized "lack of theory," as many Northern-based editors use it. While it is conceded that some work at the poorer end of the spectrum may indeed be lacking in theory, this is certainly not the case across the board. In many cases, the theory is embedded in the writing but is not made explicit. In such cases the work is undertheorized but could be strengthened by the opportunity to make the theory more explicit. This requires time, energy, and access to a broader range of intellectual resources, including texts that are often in scarce supply. Happily, the work of the AGI and the networks it has created, including the publication of the journal *Feminist Africa*, is doing much to create nurturing spaces for a confident African gender intellectual community.

In the view of some scholars and one activist, the seeming preference of African-based scholars for work that is often considered "too empirical" by Northern journals and scholars may simply be a reflection of the needs and reality that confront them. One scholar-activist suggested that the charge of being "too empirical" could reflect a degree of envy on the part of Northern scholars, editors, and others, who are often unable to produce that level of detail in their own research on Africa. But the real issue may also be that the relative balance between the theoretical and empirical dimensions is skewed. Empirical detail can be produced only by those working in the field, and the issue revolves around the relative value accorded to theory and data. In the intellectual division of labor, "empirical work or detail" is considered less worthy than "theory." This production of "difference" in intellectual work becomes a necessary prerequisite in the formation of hierarchies and divisions of labor by which "theory" becomes the high-status province of those based in the North and "empirical detail" the residual with which African scholars are preoccupied, relegating them to the position of (post)modern "native informants."

In contrast to these views and what I characterized as the abstract and surrealistic theorizing at the beginning of the chapter in the anecdote about my experience of *Signs* in the early 1980s, this chapter has demonstrated the limited but still necessary place of theory in contemporary gender work in Africa. However, many scholars and activists relate to theory that is grounded and speaks to their experiences and celebrate the wealth of empirical detail from which to create their own contributions to theory (see Collins 1990).

If, following bell hooks (2000, 32), we define theory as "a guiding set of beliefs and principles that become the basis for action," then we could argue that gender activists and trainers do not just use theory but also develop theory in their everyday work, even if they do not have the time to write it out. This is an untapped resource that can serve to refute Northern criticism of African writing as undertheorized.

Conclusion

Without a doubt, contemporary gender work in Ghana has developed in response to UN processes and donor agendas in intersection with local realities and concerns and long traditions of women's activism. Initially hijacked to state interests, gender work is now asserting its independence and has broadened its scope and strategies. While the exigencies of funding have meant that some activists and organizations appear to latch on to fashionable agendas, these agendas reflect to some extent the existential conditions in a neocolonial state. Many of the issues addressed by gender activists in Ghana and around Africa derive from the African Platform for Action agreed in Dakar in 1994 for the Fourth World Conference on Women in Beijing in 1995. These issues, which cohere around the economic, legal, political, cultural, and social rights of women, attest to the failures of dominant development agendas African states have pursued under the direction of the international financial institutions that have failed to give women and poorer people generally equal rights in the neocolony and to guarantee their livelihoods.

As is shown in the responses from the survey, gender is still a developing field for activists and scholars alike, and many of the responses are tentative. As is also hinted at in some of the responses, gender activists will increasingly need to address issues of politics and power more directly and issues of how transformative their conceptions and strategies for gender work should be. In this regard, the positions of activists and scholars vis-à-vis the practices and workings of "culture," which many see as constituting the bedrock for women's marginalization in society, will need to be addressed more frontally. In the meantime, African women activists and their (still) few male allies use gender in all its indecisiveness, uncertainties, and developing forms to do for themselves the necessary tasks of self-liberation and to create nurturing spaces to support each other and produce theory that speaks to their conditions.

Notes

I would like to thank colleagues and friends who answered questions and clarified doubts.

1. Conversation at the Berkshire Women's History Conference, June 4, 2005.
2. The economic crisis that had been simmering since the late 1960s came to a head

in the early 1980s and was compounded by political instability and drought. See Rimmer (1993) and Gyimah-Boadi (1993).

3. These include WIN (Women in Nigeria) and the several regional branches of WILDAF (Women in Law and Development in Africa). See also Abdullah, this volume.

4. Indeed, AAWORD used to be housed in the same premises as CODESRIA for many years.

5. This can be seen in the work of the African Training Centre for Women (ATRC) of the UN Economic Commission for Africa, based in Addis Ababa, Ethiopia (see Snyder and Tadesse 1995) or the Gender Unit of SADC (South African Development Community) and the Gender Unit of the African Union.

6. These were in thirteen countries: Cameroon, Ethiopia, Ghana, Kenya, Malawi, Namibia, Nigeria, Sierra Leone, South Africa, Sudan, Uganda, Zambia, and Zimbabwe. This survey is ongoing (for more, see http://www.gwsafrica.org/directory/index.html). To date, no Francophone universities in Africa offer gender studies programs. Arabic universities were not included in the survey.

7. Makerere University's Department of Women and Gender Studies is supported by a faculty of thirteen full-time and four part-time teachers who teach over 1,000 undergraduate and thirty graduate students; Boswell (2003, 7).

8. In May 2004, the University Council gave approval for the establishment of a Centre for Gender Studies and Advocacy.

9. Most degree programs in women's and gender studies are located in South Africa. While twelve universities offer master's degrees in women's and gender studies (six of them in South Africa, the others in Sudan, Uganda, Cameroon, Zambia, Zimbabwe, and Nigeria), only three institutions (out of over 300 African universities!) offer Ph.D. programs: the University of Cape Town, Makerere University, and the University of Pretoria. The University of Namibia, the University of Buea (Cameroon), and the University of Sierra Leone offer postgraduate diplomas in women's and gender studies. See Boswell (2003, 6) and Kasente (2002).

10. See the report of the Ghana Working Meeting at http://www.gwsafrica.org/workshops/index.html (accessed July 2, 2004).

11. The AGI was involved in the second CODESRIA symposium, "African Gender Research in the New Millennium: Perspectives, Directions, and Challenges," held in Cairo in 2002. The same year, the Women's Worlds Congress took place at Makerere University, Kampala, Uganda; Amina Mama gave a keynote address (2002b; see also Arnfred 2003).

12. See Aidoo (1985); Arhin (1983); Allman and Tashjian (2000); Akyeampong and Obeng (1995); and Akyeampong (2000) for accounts of these.

13. See Mensah-Kutin et al. (2000) for an evaluation of Ghana's national machinery for women.

14. P/NDC refers to the Provisional National Defence Council (PNDC), the ruling military regime from 1982 to 1993, and the National Democratic Congress (NDC), which it metamorphosed into after the return to constitutional rule in 1993.

15. During the period of military rule in West Africa from the 1970s to early 1990s, first ladies became important political players who mobilized women, ostensibly for national development and women's empowerment but ultimately in defense of the regimes of their husbands. They used state resources and were accountable to no one as they set up income-generating projects for women. See also Abdullah (1995); Baako (2003); Ibrahim (2004); Mama (1998); Manuh (1993); Okeke (1998); Tsikata (1989).

16. See Clark (1994); Clark and Manuh (1991); Manuh (1993); Robertson (1983); Sparr (1994); Tsikata (1989).

17. The announcement of the creation of the ministry failed to generate enthusiasm from many gender activists, who expressed concern about the coupling of women's and children's affairs, as if the two were synonymous. NETRIGHT issued a statement in protest of this coupling in 2001.

18. While the majority of such women were poor, patronage politics practiced by the DWM meant that many middle-class women in urban areas benefited from their projects. See Baako (2003).

19. Its members include The Ark Foundation, the Gender Studies and Human Rights and Documentation Centre, Third World Network, Actionaid, ABANTU for Development, the Development and Women's Studies (DAWS) Programme at the University of Ghana, Advocates for Gender Equity (AGE), WILDAF, FIDA, Women's Initiative for Self Empowerment (WISE), GAWU of the Ghana Trades Union Congress, Multi-disciplinary African Women's Health Network (MAWHN), and Women in Broadcasting (WIB).

20. This includes the former Minister of Women's and Children's Affairs, Mrs. Gladys Asmah, who claimed publicly that gender activists wanted to destroy families by asking for the criminalization of marital rape.

References

AAWORD. 1985. "Origins, Development and Future Prospects of Association of African Women for Research and Development (AAWORD)." Dakar: AAWORD Executive Secretariat (March).

———. 1999. "AAWORD/AFARD 1977–1999: Deconstructing Research and Development for Gender Equality." Report on AAWORD's Institutional Evolution. Dakar: AAWORD.

Abdullah, Hussaina. 1995. "Wifeism and Activism: The Nigerian Women's Movement." In *The Challenge of Local Feminisms: Women's Movements in Global Perspective*, edited by A. Basu, 209–225. Boulder, Colo.: Westview Press.

Aidoo, Agnes Akosua. 1985. "Women in the History and Culture of Ghana." *Research Review, NS* 2, no. 1:14–51.

Akyeampong, Emmanuel. 2000. "'*Wo pe tam won pe ba*' ('You like cloth, but you don't want children'): Urbanization, Individualism and Gender Relations in Colonial Ghana, c. 1900–39." In *Africa's Urban Past*, edited by D. M. Anderson and R. Rathbone, 222–234. Oxford: James Currey.

———, and Pashington Obeng. 1995. "Spirituality, Gender, and Power in Asante History." *International Journal of African Historical Studies* 28, no. 3: 481–508.

Allman, Jean, and Victoria Tashjian. 2000. *"I Will Not Eat Stone": A Women's History of Colonial Asante*. Portsmouth, N.H.: Heinemann.

Arhin, Kwame. 1983. "The Political and Military Roles of Akan Women." In *Female and Male in West Africa*, edited by C. Oppong, 91–98. London: Allen and Unwin.

Arnfred, Signe. 2003. "African Gender Research: A View from the North." *CODESRIA Bulletin* 1: 6–9.

Baako, Dede-Nako. 2003. "The Impact of African First Ladies in Their Societies: A

Study of the 31st December Women's Movement in Ghana." M.Phil. thesis, Institute of African Studies, University of Ghana, Legon.

Boswell, Barbara. 2003. "Locating Gender and Women's Studies Teaching and Research at African Universities: Survey Results." African Gender Institute, University of Cape Town. Available online at http://www.gwsafrica.org/directory/index.html (accessed July 2, 2004).

Bunwaree, Sheila. 2004. "Neoliberal Ideologies, Identity and Gender: Managing Diversity in Mauritius." In *Rights and the Politics of Recognition in Africa*, edited by H. Englund and F. B. Nyamnjoh, 148–168. London and New York: Zed Books.

Clark, Gracia. 1994. *Onions Are My Husband: Survival and Accumulation by West African Market Women.* Chicago: University of Chicago Press.

———, and Takyiwaa Manuh. 1991. "Women Traders in Ghana and the Structural Adjustment Programme." In *Structural Adjustment and African Women Farmers*, edited by C. Gladwin, 217–238. Gainesville: University Press of Florida.

Coker-Appiah, Dorcas, and Kathy Cusack. 1999. *Violence against Women and Children in Ghana.* Accra, Ghana: Gender and Human Rights Documentation Centre.

Collins, Patricia Hill. 1990. *Black Feminist Thought.* Boston: Unwin Hyman.

Gyimah-Boadi, E., ed. 1993. *Ghana under PNDC Rule.* Dakar: CODESRIA Books.

hooks, bell. 2000. *Feminist Theory: From Margin to Center.* Boston: South End Press.

Hutchful, Ebo, and A. Abdoulaye Bathily, eds. 1998. *The Military and Militarism in Africa.* Dakar: CODESRIA.

Ibrahim, Jibrin. 2004. "The First Lady Syndrome and the Marginalization of Women from Power: Opportunities or Compromises for Gender Equality?" *Feminist Africa* 3: 48–69. Available online at http://www.feministafrica.org/03-2004/2level.html.

Imam, Ayesha. 1997. "Engendering African Social Sciences: An Introductory Essay." In *Engendering African Social Sciences*, edited by A. M. Imam, A. Mama, and F. Sow, 1–30. Dakar: CODESRIA.

———, Amina Mama, and Fatou Sow, eds. 1997. *Engendering African Social Sciences.* Dakar: CODESRIA.

ISSER (Institute of Statistical, Social & Economic Research). 1998. *Women in Ghanaian Public Life.* Legon: Institute of Statistical, Social & Economic Research.

Kasente, Deborah. 2002. "Institutionalising Gender Equality in African Universities: The Case of Women's and Gender Studies at Makerere University." *Feminist Africa* 1: 91–99. Available online at http://www.feministafrica.org/fa%201/01-2002/kasente.html (accessed July 12, 2004).

McClintock, Ann. 1995. *Imperial Leather: Race, Gender and Sexuality in the Colonial Contest.* New York: Routledge.

Mama, Amina. 1995a. "Feminism or Femocracy: State Feminism and Democratisation in Nigeria." *Africa Development* 20, no. 1: 37–58.

———. 1995b. *Beyond the Masks: Race, Gender, and Subjectivity.* London: Routledge.

———. 1996. *Women's Studies and Studies of Women in Africa during the 1990s.* Dakar: CODESRIA Working Paper Series.

———. 1997. "'Sheroes and Villains': Conceptualizing Colonial and Contemporary Violence against Women in Africa." In *Feminists Genealogies, Colonial Legacies, Democratic Futures*, edited by J. M. Alexander and C. T. Mohanty, 46–62. London: Routledge.

———. 1998. "Khaki in the Family: Gender Discourses and Militarism in Nigeria." *African Studies Review* 41, no. 2: 1–17.

———. 2001. "'Challenging Subjects': Gender and Power in African Contexts." In *Identity and Beyond: Rethinking Africanity,* edited by S. B. Diagne, A. Mama, H. Melber, and F. B. Nyamnjoh, 8–17. Discussion Paper 12. Uppsala: Nordic-African Institute.

———. 2002a. "Editorial." *Feminist Africa* 1. Available online at http://www.feministafrica.org/fa%201/01-2002/editorial.html (accessed June 30, 2004).

———. 2002b. "Gains and Challenges: Linking Theory and Practice." Women's Worlds Congress: Keynote Address presented at the opening ceremony, Makerere University, July 21. Available online at http://web.uct.ac.za/org/agi/events/mama.htm (accessed July 7, 2004).

Manuh, Takyiwaa. 1991. "Women and Their Organisations during the Convention People's Party Period." In *The Life and Work of Kwame Nkrumah,* edited by K. Arhin, 101–127. Sedco: Accra.

———. 1993. "Women, the State and Society under the PNDC." In *Ghana under PNDC Rule,* edited by E. Gyimah-Boadi, 176–195. Dakar: CODESRIA.

Mensah-Kutin, Rose, Alima Mahama, Sarah Ocran, Esther Ofei-Aboagye, Vicky Okine, and Dzodzi Tsikata. 2000. "The National Machinery for Women in Ghana: An NGO Evaluation." Accra: Third World Network-Africa.

Mkandawire, Thandika, and Adebayo Olukoshi, eds. 1995. *Between Liberalization and Oppression: The Politics of Structural Adjustment in Africa.* Dakar: CODESRIA.

Nzegwu, Nkiru. 2003. "O Africa: Gender Imperialism in Academia." In *African Women and Feminism: Reflecting on the Politics of Sisterhood,* edited by O. Oyewumi, 99–157. Trenton, N.J.: Africa World Press.

Okeke, Philomena. 1998. "First Lady Syndrome: The (En)Gendering of Bureaucratic Corruption in Nigeria." *CODESRIA Bulletin* 3/4: 16–19.

Oyewumi, Oyeronke. 1997. *The Invention of Women: Making African Sense of Western Gender Discourses.* Minneapolis: University of Minnesota Press.

Pereira, Charmaine. 2002. "Between Knowing and Imagining: What Space for Feminism in Scholarship on Africa?" *Feminist Africa* 1: 9–33. Available online at http://www.feministafrica.org/fa%201/01-2002/pereira.html (accessed June 30, 2004).

———. 2003. "Locating Gender and Women's Studies in Nigeria: What Trajectories for the Future?" Revised version of paper presented at 10th General Assembly of CODESRIA, "Africa in the New Millennium," December 8–12, 2002, Kampala, Uganda. Available online at http://www.gwsafrica.org/knowledge/pereira.html (accessed July 7, 2004).

Rathgeber, Eva-Marie. 1990. "WID, WAD, GAD; Trends in Research and Practice." *Journal of Developing Areas* 24, no. 4: 489–502.

Rimmer, Douglas. 1993. *Staying Poor: Ghana's Political Economy 1950–1990.* Oxford: Pergamon Press.

Robertson, Claire. 1983. "The Death of Makola and Other Tragedies: Male Strategies against a Female-Dominated System." *Canadian Journal of African Studies* 17, no. 3: 469–495.

Snyder, Margaret C., and Mary Tadesse. 1995. *African Women and Development: A History.* Johannesburg: Witwatersrand University Press.

Sparr, Pamela. 1994. *Mortgaging Women's Lives: Feminist Critiques of Structural Adjustment.* London: Zed Press.

Taiwo, Olufemi. 2004. "Feminism and Africa: Reflections on the Poverty of Theory."

In *African Women and Feminism: Reflecting on the Politics of Sisterhood,* edited by O. Oyewumi, 45–66. New York: Palgrave.

Third World Network. 2000. *National Machinery in Africa Series.* TWN-Africa. Accra: Ghana.

Tsikata, Edzodzinam. 1989. "Women's Political Organizations, 1951–1987." In *The State, Development and Politics in Ghana,* edited by E. Hansen and K. A. Ninsin, 73–93. London: CODESRIA.

———. 1997. "Gender Equality and the State in Ghana: Some Issues of Policy and Practice." In *Engendering African Social Science,* edited by A. Imam, A. Mama, and F. Sow, 381–412. Dakar: CODESRIA.

Tsikata, Dzodzi, ed. 2001. *Gender Training in Ghana: Politics, Issues and Tools.* Accra: Woeli Publications.

United Nations Commission on the Status of Women. 1991. *National, Regional and International Machinery for the Effective Integration of Women in the Development Process, Including Non-Governmental Organizations. Report of the Secretary-General.* New York: United Nations Economic and Social Council.

8 Women as Emergent Actors: A Survey of New Women's Organizations in Nigeria since the 1990s

Hussaina J. Abdullah

Introduction

The 1990s in Nigeria can be described as the decade of nongovernmental organization (NGO) activism due to a surge of activity in that sector. This was a direct response to changes in the political and economic landscape of the country. At the political level, the widespread violation of human rights by various military regimes since 1984 coupled with political repression, extrajudicial killings, disregard for the rule of law, arbitrary arrests and detention of critics, and, finally, the annulment of the results of the 1993 presidential election, which would have ushered in a civilian government, forced Nigerians to organize to put an end to political authoritarianism and militarism. At the economic level, the negative effects of the International Monetary Fund– and World Bank–sponsored structural adjustment programs that affected incomes, market prices, employment, and social services resulted in protests against such policies and the formation of organizations to cushion the effects of the adjustments.

In addition, women's NGO activism in Nigeria, as elsewhere, was ignited by the opportunities created by the UN Decade for Women, the various international conferences organized by the UN in the 1990s, and the emergence and growth of a global feminist movement. The activities of women's NGOs in the 1990s can be traced to the UN's declaration of 1975 as the International Women's Year and the years 1975–1985 as the Decade for Women. These historic pronouncements were followed up with a UN statement that all member governments should establish ministries and commissions to aid women's integration into the development process. The functions of these departments at that time was to liaise between women's NGOs and government at all levels, coordinate all activities relating to women, advise government on women's issues, and design programs to facilitate women's integration into the development process. Thus, projects and programs to enhance women's contributions to development and improve their status in relation to men were initiated. These activities were focused mainly on home economics training, arts and crafts, skills acquisition, health and personal hygiene, adult literacy, and income-generating activities for women (Abdullah 1997, 20).

However, by the end of the Decade for Women in 1985, continued poverty and increasing gender inequality had led to a questioning of the conceptual basis of these projects and the development of a new framework to rectify the situation. The adoption of the gender and development (GAD) framework, the drafting of the Convention on the Elimination of all Forms of Discrimination against Women (CEDAW), and the publication of the 1985 Nairobi Forward-looking Strategies for the Advancement of Women took the entire global women's movement—including the African women's movement—into new terrain. Women's movements the world over began organizing around thematic issues and formed international and regional networks to lobby and advocate for gender equality. As part of this process, women began to "organise to enter into the mainstream and challenge the agendas that were discussed in the global conferences convened by the UN at the beginning of the 1990s" (Carrillo 1997, 18).

The coming together of women as an organized force meant that gender concerns were included in all UN global conferences. A special advisor on women was appointed to the UN Conference on Environment and Development (UNCED) in 1992 and Agenda 21, an official document of the conference, became the blueprint on women and the environment. At the World Conference on Human Rights in 1993, women's rights were proclaimed to be human rights and violence against women was declared a fundamental violation of human rights. Furthermore, the human rights of women were recognized as universal, interrelated, interdependent, and indivisible. The 1994 International Conference on Population and Development acknowledged the central role of women in development and agreed that equity and empowerment of women should be central components of population policies and that for every situation of subordination of women there is a component of male responsibility. Women were again able to imprint their mark at the World Summit on Social Development in 1995 as they established the centrality of their contributions to poverty reduction and social integration in the main agenda of the conference (Carrillo 1997, 19). The struggles of women's movements globally culminated in the Fourth World Conference on Women in 1995 and the adoption of the Platform for Action (PFA) as the document to lead women the world over into the twenty-first century. The PFA brought together all the commitments women had secured at the various world conferences into one document with which women could negotiate. The mission statement notes that:

> the Platform for Action is an agenda for women's empowerment. It aims at accelerating the implementation of the Nairobi Forward-looking Strategies for the Advancement of Women and at removing all the obstacles to women's active participation in all spheres of public and private life through a full and equal share in economic, social, cultural and political decision-making. This means that the principle of shared power and responsibility should be established between women and men at home, in the workplace and in the wider national and international

communities. Equality between women and men is a matter of human rights and a condition for social justice and is also a necessary and fundamental prerequisite for equality, development and peace. A transformed partnership based on equality between women and men is a condition for people-centered sustainable development. A sustained and long-term commitment is essential, so that women and men can work together for themselves, for their children and for society to meet the challenges of the twenty-first century. (United Nations 1996, 17)

While it can be argued that events at the international level contributed to the emergence and growth of new women's groups in the Nigerian sphere of women's organizing and to a change in women's organizational forms in the 1990s, the stage for the transformation in Nigerian women's engagement can be traced to the 1980s with the founding of Women in Nigeria (WIN), the country's first feminist organization. The emergence in 1979 of an elected civilian government after thirteen years of military rule led to the widening of democratic space in the country and the emergence of intellectually influential left groups such as the Zaria group, the PRP Group, and the Ife-Socialist forum (Abdullah 1994).[1] All of these were concerned with defining the way forward to a free and democratic society devoid of exploitation and oppression.

It was against this background that female academics, professionals, and activists who had been exposed to feminist writings came together to found WIN. At about the same time, a highly educated crop of women emerged in Nigeria who questioned not only the way society was organized and governed but also the way existing women's organization's were handling the problem of gender inequalities in society. These women also expressed dismay at the reductionist or dismissive attitudes of many male academics and the way social activists handled women's questions in the country. WIN was formed to fill what were considered to be serious gaps in the theory and practice of women's liberation in Nigeria. It sought to challenge the dismissiveness and complacency of leftist academics and the ineffectiveness of existing women's organizations (Abdullah 1994).

The objective of this chapter is to assess how the changing national and international environments have affected Nigeria's women's organizational forms in the 1990s. It entails an evaluation of these new women's groups in their quest for the advancement of women's rights and concerns in the emerging democratic environment. I am particularly interested in the alliances these groups have forged among themselves and with other groups in pursuing their objectives. In addition, I shall focus attention on the challenges women's organizations are confronting in undertaking their work.

Nigerian Women's Organizations in the 1990s

Before the formation of WIN, the organizational forms, activities, and discourses of Nigerian women's organizations were aimed at improving the lives of women from within the existing unequal sexual/gender division of labor. With WIN, Nigerian women's organizations in the 1990s, like others the world over, started using transformative strategies in their quest for gender equality and equitable development for women. Although Nigerian women's organizations in the 1990s were concerned with questions of emancipation and empowerment, they were just as interested in the conventional issues of women's livelihoods and welfare. The activities of Nigeria women's organizations in the 1990s can be grouped under four themes: women's human rights, reproductive health, economic advancement, and political empowerment.

With the exception of the Country Women's Association of Nigeria (COWAN), which is located in Akure, Ondo State, all of the NGOs reported upon are based in Lagos. This is because as the former capital of the Nigeria, Lagos has been the major center of NGO activism, and this was especially so in the 1990s. Most Lagos-based NGOs are more established than those in other parts of the country. Furthermore, these groups grew out of the global feminist movement and in response to the UN millennium conferences.

Following Ifi Amadiume's categorization of Nigerian women's organizations, it can be argued that it is Daughters of the Goddess as opposed to Daughters of Imperialism who are managing the organizations presented in this chapter. Daughters of the Goddess are grassroots women, female social and political activists, and left-wing female activist-scholars; Daughters of Imperialism are professional and national elite women who are the inheritors of the postcolonial state and who are perceived as "partners in corruption." Amadiume notes that in using the concepts of Daughters of Imperialism and Daughters of the Goddess in analyzing Nigerian women's activism, she was "concerned with the question of legitimate authority and the structural position of these women in relation to grassroots women's organizations and local and state systems."

> On the basis of this, I raised questions of authority and accountability in Mrs. Establishment's right to manage local women's finances through her community bank which would solicit external funding in the name of women's development. In contrast, as a trader and a traditionally titled woman, Chief Bankole, I felt, was in a structural position of legitimate authority and accountability vis à vis her local women's groups. My key interest, therefore, is in organically legitimate, organized structures of local women; [on] the basis [of] which women can reap the fruits of their labor and glory in their own success. (Amadiume 2000, 64)

I argue that since the organizations in this study have aligned themselves with poor urban and rural women in confronting the state and demanding that laws that dehumanize women be abolished, they have the legitimate authority to struggle for women's human rights because they are organically connected to grassroots women.

Women's Human Rights

Women's NGOs working for the promotion of women's rights in Nigeria focus their attention on advocacy, legal literacy, promoting and protecting Nigerian women's rights in line with international human rights instruments, and ensuring equality and nondiscrimination in law and in practice.

BAOBAB for Women's Human Rights

BAOBAB for Women's Human Rights was founded in 1996. The organization works on women's legal rights issues under customary, statutory, and religious laws. Its aim is to improve the recognition of and ability to put into practice women's human rights (BAOBAB 1999). To achieve its objectives, BAOBAB primarily undertakes the following activities: a women and laws project, a violence against women program, solidarity work and information sharing, and networking and coordination. Additionally, BAOBAB runs ad hoc projects in response to sociopolitical opportunities and threats.

The women and laws project documents the ways in which laws and practices —secular, religious, and customary, written and unwritten—are applied to and affect women as well as the strategies women use to bring about progressive change and resist reactionary trends. The project focuses on laws and practices affecting women in three areas: as family members, as citizens, and as individuals (including personal autonomy, bodily integrity, and reproductive rights). As part of this program, BAOBAB produces legal literacy leaflets (e.g., "Child Rights and Inheritance in Muslim Personal Laws," "Divorce Guardianship in Muslim Personal Laws," "Child Custody and Guardianship in Muslim Personal Laws in Nigeria," and "Violence against Women"), conducts paralegal training, organizes legal literacy outreach, and publishes analytical works and practical handbooks. The targets of its personal-empowerment, legal aid, and community-organizing projects are poor urban and rural women who live across Islamic northern Nigeria. Lessons from these grassroots efforts are then used to design public education and legal reform advocacy programs aimed nationally at building interreligious harmony, support for the advancement of gender equality, and eradication of religiously and culturally based practices and beliefs that oppress women.

BAOBAB produced a leaflet entitled "Violence Against Women" that has been used in consciousness-raising workshops with women and with the general public. The organization also participates in the annual international campaign of the 16 Days of Action Against Gender-Based Violence. It has initiated two projects within this program: one advocates women's rights through law (with the Human Rights Law Service, or HURILAWS) and the other is a public tribunal on violence against women (in collaboration with the Civil Resource Development and Documentation Centre).

A third area of the organization's activities includes circulating and responding to solidarity alerts for action and calls to join campaigns. At times BAOBAB also initiates such campaigns. In forwarding these alerts, BAOBAB usually invites recipients to join the campaigns and to mobilize international and national support through petitions, letter-writing campaigns, media strategies, and agitation for new legislation. According to the organization, solidarity work generates among women and other activists a consciousness of the strength they possess once they unite, network, and exchange resources. BAOBAB operates an e-mail discussion group on governance, democracy, human rights, and gender. It also provides individual support to women who feel that their rights have been violated.

Capacity-building, a fourth program area, is aimed at empowering women and women's groups as well as other NGOs through skill-building and capacity-enhancement activities. Towards this end, BAOBAB organized a workshop on Engendering Human Rights in February 1998 that was aimed at helping mainstream human rights organizations incorporate gender issues and gender awareness into their programs. Other activities within this program area include internships, counseling, and support skills. In the case of the latter, BAOBAB organizes workshops for its outreach teams to empower and equip them with the skills to handle the cases of girls and women whose rights have been violated. BAOBAB also provides advice and technical aid to other NGOs.

BAOBAB coordinates and participates in a number of networks as part of its effort to promote women's rights in Nigeria and internationally. At the international level, the organization hosts the coordination of the group Women Living Under Muslim Laws (WLUML) in Africa and the Middle East. This includes the production of the coalition's newsletter. BAOBAB also has a close working relationship with the Women's Health Research Network (WHRN), the International Reproductive Rights Action Group (IRRAG), and the International Council on Human Rights and Inter Rights. At the national level, since 1997 it has initiated a joint program of activities to be carried out yearly by women's NGOs to celebrate International Women's Day, initiated a network of women's NGOs and women's rights program coordinators within mainstream human rights groups to celebrate the fiftieth anniversary of the Universal Declaration of Human Rights (UDHR), and coordinated the Nigerian NGO coalition for a shadow report to the CEDAW Committee. Furthermore, in response to the adoption of Shari'a law by various states in the northern part of the country, BAOBAB initiated and coordinates a 22-member coalition to protect women's rights in religious, customary, and statutory laws (BAOBAB 1999). BAOBAB and its founding executive director, Ms. Ayesha Imam, won the 2002 John Humphrey Award for their efforts to promote and defend the rights of women oppressed by religious laws in northern Nigeria.

Women's Justice Program

Established in 1994, the Women's Justice Program (WJP) is involved in litigation and campaigns against laws and policies that discriminate against women and children. It works primarily with and for poor and socially disadvantaged women in the Lagos metropolitan area, although it also at times conducts public education and legal advocacy programs in other parts of Nigeria.

The programs and activities of the WJP include providing legal aid, counseling, and education; a prison outreach project; and enlightenment campaigns. WJP provides free legal advice—and sometimes legal representation in the courts —primarily, but not solely, for abused, battered, or sexually harassed women and for victims of harmful and discriminatory cultural practices (BAOBAB 1998b). The organization also operates the Women's Justice Centre, a legal clinic that caters to the needs of violated women and children and is open to all women and children in need of assistance. The center provides first aid care to victims along with referrals and transportation to hospitals.

In its counseling and educational programs, the WJP offers weekly lectures for women and twice-weekly lectures for children (the latter reduced to every other week during the school term). The women's lecture program focuses on issues such as harmful traditional and cultural practices against women, domestic violence, health hazards associated with female genital mutilation, family planning, primary health care, pregnancies and child-related problems, widowhood rights, sexual harassment, and oppressive religious laws. The children's program focuses on children's rights, morals, drug abuse, and how to be a good citizen.

The organization's prison project is meant to ascertain the number of women and children in the various prisons in the country. The aims of the project are to generate information to fight for better prison conditions for women, speed up the process for those awaiting trial, provide bail for those with bailable offenses, and institute a campaign to stop the housing of children and teenagers in the same jails with adults.

The WJP organizes and participates in seminars and enlightenment campaigns aimed at promoting women's rights. It has organized and participated in numerous post-Beijing conferences aimed at implementing the Beijing Platform for Action. The WJP also has an outreach project for market women to teach them about their rights, about how best to handle discriminatory situations, and about their responsibilities toward their families and the nation. WJP publishes a quarterly journal, the *Women's Rights Monitor,* which highlights discriminatory practices against women and children. The journal is distributed to government officials, the judiciary, law enforcement agencies, NGOs, international organizations, members of the diplomatic corps, and others.

The Women, Law and Development Centre, Nigeria

Founded in 1993, the Women, Law and Development Centre (WLDC) focuses on research and advocacy as well as on training women to appreciate their capacities and capabilities within the development process. The organization's program areas include human rights advocacy, community development, education and training, and research and consultancy. The center's goal is to put Nigerian women's needs and concerns on the development agenda and thus act as a link between policymakers and women and between women and the public. As part of this process, WLDC undertakes educational programs on women's human rights (focusing on health, violence against women, education, access to credit, and the role of women in decision making); organizes training and education programs (including train-the-trainer courses); pursues women's rights litigation; prepares feasibility studies (including planning and monitoring proposals); undertakes program management, appraisal, monitoring, and evaluation; promotes national and international networking for women; and conducts research into legal and developmental issues (BAOBAB 1998b; Women, Law and Development Centre 2003).

The center has also organized leadership training for women and conducted training for NGOs and community-based organizations on shared leadership, mentoring, and internal democracy. Among WLDC's publications are a simplified version of the Beijing Platform for Action, a training manual entitled *A Simple Guide for Trainers: Training in Management, Leadership and Conflict Resolution,* and the quarterly newsletter *Gender Views.* With a clear focus on urban areas and public policy, the main beneficiaries of its programs over the years have been budding women leaders, staff and members of female NGOs and community-based organizations, academics and other researchers, policymakers, and media practitioners across Nigeria, particularly in the southern regions.

Reproductive Health and Rights

The programs of women's health NGOs focus on promoting gender-sensitive initiatives in sexual and reproductive issues, fostering research and disseminating information on women's health, and increasing women's access to appropriate and affordable quality health care.

Women's Health Organisation of Nigeria

Ever since it was established in 1992, the Women's Health Organisation of Nigeria (WHON) has been strengthening the capacity of women's health groups at the grassroots level in order to enable them to respond to identified health needs of women. The organization provides technical assistance to its partners in the areas of formulating, implementing, monitoring, and evaluating reproductive health programs (BAOBAB 1998b). WHON uses concepts of gender and reproductive and sexual health in its project design and program planning. It works with over twenty groups in nine states spread across the six geopolitical zones of the country.

As part of its commitment to promoting the reproductive health and rights of Nigerian women, WHON trains traditional birth attendants (TBAs) in response to expressed needs in the communities. The training helps TBAs improve their skills in order to reduce rates of maternal and infant mortality and morbidity. They are equipped with kits to assist them in their work and are taught to provide family planning services to reduce the incidence of unwanted pregnancies. They are also taught how to recognize sexually transmitted diseases (STDs) and make prompt referrals to hospitals. Women's groups have also been assisted with an emergency obstetric transportation system to convey emergency cases to hospitals (BAOBAB 1998b).

Women in various communities are trained as volunteer health workers. They are equipped with skills to enable them to attend to minor ailments, attend to the reproductive needs of women in their communities according to primary health care principles, and make referrals in cases of emergency. They are also trained to run community-based reproductive health pharmacies. WHON has introduced and equipped community drug stores to alleviate the problem of drug inaccessibility and shortage. The profit from the drugstore is used as a revolving loan plan to boost the financial situation of participants and empower them economically.

To ensure group longevity, WHON organizes leadership training for its partners, assisting them in identifying, prioritizing, and meeting the needs of their communities. The trainees learn leadership, group management, and other skills essential to enhancing their impact on their communities.

As part of its commitment to a Nigeria that is holistically conscious of reproductive and sexual health, WHON has initiated programs aimed at adolescents and men. Its adolescent health program for both in-school and out-of-school youth is aimed at promoting reproductive health, self-esteem, and respect for women's rights. This program is pursued in collaboration with local government councils and community groups. In its program for men, WHON has been advocating for male participation and responsibility in reproductive health matters, particularly with respect to the promotion of women's health. WHON also coordinates an interdenominational health-educators project that trains people from different religious backgrounds to recognize, prevent, counsel, and manage health problems within their communities; it also teaches conflict resolution and management. The organization believes that its activities have empowered women because it gives them the information they need to make informed decisions about their reproductive health.

Community Life Project

The Community Life Project (CLP) is a community-based and community-focused organization whose mission is to improve the quality of life of the communities in which it operates. The organization's goal is to "create a community where men and women are empowered to transform their own lives by increasing the community's access to health information and sexuality education." It is therefore committed to promoting egalitarian gender values at the community level, which it considers central to the creation of its vision of a healthy and stable community (BAOBAB 1998b; Community Life Project 2000).

Since its 1992 inception, the CLP has broadened its educational activities from its original focus on AIDS to include all aspects of sexuality. Its current activities include family planning and education for parents and teenagers about STDs and sexuality. The organization works in three high-density, largely low-income communities in Lagos State: Isolo, Mushin, and Oshodi. The organization's partners in the communities include schools, private continuing education and tutorial centers, health facilities, health workers at primary health education units in the Oshodi/Isolo Local Government Area, community development organizations, market and resident associations, occupational groups (of, for example, roadside mechanics), and religious groups. The CLP currently works with thirteen community groups and twenty-three schools in Isolo as well as four community groups and four schools in both Mushin and Oshodi (BAOBAB 1998b).

The CLP uses a gender perspective in all its programs because of the importance of gender issues in the transmission of HIV/AIDS and STDs and because of the health implications of the sexual disempowerment of women. Thus, the promotion of women's health and rights is a major component of the organization's sexuality education programs (BAOBAB 1998b). The CLP's strategy for promoting women's health and rights in the community is to work with both men and women on gender issues and to discuss women's rights within the context of family health. The organization focuses on the family because of that institution's pivotal role in the community and the larger society. Moreover, the family is the first place women experience violations as daughters, sisters, and wives. These enlightenment campaigns promote harmony by emphasizing mutual respect and the protection of the rights of all members of the family, especially those of women and children. In addition, the CLP organizes community-level discussions that bring together all of its partners plus community leaders and teenagers. Drama, oral poetry, and songs are used at these events to highlight the plight of women and motivate community response in tackling discriminatory practices against women.

Other activities organized by the project include its annual celebration of World AIDS Day, International Women's Day, and the Couples Festival. At the latter, the CLP encourages the discussion of sexuality issues and highlights the sexual disempowerment of women. The CLP has also conducted research and published monographs on the sociocultural and economic factors influencing issues pertinent to women's reproductive health and rights such as women's ability to practice safe sex, religion and AIDS, and the prevention of violence against women.

Economic Empowerment

Country Women's Association of Nigeria

The Country Women's Association of Nigeria (COWAN) is a nongovernmental development organization of rural and urban poor women. When it was established in Ondo State in 1982, it had six cooperatives and 225 members; now the organization has 7,000 women's cooperative societies and a membership base of over 200,000 individuals. It operates in twenty-eight of Nigeria's thirty-six states. The organization's mandate is to empower rural and urban poor women economically, socially, and politically. Toward this end, COWAN mobilizes rural women by utilizing their traditional rotating savings cooperative structures and organizes training in productive activities and managerial skills to help free them from their powerlessness.

The organization's determination to make women active partners and participants in the national development process is based on the philosophy of self-help and the "bottom-up" participatory approach. Using this approach, COWAN works with its members to identify constraints that hinder women's development, prioritizing their needs in order to achieve a balanced system of development beneficial to women. It is around this ideology that the organization has formed its programs and activities, with a concentration on the following:

1. The African Traditional Responsive Banking Approach (ATRB) for economic empowerment
2. The Integrated Approach to Reproductive Health for Social Empowerment
3. The 100 Women Working Group for poor women's political empowerment
4. The composting of manure and the cultivation and production of mini-sets and soybeans for better nutrition and sustainable agriculture.

The ATRB was introduced because COWAN realized that lack of access to credit by its members was a major constraint to enterprise development and economic empowerment. Embodying COWAN's overall vision and mission, the ATRB is the unified product of the best of African microcredit practices, strengthened by modern knowledge and unencumbered by the harsh commercialist requirements and practices of orthodox banking institutions (Ogunleye 1997).

The ATRB operates various savings and loan devices for its members. Among them are daily savings programs, group monthly savings programs, children's savings and loan programs, a health development fund, technological/community enterprise savings programs, and a fund of enabling savings for poor women who are unable to save enough to qualify for loans. The 100 Women Working Group for poor women's political empowerment is an initiative of the Gender and Development Action (GADA) organization. It evolved from GADA-coordinated workshops on Women in Public Life in 1996. The idea behind the concept was to link individual women and women's organizations in an area, thereby creating a critical mass of individuals committed to women's political empowerment. Every member of the group was expected to sensitize 100 other women about women's political participation. These initiatives have been merged together to form what COWAN calls its "Three-Legged Approach to Poor Women's Empowerment" (Ogunleye 1997).

The impact of COWAN's work for women's empowerment nationally can be seen in the fact that in 2001, COWAN's founder and executive director, Chief Bisi Ogunleye, received from the president of Nigeria one of the highest national honors, the Officer of the Federal Republic (OFR). In addition, in 1996, Chief Ogunleye was awarded the Hunger Project Africa Leadership Prize, an award given to African women and men who have "created lasting self-reliant solutions to surmount challenges to health, education, nutrition, incomes, and women's empowerment" (Lucas 2000, 93). COWAN attracted a lot of media attention during the 2003 general elections for its efforts to mobilize women's support in Ekiti and Ondo states (in southwest Nigeria) around a number of female candidates for state and federal legislative houses.

Political Empowerment

NGOs working for the political empowerment of women concentrate their efforts on increasing women's access to and full participation in politics, decision-making, and leadership structures and positions.

Gender and Development Action

Gender and Development Action (GADA) is a national women's organization dedicated to gender equality and the pursuit of sustainable development for Nigerian women. Established in 1994, GADA promotes greater understanding and proactive responses to gender issues through research, documentation, dissemination of information, training, consultation, dialogue, advocacy, and mobilization. GADA's organizational emphasis is on networking and collaboration with various stakeholders in the society. In collaboration with its partners (government agencies, community groups, NGOs, youth networks, and international development organizations), GADA serves as a medium for developing and promoting empowerment strategies that enable individuals, particularly women, to respond effectively to development issues with a gender perspective (BAOBAB 1998b).

The organization's main focus is on women's active participation in politics and public life. Toward this end, GADA promotes cooperative networking among women at all levels, holds political and public life skills workshops for female politicians, organizes media awareness campaigns for women's political participation, and produces radio and TV talk shows. In addition, GADA initiated and developed the 100 Women Working Group concept mentioned above for women's political mobilization. The group, an informal coalition of women's civil society organizations, promotes women's consensual leadership and action in the society.

In furtherance of its work, GADA facilitated the Post-Beijing Women's Political Awareness Summits in 1996. The purpose of these summits was to sensitize women to both the goals of the Platform for Action on women's empowerment and their participation in politics and public life. The outcome of these summits was an alternative political organizing agenda for women entitled *A Political Agenda for Nigerian Women.* The *Agenda* represents a new phase in women's organizing and serves as a working document for development planners and women's rights activists (GADA 1996).

Women Empowerment Movement (WEM)

The Women Empowerment Movement (WEM) is a membership-based group of lower-middle-class women, market women, and female politicians based mainly in the southwest of Nigeria. The organization was established in 1995 to vigorously pursue the sociocultural, economic, and political emancipation of Nigerian women. Since its inception, WEM has established contacts with other women's and community-based organizations as well as research institutions working in the area of gender and development (Women Empowerment Movement 2000a).

As part of its effort to get more women into the public political space, WEM (in partnership with the Federal Ministry of Women's Affairs and Social Development) produced a radio jingle extolling the virtue of female leadership. WEM also organized political education programs, seminars on leadership skills and political campaign strategies, and workshops on fund-raising for the political activities of female politicians. It also submitted a memorandum to the Nigerian Electoral Commission (NECON) on affirmative action during the registration of political parties.

After the election of a civilian administration in May 1999, WEM organized a roundtable conference for female ministers, special advisors, and federal and state legislators in Abuja on "Female Representation in the New Democratic Government in Nigeria." The organization also submitted a memorandum of amendments to the Presidential Technical Committee on the review of the 1999 constitution (Women Empowerment Movement 2000a).

Putting Women's Issues on the National Political Agenda

From the foregoing, it can be argued that the agenda of these organizations is the total liberation of Nigerian women from patriarchal domination. In other words, the struggles of these groups are aimed at transforming existing gender relations to effect gender equality in the polity. The impetus for this change can be traced to the various UN conferences in the 1990s that culminated in the Fourth World Conference on Women in Beijing in 1995. The massive public and world awareness generated by the Beijing conference galvanized women into action. For example, after the acknowledgement of women's political importance in the Platform for Action, Nigerian women were no longer contented with organizing around their own issues but also became active participants in the struggle to end military dictatorship in the country. Once civil rule was established, they were able to build on this experience to organize and form coalitions to promote the ideals of an equitable and just society free from exploitation and gender subordination.

However, it was the adoption of the Islamic legal code, the Shari'a, by some state governments in northern Nigerian between 1999 and 2000 that brought Nigerian women's activism to both national and international attention. The sentencing of the first female victim under Shari'a law, Bariya Magazu, to eighty lashes for fornication and the later sentencing of Safiya Hussani Tungar and Amina Lawal to death by stoning for adultery by Shari'a courts spurred women into action. In spite of their action in defense of Bariya (women's groups appealed against the sentencing) the Zamfara State government went ahead with the sentence. Because of their experience with the Zamfara State government, women's groups became more organized and vigilant in the adultery cases against Hussani Tungar and Lawal. In association with civil society groups, women's groups assembled a team of lawyers to defend the victims within the Shari'a code of law. Their action was based on the conviction that the trials and sentences violated the principles of Shari'a that the states were promoting. They appealed the convictions from the lower courts up to the state Shari'a Court of Appeal. They were successful in their appeals and both women were freed. The acquittal of these women by the Shari'a Court of Appeal should be a deterrent and protect women from arbitrary arrest, conviction, and violation of their rights in an Islamic setting.

These groups, including those that are not listed in this survey, used a multipronged strategy in their effort to put women's issues on the national political and democratic agenda. The first strategy—used mainly at the organizational level—involves the organization of workshops, seminars, rallies, and community outreach programs on women's political, social, and economic empowerment and women's rights. These groups also engaged in legislative and constitutional advocacy to engender the constitution- and law-making processes. They used a multifaceted approach to reach their targeted audience: they generated press releases, interviews and conferences, e-mail campaigns, radio programs, leaflets and pamphlets, poster campaigns, and simplified versions of documents.

The second strategy involves creating networks and coalitions among themselves and with other social movements and organizations at the national and international levels to promote and defend women's rights. Examples of such networks are the National Coalition on Violence Against Women, whose objective is not only to put an end to violence against women but also to criminalize it and have it be recognized as a human rights issue. As part of this process, the group is trying to get a bill through the National Assembly and organized a public tribunal with victims of domestic violence on July 21, 2005, in Abuja to sensitize the general public and the legislature on the issue. Women's Organization for National Conference Representation is a coalition of 167 NGOs, including men, that was formed in response to the low number of female appointments to the 2005 national political reform conference. The group organized a parallel conference to the government-sponsored meeting and is demanding that a specific provision of 30 percent of all appointed and elective positions be reserved for women be included in the amended constitution. Also, a Womanifesto, a manifesto of women's demands for total equality, is being drafted. The Coalition of NGOs for the Protection of Women's Rights in Religious, Customary and Statutory Laws is a 22-member group concerned with the rights of women under religious, customary, and statutory laws. It was created to protect and promote women's rights after the adoption of Shari'a acts by various states in northern Nigeria. The Citizen Forum for Constitutional Reform (CFCR) is a national coalition of over ninety civil society organizations that are committed to a process-led and participatory approach to constitutional reform in Nigeria. The Electoral Reform Network (ERN), a network of over forty organizations, advocates for changes in electoral law and the registration of political parties. Toward that end, the coalition organized nationwide electoral hearings on the Electoral Bill and presented its findings to both the Independent Election Commission and the National Assembly.

The third strategy employed by women's organizations in the 1990s entailed engaging the state and its allies in their struggle for women's emancipation and empowerment. The methods used within this framework included lobbying and submitting memoranda, petitions, and amendments to bills to various government bodies (including the Presidential Technical Committee on the review of the 1999 Constitution).

The fourth strategy of educating the populace (both women and men) on women's rights issues and gender discrimination was aimed at creating a popular base from which they could engage the state and its allies in their struggle for gender equality and social justice.

Due to their concerted efforts, the Nigerian social and political landscape is no longer the same. The National Policy on Women has been signed into law; Edo, Cross River, Ekiti, and Enugu state legislatures have enacted laws prohibiting female genital mutilation, child marriages, and the disinheritance of widows.[2] Furthermore, issues regarding wife battering, marital rape, sexuality, and reproductive health that were once viewed as private matters are now part of public political discourse. In addition, the Electoral Bill was amended to reflect the position of the ERN.

It must be noted that in spite of women's activism there has been no significant policy shift at the national level to ensure gender equality. Apart from the National Policy on Women, no major policy statement has been made. However, the fact that the Federal Ministry of Women's Affairs is no longer beholden to the wife of the head of state is a step in the right direction. The ministry now sees women's NGOs not as rivals but as partners in promoting and defending the rights of women.

Challenges Confronting Women's Organizations in the 1990s

The 1999 opening up of democratic space after sixteen years of brutal military dictatorship created opportunities for the advancement of human (especially women's) rights, but it also brought up forces that are trying to thwart the efforts of women and their allies as they strive to put women's rights issues on the national political and democratic agenda. The current challenge confronting women's associations is twofold: they must both consolidate the gains they have achieved so far and defeat the emerging anti-women forces in the emerging democratic landscape (the Shari'aists and the anti-women forces within the legislature). This is definitely not an easy task. But with the alliances women's associations have forged at both the local and international levels and with the popular base they have built among the citizenry, they should continue to move ahead in their struggle for gender equality and in their efforts to put women's rights issues on the national political and democratic agenda.

Concluding Observations

Women's organizations in the 1990s have successfully intervened in the lives of poor urban and rural women through human rights advocacy, credit plans, income-generating projects, and programs on personal empowerment, political sensitization, legal literacy, and legal aid. Some states have signed bills prohibiting female genital mutilation, child marriage, and the disinheritance of widows. Additionally, issues such as marital rape, wife battering, and violence against women, which were once viewed as private matters, are now part of the public political discourse.

Through the efforts of BAOBAB regarding women's human rights, the rights of Muslim women under Shari'a law and the violations of such rights by some northern states are now part of national and international gender and human rights discourse. Furthermore, the research activities of these organizations have generated data for policymakers and researchers on Nigerian women.

The achievements of these organizations lie in the fact that they have used a gendered perspective aimed at transforming existing gender inequalities in Nigeria and have built coalitions among themselves and with like-minded organizations at the national and international levels.

The activities, discourse, and organizational forms of women's engagement in Nigeria began to change in the 1980s. But a total transformation occurred in the 1990s with the emergence and growth of new women's groups that were influenced by the UN's development agenda for women and a global feminist movement. As a result, women's organizations stopped organizing for an improvement in their status and started organizing and demanding total transformation of the existing unequal gender relations. While these organizations have not completely succeeded in overthrowing the structures of patriarchal domination, they have posed serious and significant challenges to it.

This chapter did not cover organizations that are founded, funded, and controlled by wives of the political establishment,[3] a trend that developed in the late 1980s and is now firmly entrenched in the national political landscape. These organizations were not included because they do not focus on eliminating gender inequalities in society. The new feminist organizations that emerged in the 1990s were the focus of this discussion because of their transformatory objectives.

Notes

1. Composed of Marxist scholars teaching at Ahmadu Bello University, Zaria; nationalist scholars, mainly from Ahmadu Bello University, Zaria (as well as northern politicians opposed to the conservative northern ruling class); and Marxist scholars based at the Obafemi Awolowo University, Ile-Ife, respectively.

2. It must be noted that all the states that have enacted laws to end some dehumanizing practices against women are in the southern part of Nigeria, which has a history of female activism. Rather than follow the examples of its southern counterparts, state governments in the predominately Muslim northern region have reintroduced retrogressive Shari'a laws curtailing the rights of women.

3. The Better Life for Rural Women Programme (BLP), The Family Support Programme (FSP) and the Women's Rights Advancement and Protection Alternative (WRAPA) were established during the military era, 1986–1999. These projects were centralized from the federal government to state and local government councils. When civil rule was established, the whole project became decentralized and the wife of the president, the wife of the vice president, and the wives of state governors each initiated their own projects. For example, the president's wife's project is the Child Care Trust and the vice president's wife's project is Women's Trafficking and Child Labor Eradication Foundation (WOTCLEF).

References

Abdullah, H. J. 1994. "Between Emancipation and Subordination: A Study of the Women's Movement in Nigeria." A Consultancy Report for the Ford Foundation.

——. 1997. "Overview of the Gender Discourse in Women's Studies." In *Taking the African Women's Movement into the 21st Century : Report of the First African Women's Leadership Institute, February 22nd to March 14th, 1997,* edited by Bisi Adeleye-Fayemi and Algresia Akwi-Ogojo. Kampala, Uganda: Akina Mama wa Afrika, Africa Office.

Amadiume, Ifi. 2000. *Daughters of the Goddess, Daughters of Imperialism: African Women Struggle for Culture, Power and Democracy.* London: Zed Books.

BAOBAB. 1998a. *Annual Report.* Lagos, Nigeria: BAOBAB.

———. 1998b. "Building a Culture of Women's Rights in Nigeria." *BAOBAB News Sheet* 1 (December 10, 1998). Special edition for the 50th Anniversary of the UDR.

———. 1999. *Annual Report.* Lagos, Nigeria: BAOBAB.

Carrillo, R. 1997. "Summary of the Opening Plenary Session: Global Movements Organising towards the 21st Century." In *Taking the African Women's Movement into the 21st Century: Report of the First African Women's Leadership Institute, February 22nd to March 14th, 1997,* edited by Bisi Adeleye-Fayemi and Algresia Akwi-Ogojo. Kampala, Uganda: Akina Mama wa Afrika, Africa Office.

Community Life Project. 2000. Information Brochure and Annual Report. In author's possession.

COWAN (Country Women's Association of Nigeria). 1993. Information Brochure. In author's possession.

———. n.d. *Rural Development Is a Must.* Akure, Ondo State: COWAN.

GADA (Gender and Development Action). 1996. *A Political Agenda for Nigerian Women.* Lagos: Gender and Development Action.

Lucas, E. T. 2000. "We Decide, They Decide for Us: Popular Participation as an Issue in Two Nigerian Women's Development Programmes." *Africa Development* 25, no. 1–2: 75–98.

Mukasa, S. 1997. "Thematic and Conceptual Issues Affecting the Women's Movement in Africa." In *Taking the African Women's Movement into the 21st Century : Report of the First African Women's Leadership Institute, February 22nd to March 14th, 1997,* edited by Bisi Adeleye-Fayemi and Algresia Akwi-Ogojo. Kampala, Uganda: Akina Mama wa Afrika, Africa Office.

Ogunleye, B. 1997. "African Traditional Responsive Banking Approach: An African Innovation for Poverty Eradication." Paper presented at the Micro-Credit Summit, Washington, D.C., February 2–4.

Toyo, N. 1997. "Women, Organisations and Political Developments." Paper presented at the Centre for Research and Documentation Workshop on "Women's Rights, Politics and Democratisation," Kano, Nigeria, December 26–28.

United Nations. 1996. *The Beijing Declaration and the Platform for Action.* New York: UN Department of Public Information.

Women Empowerment Movement. 2000a. Constitution. Lagos, Nigeria.

———. 2000b. Information Brochure. Lagos, Nigeria.

Women, Law and Development Centre Nigeria. 2003. *The Journey So Far, 1992–2003.* Lagos: Women, Law and Development Centre.

Part Three   *Gender Enactments,*
Gendered Perceptions

9 Constituting Subjects through Performative Acts

Paulla A. Ebron

A chasm between North and South has worked its way into much of contemporary feminist theory. On one side of the divide, proponents generate notions in which the very definition of theory is that which "speaks" to the universals of humanity; on the other side of this gulf, proponents are forced to address specific and concrete issues of colonialism, culture, and conventions of representation. Yet what if this imagined geography of difference could be reconfigured so that these two sources of gender analysis were brought together in a productive conversation? I attempt to prompt such a discussion in this chapter by analyzing the notion of gender as performance as it is currently developed within feminist theory. I engage the resonances of this analytic with three West African contexts.

This essay brings together notions of performance and performativity as they have developed within gender studies over the last fifteen years. In the 1970s, popular discussions of feminism entered the academy and programs in women's studies were established with the goal of making systems of gender differentiation important sites of social analysis. This early history, however complex and diverse, reified conventional notions about what constituted theory. But as many have already suggested, the time has come to engage in a more diverse discussion about gender. Some scholars of Africa have argued that the primacy of gender as a significant category of differentiation is an imposition.[1]

I suggest here that West African studies of gender and Northern feminist studies have a great deal to exchange in a dialogue about performance and performativity. Both "fields" share a critique of binary and stable figurings of male and female. They each argue that performance-based approaches move us away from gender essences toward an appreciation of gender in action. Yet these fields cease to address one another when it comes to the relationship of theory to ethnography. Theory is often imagined as a transcendent, reflexive stance that allows the analyst to stand above context, while ethnography is thought to be located in a single milieu and thus unable to provide a wide-ranging perspective.

Yet beyond the sense that scale or range is what separates the two, I want to suggest that if one accepts the notion that all theories are partial and situated (see Haraway 1988), then the radical distinction between theory and context becomes less significant. Furthermore, this acknowledgment allows us to better appreciate the theoretical insights offered by the dialogue between geographical regions. Without this shift in how theory is conceptualized, our interlocutors can only be imagined as mute *objects* of theoretical investigation. Their insights will only be understood as those created by others from powerful places. The importance of what is being conveyed will not be seen as significant as a contribution to theory. I propose that naturalizing the gulf between North and South has restricted the development of theories of performance and performativity to a particular ethnographic site, the North, by espousing Northern cultural frameworks as if they were universals. Undoubtedly, this point resonates with ongoing critiques of feminism made by women who are not part of a dominant group. Class, race, and global positionings have continually posed a challenge to universalist notions about the subordination of women to men.[2]

In turning to examples of performance of gender in Ghana and Senegambia, I emphasize the importance of a regional knowledge that accentuates genre, style, and the enactment of gender and other social roles as the bases of sociality. The examples I draw upon suggest that people articulate this knowledge not only to each other but also in their dialogues with foreigners in which their representation within international circles is at stake. In the pages that follow, I begin by considering the work of ethnologist and filmmaker Safi Faye in dialogue with that of philosopher Judith Butler, whose theories of gender as performance have been particularly influential in Northern feminist theory. I then apply the theory of gender performance to West African ethnographic projects centered in the regions of Senegambia and Ghana. The Gambia is the site of my own research. In an effort to create the possibility of a wider dialogue, I go beyond an orthodox reading of the theoretical actants; my approach here requires a particular rethinking of ethnographic research and strategies of representation—my own as well as those of others.

Scholars of Africa already tend to engage the performative enactments of West African interlocutors with some self-consciousness. We have re-performed ideas about West African gender systems, explaining to our audiences the complexity of multiple social issues: class, caste, ethnicity, age hierarchies, nation-building, and transnational encounters. Our representations of gender systems have been successful to the extent that they have been persuasive performances —that is, performances informed by regional theories and articulations of gender systems. Northern audiences, however, are not always attentive to this layer of significance. I have found that when they encounter an ethnographic film or text, nonspecialized viewers are quick to imagine "Africans" as authentic embodiments of culture. This view is perhaps encouraged by the prevalent mode of presentation—the documentary. To the extent that international audiences imagine Africans as always already ethnographic subjects, they are apt to pay little attention to the reflexive commentary of the interlocutor, instead waiting for the author's authoritative conclusions to make some generalized statement about the film's message. Yet once we attune ourselves to what respondents are explaining, it is possible to see how interviewees are suggesting a great deal about the relationship of performance to the forms and constraints of social life. I suggest, then, that we need to learn not only how to read ethnographic texts differently but also how to elevate the role of the audience from passive to active viewers. The position of the viewers and the *role* they perform in making interview subjects real is critical, for audiences "perform" the role of reinscribers of taken-for-granted ideas. Our consciousness has been formed through representations about the subject that precede the visual encounter—we are not innocent of preconceived notions.[3] This then allows me to assert the importance of form and the role it plays in the conventions of representation.

Performing Difference

Film is a particularly powerful medium, an "encounter" with the lives of non-Western people for wide-ranging audiences, including academics and students in North America and Europe. Visual texts usefully present a variety of people who appear to "speak" directly to the audience. One is brought into the immediacy of people's lives even while being thousands of miles away. Often overlooked by social science analysts, however, are questions about genre, point of view, and the strategies at work in (re)presenting an individual's life. In taking the films' stories as transparent facts, the inattentive spectator finds unmediated "truth." This same material, when informed by the question of how there might be a theory about the world embedded therein, moves polarized notions of theory and data into closer proximity.

Safi Faye's film *Selbe et tant d'autres* (*Selbe: One Among Many;* Faye 1982) is part of a series of significant films made by Third World women filmmakers. Faye takes as her subject the lives of villagers in the Casamance region of southern Senegal. She wants to tell her audience about the challenges confronting women caught at the far peripheries of the global system. For instance, we learn that women often bear double responsibilities: they must perform the tasks traditionally assigned to women and they must increasingly combine these duties with the added responsibility of their husbands' duties as village men seek employment in urban areas. Faye shows women caring for their children, preparing food, and trying to find money to support their families. The film is not a paean to female tradition but rather a cry of outrage against the burdens of women as they are accentuated by global capitalism. Faye thus urges viewers to imagine and confront the everyday burdens of women who are struggling simply to survive.

Without doubt, these daily concerns are serious matters. Yet the challenges of representation are particularly relevant to the goals of this chapter. Faye uses the images of women's work to *perform* their burdened plight. She creates multiple layers of activities, showing their cumulative impact—the repetition of task after task, duty after duty, thus dramatizing for viewers the oppressive effects of everyday circumstances. Faye draws our attention with striking, even stereotypic images: women with enormous loads of wood carried on their heads, the endless pounding of grain, the enduring need to prepare children's meals and tend to their small comforts. Men, in contrast, are shown as idle; they appear to contribute little toward sustaining daily life. In light of the men's idleness, the women's tasks seem even more arduous and overwhelming. Faye emphasizes this laboriousness by piling image upon image; the images themselves create performative excess.

If viewers are not attuned to the visual strategies Faye is using, they will perceive this film's images as simply "real." The film appears to be about the complaints village women have against men instead of reflectively creating or being created by mediating factors. The technologies of self-making[4] go unacknowledged as ethnographic subjects are injected into an international discussion of the variety of roles of men and women cross-culturally. The drama created by the juxtaposition of filmic images is the means by which Faye communicates her message. Only if our attention as viewers is turned toward the strategies of dramatic enactment can we enter into a direct dialogue with Faye's insights about performativity and the construction of gender.

Thus, one possible "reading" of Safi Faye's film, among many, suggests that *Selbe* offers a metacommentary on gender performance. In this reading, *Selbe* and other ethnographic texts about West Africa urge an expansion of the canon of feminist theory that is configured as Western. For the performance of women's burdens, Faye tells us, is a complaint not just about the plight of women but also about the organization of the global political economy. The domestic scene refers us to international questions of development and inequality. Through her use of repetition in her images of women's burdens, Faye appears to ask her viewers Why are women in Senegal working so hard when you, viewer, have an easy life? Are you like the men caught in your idleness as spectators of the village women's daily struggles? The performance of gender, then, extends beyond local social dynamics to include the global economy, articulating social divisions in the global position of Africa and the world—not an idea that is generally developed in Northern theories of performance. This is an important and instructive insight Faye offers for understanding the making of gendered subjects.

Performance and Performativity

Theories of performance have been put to use in a number of ways. Some use the notion of performance to emphasize the agency of subjects. Supporters of this position highlight the ability of subjects to have a degree of *choice* in how they respond to structures of power. Thus, for example, subjects sometimes appear to speak back defiantly to powerful figures, challenging the structures that dominate their lives. For these theorists, life is a stage, with individuals playing roles strategically in order to get what they want (see Goffman

1959). The key element in this interpretation is consciousness. Subjects are imagined as fully aware of the circumstances to which they are subjected and against which they choose to act.

Other performance theorists emphasize the constitutive nature of performance. In their view, subjects do not choose their roles; rather, those roles are made by a social set of rules. In this model, the "structures of domination" are enacted, as well as evaded, in performance.[5] The notion of performativity challenges the notion of individuals as free-will actors to show how these individuals are enmeshed in the logics of a given society. Theories of performativity stress the pervasiveness of genre conventions through which subjects come to "know" how to express themselves. Their performances must be socially comprehensible, and it is through those performances that we *know* who subjects are. No one has been more influential to these theories of performance and performativity—particularly in feminist circles—than philosopher Judith Butler.

In *Gender Trouble* (1990a) and *Bodies That Matter* (1993), Butler develops the notion of gender performance in order to disrupt the simple binary understanding of gender in the Western imagination. Stimulated by and yet critical of Simone de Beauvoir's assertion that women are not born but made, Butler argues in these two works that gender dispositions are constituted through a set of acts that constantly inform gender identity. Thus she brings performance into everyday life: "Gender is in no way a stable identity or locus of agency from which various acts proceed; rather, it is an identity tenuously constituted in time—an identity instituted through a *stylized repetition of acts*" (1990b, 140).

Butler's argument moves beyond a notion of performance as intentionality. Although many early readers initially interpreted *Gender Trouble* as suggesting that subjects chose what gendered subject they could become, Butler in fact argues something quite different. In affinity with other poststructuralist thinkers, she suggests that social subjects are interpellated, to use Althusser's term, in social orders; they are "hailed" into an ideology (1971). The social matrix becomes a habitus, as Pierre Bourdieu might suggest (1977). Most significant, social structures produce effects. They work their way into subjects, and thus there is no subject without the social realm or, more specifically, without discourse. Butler writes:

> In opposition to theatrical or phenomenological models which take the gendered self to be prior to its acts, I will understand constituting acts not only as constituting the identity of the actor, but as constituting that identity as a compelling illusion, as an object of *belief*. (1990b, 271)

The subject is formed through these performative acts, even though the acts themselves are not scripted in advance. Thus, the social order is made in performance even as it precipitates performative subjects.

Butler's concern about the tendency to naturalize gender roles and attribute sex differences to bodies—believed to be manifested in certain social functions—

leads her to ask what it would mean to see the ways these "social roles" are formed through a repetitive making of subjects. Her attention to gender performance works against the invisibility of performance in the Northern contexts with which she appears most familiar. In fact, Butler's work helps make the invisible visible. Yet in the contexts with which this essay is concerned, gender performance, as this is the means by which research interlocutors were gathered, is so visible that it can be used as a model for other, perhaps less visible, social distinctions. In the West African examples I draw upon here, gender performance is used both to normalize and denormalize other social categories. Gender performance dramatizes social distinctions more generally; it asks interlocutors to pay attention to the making of society. Rather than making transcendent the individual subjects who hide their social dependencies on audiences, they present social dependencies in the sharp light of drama.

To see this, Butler's insights on performance (1990b) may need to be extended to the performance qualities of ethnographic representations, as I argued in considering Safi Faye's film. We are required not only to read ethnographies as performance but also to appreciate the performances enacted within them as themselves theoretical commentaries about the making of subjects and society. Butler and Faye both set us on this path; the work of J. L. Austin carries us further on it. Austin's work—particularly his *How to Do Things with Words* (1975/1962)—is one source of inspiration for Judith Butler. Austin develops the notion of performativity with particular regard to language. He says of philosophers:

> It was for too long the assumption of philosophers that the business of a "statement" can only be to "describe" some state of affairs, or to "state some fact," which it must do either truly or falsely. Grammarians, indeed, have regularly pointed out that not all "sentences" are (used in making) statements: there are, traditionally, besides (grammarians') statements, also questions and exclamations, and sentences expressing commands or wishes or concession. (1)

Austin's theories are easily extended to ethnography. For as long as we imagine ethnographers' and informants' descriptions of gender to merely "state some fact" or function, we miss what these descriptions *do*—enact and perform gender, making gender speak, variously, to domestic and foreign interlocutors.[6] Indeed, Austin's work is essential to the distinction between self-conscious performance and unself-conscious performativity. Gender is performative rather than performance because we learn to do it "naturally," just as we learn to speak without following a text. But language use may or may not be unself-conscious. It crosses the line between self-conscious and unself-conscious, forming a zone in which this distinction is just not the most relevant marker. Butler's Derridean use of Austin draws on the habitual aspects of language use because she applies it to *gender,* a folk category understood in the places she knows best as a category of "nature." But what if we began our theoretical musings somewhere else? What if, for example, gender was locally understood to be a pedagogical category rather than a natural one?

176 *Paulla A. Ebron*

In many places in West Africa, gender is not something that newborns are fully equipped with. The making of women and men is formally performed through age-grade systems that usher children into women and men.[7] Prior to the formal event, children are often viewed as unmarked in any significant way. They remain so until the social work of making gendered subjects is accomplished. "Making" gender is a local system, not a counterintuitive idea that philosophers must establish. Gender does not have to be rescued from nature.

This starting point reminds us that the distinction between performance and performativity is important only because of particularly positioned theories of subject-making. Eighteenth-century European philosophy established that conscious minds are different from unself-conscious bodies and that freedom is that which is not nature. It is within this set of distinctions that performance and performativity appear so different; they repeat the distinctions between body and mind, nature and freedom. However, not all of daily life in the global North has been structured by these distinctions. If we think of table manners, for example, we can see both the importance of self-conscious instruction and the unthinking habits of propriety. Table manners are both performance and performativity. Much of daily life has this quality. It is only the importance of the distinction within philosophy, indeed, that makes it the frame for further philosophical thought—within the same regional genealogy.

Beginning in West Africa frees us from this constraint. Everyday theories of subject-making do not contrast nature and freedom. Instead, the line between performance and performativity is blurred and much happens in the overlapping, alternating, and undistinguished space between them. This space is large enough to include daily habits, community rites, caste knowledges, self-reflection, and exceptionally well-developed forms of personal style. Gender performance in particular is simultaneously taken for granted, carefully taught, and wildly exaggerated—or reversed—for effect. Indeed, within this blurred space between performance and performativity, gender can do kinds of work that have been ignored in Northern theory.

Because gender is both self-consciously and unself-consciously performed, it can teach people about society more generally—just as table manners, both taught and inhabited, can teach Northerners to be civilized. Gender performance is a pedagogical tool that reminds both children and adults of the tensions and distinctions of social life. Perhaps West African theories of the pedagogical qualities of gender performance can open up new research trajectories in the North as well as the South—beyond the fetters of Kant and Descartes.

Austin, Butler, and Faye all inspire a set of questions relevant to our North-South dialogue: What can we learn from the performative visibilities of gender in studies of West Africa? If we move beyond assumptions of straightforward descriptions, how might we re-view the performative qualities of ethnographic representations of West Africa? In the following section, I engage these questions in relation to three ethnographic genres: the interview, the documentary film, and the ethnography. Here, genre is as critical to the process of shaping subjects as is what those subjects actually say about their lives.

Jali Interviews as the Performance of Profession

> To be a heroic *jali* is not only a matter of songs; it is part of your [ordinary] speech.
>
> Woman praise-singer interviewee, Gambia, 1989

In 1989 and 1990, I conducted research in the Gambia with Mandinka *jalis*, praise-singers once tied to royal courts in medieval West Africa. A distinctive class niche within the Gambia and other societies with similar social stratification, this group illuminates how social status is a performance. The contemporary professional role of *jalis* is to sing the praises of their important patrons and act as mediators between families as well as between communities and political figures. *Jalis* figure prominently in a number of ceremonial activities, including naming rituals and weddings. They see their own position as involving performance in two senses: first, they act as musicians, oral historians, and poets; second, they urge patrons to properly perform their roles as important people, and they do this through their own continual performance of status. Thus, their social roles highlight their responsibility in two areas of concern for this essay: in the organization of social life and in performance. *Jalis* bring these together through a continual commentary on the performative nature of social roles.[8]

My initial interest in *jalis* was very much influenced by debates within feminist studies in the late 1980s in the United States, particularly among those who were working to challenge a monolithic representation of women. Determined to move beyond assumptions of the singularity and universality of the category "woman," I planned a research project that would address the multiplicity of kinds of women across social divisions of class, race, ethnicity, nationality, religion, and culture, all of which crosscut gender. Existing literature suggested that Gambian society was divided not only by class and ethnicity but also by hereditary rank—*jalis* are born to their roles. I thought that a study of gender roles among *jalis* might offer important insights about the intersection of caste and other social categories in the construction of gender.

I also appreciated that *jalis* were unlikely to explain inequality in the way Northern feminists understood it. First, the very nature of speaking was differently understood in Mandinka culture. *Jalis* are said to have a liminal social status because they are speakers; those with actual authority do not speak but have others speak for them.[9] The principle aim of Western feminism, by contrast, has been to give voice to women who were perceived as having less power because of their lack of voice.

I imagined that I could gather socially positioned "perspectives" from *jali* women that would clarify the dilemmas of their position. Little had been published at that time on the professional activities and perspectives of *jali* women; thus, I imagined my job, in part, as gathering data.[10] I hoped to use interviews, in particular, thinking that they would offer me intimate and straightforward facts about gender and *jalis*.

I was encouraged in my plans by a young Mandinka woman who agreed to work with me as a research assistant. She was even more determined to gather the facts than I was. As a woman from a highly ranked family, she was curious about the role of *jalis* but was also dubious about whether we would learn the whole truth. Mariama thought that by bringing rationalized, modern research methods to our interviews, as she was trained to do to obtain the truth from her interviewees, we would be able to *make* our *jali* interlocutors tell us everything, even their secrets. "I am going to get the facts out of those *jalis,* Paulla," she would say.

Within a few days of conducting interviews, it became clear that the interview questions that Mariama and I had so carefully prepared were not going to work in the way either of us had naively hoped. We often heard the same answers in interview after interview and, curiously enough, whatever we asked, we received replies that told us about the proper relationships between patrons and *jali* clients. I soon abandoned working so intensely to acquire the factual picture of Mandinka society I might have initially imagined. It was only then that I could begin to hear what the *jalis* we interviewed were actually telling us. *Jali* were explaining to us *our* responsibilities as patrons to them. But more significantly, the *jalis* we interviewed were *enacting* the social distinctions they were describing in telling us the details of their professional lives. They commonly used the interviews as a site of their praise-singing profession. Even in their negotiation of our straightforward questions, they were showing us how social statuses could be performed in ways that were not simply random acts of individual choices but the reproduction of the social categories that framed their lives.

One illustrative example of this performance could be seen in a curiously consistent feature of several interviews. Although I initially addressed the people we were interviewing in Mandinka—or, when it was appropriate, in English—most of the *jalis* directed their responses toward my research assistant, even when I had initiated the question! Why was I being dismissed? I wondered at first. But of course, I was not being slighted; later I would observe this practice as a form of respect generally granted an important person. This was how *jalis* showed us how to differentiate social categories by status. As a foreigner—who was accorded greater respect than my graduate student status ever commanded at home—I was treated as a powerful patron; it was assumed as a matter of course that I would have my assistant do the talking for me.

Matters were somewhat complicated by the fact that my research assistant, because of family background, could herself be a patron. When *jalis* who did not immediately know her found out her family background, as they were likely to do during the course of our conversation, they often began to praise her family name and would not stop until she gave them the monetary compensation that is expected of such praises. My assistant, then, was no longer treated simply as a young woman but rather as a descendent of an illustrious lineage and an individual who needed to be reminded and socialized into the proper role of a patron. In short, interviews, for many of the *jalis* we spoke to, were another opportunity to perform their own status and show those around them—in this case, Mariama and myself—how to *perform* status properly.

In accepting that the interviews would be sites for witnessing and training in performance, I eventually learned about the social intersections of which gender forms a part, but again not as I had originally imagined. A particularly emphatic performance of gender, I learned, can point interlocutors toward the importance of other social divisions, such as age hierarchies or status distinctions among lineages. Thus, for example, a performative rendition of the unfairness of women's subordination was used on several occasions during the interviews to highlight the importance of the individual woman's personal power to overcome such disadvantage. One *jali* woman lamented women's inability to be heard when they speak as *jalis. Jali* women's ability to "speak" and "act" outside of the conventions prescribed for other women in the society would seem to suggest that they have considerably more flexibility, yet differences between men and women exist. *Jali* men's performance of histories, one interviewee complained, is valued over those of *jali* women. *Jali* women's activities are curtailed by gendered expectations; most women cannot, for example, travel as extensively and as freely as men can.

Yet my interviewee made this lament in the context of offering her own expertise as a speaker, historian, and traveler. As the *jali* woman explained, as a daughter of a famous *jali* man, she knew all those histories and genealogies that most women were not allowed to tell outside of the presence of the men with whom they performed. Her superior knowledge and performance, she suggested, were products of her own bold style. Indeed, I found her to be a woman with great flair and thus impossible to ignore. The *jali* explained the aspects that contributed to her style by saying that she owed her skills to great teachers, including her lineage members, as well as to her confidence as a woman with the rights of age and accomplishment. Thus, this *jali* drew our attention to her lineage status and to her status as an older person.

Another influential *jali* woman drew our attention with a different performance style. With mixed dignity and enthusiasm, she explained the stylistic requirements for receiving respect as an older woman from a distinguished *jali* lineage. Of course, she was speaking to us—two younger women who owed her that respect even as she owed us the deference of a *jali*. She explained that if she performs with a group of men who are younger than she, they commonly offer her the money they have received for the performance as a sign of their respect for her age. The woman expresses her appreciation but then returns the money to them. She continued with a parable of lineage, reminding us that the Kouyates rank first among *jali* families. *Jalis* must pay respects to them. This *jali* was not a Kouyate, but she held up the status of her own lineage by observing this rule. So too might we both protect and defer to her.

Jali women proved effective interlocutors in helping explain the intersection of multiple social categories at play among various groups within the Gambia. But, here again, it was not because the *jalis* wanted to share their secret vulnerabilities with us. Instead, they showed how gender performance could remind everyone present of the performative obligations of social interactions and their privileges and dependencies. I was led to this insight only by reinterpreting the interviews themselves as sites of performance. Revisiting the interview material has encouraged me to reread other ethnographic representations of West Africa as offering insights about performance. If we stop looking for unmotivated descriptions of gender roles, we see men and women performing gender to remind others of their social obligations.

"Obaa to you": Performing for the Camera

One of the most striking examples of gender performance in the West African ethnographic accounts is *Asante Market Women* (1982), produced and directed by filmmakers Claudia Milne and anthropologist Charlotte Boaitey (herself a member of the Asante people). Obaa is one of the powerful Asante queenmothers featured in the film. Her ability to pull her group of market women into singing a song about her, urging the women to sing, hitting at those who do not join in the spectacle, easily captures the attention of audiences. This documentary tells the life stories of three market women in Kumasi, Ghana. The central question for the directors is how social positions are constituted along gender lines. As the film proceeds, it becomes impossible to reduce all of society to a binary power relationship in which male equals power and female equals lack of power. Factors such as class, age, and seniority turn social positionings into complicated categories.

Each of the film interviewees is shown to have a significant public role as the head of a division at the central market in Kumasi. West African market women are well known for wielding substantial power and authority.[11] Market women are considered such a formidable bloc within Ghanaian society that they are often the targets of the anger of both politicians and consumers. Yet the filmmakers use the portraits of the three market leaders to argue that these same women lack a parallel authority in the domestic sphere. Contextual material in the film helps orient the analysis of power and authority. Women who are organized into associations administered by a commodity queenmother and her council of elders dominate the market. The duties of the queenmother include setting the prices of her particular line of produce and adjudicating disputes among the market women. In explaining the role of the queenmother, the filmmakers give viewers a glimpse of the lines of power and rank among women as well as between women and men. In the market, the only positions open to men are those of secretary and laborer. The secretary handles market accounts; laborers are hired to carry the produce once the women fix the prices. Notably, the secretary inherits his position from the female members of his family.

The role of queenmother is crucial to the operation of the market, and she is noted for her ability to resolve disputes among the market women. As an elected official of the market, the queenmother also serves as a representative to the state government. An individual who clearly compels the attention of the ethnographers, Queenmother Obaa adroitly used the camera to draw upon the audience's sympathies and win converts to her side. Obaa is tremendously personable. She captures the attention of the filmmakers with her charisma and animated responses.

Obaa urges us to believe that she gets what she wants, though things are not always gained without struggle. In one scene, Obaa arrives at the site of a dispute and calls everyone to attention. The women answer her, she repeats her call, and they answer again. By such gestures, Obaa instructs her constituents in her ultimate authority. Still, her resolution of the dispute is not welcomed by all of the women; some complain that she did not even consult a committee of elders. The narrator also informs us that Obaa has been accused of taking more than her fair share of the profits. Such criticism notwithstanding, Obaa commands her audience with a sense of assurance and confidence. The women ultimately agree to abide by her decision, someone in the background affirming that she is the queenmother and must be respected.

Although the other queenmothers have equally compelling stories to tell, they do so in a different, though no less performative, manner. One of the other queenmothers is seen listening attentively to her council of elders. After hearing all sides, she offers her reflections about the issue and suggests a plan of action. This performance of status through a reserved manner is perhaps not so readily available to one who, like Obaa, rose to power without election to office by the market women.[12]

Feminist scholars with an interest in women's roles in West African societies have argued that the public presence of market women attests to women's considerable power in the public sphere. While the ethnographic record in many places in West Africa indeed seems to point to women's power in the public sphere, their power is not ubiquitous. As the narrator of *Asante Market Women* tells us, "While women like Obaa can settle the most difficult disputes in the market, in the home she would have no such role." An older woman in the film sings of the challenges she finds as a woman living in a polygamous society.

> You have caught a younger tadpole
> Now you regard me as an old crab.
> Well, I think I have something still to offer
> All you can say to me is, "Hey you
> It's the way things are in a marriage."
> You treat me like a piece of discarded cloth
> And I can't take such cruelty any longer.

In scholarly terms, this lament might fit within the rubric of "subordinate discourse"; that is, a subversive commentary on hegemonic discourse.[13] But here the refrain can also be seen as itself a hegemonic discourse. Indeed, this lament is part of the production of gender as discord and drama.

This point becomes even more apparent in a scene in which the men convey their thoughts. A younger man, gesturing animatedly, is discussing his dilemma with some of his male relatives:

My wives inevitably fight. Even the teeth and tongue quarrel and fight. When they argue, I judge the case.

[Another man speaks] Then I will report the guilty one to her family. All you have to do is run and find an elder and say to him, "Look at what's happening. Please come and stop my wives fighting each other."

[Younger man, using hand gestures to emphasize his points] I don't separate them myself. Before, if I restrain my senior wife, she accuses me of helping the junior wife to beat her up. And if I hold the junior wife, there is trouble. So I find someone to help to cool their hearts. When they have calmed down I call my two wives. Both the senior and the junior.

In this scene, too, we see the performance of gender as discord. Husbands are tested to control their wives, thus showing their own worth within male as well as male-female hierarchies. The use of dramatic tension to produce the sociality of gender is created through play, manipulation, and performative rhetorics that help establish one's ground. In another scene in the film, a group of women gather for the filmmakers' questions and they talk about their relationships with their husbands. One woman comments on how useless men are; the other women laugh in agreement. Obaa's thoughts about her marital situation are telling. Away from the market, she narrates her story in a personalized interview, provoked into conversation by a member of the film crew.

> The marriage was never happy. Marriage, no matter how much time you spend, there is still a lot to discuss. It really is a long, long, long story. You could talk about it—walking all the way from here to Europe—and still have more to say about marriage. Men in Asante are very, very, very bad.

Note the extended emphasis—"long, long, long" and "very, very, very"—and the distance one would have to travel to get at the story of marriage. Overemphasizing the differences between men and women, she rhetorically creates gender difference as a dramatic and much-fought-over social category.

Their domestic complaints notwithstanding, market women enjoy considerable public control over the activities of the laborers and secretaries, men who have virtually no power in the market. Thus, it becomes difficult to easily frame as a universal precept the concept of men as those with power and women as those without power. Indeed, one of the insights gleaned from research conducted in West African societies is that power and authority are not determined solely on the basis of one's rank. Patrons of considerable status regularly defer to their clients of lesser status to negotiate certain situations for them. Among the market women, age distinctions are clearly present and serve to establish lines of authority. Queenmothers and the council of women oversee the association. In this instance, older market women control the labor of younger women and men. Yet if one is attentive to their discussions about marriage, one can see that junior women have a momentary advantage over older women when they become the latest co-wife chosen by their husbands. Strikingly absent from the discussion, however, is the fact that older wives can require that junior wives perform certain tasks—another case in which the labor of junior women is under the authority of senior women. Here again, then, a focus on gender highlights the relevance of other social categories, such as age.

Performative Encounters in an Ethnography of Development

Each of these ethnographic interlocutions allows for an appreciation of the ways it is possible to be aware of the available performative genres and their significance in creating gender performance in the process of conducting interviews. My last example addresses the question of how gender systems get configured in an ethnographic text. Richard Schroeder's ethnography of development projects in the Gambia, *Shady Practices* (1999), suggests how gender performance is central to social science research in Africa and in international development agencies. Schroeder analyzes two development projects that draw men and women in divergent ways: a men's agroforestry project and a women's garden project, both in a village in the Upper River Division of the Gambia. The organization of labor and land created by the projects caused the two groups to compete for resources, and much of the subsequent drama is played out in marital metaphors and contests. For the purposes of my discussion, I focus on the women's projects.

Schroeder portrays development as negotiated in rhetorical battles between women and men in which each use gender performance to formulate a vision of proper social goals and practices. The expectation that men and women might perform the tasks of development differently is used to consider possible village futures. The differences between men and women are sharpened and dramatized in order to discuss the opportunities and costs of development. In other words, ordinary habits of gender performance are brought to bear on particular historical social events, bringing them into ongoing discussions of self and society.

The drama of daily life in the village that Schroeder describes centers on the impact of the women's so-called second husbands. In the 1980s, a number of women's garden projects were sponsored by international development agencies and they became a lucrative business, particularly for women who organized collective work teams or horticultural groups to cultivate the cash crops. Yet not everyone in the village celebrated the success of the garden plots. Most notably, it became a contentious issue between village men and women. Schroeder recounts:

> Many men publicly ridiculed the gardens, dismissing them derisively as a waste of time. They also often impugned their wives directly for what they saw as a lack of commitment to their marriage. It became commonplace for men to complain that the women had taken new "husbands." Thus if a man's wife was busy working in

her garden and someone asked her whereabouts, he often replied, "She's gone to her husband." (1999, 41)

The "second husbands" were thus the garden plots women tended in addition to performing their other regular household duties, including family farming activities. In the ensuing drama between the sexes, men argued that the tasks that were sacrificed to accommodate the garden work were the women's marital duties. Men lamented the fact that women no longer brought water to their guests or played the role of proper hostesses. According to the men's dramatic renditions, these responsibilities had now fallen—unthinkably—on the husband. The women joined in the fray. Rather then countering the men's claims that they had taken "second husbands," they agreed—albeit sardonically. Schroeder writes:

> One grower underscored the point dramatically by asserting that not just her garden but also the well bucket she used to irrigate her vegetables was her husband, because everything she owned came from it. Playing to the laughter of several women gathered nearby, she spoke with her voice rising in mock rage: This [indicating her shoes]; this [her earrings]; this [miming the food she put into her mouth]; and this [clutching her breast to indicate the food she fed her children]— they all come from this bucket! That's why the bucket is my husband!! (43)

To call a bucket a second husband is even more insulting than it might first appear, because it is conventionally assumed in this society that people marry first for family arrangements and second for choice.

The women's garden plots yielded considerable cash flow, particularly when compared to the resources the husbands were able to generate from their farming activities. The husbands, upset by what they saw as their wives' abandonment of their domestic responsibilities, responded in various ways. Schroeder's informants provided two possible scripts that men were said to follow:

> The husband returned home unannounced from a firewood-cutting expedition, or a hard day of work on the family's fields. He arrived at a time when he knew his wife was either in her garden or had yet to draw the evening water supply from the town tap. He then demanded to know why there was no bath water waiting for him, complaining: "I came from the farm very tired and dirty, and this woman wouldn't even help me with bath water!" (53)

Or a second scenario:

> He intervened as his wife administered a beating to one of his children for some obvious infraction: "How can you be so cruel to your daughter!" The development of these scenarios provoked a great deal of laughter among my informants. When asked why they found these stories so funny, they explained [that] they are so typical! (53)

In these situations, we can see that internal domestic negotiations are conducted through a performance of gender conflicts—"a bitter war of words," as Schroeder characterized it. Through these rhetorical challenges, the social places of men and women become important markers of the ways in which gender is negotiated both through speech acts and in the actual practices of the everyday. In turn, through such speech acts and everyday practices, gender is itself negotiated. In addition to its relevance to the contest of roles within the family, gender performance, as Schroeder's study reveals, is also a feature of the international development scene. Both women and men tapped international development projects to make their points about local society. Through their conflictual gender performances, they hoped not only to establish livelihood practices that would benefit them but also to teach villagers—both men and women—a better vision of village life. Development, indeed, was pedagogical, but not perhaps as its international agents had intended.

Schroeder's text also reveals something about ethnographic research as performance and about the performative position of the ethnographer. Schroeder recounts how he practiced what he refers to as "cross-gender" research and comments upon his inability to escape his performance of social location. He notes that Western women ethnographers commonly assume the role of honorary male, a status that affords them, as outsiders, access to arenas from which most other women in the society are excluded. The issue for Schroeder was problematic in a different way: How does one gain trust among a group with which one is not supposed to be associating? In negotiating a working relationship with the village women, Schroeder and his male research assistant took care to ensure that all their arrangements were made in public view; in one case, this involved access to an informant husband.

Prior to this particular research project, Schroeder had previously worked in the Gambia, and his fluency in Mandinka helped him to gain the confidence of the women gardeners. But as their work with the women developed, Schroeder and his research assistant found themselves shunned by the men of the village. The men became suspicious of him and referred to him as an outsider, or *toubob,* because he broke with local understandings about the proper place of men vis-à-vis women. The idea that Schroeder and his research assistant were at all interested in women's activities opened them up to ridicule by the village men. The men even suggested that his research would be worthless without their input. At one point, some of the men in the village invoked his authority in an effort to get back at the women, but the women chose not to fall for their ploy and asked Schroeder about the issue directly. In this instance, men and women were both trying to enlist a researcher in their dramatic enactment of male-female conflict.

Schroeder's research experience was both a self-conscious strategy and an interpellation into local practices that went beyond his control. In deciding to work with women, he entered the rhetorical gender wars through which development itself was discussed and negotiated. He could not stand by and watch in this pedagogical process of gender performance. His own actions were interpreted as both performance and performativity and his research required learning just what this blurred space entailed.

Conclusion

The three examples discussed here provide a sense of the negotiation and performance of gender in a variety of encounters. In each case, subjects use gender performance as a way of explaining social dilemmas more generally, dramatically illustrating how performance creates social divisions, conflicts, and communities. In this way, gender becomes a way into understanding other forms of social distinction. It is my hope that these perspectives can enlarge and deepen "Northern" feminist theory in ways that allow researchers to "use gender as a category of analysis."[14] They allow us to see the ways in which performance and performativity are not the separate analytic categories they are often assumed to be in Western contexts. Instead, the blurred or undifferentiated zone between performance and performativity turns out to be a productive space for theories of gender. In particular, I have shown the importance of pedagogical and rhetorically dramatic gender performances as elaborated in West Africa. I imagine such performances are important in other places as well, although they are not always at the center of local theories of the self and society.

Gender performance in some societies in West Africa instructs about social categories, including class, age, and rank, as well as the possibilities of development projects and global economic inequalities. This attention to multiple differences offers a useful dialogue with the agenda of feminists of color in the West and international feminists who pushed for an expansion of the men/women binary to include categories of race and class as mediating factors in the formation of gender identities. In the spirit of challenging the non-sited aspects of theory, the ideological primacy of the transcendent, I note the efforts of Bourdieu (2001) to analyze the reproduction of male power in Western society. In one of his last works before his death, Bourdieu engaged the question of the habitus that so naturalizes gender relations in Western societies. His attempts form a nice bridge between the culture-bound assumptions of the West by making them the subject of ethnographic inquiry as part of a larger effort to generate a cross-cultural dialogue about gender performativity. Those Western assumptions make it difficult to see that gender dynamics and the constitution of subjects are mired in some of the same processes that one can observe in the instances discusses throughout this chapter. Each of the cases presented here makes critical suggestions about the methodological considerations when analyzing gender as a performative category.

Notes

My sincere appreciation to the volume's editors for their thoughtful suggestions. I also express my gratitude to Gracia Clark and her assistance in translating the words of the song in *Asante Market Women,* "Obaa to you." Thank you also to Anna Tsing and Kathryn Chetkovich for their insightful comments.

1. For recent discussion of the applicability of gender as a privileged site of analysis see the collection *Africa Gender Scholarship* (Arnfred et al. 2004).

2. Among the most prominent anthologies see Hull, Bell-Scott, and Smith (1982); Imam, Mama, and Sow (1997); Alexander and Mohanty (1997); and Kaplan, Alarcón, and Moallem (1999).

3. While the emphasis in cultural studies has been on the radical potential of audiences to remake hegemonic discourse, I am at this moment less inspired by this investment in audience potential. I want to look at the structural position of audiences along national interest lines, parallel to class formation. Of concern to me is process of the "manufacturing of consent" on the part of U.S. citizens through representations of the Other. Of course there are fissures in this bloc. But it is first necessary to ask how a certain kind of consensus is achieved among the general public.

4. Technologies of self-making is a phrase I use in the Foucauldian sense of the disciplinary techniques bound to social practices that "make" the modern subject.

5. Althusser's classic example of subjects being hailed by police and the subject responding even when they have not committed a crime introduced the notion of interpellation. Giddens offered a key term in articulation between society and subjects, structuration. Here the notion of individual acts is part of a social contest that helps inform how one relates to the society they are a part of. Bourdieu's notion of a theory of practice where "doxa" is sustained through habitus also notes the close tie between social rules and subject formation. See Althusser (1971); Bourdieu (1977); and Giddens (1987).

6. A point of confusion, I submit, for Western readers of texts and viewers of films, is the reification of a body-mind split, the Cartesian divide that posits a distinction between consciousness and acts, between performativity and performance.

7. A classic source is Boone's *Radiance from the Waters: Ideals of Feminine Beauty in Mende Art* (1986), which offers a compelling look at women's initiation ceremonies in Sierra Leone.

8. A longer account of this discussion can be found in Ebron (2002).

9. See Camara (1976), Irvine (1973, 1989), and Wright (1989).

10. Since this time, several good sources on *jali* women have appeared. Thomas Hale's studies of griots (1991, 1998) are valuable sources. Duran's dissertation (1999) of women *jeli* musicians from Mali is also extremely informative.

11. Several classic texts substantiate the importance of market women. Among these are Clark (1994), White (1987), and Robertson (1984).

12. According to Clark (1994), the usual means of becoming a queenmother is through election to office by the other market women within one's commodity sphere. In practice, however, the positions are usually secured at least in part by political moves, even though these moves are made to appear as if they were generated by the market women themselves. Being elected and supported by the reigning state political party, however, requires a different sort of negotiation. Obaa is in a difficult position, for her stability depends upon the favor of this elected party, which is itself vulnerable to dismissal.

13. See, for example, Boddy (1989) and Abu-Lughod (1986).

14. This is a reference taken from Joan Scott's (1988) essay of the same title in *Gender and the Politics of History.*

References

Abu-Lughod, Lila. 1986. *Veiled Sentiments: Honor and Poetry in a Bedouin Society.* Berkeley: University of California Press.

Alexander, M. Jacqui, and Chandra Talpade Mohanty, eds. 1997. *Feminist Genealogies, Colonial Legacies, Democratic Futures.* New York: Routledge.

Althusser, Louis. 1971. "Ideology and Ideological State Apparatus." In *Lenin and Philosophy and Other Essays,* 121–173. Translated by Ben Brewster. London: New Left Books.

Arnfred, Signe, Bibi Bakare-Yusuf, Edward Waswa Kisiang'ani, Desiree Lewis, Oyeronke Oyewumi, and Filomina Chioma Steady. 2004. *African Gender Scholarship: Concepts, Methodologies, and Paradigms.* Dakar: CODESRIA.

Austin, J. L. 1975/1962. *How to Do Things with Words.* Cambridge: Harvard University Press.

Boddy, Janice. 1989. *Wombs and Alien Spirits: Women, Men, and the Zār Cult in Northern Sudan.* Madison: University of Wisconsin Press.

Boone, Sylvia. 1986. *Radiance from the Waters: Ideals of Feminine Beauty in Mende Art.* New Haven, Conn.: Yale University Press.

Bourdieu, Pierre. 1977. *Outline of a Theory of Practice.* Translated by Richard Nice. Cambridge: Cambridge University Press.

———. 2001. *Masculine Domination.* Translated by Richard Nice. Stanford, Calif.: Stanford University Press.

Butler, Judith. 1990a. *Gender Trouble: Feminism and the Subversion of Identity.* New York: Routledge.

———. 1990b. "Performative Acts and Gender Constitution: An Essay in Phenomenology and Feminist Theory." In *Performing Feminisms: Feminist Critical Theory and Theatre,* edited by Sue-Ellen Case, 270–282. Baltimore, Md.: Johns Hopkins University Press.

———. 1993. *Bodies That Matter: On the Discursive Limits of "Sex."* New York: Routledge.

Camara, Sory. 1976. *Gens des Parole: Essai sur la condition et le role des griots dans la societe malinke.* Paris: Mouton.

Clark, Gracia. 1994. *Onions Are My Husband: Survival and Accumulation by West African Market Women.* Chicago: University of Chicago Press.

Duran, Lucy. 1999. "Stars and Song Birds: Mande Female Singers in Music, Mali 1980–99." Ph.D. diss., University of London, School of Oriental and African Studies.

Ebron, Paulla. 2002. *Performing Africa.* Princeton: Princeton University Press.

Faye, Safi. 1982. *Selbe: One Among Many.* New York: Women Make Movies.

Giddens, Anthony. 1987. *Social Theory and Modern Sociology.* Stanford, Calif.: Stanford University Press.

Goffman, Erving. 1959. *Presentation of Self in Everyday Life.* New York: Doubleday.

Hale, Thomas. 1991. *Griottes of the Sahel.* Video. Pennsylvania: Penn State University.

———. 1998. *Griots and Griottes: Masters of Words and Music.* Bloomington: Indiana University Press.

Haraway, Donna J. 1988. "Situated Knowledges: The Science Question in Feminism and the Privilege of Partial Perspective." In *Simian, Cyborgs, and Women: The Reinvention of Nature,* edited by Donna J. Haraway, 183–201. New York: Routledge.

Hull, Gloria, Patricia Bell-Scott, and Barbara Smith, eds. 1982. *All the Women Are White, All the Blacks Are Men, But Some of Us Are Brave.* Old Westbury, N.Y.: Feminist Press.

Imam, Ayesha, Amina Mama, and Fatou Sow, eds. 1997. *Engendering African Social Sciences.* Dakar: CODESRIA.

Irvine, Judith. 1973. "Caste and Communication in a Wolof Village." Ph.D. diss., University of Pennsylvania.

———. 1989. "When Talk Isn't Cheap: Language and Political Economy." *American Ethnologist* 16, no. 2: 248–267.

Kaplan, Caren, Norma Alarcón, and Minoo Moallem, eds. 1999. *Between Women and Nation: Nationalisms, Transnational Feminisms and the State.* Durham, N.C.: Duke University Press.

Milne, Claudia, with Charlotte Boaitey. 1982. *Asante Market Women.* New York: Filmmaker's Library.

Robertson, Claire. 1984. *Sharing the Same Bowl: A Socioeconomic History of Women and Class in Accra, Ghana.* Bloomington: Indiana University Press.

Schroeder, Richard. 1999. *Shady Practices: Agroforestry and Gender Politics in the Gambia.* Berkeley: University of California Press.

Scott, Joan Wallach. 1988. "Gender: A Useful Category of Historical Analysis." In *Gender and the Politics of History,* edited by Joan Wallach Scott, 28–50. New York: Columbia University Press.

White, E. Frances. 1987. *Sierra Leone's Settler Women Trader on the Afro-European Frontier.* Ann Arbor: University of Michigan Press.

Wright, Bonnie L. 1989. "The Power of Articulation." In *Creativity of Power: Cosmology and Action in African Societies,* edited by W. Arens and Ivan Karp, 39–57. Washington, D.C.: Smithsonian Institution Press.

10 Gender After Africa!

Eileen Boris

I want to turn the question "What impact has gender as a category of analysis had on the study of Africa?" upside down, so to speak, and ask, if somewhat flippantly, "What can Africa do for gender?" I make this move not to replicate the colonialist expropriation of African peoples and land, long a characteristic of Western investigation that found objects/subjects of research in the subcontinent and forced its intellectual framework on them. Rather, I enter this conversation in debt to Africans and others whose labors challenge essentialist conceptions of gender that have enmeshed women's studies in the very binary oppositions that research on women, gender, and sexualities had sought to escape. Informing my analysis is the proposition that those from other fields who seek to develop women's studies as a site of knowledge production have much to learn from the work of Africanists.

Feminist theory has consisted of writings by Westerners attached to an intellectual tradition that, until recently, misunderstood its own concrete, historically constructed gender systems as universal. By the early 1980s, an initial challenge to this feminist epistemology had come from within by women—especially black women, lesbian women, and black lesbian women—whose identities always appeared with a modifier that branded them as "other" to the white, middle-class, heterosexual standpoint that remained unarticulated. A second critique developed from those labeled "Third World women," who not only saw the reigning knowledge systems as partial but strenuously protested their own objectification as victims of backward gender relations and sexual oppression in need of saving by Western feminists. Intersectionality and transnationalism became the new catchwords of gender analysis in response to these critiques (Mohanty 2003). But theory remained abstract, subject to timelessness and prone to essentialism. To combat ethnocentrism, I argue, we need to view gender as a product of location, negotiated by women and men with discursive and performative vocabularies that they deploy but do not command into existence. In short, we need to take the historicity of gender seriously. That Western knowledge was and continues to exist as a construction becomes apparent when we turn to formulations derived from distinct contexts that present alternative meanings of and ways of doing gender.

Here Africa with a continent's worth of multiple indigenous, colonial, and national pasts enters my analysis. Such diversity complicates any tendency to flatten gender analysis to a single presentation, illuminating even while questioning gender as we in women's studies have come to define the term. In this chapter, I reflect on three crucial interventions African scholarship brings to the reconsideration of gender as a category of analysis: an unsettling of the relationship between the biological and social that reinforces trends within feminist thought; a questioning of the privileging of gender over other social attributes, especially age, lineage, kinship, and wealth, thus complicating understandings of "intersectionality"; and a revealing of gender as an expression of power through historical struggles over colonization and liberation. The following discussion makes no claims to comprehensiveness but rather draws upon a selective reading of Africanist scholarship to rethink the engagement of women's studies with gender.[1]

The Biological and the Social

Social constructionist to its core, much of contemporary Western feminist thought refutes Freud's dictum that biology is destiny. By the early 1980s, "gender" as a category of analysis had come to distinguish the biological, which initially referred to male and female, from the cultural, which was associated with masculine and feminine. As Joan Scott (1988, 2) explained, "Gender is the social organization of sexual difference. But this does not mean that gender reflects or implements fixed and natural physical differences between women and men; rather gender is the knowledge that establishes meanings for bodily differences."

Nonetheless, as Linda Nicholson (1994, 82–83) points out, Scott and most social constructionists remain tied to a "biological foundationalism" that not only privileges the body but assumes "that distinctions of nature, at some basic level, manifest themselves in or ground sex identity, a cross-culturally common set of criteria for distinguishing women and men." Nicholson more fruitfully argues that "we cannot look to the body to ground cross-cultural claims about the male/female distinction" nor can we forget that the body and how people think about it constitute in themselves historical and culturally constituted variables. Her insight that bodies, whether consisting of two sexes or reflecting multiple genders, generate identities but only in terms of specific historical contexts seems particularly salient when we turn to Africa.

Since the mid-1980s, feminist theorists in the West also have focused on the study of men and masculinities in order to sever the denotation of gender with "woman." Scholarship has, as Robyn Wiegman notes, "draw[n] our attention to the constructedness of masculinity and its complex dependence on discourses of sexual difference (sometimes with and sometimes without the figure of women), thereby making visible and theoretically credible analyses of the constitutional performativity of a variety of masculinities" (2001, 355–388). This shift came with those "post" moves—postmodernism, poststructuralism, and postcolonialism—that considered desires, identifications, and subjectivities (Hunt 1996). The sexed body and regulatory discourses that discipline that racialized gendered body, a body marked by class and nation as well, replaced an earlier language of sex roles and even the sexual division of labor, certainly that of separate spheres, that previously had dominated scholarship. Current approaches emphasize subjectivities that derive from the body (Canning 1999).

Much of this literature belongs to queer projects that seek to deconstruct heteronormativity and provide a critical praxis for female masculinity or for masculinity without biological maleness, for drag kings and queens and other performances that subvert the feminine and masculine, that separate bodies from identities (Jagose 1996). As exemplified by the work of Judith Halberstam (1998), identification replaces corporeality as masculinity disconnects from a male body. This very powerful insight refuses to make biological sex a precondition for gender as it separates sex from gender and sex from reproduction—an anti-fertility stance out of keeping with many African societies that suggests how a multiplicity of uses stems from disconnecting the biological from the social.

Perhaps Africanists exaggerate when contending that "the distinction between gender and biological sex has come as something of a revelation to Western scholars" (Herbert 1993, 19). For over two decades, U.S. feminists have recognized what, according to Herbert, "Africans have known all along[,] that gender is socially, not biologically, created and that it evolves over the life cycle."[2] Though more influenced by Marxism than most work in women's history,[3] scholarship on Africa partook of the linguistic or gender turn simultaneously with other historical and feminist writing. Its attention to culture, language, and representation perhaps was overdetermined, as appropriate for an interdisciplinary practice drawing heavily on anthropology and ethnographic methodology that has focused on words and things. But in contrast to research on Western societies, approach and place have reinforced each other to illuminate a separation between biology and gender that apparently distinguished numerous precolonial settings.

This distinction between the biological and the social particularly comes through the pioneering work on gender by Ifi Amadiume (1987) on the Igbo and Oyeronke Oyewumi (1997) on the Yorùbá. Both African scholars challenge Western epistemologies as applied to their cultures of origin, blaming colonization for disrupting modes of thought no less than ways of living. Both make much of gender-neutral pronouns and designations, such as child and adult, within indigenous languages. However, it is difficult to derive gender ideology from grammatical neutrality. This linguistic characteristic also exists, for example, in Finnish, the language of a culture and society where greater gender equality (relative to Anglo-American countries) lays nestled within an embodied gendered system similar to other Western formations (Rantalaiho 1997, 16–30). That is, linguistic conventions and gendered embodiments lack any automatic correspondence, though they very well may hold keys to a people's mindset.

Nonetheless, epistemology apparently distinguished the precolonial Igbo and Yorùbá from Western thought. As Oyewumi explains, "body-reasoning" stems from Western enlightenment privileging of sight over other senses and rejection of an overlapping between the worlds of ancestors and spirits and this one. Claiming to speak from the Yorùbá standpoint, Oyewumi perhaps equates elite understandings with an entire "frame of reference," but she certainly differentiates Yorùbá ontology from Western. "The social category 'woman'—anatomically identified and assumed to be a victim and socially disadvantaged—did not exist," she declares (1997, 79).

Amadiume (1987) too rejects any necessary equation of the social with the physical body. "The flexibility of Igbo gender construction meant that gender was separate from biological sex. Daughters could become sons and consequently male. Daughters and women in general could be husbands to wives and consequently males in relation to their wives," she asserts (15). Women who became male chiefs or kings married wives, though they might have male lovers.[4] As Judy Rosenthal has concluded from the "cross-gender possession" and "same-gender ritual marriage" among southern Ewe and Mina practitioners of Vodu, gender could travel as a "sort of trope rather than a reality stuck to the bodies of real women and men" (1997, 194, 199), an insight quite in keeping with the performative understandings of gender associated with Judith Butler (1990) and now prevalent within women's studies. But physicality could matter: as Nwando Achebe (2003) has shown, a female king, Ahebi Ugbabe, undermined her structural masculinity by trying to appropriate "physical *manhood*" by sponsoring a masquerade belonging only to men.

But lest we label such designations as gender-bending, Amadiume and Oyewumi quickly—perhaps too quickly—dismiss attempts to find a queer past in such social relations.[5] They reunite sexuality with biology, even as they separate sexuality from gender when it comes to female bodies performing male-designated roles. Yet purely functionalist explanations for female husbands—such as lack of an elder son, the need for labor power, or protection of land for the lineage—actually impose "a 'male' characterization upon a situation where none necessarily exists," maintaining "male-identification regarding their roles," Wairmū Ngarūiya Njambi and William E. O'Brien have argued (2000, 2). Typical of such analysis, Leslie Gray and Michael Kevane trace how Kenyan women even in the 1990s "circumvent male authority and gain or maintain control over land through the institution of female husbands" (1999, 31). Such characterizations ironically reinforce the gender dimorphism of the West by elevating the male social position (Njambi and O'Brien 2000). Oyewumi, however, would respond that only a Western standpoint would equate male with husband in the first place.

And perhaps only an Africanist would connect the male with fertility. Iron smelters in Herbert's own study contain "both sides of the procreative equation, male and female, father and mother." They were symbolically like the king, "responsible for the fertility of his people in the widest sense," whether embodying "masculinity and femininity within himself" or by gaining authority through designation by a queen mother or marriage to "a female emblem." Herbert contends that "like smiths, kings and hunters must be able to move back and forth between the domains of gender and age that hem in ordinary people; it is necessary to the exercise of their power and at the same time evidence of that power" (1993, 228). Still, gender only accounts for part of their power, for "the true fathers are ancestral, the dead smelters of the past." This emphasis on the ancestors reinforces analysis that refuses to stress gender as if gender exists alone.

Others argue for notions of equality more in tune with "difference" cultural-ists and African American womanists than with the dominant equal rights tra-dition of Western feminism. Nkiru Nzegwu (2001) provocatively has claimed that the West embraced "a mono-sex system" that privileges what is male, judg-ing equality by characteristics or standards shaped by men's lives. "Equality as equivalence stacks the odds against women." But an African "dual-sex" system emphasizes complementarity based on separate but equally significant contri-butions to the well-being of the society. Like kinship categories, it is relational, while the Western hegemonic binary male/female is absolute (Arnfred 2002).

Unprivileging Gender

To the extent that gender is the subject of women's studies, it tends to overshadow other markers of social identity and individual subjectivity that ex-ist in tandem to form the category "woman" or "man" and forge actual women and men. Critical race—and other women of color—feminists introduced the concept of "intersectionality" to move beyond additive conceptions of gender, race, class, and nation.[6] I have argued that we are not only gendered or raced but racialized and gendered in specific culturally and historically determined ways: class, age, sexuality, ethnicity, disability, and a host of other attributes combine with racialized gender, even though one or more factors might be sa-lient in a given situation or relation. And identity is made and remade through interaction, relation, and political struggle as well as through discourse and rep-resentation (Boris 1995).

Africanists especially stress the significance of kinship for understanding gender, thus further undermining essentialism. They have linked identity to town of origin, which is associated with lineage, and have measured status spa-tially in terms of distance from the center of the family compound, which is related to kinship position (Sudarkasa 1986, 91–103). In a pioneering contribu-tion to the field of women's studies, Marxist feminist anthropologist Karen Sacks (1979, 9–10) made theory out of such African particularities. Complicat-ing Engels on the origins of women's oppression, in 1979 she turned to the gatherer-hunter Mbuti of Zaïre, the nonstate Lovedu and Mpondo societies of South Africa, the East African kingdom of Buganda, the city of Onitsha, and the kingdom of Dahomey to chart the relationship between kinship position and mode of production. The Mbuti stressed nongendered age relationships, "the most central of which was that of parent-producer-adult" instead of dis-tinguishing between sisters and wives. In contrast, the Lovedu and Mpondo in differing ways "had kin corporate modes of production with patrilineal corpo-rations; wives lived on and labored for the husband's estate" and so, she concluded, "sister and wife were contrasting productive relationships." With the undermining of corporate kin groups in Buganda, the status of wife became more significant than that of sister. Where corporate lineages retained control of land, as in Onitsha, sisters retained more power than where lineages became weaker, as in Dahomey. Market or trader associations contained the remnants of such power.

Later comparisons of wives to daughters, in contrast, generally elevate kinship itself over its centrality in constructing economic relations. Oyewumi stresses "the mode of recruitment into the lineage, not gender" (1997, 44–45). The embodied female born into a lineage shared "social distinction" with the anatomical male also born into the lineage. Indeed, women possessed multiple identities: as "an *aya* (in-marrying resident) and usually also an *ìyá* (mother) in her marital lineage" but also "an *ọmọ* (offspring/member of the lineage) and an *ọkọ* (owner/member) in her natal home." The latter, Oyewumi notes but fails to elaborate, "gave her access to its means of production" (60). Amadiume records the answer of a Nnobi elder to the question, "Why are patrilineage daughters given so much power?"—"Because, had they been men, they would have had the same power as lineage men. . . . For this reason, lineage wives will bow down their heads to lineage daughters" (1987, 60). Confirming distinctions between women, this response ironically reinscribes the primacy of men, if not gender.

"Relation" became a key term for breaking through static notions of intersectionality. Before colonial disruptions, as Dorothy L. Hodgson (1999) shows, the Maasai in Tanzania produced a gender system where women's "prestige, respect, and economic security" depended not only on their own age but also on the status of their sons as *ilmurran,* "the circumcised ones," or warriors. Then they could wear "special earrings." Among men, a generational hierarchy distinguished between the *ilayiok,* or uncircumcised (boys), the *ilmurran, ilpayioni* (or junior elders), and elders/senior elders. Hodgson explains "the structural tension and contrasts between *ilmurran* and elders" through a set of binaries— "communal/individual, wild/domesticated, freedom/authority, sex for pleasure/ sex for procreation"—symbolized by the displayed genitalia of the *ilmurran* in contrast to the covered genitalia of the elders. Women developed their position in relation to men's: uncircumcised girls gained freedom from relationships with *ilmurran* lovers, even as respect depended on working for mothers and obeying parents; wives joined husbands in household management, winning additional respect when the boys in whom they had instilled "the ideals of warriorhood" became circumcised and entered the ranks of *ilmurran.*

Age itself appears relational and thus social. For Oyewumi, pronoun distinctions reveal "age relativity" as "the pivotal principle of social organization." Seniority thus becomes "situational in that no one is permanently in a senior or junior position; it all depends on who is present in any given situation" (1997, 40, 42). Rather than defined chronologically, then, age is measured temporarily by when an individual enters a lineage, and it confers power and prestige. Emphasizing how gender alters over the life course, Stephan Miescher (this volume) shows elderhood, as with senior masculinity or the position of ɔpanyin in twentieth-century Kwawu, to be open to women as well as men. Ɔpanyin represents a social rank rather than a chronological age. It signifies experience and maturity; holders of this status often engage in "dispute resolution," sometimes serving as an appointed or elected government or church official. Women particularly became noted for their mediation skills. Recognized by the community, one became an ɔpanyin in relation to others and on the basis of specified attributes rather than primarily on account of age or gender.

Obtaining wealth or attaining age rather than maleness or femaleness, then, could determine rank. Amadiume offers the example of women who became ekwe, a title available only to women of economic means able to command the labor of others to generate additional wealth—either through the practice of igbu ohu (woman-to-women marriage) or through the services of volunteers convinced that the goddess had designated a woman claiming the title for this honor. Such wealthy women could hand over domestic labor to wives. This arrangement provides new perspective on the practice throughout U.S. history of employers of household labor referring to their servants as family and helps deconstruct the women's liberation lament, "I need a wife." Labor that itself represented wealth but also directly produced wealth for female husbands among the Igbo finds an equivalent in the United States, where household labor has enabled the employment of professional women, generating an indirect contribution to wealth formation that reinforces economic inequalities (Ehrenreich 2002). In some precolonial societies, differences among women become expressed in terms of kinship position in some precolonial societies, but in the United States, racialized and gendered class relations distinguish women, no matter what terms of endearment women use to describe their maids.

Similarly, maleness alone failed to make a "Big Man"; for that designation, a man needed wealth and extensive household personnel, including wives, themselves a form of wealth (Amadiume 1987, 42–46; Lindsay 2003, 42). In such ways, gender has worked along with, rather than apart from, age, wealth, lineage, and other social factors. And womanhood as well as manhood was multiple, intertwined with life cycle and additional social positions. With emphasis on lineage and kinship, as well as age, African studies expands the repertoire for intersectional analysis beyond gender, race, class, and nation.

Gendered Expressions of Power

As a signifier of power, gender has provided a terrain upon which to enact other struggles over power. Especially in encounters or, more appropriately, contestations and negotiations with the West, African societies faced states whose division of social life into gendered binaries provided a weapon to reinforce inequalities and hierarchies. Feminist appropriations of Foucault may very well need to step back in contexts where force is more overt, surveillance more obtrusive.[7] Yet disciplining in the Foucauldian sense occurred, though not without generating resistance and not without unintended hybridity, as Nancy Hunt's (1999) magisterial study of biopolitics in the Congo reveals.

Marc Epprecht explains, "Colonial rule and racial capitalism emasculated African men in the sense that they undermined Africans' ability to attain the sig-·nifiers of social manhood," such as land and other forms of wealth (1998, 641). As in the United States under Jim Crow's racial division of labor, new markers of manhood emerged in Southern Africa to compensate for such economic barriers: "sports, clothes, faction fighting, gangs, ostentatious consumption of European products (liquor, notably), more conspicuous exercise of power over (and sexual consumption of) women, and achievement in the white man's terms (school, church, police, master farming, hygiene)" (642). Subsequent liberation struggles rallied against feminization and impotency, denounced homosexuality as a Western (or white) import, and lessened the space for alternative sexualities, including the mine marriages of the past.[8]

In colonial Zimbabwe, Teresa Barnes (1997) documents, passes or identity cards not only distinguished Africans from Europeans but further "served as markers of gender difference" because the law required them only of men. African men understood the disciplining power of passes even as they resented the humiliation that the requests to see them brought: "there [was] no longer any status of manhood in a man of Black Africa," declared members of the Zimbabwean African Universal Benefit Society in 1923. Yet passes marked coming of age and established a legal personality denied to women. Reflecting its own contradictions, even as the colonial law designed an African woman a legal minor, no matter what her other attributes, the state undermined the power of village elders by leaving the travel of African wives and daughters unregulated. However, by the 1950s, colonial authorities differentiated women by whether they had "a baby on your back." Wives and mothers were assumed to be with husbands, while unmarried women without work permits became undesirable migrants to cities; that is, prostitutes (61, 72, 70). Here the state built upon previous African distinctions to reinterpret gender as a form of control, though administrative weaknesses interfered in the carrying out of its plans. In viewing "the gendered application of pass laws" as "contributing to new cultural understanding of the dichotomies . . . male/female, productive/unproductive, adult/child and perhaps even significant/insignificant," Barnes offers a model gender analysis of power relations (76).

State policy could both disrupt and recreate the production of gendered personhood. Among Mpiemu laboring for French companies, Tamara Giles-Vernick shows (1999), when the rubber came out of the tree, manhood arrived as well. This mobile group defined personhood through use of natural resources even after colonization. "For generations of young men who worked in the 1930s, 1940s, and 1950s, becoming a male person now meant laboring—not for elders, but for European enterprises—to acquire bridewealth and consumer goods" (327). But when in the late 1980s the Central African Republic and the World Wildlife Fund restricted hunting and gathering activities, they undermined Mpiemu personhood as well as "gender and generational relations" (337).

State intervention had to overcome these "relations of gender and genera-tion" (Thomas 1996, 356; 2003). State authorities in Meru, Kenya, for example, failed to predict the resistance to their 1956 ban on clitoridectomy, a practice that turned girls into women and cemented the power of adult women. In the process of defying male authorities, waves of prepubescent girls circumcised themselves, temporarily grabbing control over becoming a woman away from female elders. According to Lynn M. Thomas, "the Meru remember *Ngaitana* as a time of profound change, when female initiation was driven 'underground,' stripped of its attendant celebrations and teachings, and reduced to the clan-destine performance of excision" (1996, 348).

Colonialism particularly exacerbated generational struggles, as between "se-nior men," considered social fathers, and "junior" men. Missionaries and colo-nial administrators also attacked rituals that transformed boys into men while offering substitutes through participation in the school and the church to the landed economic base necessary for adult manhood. Hodgson (1999), for one, traces the complex process by which British colonials associated Maasai eth-nicity with certain permeations of maleness—the herder, nomad, and warrior— that relegated these men to the realm of the primitive while simultaneously re-serving the statuses of taxpayer, household head, and native authority to men, thus incorporating some into the modern state. Introduction of a cattle mar-ket made men, rather than women, the owners of the animals. Thus, "Maasai women have not only lost economic rights of control over pastoralist resources and access to new economic and political opportunities, but they have been dis-enfranchised from a sense of Massai identity" (122).

However, resistance to colonial practices constituted new definitions of man-hood, which in turn supplanted dominant masculinities. The stigmatized term *ormeek,* which had referred to non-Maasai Africans, became directed to "those Africans who were educated, spoke Swahili, worked in the government, or were baptized" (135). This insult questioned the masculinity of men, no matter what their age, who served the government as headmen or accepted attributes of Western modernity, such as schooling or Christianity. In time, however, men who embraced modernity reworked *ormeek* into a term of honor, even as a changing political economy made senior and venerable elders judge themselves *emodai* (stupid) for being ignorant of the ways of schools and courts.

Certainly Hodgson's theoretical point—that "a dominant masculinity is less a construction than a production, and thus always in tension, always relative, and always a site of mediation and negotiation"—is one worth centering a femi-nist analysis of gender around (144). Lisa A. Lindsay (2003) shows this pro-cess in her discussion of Nigerian rail workers in the twentieth century. The male breadwinner norm of British gender ideology turned into a discursive strategy among trade unionists fighting for higher wages even as they supported extended kin, entered polygamous relationships, and depended on income-earning wives to maintain themselves, Lindsay introduces agency into "working with gender" under colonialism. "Nigerian wage and salary earners consciously grappled with their roles as men, engaging with, adopting, and discarding various aspects of what were perceived as European, Yorùbá, Nigerian, 'modern,' elite, or working-class masculinities," she argues. They selectively embraced borrowings from other cultures, including Western "modernity." Before the 1940s, British officials saw "kin and hometown networks as sources of support for workers," and growing labor militancy turned local gender and family systems into contributors to "urban overcrowding and unemployment" (72). Embrace of the male breadwinner role countered such charges even as it undermined the consideration of women traders as "workers."

Colonialism's impact on gender ultimately requires disaggregation. The politics of the womb, to borrow from Lynn M. Thomas (2003), called forth competing understandings of proper gender behavior both among Africans and between colonizers and colonized as much as struggles over land and labor did. The "man in the village" became "a 'boy' in the workplace" when European managers "feminized and infantilized" African men, even those laboring in extractive industries rather than domestic service (Lindsay 2003, 12). Jean Allman and Victoria Tashjian specify how "broader economic and political forces—for example, cash cropping, production for the market, monetization, native courts, mission schools—recast the domestic terrain of conjugal production and reproduction, both before and after 1900" (2000, 222). Only through such specifications then can we realize the promise of gender analysis for understanding globalization and exploitation.

Conclusion

The interrogation of masculinity by U.S. feminist scholars and the development of queer theory exposed the contingency and fluidity of identities and categories once taken for granted, paralleling the epistemological insights that women's studies gains from African studies. But if a gender studies with multiple genders sometimes risks its own version of essentialism, research on Africa serves as a corrective by grounding gender systems, identities, practices, and ideologies in time and place. In the deconstruction of masculinities by Lisa A. Lindsay and Stephan Miescher (2003), Luise White (1990), and others,[9] the production of gender moves from abstraction to process.

African studies might serve as a corrective in another way. Sexualities take up much of the current explorations of women's studies into gender, power, discourse, desire, and subjectivities. As important as this project is, it can lead to the neglect of other manifestations of gender, such as gender as social position. Many African feminists have linked their analysis to the ongoing issues faced by their countries, to what the Nigerian poet and author Molara Ogundipe-Leslie has named STIWA—"Social Transformations in Africa Including Women." This linkage has led to a shift in focus away from gender by itself to analysis that is systemic, ". . . [and allows for] transform[ing] the continent structurally within states and within families, and that this historical activity should happen with the collaboration of both men and women" (Ogundipe-Leslie and Lewis 2002). African studies reminds us that there is more to gender performance than sexualities or even sex. And it emphasizes that just because gender is a compulsory practice, it does not follow that the constant production of gender is not without openings for subversion or alternatives. The competing masculinities and femininities of colonial governments, guerillas, militias, missionaries, and various local peoples themselves reveal processes of gender production that illuminate the creativity of the human spirit. As women's studies enters an era of internationalization, a critical engagement with Africa offers compelling models through the thickets of positions and positionality.

Notes

I would like to thank Bianca Murillo, Linda Heywood, and the editors of this volume for their support and comments.

1. The literature on women and gender in Africa has grown enormously. For a sample, see Allman, Geiger, and Musisi (2002); Grosz-Ngate and Kokole (1997); and Ogundipe and Lewis (2002).
2. Herbert quoted in Berger (2003). See also Hodgson and McCurdy (2001, 3–5).
3. Hunt (1989, 323–337) traces the contours of the field. See also Robertson (1987, 97–137).
4. For a number of examples, see Herbert (1993, 229).
5. In contrast, see Murray and Roscoe (1998).
6. For a classic statement, see Crenshaw (1989, 139–167) and Wing (1997).
7. For a critique of feminist reliance on Foucault, see Bordo (1999).
8. See also E. Frances White (1990, 80); Matthews (2001).
9. See Morrell (1998) and the rest of the special issue of *Journal of Southern African Studies* entitled "Masculinities in Southern Africa" (24, no. 4).

References

Achebe, Nwando. 2003. "'And She Became a Man': King Ahebi Ugbabe in the History of Enugu-Ezike, Northern Igboland, 1880–1948." In *Men and Masculinities in Modern African History,* edited by Lisa A. Lindsay and Stephan F. Miescher, 52–68. Portsmouth, N.H.: Heinemann.

Allman, Jean, and Victoria Tashjian. 2000. *"I Will Not Eat Stone": A Women's History of Colonial Asante.* Portsmouth, N.H.: Heinemann.

Allman, Jean, Susan Geiger, and Nakanyike Musisi, eds. 2002. *Women in African Colonial Histories.* Bloomington: Indiana University Press.

Amadiume, Ifi. 1987. *Male Daughters, Female Husbands: Gender and Sex in an African Society.* London: Zed Books.

Arnfred, Signe. 2002. "Simone De Beauvoir in Africa: 'Women=The Second Sex?' Issues of African Feminist Thought." *Jenda: A Journal of Culture and African*

Women's Studies 2, no. 1. Available online at http://www.jendajournal.com/
    vol2.1/arnfred.html (accessed July 19, 2005).
Barnes, Teresa. 1997. "'Am I a Man?' Gender and the Pass Laws in Urban Colonial
    Zimbabwe, 1930–80." *African Studies Review* 40, no.1: 59–81.
Berger, Iris. 2003. "African Women's History: Themes and Perspectives." *Journal of
    Colonialism and Colonial History* 4, no. 1. Available online at
    http://muse.jhu.edu/journals/journal_of_colonialism_and_colonial_
    history/v004/4.1berger.html (accessed July 20, 2005).
Bordo, Susan. 1999. "Feminism, Foucault and the Politics of the Body." In *Feminist
    Theory and the Body,* edited by Janet Price and Margrit Shildrick, 246–257.
    New York: Routledge.
Boris, Eileen. 1995. "The Racialized Gendered State: Concepts of Citizenship in the
    United States." *Social Politics* 2, no. 2: 160–180.
Butler, Judith. 1990. *Gender Trouble: Feminism and the Subversion of Identity.* New
    York: Routledge.
Canning, Kathleen. 1999. "The Body as Method? Reflections on the Place of the Body
    in Gender History." *Gender & History* 11, no. 3: 499–513.
Crenshaw, Kimberle. 1989. "Demarginalizing the Intersection of Race and Sex: A
    Black Feminist Critique of Antidiscrimination Doctrine, Feminist Theory
    and Antiracist Politics." *University of Chicago Legal Forum:* 139–167.
Ehrenreich, Barbara. 2002. "Maid to Order." In *Global Woman: Nannies, Maids, and
    Sex Workers in the New Economy,* edited by Barbara Ehrenreich and Arlie
    Russell Hochschild, 85–103. New York: Metropolitan Books.
Epprecht, Marc. 1998. "The 'Unsaying' of Indigenous Homosexualities in Zimbabwe:
    Mapping a Blindspot in an African Masculinity." *Journal of Southern African
    Studies* 24 no. 4: 631–651.
Giles-Vernick, Tamara. 1999. "Leaving A Person Behind: History, Personhood, and
    Struggles over Forest Resources in the Sangha Basin of Equatorial Africa."
    International Journal of African Historical Studies 32, no. 2–3: 311–338.
Gray, Leslie, and Michael Kevane. 1999. "Diminished Access, Diverted Exclusion:
    Women and Land Tenure in Sub-Saharan Africa." *African Studies Review* 42,
    no. 2: 15–39.
Grosz-Ngate, Maria, and Omari H. Kokole, eds. 1997. *Gendered Encounters: Challeng-
    ing Cultural Boundaries and Social Hierarchies in Africa.* New York: Routledge.
Halberstam, Judith. 1998. *Female Masculinity.* Durham, N.C.: Duke University Press.
Herbert, Eugenia W. 1993. *Iron, Gender, and Power: Rituals of Transformation in Afri-
    can Societies.* Bloomington: Indiana University Press.
Hodgson, Dorothy L. 1999. "'Once Intrepid Warriors': Modernity and the Production
    of Massai Masculinities." *Ethnology* 38, no. 2: 121–50.
———, and Sheryl A. McCurdy. 2001. "Introduction: 'Wicked' Women and the Re-
    configuration of Gender in Africa." In *"Wicked" Women and the Reconfigura-
    tion of Gender in Africa,* edited by Dorothy L. Hodgson and Sheryl A.
    McCurdy, 1–24. Portsmouth, N.H.: Heinemann.
Hunt, Nancy Rose. 1989. "Placing African Women's History and Locating Gender."
    Social History 14, no. 3: 359–379.
———. 1996. "Introduction." *Gender & History* 8, no. 3: 323–337.
———. 1999. *A Colonial Lexicon: Of Birth Ritual, Medicalization, and Mobility in the
    Congo.* Durham, N.C.: Duke University Press.

Jagose, Annamarie. 1996. *Queer Theory: An Introduction.* New York: New York University Press.

Lindsay, Lisa A. 2003. *Working with Gender: Wage Labor and Social Change in Southwestern Nigeria.* Portsmouth, N.H.: Heinemann.

———, and Stephan F. Miescher, eds. 2003. *Men and Masculinities in Modern African History.* Portsmouth, N.H.: Heinemann.

Matthews, Tracye A. 2001. "'No One Ever Asks What a Man's Role in the Revolution Is': Gender Politics and Leadership in the Black Panther Party, 1966–71." In *Sisters in the Struggle: African American Women in the Civil Rights–Black Power Movement,* edited by Bettye Collier-Thomas and V. P. Franklin, 230–256. New York: New York University Press.

Mohanty, Chandra Talpade. 2003. *Feminism without Borders: Decolonizing Theory, Practicing Solidarity.* Durham, N.C.: Duke University Press.

Morrell, Robert. 1988. "Of Boys and Men: Masculinity and Gender in Southern African Studies." *Journal of Southern African Studies* 24, no. 4: 605–630.

Murray, Stephan O., and Will Roscoe. 1998. *Boy-Wives and Female Husbands: Studies in African Homosexualities.* New York: St. Martin's Press.

Nicholson, Linda. 1994. "Interpreting Gender." *Signs: A Journal of Women in Culture and Society* 20, no. 1: 79–105.

Njambi, Wairmū Ngarūiya, and William E. O'Brien. 2000. "Revisiting 'Woman-Woman Marriage': Notes on Gīkūyū Women." *NWSA Journal* 12, no. 1: 1–23.

Nzegwu, Nkiru. 2001. "Gender Equality in a Dual-Sex System: The Case of Onitsha." *Jenda: A Journal of Culture and African Women's Studies* 1, no. 1. Available online at http://www.jendajournal.com/vol1.1/nzegwu.html (accessed July 19, 2005).

Ogundipe-Leslie, Molara, and Desiree Lewis. 2002. "Conversation." *Feminist Africa,* no. 1. Available online at http://www.feministafrica.org/fa%201/2level.html (accessed July 23, 2005).

Oyewumi, Oyeronke. 1997. *The Invention of Women: Making an African Sense of Western Gender Discourses.* Minneapolis: University of Minnesota Press.

Rantalaiho, Lisa. 1997. "Contextualising Gender." In *Gendered Practices in Working Life,* edited by Lisa Rantalaiho and Tuula Heiskanen, 16–30. New York: St. Martin's Press.

Robertson, Claire. 1987. "Developing Economic Awareness: Changing Perspectives in Studies of African Women, 1976–1983." *Feminist Studies* 13, no. 1: 97–137.

Rosenthal, Judy. 1997. "Foreign Tongues and Domestic Bodies: Gendered Cultural Regions and Regionalized Sacred Flows." In *Gendered Encounters: Challenging Cultural Boundaries and Social Hierarchies in Africa,* edited by Maria Grosz-Ngate and Omari H. Kokole, 183–203. New York: Routledge.

Sacks, Karen. 1979. *Sisters and Wives: The Past and Future of Sexual Equality.* Westport, Conn.: Greenwood Press.

Scott, Joan. 1988. *Gender and the Politics of History.* New York: Columbia University Press.

Sudarkasa, Niara. 1986. "The Status of Women in Indigenous African Societies." *Feminist Studies* 12, no. 1: 91–103.

Thomas, Lynn M. 1996. "'*Ngaitana* (I will circumcise myself)': The Gender and Generational Politics of the 1956 Ban on Clitoridectomy in Meru, Kenya." *Gender & History* 8, no. 3: 338–363.

———. 2003. *Politics of the Womb: Women, Reproduction, and the State in Kenya.* Berkeley: University of California Press.

Wiegman, Robyn. 2001. "Object Lessons: Men, Masculinity, and the Sign Women." *Signs: A Journal of Women in Culture and Society* 26, no. 2: 355–388.

White, E. Frances. 1990. "Africa on My Mind: Gender, Counter Discourse and African-American Nationalism." *Journal of Women's History* 2, no. 1: 73–97.

White, Luise. 1990. "Separating the Men from the Boys: Constructions of Gender, Sexuality, and Terrorism in Central Kenya, 1939–1959." *International Journal of African Historical Studies* 23, no. 1: 1–25.

Wing, Adrien Katherine. 1997. *Critical Race Feminism: A Reader.* New York: New York University Press.

11 When a Man Loves a Woman: Gender and National Identity in Wole Soyinka's *Death and the King's Horseman* and Mariama Bâ's *Scarlet Song*

Eileen Julien

> The world is like a Mask dancing. If you want to see it well you do not stand in one place.
>
> Chinua Achebe, *Arrow of God*

Literature as we know it today is a gendered practice. This is not because gendered lives are its referents: the study of those real lives is primarily the work of historians, sociologists, and anthropologists. Rather it is through the workings of the material worlds of publishing, teaching, and criticism, through narrative processes of selection and omission and strategies of representation, that literature is gendered. These processes and strategies will be our focus here: Readers, teachers, and critics who are conscious of the logic of gender are able to foreground both critical aspects of texts that typically are overlooked and the conditions that push certain texts into the limelight while obscuring others.

This does not mean that gender is *the* most powerful explanatory category of analysis nor a category that is complete unto itself. In fact, gender's high visibility as an analytical tool and the mostly celebratory readings of African women's writing in recent African literary scholarship may have obscured other discreet, if not unrelated, factors of stratification, such as class or access to education, that have equal relevance for understanding the lives of women and men that are drawn in texts we read. Whatever their specific arguments or the debates they have generated, the work of Ifi Amadiume (1987) on "traditional" Igbo gender roles and that of Oyeronke Oyewumi (1997) on the absence of gender categories in the Yorùbá language serve as reminders of the importance of taking into account the multiple factors at play in identity.

No mode of analysis, and certainly not *gender*, exists in a vacuum. If there is a debate on the epistemological merit of gender as a category within African studies, is it not precisely because the preoccupation with gender is felt to come from "somewhere" and that somewhere might not be Africa? Thus the question "Whose African studies?" is also germane. If one refers to the study of Africa practiced within *American* institutions of higher learning, then this location, as they all do, comes with baggage—the initial post-Sputnik tensions and rivalry (which is to say U.S. foreign policy concerns) that gave rise to African studies programs in the 1960s; the centrality of Title VI funding, which structures such programs around outreach and language training and has tended to privilege the social sciences; and the divergent trajectories, the often separate and typically unequal resources, the frequently tense relations between African studies and African-American (or Afro-American) studies.

In fact, "African studies," some have argued, is inherently and uniquely a U.S. formulation, in which Africa—like Latin America and Asia and perhaps even more than them—is appended to discipline-based university curricula and suffers from marginality and second-class citizenship. I am alluding to arguments set forth in *Africa Today* (1997) over the decline of the area studies model in the United States and the debate at the University of Cape Town in the late 1990s over the relevance of "African studies" as a way of conceptualizing and packaging the study of Africa.

Is the theme "Africa after gender?" about the aptness and merits of attention paid to gender in the study of Africa *within universities in the United States,* where a prevailing feminist consciousness may obscure North American women's own collusion with global processes and other forms of oppression that affect African women adversely? Or is it about gender and the study of Africa more generally *outside* Africa, since "African studies," as the marginal unit described above, presumably does not exist in Africa? Or is it rather about the study of Africa *everywhere,* including Africa first and foremost? There is strong evidence that gender has become an important category of analysis on the continent. Since 1994, for example, the Council for the Development of Social Science Research in Africa (CODESRIA) has sponsored an institute on gender each summer with the participation of twelve to fifteen researchers from around the continent and in every field.[1] On a personal level, I witnessed the interest and demands of students at the University of Yaoundé in fall semester 1998: whether because it was fashionable to do so or because it resonated with their own lives, students clamored for readings and coursework on feminism and gender.

Whatever its origins, whatever the systems of categorization and hierarchy of which it is a part, whatever the care with which it must therefore be handled, gender as a mode of analysis is felt to be important by many African scholars, students, and activists on the ground. It is here to stay. My question, then, is this: How specifically does gender shape literature and our understanding of literary processes?

Among the perspectives on literary practice offered by a consideration of gender, there are two that I find compelling and to which I return time and again in my own readings of African texts. The first is offered by Florence Stratton (1994), the second by R. Radhakrishnan (1992), whose case study is India but whose argument I find to be relevant to African literatures. Stratton shows that "African literature" at its inception in the world of publishing and the academy is a field constituted on the basis of gender bias. In particular, she makes clear the ways in which critical reception and scholarship have worked to marginalize African women writers and valorize male writers and male preoccupations or formulations. From the standard tripartite periodization of African literature—the age of anticolonial struggle, the age of independence, and the age of neocolonialism—to Fredric Jameson's (1986) claim of the predilection in "third world" literature for "national allegory" to Abdul JanMohamed's (1983) privileging of "race" as the constitutive category of African literature, Stratton demonstrates that gender differences are entrenched and ignored. For even as women wrote against colonial domination, they—unlike men, on the basis of whose works these parameters came to be seen as doctrine—set about critiquing differences *internal* to African nations. In the standard chronology, this self-critique is a characteristic of what is normally taken to be the last phase, the age of neocolonialism. The standard definition and periodization resulted in skewed criticism by the male establishment of the works of women writers, which led Ghanaian writer Ama Ata Aidoo to complain that she and other women writers had been deprived of vital critical commentary on their work.[2]

Stratton demonstrates likewise that the "mother Africa" trope operates to present women as what she calls "the pot of culture" and that male writers, who are often viewed as progressive, call them into service as prostitutes to condemn the degradation of contemporary Africa associated with the "sweep of history." While I might quarrel with her denunciation of particular texts and writers or specific interpretations, the overall vision is an important and useful one.

R. Radhakrishnan (1992) expands on the first avatar of this trope in an article that seeks to understand the exclusion of "the woman question" from the nationalist debate and agenda at the moment of decolonization in India or its relegation to a second order of importance. Building on the work of Partha Chatterjee (1993) and Kumkum Sangari and Sudesh Vaid (1990), Radhakrishnan begins with the important observation that in the context of third world nationalisms, the nation is seen as foreign:

Western nationalisms are deemed capable of generating their own models of autonomy from within, whereas Eastern nationalisms have to assimilate something alien to their own cultures before they can become modern nations. Thus in the Western context, the ideals of Frenchness, Germanness, or Englishness—national essences rooted in a sense of autochthony—become the basis of a modernity that re-roots and reconfirms a native sense of identity. On the other hand, Eastern nationalisms, and in particular "Third World" nationalisms, are forced to choose between "being themselves" and "becoming modern nations" as though the universal standards of reason and progress were natural and intrinsic to the West. In this latter case, the universalizing mission is embued with violence, coercion, deracination and denaturalization. We can see how this divide perpetuates the ideology of a dominant common world where the West leads naturally and the East follows in an eternal game of catch-up where its identity is always in dissonance with itself. (1992, 86)

The choice between "becoming modern nations" and "being ourselves" can be seen as a form of politicocultural schizophrenia. In this tug of war, women become, in Christine Obbo's words, "the mediators between the past and the present, while men see themselves as mediators between the present and the future" (Stratton 1994, 8). Women are the symbolic markers of "true identity." Radhakrishnan explains this phenomenon in detail:

By mobilizing the inner/outer distinction against the "outerness" of the West, nationalist rhetoric makes "woman" the pure and ahistorical signifier of "interiority" . . . the mute but necessary allegorical ground for the transactions of nationalist history. . . . Nationalism could neither ignore the West completely nor capitulate to it entirely: the West and its ideals of material progress had to be assimilated selectively, without any fundamental damage to the native and "inner" Indian self. In other words, questions of change and progress posed in Western attire were conceived as an outer and epiphenomenal aspect of Indian identity, whereas the inner and inviolable sanctum of Indian identity had to do with home, spirituality, and the figure of Woman as representative of the true self. (1992, 84)

In texts written under the sign of nationalism, then, if one follows the scholars I have cited, women are inscribed as correlatives of the "inner sanctum"— home, tradition, and thus the wholesomeness of the body politic. These scholars do not address the roles of men in comparable detail, but I assume that within this model the forms of progress associated with "outerness" (the West)—such as the state and public space—lie in the province of men. Given these assumptions, I shall offer a gender-sensitive reading of two texts frequently taught in undergraduate literature courses in the United States, Wole Soyinka's *Death and the King's Horseman* (1975) and Mariama Bâ's *Scarlet Song* (*Un chant écarlate*, 1981). Both involve a man's marriage to an additional wife; in Soyinka's text, the new wife is young enough to be his daughter. Men in these texts regard such marriages, implicitly or explicitly, as emblems for "African tradition." While *Death and the King's Horseman* deploys this marriage to defend African essence and honor, *Scarlet Song* treats this perspective with irony. Soyinka's text is an act of archeological and utopic recovery, whereas Bâ offers a stringent critique of patriarchal privilege in the present.

While the works of Bâ and Soyinka are different in genre, language, and national context, concepts of gender are critical to and circulate through them. *Scarlet Song* is a French-language novel by a Senegalese woman; *Death and the King's Horseman* is an English-language play by a Nigerian man. In the latter, traditional Yoruba rituals, myths, and social practices are central to the theatrical language. By contrast, Bâ's ethnic origins—Bâ is a Fulbe name—are rarely mentioned in discussions of her work: Her choice of form, the dilemmas she constructs, her strategies of representation are not particularly conditioned by ethnicity. What the two works share is a preoccupation with woman as signifier of the past and, consequently, as anchor in a turbulent present. Thus, Soyinka relies on gender constructs to defend Yorùbá civilization in the face of Western colonialism. Bâ demonstrates that such constructs are incompatible with a truly progressive society or at least with middle-class women's welfare.

Death and the King's Horseman is an acclaimed, now canonical, play, the object of significant critical commentary and debate. The play is composed of five acts. In the first, Elesin Oba, the King's Horseman, is accompanied by his praise-singer to the marketplace, where the market women are closing their stalls for the day: "This market is my roost. When I come among the women I am a chicken with a hundred mothers. I become a monarch whose palace is built with tenderness and beauty" (1975, I:10). It is here that Elesin intends to die so as to follow the immemorial tradition of accompanying the King, who has recently died, to the other side.[3] Elesin and the praise-singer banter through rich, dense metaphor and parables about Elesin's exuberance and great love of life, his privilege as the King's Horseman, the human fear of death, the importance of the ritual to come, and Elesin's determination to follow through as a man of honor. After his prodding, Iyaloja, the mother of the market, consents to marry off her intended daughter-in-law to Elesin as a sign of the market women's love and admiration for him and warns him, much to his displeasure, that failure to follow through on the ritual once the marriage is consummated would be disastrous for the community and Elesin's legacy.

In contrast to the brilliantly lyrical Act I, Act II is prosaic and comic, as the action switches to the residence of the British administrator Simon Pilkings and his wife Jane. The couple are preparing for a masquerade ball that will feature a surprise visit by the British prince, and for the occasion they have donned ritual clothing confiscated from the Yorùbá. Their Christian servant Joseph and Muslim subaltern officer Amusa are intimidated and disapproving. Worried by distant drums whose message—Is it death? Is it a marriage?—cannot be determined, Pilkings and Jane nonetheless set off for the ball and send Amusa to forestall any trouble.

Amusa and his men arrive at the market in Act III and are not allowed by the market women to arrest Elesin, who will shortly "commit death" but who is still in the bridal chamber. The women's daughters parody British settlers in an uproarious manner and draw Amusa into their performance. As the errand boy of the British, he is belittled and labeled a nonman ("he has no weapon") in comparison to Elesin. Act III closes in semi-darkness, as Elesin, under the spell of the drum and poetic chant of the praise singer, is in the passage to death.

Act IV finds Pilkings and Jane at the ball, where they learn that Elesin has been captured. Olunde, Elesin's son, appears, having returned from England, where he had gone to obtain training as a doctor. When he learned that the King had died, he booked passage back to Nigeria to bury his father who he knew would accompany the King in death. Olunde confronts Jane and they clash over the meaning of "civilization" and "primitivism." The captured Elesin is dragged on stage and grovels before his son.

In Act V, a shamed and contemplative Elesin, his young bride at his side, speaks from his jail cell with Pilkings, who is satisfied to have prevented a primitive ritual and avoided embarrassment during the Prince's visit. Iyaloja appears, rebuking Elesin and delivering a mysterious bundle. His father having failed to die, Olunde has desperately and perhaps ineffectively followed through on the immemorial cultural ritual in his father's stead. When Elesin realizes that before him lies the body of his son, he strangles himself.

Soyinka tells us in his "Author's Note" that *Death and the King's Horseman* is based on an incident that took place in Nigeria in 1946 but that for purposes of dramaturgy he has taken a number of liberties, among them, changing the date of the action to the early 1940s, during World War II. This enables both the wartime visit of the British prince to the colony—escalating the stakes for Pilkings—and comparisons in Act IV between a British ship captain's self-sacrifice in wartime and ritual suicide among the Yorùbá.

The representation of woman and man in *Death and the King's Horseman* is thus subsumed under a "larger" project of defending an African civilization that is none other than a form of nationalism. In this sense the play demonstrates that nationalism is a gendered construct and that women are the stable ground upon which—if we take Soyinka to be exemplary—masculine nationalism is built. What is of particular interest here is, first, the trio of Iyaloja, the daughters of the market women, and the young virginal Bride whom Elesin takes shortly before he will die, and, second, the Elesin-Amusa pair. There are important contradictions in these groupings that suggest the instability of gendered nationalism and foretell its crises.

Significantly, as Radhakrishnan's model of the politicocultural division of spheres in anticolonial or postcolonial societies predicts, the play sends Olunde off to England, the outside world of apparent modernity and progress, to obtain medical training, a by-product of colonialism. And it places local traditions under the sign of the feminine. Elesin Oba's death, which will assure continuity between the worlds of the living, the dead, and the unborn and will therefore keep the Yorùbá world "on its course," is prepared by and is to take place among the market women, of whom Iyaloja is the leader. Iyaloja represents the considerable social and commercial stature of women within patriarchy before and even during European intervention in West Africa. She makes the decision to grant Elesin, the community's revered ambassador to the land of the ancestors, his final wish and dictates the terms of that gift. Except for the praise-singer, the Yorùbá community is represented in the play entirely by women.

The daughters of the market women who are attending British or missionary schools and the Bride represent the next generation, but there is a deep split between their socially critical positions. The spiritual, traditional, indigenous sphere is emphatically embodied in the person of the young bride, the "gift of the living to their emissary to the land of the ancestors," the "earth" into which Elesin will sow seed, the "abyss" across which his body will be drawn. The Bride has no name and never speaks. She thus stands outside of time and represents the pure and unchanging Tradition of which Iyaloja and the girls are vociferous defenders. The Bride is modest and self-effacing and assumes postures of submission and obedience at every moment. Elesin calls her "little mother." In the final act she weeps, Elesin observes, and her only gesture comes at the very end of the play when, under the authority of Iyaloja, she closes Elesin's eyelids and pours earth over each of them.

The static role of the Bride is in textual tension with the dynamic role of the other girls, presumably her age, who attend school. An important implication is that whatever British protocols, "rational" arguments, or technological feats they have mastered at school, the indigenous cultural and metaphysical moorings of the daughters of the market women, like those of Olunde, remain unshaken.[4] There is no incommensurability, the play suggests, between local beliefs or rituals and world knowledges: "foreign" technology and knowledge can be assimilated and indigenized without damage to cultural identity. Thus, not only do the schoolgirls mock the British colonizers, they also ridicule the colonial lackeys, Amusa and his men, who appear to have lost their cultural identity.

But the play offers no explanation as to why the young bride should represent the past and be unable to speak of it. She gives no signs of the dexterity of movement and thought implicit in the girls' parody of British colonial civility. This is all the more striking because two of the market women express pride in their daughters' accomplishments. Their decision to send their daughters (Apinke and Wuraola) to school is justified by the girls' theatrical triumph:

> (The women strike their palms across in the gesture of wonder.)
> **WOMEN:** Do they teach you all that at school?
> **WOMAN:** And to think I nearly kept Apinke away from the place.
> **WOMAN:** Did you hear them? Did you see how they mimicked the white man?
> **WOMAN:** The voices exactly. Hey, there are wonders in this world!
> **IYALOJA:** Well, our elders have said it: Dada may be weak, but he has a younger sibling who is truly fearless.
> **WOMAN:** The next time the white man shows his face in this market I will set Wuraola on his tail. (40)

The girls are firmly anchored in history, while the Bride is systematically referred to as the earth into which Elesin will sow his seed and is associated with earth in the final act. There are two ironies here. First, the girls, like Olunde, are articulate and effective defenders of Tradition precisely because they are no longer pure embodiments of those traditions themselves. Thanks to their colonial education, they will one day challenge colonial arrogance on its own terms and *be heard* ("Fearless Wuraola will be on the white man's tail"). In fact, Olunde and the schoolgirls are hybrids, as is the ridiculed Amusa, who can be seen as more faithful to Yorùbá traditions in some respects than is Olunde (George 1999, 67–91). The second irony is that in their fierce defense of tradition for tradition's sake, the schoolgirls are able to consign a girl like themselves to a silence and a role that seem to be terribly at odds with their own lives. The girls put African nationalism first, while they relegate "the woman question" to the back burner. Is this the playwright's nationalist wishful thinking? Or prescience? Does this invisibility of some women to others signal a troubled stratification to come? Is the Bride the subaltern for whom postcolonial women intellectuals will speak?

The conflation of masculinity and nationalist resistance is similarly exposed in a comparison of Elesin and Amusa. From the opening lines of the play, Elesin is cast as a man with an appetite for all of life's pleasures. In an extended series of metaphors, the praise-singer proclaims Elesin's prowess as hunter, warrior, and lover:

> PRAISE-SINGER: Who would deny your reputation, snake-on-the-loose in dark passages of the market! Bed-bug who wages war on the mat and receives the thanks of the vanquished! When caught with his bride's own sister he protested— but I was only prostrating myself to her as becomes a grateful in-law. Hunter who carries his powder-horn on the hips and fires crouching or standing! Warrior who never makes that excuse of the whining coward—but how can I go to battle with- out my trousers?—trouserless or shirtless it's all one to him. Oka-rearing-from-a- camouflage-of-leaves, before he strikes the victim is already prone! Once they told him, Howu, a stallion does not feed on the grass beneath him: he replied, true, but surely he can roll on it! (I:19)

It comes as no surprise, then, that Elesin desires the beautiful young woman he sees in the market, although it is construed as a spiritual union that will com- plement and bring to fulfillment his passage to the world beyond. Given his role and the community's reverence for him, it likewise makes sense that Iyaloja should agree to his marriage to the girl who was to become her son's wife. In Act 3, when Amusa comes to arrest Elesin for the suicide he is to commit, Iyaloja, voicing an anticolonial critique, conflates Elesin's death on behalf of the com- munity with the consummation of the marriage:

> IYALOJA: What gives you the right to obstruct our leader of men in the performance of his duty.
> AMUSA: What kin' duty be dat one Iyaloja.
> IYALOJA: What kin' duty? What kin' duty does a man have to his new bride?
> AMUSA (bewildered, looks at the women and at the entrance to the hut): Iyaloja, is it wedding you call dis kin' ting?
> IYALOJA: You have wives haven't you? Whatever the white man has done to you he hasn't stopped you having wives. And if he has, at least he is mar- ried. If you don't know what a marriage is, go and ask him to tell you.
> AMUSA: This no to wedding.
> IYALOJA: You want to look inside the bridal chamber? You want to see for yourself how a man cuts the virgin knot? (III:36)

It is hard to imagine a more potent use of Woman as embodiment of tradi- tion and, conversely, of masculinity *via heterosexual intercourse* as traditionalist, heroic, nationalist. For this is not simply a double entendre or metaphor: the physical consummation of the marriage has become part of the ritual, bloodstained white cloth and all. In contrast, Iyaloja then suggests Amusa's lack of manliness, thereby extending the earlier taunts of the other market women: "white man's eunuch," "You mean there is nothing there at all," "you come to show power to women and you don't even have a weapon" (III:34–35). The great irony, of course, is that while in this scene Elesin does have a "weapon" and is fully a man in the community's terms, it is he nonetheless who will lose his status as a man of honor. Ultimately, the equating of sexual prowess in the bridal chamber to manliness and the defense of tradition—despite the case made for this reading by the play—can be seen to be a sham.

Soyinka insists in his foreword that the colonial factor is a mere "catalytic incident" and that this failure should be attributed solely to Elesin, who self-servingly chooses to read the colonial intervention as a sign that he might escape his destiny. But the spectator or reader is in her rights to ponder the significance not only of the colonial intervention in this failure, as Anthony Appiah (1992) and Olakunle George (1999) have argued, but also of the gendered construction itself, the conflation of anticolonial resistance and manliness.

Elesin, who undoubtedly sees Olunde's cultural "hybridity" as incompatible with manhood and has dismissed his son, finds himself admitting in response to Olunde's contempt for him: "I know now that I did give birth to a son" (V:63). But the play does not authorize a reading of Olunde as particularly manly. Olunde is rather consistently referred to as "the younger shoot" in contrast to Elesin, "the parent shoot." Even Iyaloja's final castigation of Elesin and honoring of Olunde rests as much on a rhetoric of age and maturity as one of masculinity: "There lies the honour of your household and of our race. Because he could not bear to let honour fly out of doors, he stopped it with his life. The son has proved the father Elesin, and there is nothing left in your mouth to gnash but infant gums" (V:75). This defense of "African culture and tradition" is shaken by the many contradictions surrounding its reliance on gender identities.

It is precisely against such gendered representation of national and cultural identity that Senegalese writer Mariama Bâ rebels. This is implicit in her first novel, *So Long a Letter* (*Une si longue lettre,* 1980) for which Bâ received the first annual Noma Award for the best work published in Africa (Harrell-Bond, 1980),[5] but it is powerfully articulated in her posthumous second novel, *Scarlet Song,* which has received less critical attention. *So Long a Letter* is a tract against polygyny, which Bâ presents as backward, distinctly unmodern and unprogressive. Ramatoulaye, the heroine, who has grown up in the era of colonialism, is enamored of books, writing, and the sense of possibility which they afford her, an African woman. In post-independence Senegal, Rama is a married woman, a mother of twelve, a schoolteacher. Her world is devastated when her husband of many years abandons her in taking a second wife, Binetou, a schoolgirl who has been manipulated by her status-seeking mother. Upon her husband's death, Rama writes a series of letters to her childhood friend Aïssatou, who lives in New York. Aïssa, a mother of four, has chosen divorce rather than accept the co-wife status imposed on her by her husband and mother-in-law, for whom stratification by caste is paramount. The entire story is told through Rama's letters, which are more akin in fact to a diary or journal. Rama takes up her pen to examine her life, her relationship to her deceased husband, and her future.

Bâ's second novel, *Scarlet Song* (1986), is the story of two adolescent sweethearts, Mireille de La Vallée, daughter of a French diplomat assigned to Senegal, and Ousmane Guèye, the good-hearted son of a poor Muslim family in urban Dakar. Students at Cheikh Anta Diop University in the 1960s, they fall in love and keep their love secret from their families. When Mireille's father discovers his daughter's relationship, he whisks her back to France, where she finds herself in the midst of the tumult of May 1968. Mireille and Ousmane keep up their relationship through letters in which they affirm their commitment to each other and to progressive politics. His diploma in hand, Ousmane flies to France for a vacation, so his parents think, but he and Mireille are wed. The couple write to their respective parents to give them the news and create consternation on every side.

Upon their return to Senegal, Mireille strives to adapt to Senegalese family life, but the marriage is soon under strain; Ousmane's mother in particular rejects all of Mireille's efforts. Even the son born to them is dismissed by Yaye Khady as a café-au-lait mongrel. Ousmane loses interest in his son and wife, whose Western assumptions and values he now finds constraining and demeaning of his identity as a black African. He prefers the companionship of his male friends and shows solidarity with his mother against Mireille. Ouleymatou, a young woman with no future prospects of husband or work, sees an opening and makes the most of it. An old flame who had rejected Ousmane as something of a mother's boy when they were younger, she now pursues him on every front—working her way into Yaye Khady's good graces and seducing Ousmane with an arsenal of charms and cultural rituals. Unbeknown to Mireille and much to Yaye Khady's pleasure, Ousmane starts a second family and takes Ouleymatou as his second wife. Mireille's suspicions of Ousmane's infidelity are confirmed by his younger sister. Mireille goes mad, killing their son and leaving Ousmane to ponder unhappily the chaos he has created.[6]

Most commentators on *Scarlet Song* are unanimous: they read the novel as an accurate portrayal and assessment of the difficulties of interracial marriage in early post-independence West Africa. Class expectations and the specific gender configuration—the woman is white and the man black—are important compounding factors in the couple's demise, although in initial critical responses at least, these factors, especially gender, were signaled less often. But clearly the social burden, the competition menacing the foreign spouse, would not arise were the man white and the woman black. Ousmane's and Mireille's racial difference alone, then, is read as a metonymy for the impossibility of transcending culture or—in this text's terms—origins.

Commentators thus assume (or imply that Mariama Bâ assumes) the exclusive and imperative nature of cultural heritage and that, even if unfortunate, the influence of culture is "normal."[7] Clearly, Mireille and Ousmane *should* have heeded the call of origins, they *should not* have married outside their race and class. One such commentator, whose publication in the popular press may help ground her particular assumptions, goes still further, seeing Ousmane's ultimate rejection of Mireille as justified: "Bâ . . . as an African . . . identifies with the forces that motivate Ousmane. After repudiating his background and culture to marry Mireille, he is expected to conform with her Western conception of marriage. . . . His decision to marry the woman he was in love with as an adolescent signifies his need to return to his roots" (Toupouzis 1998, 70–71).

The cracks in this argument are quite apparent, however, if one chooses to look. The argument can only be made if one accepts a number of omissions and contradictions. For example, the narrator of Scarlet Song states explicitly with respect to the supposed expectation that Ousmane conform to a Western conception of marriage that Mireille was willing to work at a mutually satisfactory marriage and insinuates that Ousmane chose not to: "Between the two extremes, it would have been easy for Ousmane to create . . . a home [with tolerance and respect for differences], since his wife, while retaining her own personality, did not attempt to make him her slave. But, when all was said and done, was Ousmane really interested in the peace and equilibrium of his household?" (Bâ 1986, 123).

Similarly, Ouleymatou cannot be called simply the woman Ousmane "was in love with as an adolescent." To do so is to ignore the crucial fact that Ousmane did not just stop loving Ouleymatou and then start loving her again, as one might be led to believe. It was Ouleymatou who rejected Ousmane, and she did so because he was too "feminine," too much his mother's helper. In fact, the narrator goes to great lengths to cast Ouleymatou as entirely self-interested. One can come to the conclusion that Bâ identifies with Ousmane's quest for returning to "his roots," for renewing a bond with essential Africa, only if one elides these dimensions of the story.

I cite these assorted interpretations because they exemplify a pervasive preoccupation on the part of readers with racial-cultural conflict and an assumption that cultural traditions, be they African or European, are imperative—a sort of call of the primal—and, in any event, socially enforced. But a careful reading of the text shows that Bâ's critique of polygyny is as unwavering in this second novel as it is in her first. Moreover, the novel is up to the still more important work of critiquing the conflation of masculinity, cultural nationalism (négritude), and the mystification of the black woman, as we see it in Léopold Senghor's "Femme noire" or Soyinka's Death and the King's Horseman. In So Long a Letter, the cultural signification of the "black woman" cannot be raised because all the women are black. Ironically, the racial difference of the couple in Scarlet Song mystifies Ousmane's abandonment of his wife and obscures the critique of polygyny, but Mireille's whiteness is absolutely crucial to the critique of the role of the black woman in forms of cultural nationalism such as négritude, for there is no such thing as "black woman" where there is no "white woman."

Mireille is in my reading but an avatar, a more intense version of Aïssa and Rama, those Senegalese black women who "keep clean houses," "like books," and, not coincidentally, want monogamous husbands. Being white, Mireille is simply "the extreme" of the type. It is helpful to think of Bâ's novels, then, as images on a "silk screen." In the first image/printing (which corresponds to *So Long a Letter*), the second wife's appeal is her pliability or docileness, a product of her "noble" education in the case of Aïssatou's rival, Nabou, or, in the case of Binetou, her inferior class status and quest for material improvement. For whatever motives, then, the second wife accepts the role of handmaiden to man. The narrator insists on the backward nature and atavistic behavior of these women or their mothers and contrasts these qualities with the enlightened and autonomous choices of the highly educated Aïssa and Rama in their presumably equal partnerships with Mawdo and Modou, respectively.[8]

In the second image/printing that is *Scarlet Song*, then, Bâ launches the same scathing attack on what the novel presents as the innate sexual greed of men and the material hunger of lower-class women (Ouleymatou and Yaye Khady) that helps fuel polygynist logic. Because Mireille is white, the limits of the cultural nationalist representation of the black woman become visible. In Ouleymatou, Ousmane experiences sexual comforts, in addition to or because of a shared past and culture: "Night after night passed. Incense rose in clouds. They feasted on highly spiced dishes, nostalgically reliving the kingdom of childhood. Mabo the Dialli plucked at the strings of his Khalam. The compound flourished at Ousmane's expense" (121). Ouleymatou, incense, traditional foods, and music: for Ousmane, loving Ouleymatou is a synesthetic experience of culture and history.

Frequently the narrator slips into a favored mode of narration, indirect free speech, to share Ousmane's intoxication:

> Ouleymatou had become his true soulmate, the woman in whom he recognized the extension of himself. She was, as Mabo Dialli so rightly sang, at one and the same time his roots, his stock, his growth, his flowering. They were linked by their childhood, spent in the maze of dusty streets. Most important, they were linked by their common origins: the same ancestors, the same skies. The same soil! The same traditions! Their souls were impregnated with the sap of the same customs. They were excited by the same causes. Neither Ousmane nor Ouleymatou could disclaim this common essence without distorting their very natures. Cultural heritage was taking its pitiless revenge. It was reclaiming its due and revealing to Ousmane the end-point of his flight. (121)

Because Mariama Bâ has a predilection for indirect free speech and uses it forcefully and systematically to convey interior thoughts and perspectives, it is easy to read the novel as approving of Ousmane's choice to "return to the source" via his love for Ouleymatou and to resist Western cultural domination. But there are significant passages in which the narrator attacks Ousmane's behavior in forthright terms. Ousmane's rapture, Ouleymatou's seduction are rarely narrated without mention of their material causes and effects. Thus, in the passage where Ousmane is under the spell of music, incense, and food, the narrator points out that the compound is aware of the illicit relationship—

Ouleymatou's father's first wife slips incense and aphrodisiac powders to Ouley-matou; her father is conveniently sunk in his world of prayers, unaware of the whispers around his daughter's behavior; and everyone is flourishing materially from their complicity. In this way, Ouleymatou's mystique is continually de-mystified by the narrator's references to "manna from heaven" and by the os-tentatious waste triggered by this call of origins (125).

Moreover, the narrator's judgment of Ousmane's morality is absolute: "In Usine Niari Talli Ouleymatou was admired: a suitor's moral qualities carry-ing little weight in people's judgment, money alone being at the heart of their raptures over Ouleymatou, merchandise that had gone to the highest bidder!" (134–135). Ousmane's friend, Ali, is similarly revolted by Ousmane's abandon-ment of Mireille, his misuse of her property, and his "trying to find cultural justifications" (139) for a physical infatuation. Ali seethes with disappointment: "Ousmane Gueye, the uncompromising disciple of 'Negritude', who used to ad-vise them to 'open up,' was now turning in on himself, with the excuse of not betraying 'his roots!'" (135).[9]

The narrator spells out the stakes, then, for the black man in a culturalist reading of the black female body:

> "Ouleymatou, the symbol of my double life!" Symbol of the black woman, whom he had to emancipate; symbol of Africa, one of whose "enlightened sons" he was.
>
> In his mind he confused Ouleymatou with Africa, "an African [sic] which has to be restored to its prerogatives, to be helped to evolve!" When he was with the African woman, he was the prophet of the "word made truth", the messiah with the unstinting hands, providing nourishment for body and soul. And these roles suited his deep involvement. . . . When those gentle black hands massaged his muscles with infinite tenderness, a deep affinity was established. It ate into his innermost being, shook him to the core, disturbed his very soul, and set him up as a "fighter," "an ambassador of his people". . . . (149–150)

In a clairvoyant glimpse of postcolonial theorizing to come, Mariama Bâ has drawn the portrait of feminine and masculine identities under decolonizing na-tionalism, located them in their respective private and public spaces, and sig-naled their distinct relationships to the past and the present/future.

But even as *Scarlet Song* critiques polygyny and the mystique of the black woman under cultural nationalism, it reveals a certain ambivalence: it indulges in this mystique and simultaneously views the sexuality of Ouleymatou and the women she represents with suspicion, if not hostility.

Both *So Long a Letter* and *Scarlet Song* suppress the representation of middle-class women's sexuality—in correlation perhaps to their espousal of monogamy and the quest for female dignity. Sexual desire or behavior is absent in the por-traiture of the enlightened, middle-class Rama and Aïssatou—whether an effect of caste or ethnic stereotyping or an expression of Islamic or colonial models of femininity.[10] Simultaneously, a menacing sexuality is explicitly assigned to the naive or lower-class antagonists who become second wives in *So Long a Let-ter* and *Scarlet Song*. Significantly, descriptions of Mireille are limited to the mention early on in the novel of the young woman's *uncontrived* appeal: her "green eyes," "long hair," and "enchanting beauty." The white woman's "God-given" unbeguiling beauty is in counterpoint to *Scarlet Song*'s titillating scenes of Ouleymatou's toilette and her arsenal of seductive weaponry. The lower-class, uneducated, and man-hungry Ouleymatou works at seduction. Ironically, she is in this novel—as "black woman" is more generally for many a male writer—the occasion for lyrical expression. The following passage in which Ouleymatou prepares to seduce Ousmane for the first time is a veritable space of textual/sexual play (and possibly pastiche). Parting ways with the ponderous issues we associate with "Literature," this description would easily be at home in the romance novel of popular culture (and therefore blurs the distinction between "elite" and popular forms):

> She smeared a scented salve over her whole body till it shone and her oiled skin clothed her like a velvety film, which followed the swellings of her small firm breasts, curved over her hips to cover her firm, rounded buttocks.
>
> Clouds of incense rose up from a clay vessel and spiraled round her parted legs; she offered her whole body to its warm, fragrant caresses.
>
> She took strings of white beads from a box and draped them tinkling round her hips. She chose a pagne of light material, transparent enough to suggest her curves, while still remaining decent. She unfolded a new white bra that she had bought specially to emphasize her bust.
>
> She tied a little *gongo* powder in a piece of muslin and slipped the sweet-scented aphrodisiac between her breasts. . . .
>
> As she moved, a gauzy boubou allowed a glimpse, now of a plump shoulder, now of her breasts in their lacy prison, now the strings of beads, standing out round her hips. (108–109)

This voyeuristic passage is not unlike several in Pierre Loti's *Roman d'un spahi* (1870/1992), in which the native Senegalese girl Fatou-gaye seduces the *spahi* with her body, clothing, fragrance, and sexual savoir-faire. While such passages in Loti and other colonial writers draw on and extend racial and imperial discourse of the era with the effect of "othering" Africa, the effect of such passages in *Scarlet Song* is to "other" the lower-class or uneducated black woman on whom the novel foists sexuality and who in the current context represents a menace to middle-class family stability and the progressive nation.

The rift between the middle-class writing heroines and their antagonists can be understood in relationship to socioeconomic pressures and the lack of opportunities for women. This is one reason that Sembène's short novel (1973) and film (1974) *Xala,* which are intertexts for Bâ's novels, are helpful. They tie the representation of polygyny and gender roles to a portrait of neocolonialism, even though the film fails to portray the financial strain of the family of the new bride as it is depicted in the written text. Here, then, I take issue with Florence Stratton, who implies, if I read her correctly, that a male writer's (or filmmaker's) simultaneous portrayal of a woman prostitute (or, presumably, a second or third wife) *and* the multiple mechanisms of social anomie lead to an eclipse of women's specificity in favor of supposedly larger oppressions of global politics or totalitarian political regimes. I would argue, on the contrary, that failure to represent the social dynamic within which women's oppression is realized may put women center stage but can be terribly misleading.

To the extent that *Death and the King's Horseman,* in its defense of Africa, deploys a certain mythology of masculine and feminine roles, perspectives on gender have allowed us to reveal the asymmetries of its vision. With regard to *Scarlet Song,* reading with attention to gender has allowed us to go beyond the conventional view of Bâ's novel as a reflection on the impediments to interracial marriage. The novel is itself gender-aware: Mariama Bâ points to the dangerous mystifications implicit in Soyinka's and all such readings of the African woman as bridge to the past or to cultural origins. But a consideration of the dynamics of class in *Scarlet Song* forces us to unpack the way that intellect and body, cosmopolitanism and backwardness (the lack of true "modern" ambition associated with formal or Western-style education) nonetheless inform Bâ's deployment of women. *Scarlet Song*'s revolt is incomplete. It pleads thematically for the importance of education and other fruits of modernity for all women, as does *So Long a Letter,* but it unwittingly projects a representational bias against lower-class and poor women. Bâ's gender-sensitive vision reveals the limits of négritude's space for Woman, but the lens of gender through which she writes is insufficient to clear a textual space for the poor or uneducated women whom it leaves in limbo. Ironically, both *Death and the King's Horseman* and *Scarlet Song* reveal the difficulty in imagining a truly progressive egalitarian society.

Gender analysis is one of several critical approaches that have challenged the notion of literature as pure, transcendent, and sacred. This matters because literary texts become our authorities on history, on the present, and on possibilities for the future. We need to see these texts as inquiries and experiments with all their contradictions: As long as social hierarchy informs and is normalized by creative processes, gender will remain a critical point of entry into complex social and aesthetic dynamics.

Notes

I am grateful to Susan Andrade, Sandra Zagarell, and the editors for helpful comments on earlier drafts of this essay.

1. See http://www.codesria.org/Links/Training_and_Grants/Gender_institute.htm (accessed August 15, 2003).
2. Roundtable at Festival of African Writing, Brown University, November 1991.
3. Scholars have critiqued the ideological aspects of the play, the choice of this particular ritual from "class entrenched" ancient Oyo kingdom as the centerpiece of a defense of African civilizations, and the metaphysical vision of African unity that the play proposes (Jeyifo 1985). See also Appiah (1992, 73–84) and George (1999).
4. Tejumola Olaniyan has argued that for Soyinka, "The animist world-view is not inherently reactionary or anti-progress" (1992, 495). Soyinka himself writes that super-

stition, which includes "animism" and all the great religions, Buddhism, Roman Catholicism, Islam, and so forth, "has never yet prevented the rise to technological heights of any society" (1988, 74).

5. The Noma Award for publishing in Africa was created by the late Shoichi Noma, formerly president of Kodansha Ltd., the Japanese publishing house. Established in 1979, the award is open to African writers and scholars whose work is published in Africa. For more information, see http://www.nomaaward.org (accessed July 30, 2005).

6. There is little in their years of separation and tenacious commitment to suggest Ousmane's future change of heart and Mireille's fragility. Likewise, Ousmane's sister appears on the scene to deliver the fatal message of Ousmane's second marriage and then just as quickly and implausibly disappears. I read these textual discrepancies and excesses as signs of Bâ's will to contrive an impervious moral.

7. The editor of the novel, writing a tribute to Bâ that appears in the French text but is left out of the English version, draws a broad lesson about human nature: "Love does not always triumph over [the] prejudice and misunderstandings that are part of the cultural heritage that each of us carries as both wealth and burden" (my translation).

Mbye Cham (1987) sees the novel pragmatically as a cautionary tale about the dangers of ignoring the sway of race, class, and culture, while Aminata Maïga Kâ (1981) writes that all Bâ's heroines are punished for disobeying their parents and defying social norms.

For a reading that focuses on the couple's cultural differences but breaks with this pattern, see Juliana Makuchi Nfah-Abbenyi (1997, 110–123). Susan Stringer also argues that Bâ's heroines are presented "as victims of their male partners rather than of their own lack of judgment" (1996, 62).

8. On the question of polygyny, modernity, and the nation, see Uzo Esonwanne (1997, 82–100).

9. Ali is recalling an oft-forgotten dimension of Senghorian négritude that is also rearticulated in the novel: the "return to the source" is complemented by cultural mixing and participation in the creation of a universal civilization. For Ali, Ousmane makes an excuse of the first to deny the second.

10. Ouleymatou's ethnic or caste status is never mentioned, but her sexualization by the narrator recalls the stereotyping of Laobé women performers by Wolof women (McNee 2000, 47–48).

With respect to Islam, Calloway and Creevey write that "husbands are obligated to provide food, clothing, shelter and sexual satisfaction (*defined as producing children*)" (1994, 36, my emphasis).

As for the colonial factor, there are interesting parallels in other contexts to the production of "enlightened" women in Bâ's novels. Kumari Jayawardena writes that the decolonized Asian bourgeois man, "himself a product of Western education or missionary influence, needed as his partner a 'new woman,' educated in the relevant foreign language, dressed in the new styles and attuned to Western ways. These women had to show that they were the negation of everything that was considered 'backwards' in the old society: that they were no longer secluded, veiled and illiterate with bound feet and minds, threatened with death on their husband's funeral pyre" (1986, 12–13). Ironically, in Bâ's Senegal, it is the men who collude—conveniently with lower-class women or to maintain caste privilege—to hold on to the atavistic practice of polygyny.

In the context of the United States, Hazel Carby (1999) argues that against the backdrop of twentieth-century racial politics and the legacy of slavery, black female sexuality was perceived by middle-class black women as degenerate. Carby cites Jane Edna Hunter's

A Nickel and a Prayer (1940) to the effect that black women's sexual behavior threatened to "tumble gutterward," menacing the "headway which the Negro had made toward the state of good citizenship" (27). Carby concludes that "Hunter secures her personal autonomy in the process of claiming the right to circumscribe the rights of young black working-class women and to transform their behavior on the grounds of nurturing the progress of the race as a whole" (29).

References

Africa Today. 1997. 44, no. 2.

Amadiume, Ifi. 1987. *Male Daughters, Female Husbands: Gender and Sex in an African Society.* London: Zed Books.

Appiah, Kwame Anthony. 1992. "The Myth of an African World." In *My Father's House: Africa in the Philosophy of Culture,* 73–84. New York: Oxford University Press.

Bâ, Mariama. 1981. *So Long a Letter.* Translated Modupé Bodé-Thomas. London: Heinemann. First published as *Une si longue letter.* Dakar: Nouvelles Editions Africaines, 1980.

———. 1986. *Scarlet Song.* Translated by Dorothy Blair. Essex: Longman. First published as *Un chant écarlate.* Dakar: Les Nouvelles Editions Africaines, 1981.

Calloway, Barbara, and Lucy Creevey. 1994. *The Heritage of Islam: Women, Religion, and Politics in West Africa.* Boulder, Colo.: Lynne Rienner.

Carby, Hazel. 1999. "Policing the Black Woman's Body." In *Cultures in Babylon: Black Britain and African America.* London: Verso.

Cham, Mbaye. 1987. "Contemporary Society and the Female Imagination: A Study of the Novels of Mariama Bâ." In *Women in African Literature Today: A Review,* edited by Eldred Durosimi Jones, 89–101. Trenton, N.J.: Africa World Press.

Chatterjee, Partha. 1993. *The Nation and Its Fragments.* Princeton, N.J.: Princeton University Press.

Esonwame, Uzo. 1997. "Enlightenment Epistemology and 'Aesthetic Cognition': Mariama Bâ's *So Long a Letter.*" In *The Politics of (M)othering: Womanhood, Identity, and Resistance in African Literature,* edited by Obioma Nnaemeka, 82–100. London: Routledge.

George, Olakunle. 1999. "Cultural Criticism in Wole Soyinka's *Death and the King's Horseman.*" *Representations* 67 (Summer): 67–91.

Harrell-Bond, Barbara. 1980. "Mariama Bâ: Winner of the First Noma Award for Publishing in Africa." *African Book Publishing Record* 6: 209–214.

Jameson, Frederic. 1986. "Third World Literature in the Era of Multinational Capitalism." *Social Text* 15 (Fall): 65–88.

JanMohamed, Abdul. 1983. *Manichean Aesthetics: The Politics of Literature in Colonial Africa.* Amherst: University of Massachusetts Press.

Jayawardena, Kumari. 1986. *Feminism and Nationalism in the Third World.* London: Zed Books.

Jeyifo, Biodun. 1985. "Tragedy, History and Ideology: Soyinka's *Death and the King's Horseman* and Ebrahim Hussein's *Kinjeketile.*" In *Marxism and African Literature,* edited by Georg M. Gugelberger, 94–109. London: James Currey.

Kâ, Aminata Maïga. 1985. "Ramatoulaye, Aïssatou, Mireille et . . . Mariama Bâ." *Notre Librairie* 81: 129–34.

Loti, Pierre. 1870/1992. *Roman d'un spahi.* Paris: Gallimard.

McNee, Lisa. 2000. *Selfish Gifts.* Albany: State University of New York Press.

Nfah-Abbenyi, Juliana Makuchi. 1997. *Gender in African Women's Writing: Identity, Sexuality, and Difference.* Bloomington: Indiana University Press.

Olaniyan, Tejumola. 1992. "Dramatizing Postcoloniality: Wole Soyinka and Derek Walcott." *Theatre Journal* 44, no. 4: 485–499.

Oyewumi, Oyeronke. 1997. *The Invention of Woman: Making an African Sense of Western Gender Discourses.* Minneapolis: University of Minnesota Press.

Radhakrishnan, R. 1992. "Nationalism, Gender, and the Narrative of Identity." In *Nationalisms and Sexuality,* edited by Andrew Parker, Mary Russo, Doris Sommer, and Patricia Yaeger, 77–95. New York: Routledge.

Sangari, Kumkum, and Sudesh Vaid, eds. 1990. "Introduction." In *Recasting Women: Essays in Indian Colonial History,* edited by Kumkum Sangari and Sudesh Vaid. New Brunswick, N.J.: Rutgers University Press.

Sembène, Ousmane. 1973. *Xala.* Paris: Présence Africaine.

———. 1974. *Xala.* New Yorker Films.

Soyinka, Wole. 1975. *Death and the King's Horseman.* New York: Hill and Wang.

———. 1988. "Who's Afraid of Elesin Oba?" In *Art, Dialogue and Outrage: Essays on Literature and Culture,* edited by Biodun Jeyifo, 62–81. New York: Pantheon.

Stratton, Florence. 1994. *Contemporary African Literature and the Politics of Gender.* London: Routledge.

Stringer, Susan. 1996. *The Senegalese Novel by Women: Through Their Own Eyes.* New York: Peter Lang.

Toupouzis, Daphne. 1988. "Women of Substance." *Africa Report* (May/June): 70–71.

12 Representing Culture and Identity: African Women Writers and National Cultures

Nana Wilson-Tagoe

Dominant Narratives of Nation and Culture

The problem with the notion of culture in African literature is that it is often embedded in representational narratives of the nation and shaped by the politics of national emergence. In such narratives, "culture" becomes part of a political process of constructing the distinctive identity of a national collective through the representation of its history and the creation of new knowledge about its place in world history. When culture is so determined by the exigencies of anticolonial discourse, linking nation and culture runs the risk of presenting culture as coherent and homogenous instead of continually contested and renewed.

As prominent twentieth-century commentators on African culture, both Frantz Fanon (1961/1967, 166–199) and Amilcar Cabral (1980, 138–154) recognize this risk when they reject tendencies to define culture in terms of concrete behavior patterns and customs and focus instead on people's fluid movements throughout the course of their political and economic history. Fanon also anticipates the paradoxes we confront in representing culture in literature. On the one hand, he sees culture as "the whole body of efforts made by a people in the sphere of thought to describe, justify, and praise the action through which that people has created itself and keeps itself in existence" (1967, 188). On the other hand, he recognizes that this "body of efforts" can never be stable and fixed, that it is from the "instability of cultural signification that the national culture comes to be articulated as a dialectic of various temporalities—modern, colonial, postcolonial, native" (Bhabha 1994, 152). Fanon's warning against the reification of culture stems from his sense of culture's contemporariness and its continually transforming and contested aspects.

In spite of their sense of culture's fluidity and presentness, neither Cabral nor Fanon pursues the ramifications of cultural fluidity in relation to gender. For Fanon, the major power struggle in colonial relations is between colonizer and colonized and between black and white. Women's liberation and agency become part of the radical and revolutionary history of the anticolonial struggle and require no separate elaboration. The likelihood that men may seek to subordinate women even within the revolutionary movement is certainly not a consideration in Fanon's major text, *The Wretched of the Earth* (1961/1967). Even where Fanon broaches the question of gender in his short piece, "Algeria Unveiled" (1965, 32–67), the fluctuating history of the veil as a mechanism of resistance completely overshadows the subtext of the abuse and humiliation of the unveiled Algerian girl by her male compatriots, and the exploration of the local politics of the veil goes no further than the fact that "traditions demanded a rigid separation of the sexes" (65).

For Fanon, then, the possibility of a distinct history of women's agency (in terms of its sources, motivations, and dynamics) is never fully theorized, even though he recognizes the heterogeneity of national agency and the various temporalities within which national cultures are articulated. In *The Wretched of the Earth,* Fanon envisages the future of the postcolonial nation when he ponders the quality of its social relations and the future of humanity within the new nation (1961/1967, 189). Yet he never anticipated the new interrogations that an interpretive concept such as gender would soon provoke in women's rethinking of nationhood and national culture. Anne McClintock astutely describes the suppression of gender in his theorizing when she claims that "gender runs like a multiple fissure through Fanon's work, splitting and displacing the 'Manichean delirium' to which he repeatedly returns" (1997, 96).

In Cabral's theorizations, an emphasis on culture as both the product and determinant of national liberation inspires a comprehensive and dynamic view of culture in which the positive cultural values of different social groups create a popular and national culture. Though Cabral suggests that the social inferiority of women would limit such a culture, he leaves the resolution of such contradictions to "the balances and solutions which society engenders to resolve conflicts" (1980, 152, 149). Within his generalized and collective view of culture, therefore, gender disappears as a constitutive factor of social/sexual relations and as a determinant of power. Robert Young (2001) has argued that the dialectical form of identity that culture preserves is, in Cabral's account, very different from the performative kind of identity described by modern commentators. Cabral's notion of identity, Young argues, "results from the place of an individual within a framework of a culture that operates as a constant form of resistance, passive or otherwise" (291).

Nation, Culture, and Gender

It is precisely the conceptual challenge offered by the performative that problematizes Cabral's discourse and opens avenues for rethinking culture in terms of gender, especially in a postcolonial era. The work of critics such as Molara Ogundipe-Leslie, which is frequently overshadowed by the dominant theories of Fanon and Cabral, challenges the assumption that the history of women's agency should be read exclusively in terms of the liberation discourse of the national struggle. Fanon may talk in general terms of how traditions become unstable and "shot through by centrifugal tendencies" in national struggles (1961/1967, 180). But it is the work of theorists such as Ogundipe-Leslie (1994) and the imaginative writing of African women that relate these transformative possibilities to the complexities, contradictions, and ambiguities of women's histories and illustrate how women may be located differently within nationalist struggles.

Ogundipe-Leslie's focus on women's condition as a process presents a crucial framework for exploring culture from the perspective of women's lives. In situating women's quests for transformations within broader economic, social, and political transformations in Africa, Ogundipe-Leslie interrogates the generalizations of Fanon and Cabral by addressing the contradictions between women's inherited cultures and their modern conditions of life. Her questions and explorations expose gaps in the accumulated knowledge of history and culture and reveal the extent to which gender ideologies permeate the politics of culture, history, and nationalism.

These varying perspectives on culture and identity demonstrate that there cannot be a single narrative of culture within a national construct. We need a wider interpretive framework not only for reading contemporary texts of culture against the grain of nationalist theorizations but also for exploring productive tensions between social science discourses on culture and the performative narratives that enact contending and liberating forms of cultural identification.

The "traditional" opposition between the empirically centered social sciences and the generally imaginative thrusts of literature has been blurred by recent moves toward narrative in the social sciences and the increasingly sociohistorical focus in literary studies. Yet the two disciplines still have distinct epistemologies and equally different expectations from language and narrative. On the one hand, the constative language indispensable to the empirical methodologies of the social sciences describes reality as it exists, independent of linguistic reference. On the other hand, performative language as a speech act creates its own reality and wills new states of existence into being. In the social sciences, language represents objective facts and works to produce explicatory concepts about reality; in the imaginative arts, it produces meanings about reality instead of representing it.

Explorations of culture and gender benefit from both disciplines in spite of their different approaches to language and narrative. It is the tension between the constative and the performative in imaginative writing that allows texts to engage with historical, sociological, and cultural contexts and at the same time project their alternative possibilities. It is also within the performative that we uncover repressed aspects of everyday culture and in the process illuminate the psychodynamics of cultural identification and their implications for how we internalize gender ideologies.

This chapter focuses particularly on Ama Ata Aidoo and Yvonne Vera because their narratives consistently explore history and culture in terms of women's struggles for agency and confront ideologies of femininity and masculinity entrenched in normative gender norms. Their works place these struggles in different historical contexts and create histories of women that question both a fixation with the nationalist struggles of the mid-twentieth century and the masculinist ways in which they have been represented. Aidoo's play *Anowa* (1970) investigates the possibilities and contradictions of women's ambiguous position in a nineteenth-century Ghanaian world touched by a new capitalist modernity. Vera's novel *Nehanda* (1993) dramatizes the impact of a woman's spiritual leadership on a patriarchal Shona world destabilized by colonial incursions, while in *Butterfly Burning* (1998) she focuses on a colonial urban Zimbabwean world that reshapes women's traditional roles and aspirations.

Aidoo and Vera resist the tendency to subsume and foreclose women's histories within patriarchal views of nationalist struggles. In both *Anowa* and *Butterfly Burning*, the colonial worlds are at once sites of modernity and disruptions of traditionally regulated gender relations, with the authors confronting both sites simultaneously. In situations where political upheavals throw old orders into chaos and bring new ones into being, the terms and organization of gender and culture may be revised. But they also may not be (Scott 1986, 1075). This is the ambiguous process anticipated in *Butterfly Burning*. The old world is transformed by the dreams of white settlers and survives only precariously in the transformed city. The urban world is thus almost entirely the novel's context. Its chaos and newness present a chance for recreation, with Vera insisting that the process within this flux should involve both gender transformation and the community's collective self-creation. Because it encapsulates both a struggle against oppressive gender codes and the community's larger colonial struggle, the quest of the woman protagonist, Phephelaphi, becomes a paradigm for the national quest itself.

In the nineteenth-century world of Aidoo's *Anowa*, the context of confrontation with gender and culture is slightly different. The old traditional world seems like an impregnable force whose systems of social and sexual relations rigidly define a woman's place and possibilities. Yet the social power on which this world is based is not as unified and coherent as it appears to be. It is disrupted by the contending perspectives of an old man and an old woman, who are representative voices of culture, and the values of a new capitalist modernity that has already created an exploitative new class. These fissures are conveyed through the dialogized voices of the play and suggest important connections between colonialism, the language of male dominance, economic exploitation, and the history of slavery in terms of an expanded view of gender and culture.

In exploring women's relationships to their bodies, to home, to nation, and to language, Aidoo and Vera often point to moments of resistance and reinterpretation in terms of "the play of metaphoric invention and imagination" (Scott 1986, 1067). The emphasis on invention and imagination exemplifies the fact that art, rather than simply "expressing" culture, sometimes works against culture. By redefining and reimagining the social signs of culture and everyday communication, art can transform cultural and gendered meanings even if such transformations are achieved more through style and mode of narration than through the actual representations of alternative societies. I show, especially in the last section of this chapter dealing with the writers' later works, that Aidoo and Vera continually engage in such imaginative transformations.

Aidoo's *Anowa*

Anowa is a play about the life and death of Anowa, a visionary woman who transgresses familial and community codes by insisting on choosing her own husband as well as the terms on which she will relate to him as a wife. Inspired by an egalitarian vision, Anowa's marriage to Kofi Ako begins well when the pair leaves the village to make their fortunes trading with British merchants in the developing capitalist economy in coastal Ghana. The marriage falters, however, when Kofi Ako buys slaves to help with their expanding business and counters Anowa's objections by asserting his masculine power and threatening to send Anowa back to the village.

Disappointed and disoriented, Anowa sees a connection between her husband's exploitation of slaves and the greed that made her community complicit with the bigger crime of the slave trade. In a dream, she takes on the historical burden of the slave mother and relives the moment of enslavement as a terrible wrenching and a loss of her community's creativity. From this illumination, she is able to connect Kofi Ako's sexual impotence with his acquisitiveness and greed, and she publicly exposes him. Shamed, Kofi Ako kills himself. Anowa, still disoriented and dazed, drowns herself.

The tragedy of Anowa's marriage unravels against the unequal marriage of Anowa's father, Osam, and her mother, Badua, and in the context of a community represented by the opposing views of an old woman and an old man. The two contradictory perspectives—the old woman's fixed ideas about gender norms and the old man's more fluid view of change and possibility—dramatize the paradoxes within which the play imagines change and transformation.

Anowa confronts the conflation of imperial and male domination by forcing us to read the normative gender-inflected signs and symbols of culture against contradictory languages within the culture. The play suggests that the ascendant patriarchal norms that construct the place of Anowa and other women in the community remain "natural" only because they suppress contradiction, opposition, and ambiguity. Rather than simply presenting masculine perspectives as dominant values, therefore, the play creates a battleground of meaning in which the very norms that marginalize and oppress women are undermined within the society. For instance, the masculine perception of women's language as babble "that no real man can take seriously" (Aidoo 1970, 92) is counteracted by Anowa's monumental and transformative vision of history and gender. Similarly, various attempts by Osam, Badua, and the old woman to define Anowa strictly in terms of the community's myths of continuity and domesticity are countered by the old man's open view of the instability of such constructions.

Indeed, the very notion of "home" as the location of culture-specific modes of perceiving the world and the locus of identity is called into question when Anowa distinguishes between her destiny and "home" and claims her identity as a wayfarer: "A wayfarer is a traveler. Therefore, to call someone a wayfarer is a painless way of saying he does not belong. That he has no home, no family, no village, no stool of his own, has no feast, no holidays, no state, no territory" (97). Here she refuses the connotations of identity through which her father and others envision her destiny and possibilities and sees her own developing vision as an intervention into the meanings of home and culture. Carole Boyce Davies helps us understand Anowa's rebellion when she describes stable notions of home as an "illusion of coherence and safety based on the exclusion of specific histories of oppression and resistance, the repression of differences even within oneself" (1994, 65).

Anowa's critique of home encodes a transforming vision. The split between self and home is a tension between the normative gender values of the collective and the conceptual language of gender transformation contained in Anowa's vision. I show later that such a concept of language is specifically elaborated in Aidoo's novel *Our Sister Killjoy* (1977), but it is also applicable to the play and demonstrates Aidoo's desire not only to create histories of women's agency but also to explore the dynamic social and historical contexts of national transformation. Language in this sense encompasses all the "meaning-constituting systems" through which we organize cultural practices and construct meanings. This language can articulate the future and is one in which men and women can share fears, fantasies, histories, and anxieties. This is the language Anowa seeks even in the nineteenth-century setting within which the play explores her predicament. It is central to her experiment with an idea of marriage based not on unequal power relations between men and women but on a shared partnership of work, history, anxiety, and fantasy. The play postulates a kind of neutral ground for the working out of a relationship of equality.

But at the same time it also shows how gender hierarchies are kept alive. Both Kofi Ako's notions of masculinity and the community's gender perspectives are seen to mediate Anowa's new experiment in gender relations, and the play demonstrates their power even in the face of Anowa's radical vision. Her experiment therefore collapses with the failure of her marriage, although this failure is less significant than the growth, insights, and possibilities that her experiment opens up. It is, for instance, through her unraveling sense of displacement, alienation, and homelessness that Anowa acquires a view that connects the community's gender regulations, Kofi Ako's exploitative business ventures, and the community's willed amnesia about the slave trade.

Anowa's ability to resituate the memory of the slave trade is crucial. By filling the gaps in the community's history narrated in the opening section, it broadly explores political, cultural, and gendered processes by making connections between slavery, perverted fertility, and sexual impotence. Anowa's prophetic dream, the psychic means through which she internalizes and relives the story of enslavement, illustrates this. It is significant that the play recalls it at a point when Kofi Ako has become the ultimate manifestation of the new colonized class. Anowa's own identity is a subject of debate, and perceptions about her are split between the unyielding views of the old woman (who cannot accept how a woman can know better than her husband) and the more tolerant vision of the old man (who believes that the children of a latter day might know what has remained hidden from previous generations). Though the dream presents Anowa as the mother whose children are brutalized and enslaved, it does not symbolize the common nationalist vision of the African woman as bearer of the nation's children. Anowa relives not the teleological history of the nation but its sordid and expunged past. We have moved away, it seems, from the unproblematized past of the nation's history into what Fanon would call "the zone of occult instability where the people dwell" (1967, 183), the fluctuating movement of history that the people shape and within which everything can be called into question.

For Fanon and Homi Bhabha, this instability merely marks the various temporalities from which national cultures come to be articulated (Fanon 1967; Bhabha 1994, 152). For Aidoo, however, it is the point of gender mediation. It connects motherhood and slavery and marginalization and oppression and points to a differentiated female history that disrupts the homogeneity of a national culture. Importantly, Anowa's dream vision of herself as the mother whose children are enslaved and brutalized by white slavers is a reinstatement of her prophetic and priestly role, since only a powerful visionary figure can move beyond the huge and tantalizing structures of the new modernity to unravel its aberrations. The play's linking of motherhood and slavery gives a dual view of Anowa and highlights the possibilities of her ambiguous position.

In an interview with Adeola James in 1990, Aidoo explains the immense significance of a gender perspective in discourses of culture in the following way: "I think part of the resentment which our brothers feel about any discussion on women is because they feel it diverts from the 'main issues.' On the contrary, I feel the revolutionizing of our continent hinges on the woman question. It might be the catalyst for development, but people feel very nervous about it" (James 1990, 26). What Aidoo calls "the woman question" is more complex than the issue of sex roles. It involves larger issues of social, cultural, and economic relations and therefore becomes a paradigm for exploring national culture and agency as a whole.

Vera's *Butterfly Burning*

Butterfly Burning captures a transitional moment in Zimbabwe's history and uses it to explore possibilities for national and individual self-creation. Set in the emerging "modern" city of Bulawayo, it tells the love story of Phephelaphi, a young woman born and bred in the city, and Fumbatha, an older man of fifty with an inherited legacy of resistance. Their intense relationship survives until Phephelaphi seeks to extend herself by applying to train as a nurse. Her quest sets her in collision with Fumbatha, especially when she aborts a pregnancy in order to free herself to enter college. When she becomes pregnant for the second time, Phephelaphi sets herself on fire and burns in her own storm. The couple's tragic story is linked to the stories of other African characters in the same way as Phephelaphi's quest for agency becomes a paradigm for the community's own struggle for freedom.

In *Butterfly Burning*, national culture and cultural identification become more a matter of creating "the Word" from what is torn, frayed, and new than a matter of cultural consolidation or deconstruction. The city and township of Bulawayo in the 1940s are paradoxical and contradictory worlds, suspended between the first *chimurenga* of 1896 and white settlers' transformation of the land. In the 1940s, Vera's characters live suspended between submission to settler rule and latent resistance and creation. It is within the limits and possibilities of this transitional moment that Vera explores the meaning of a community's culture and its implications for women. Her evocation of city and township life of the 1940s enacts the paradox of limitation and possibility. In this period of European transformation of Zimbabwe, culture is explored in terms of creation rather than deconstruction. The townships, built specifically to confine and limit Africans, are ironically the very context for the creation of new languages of culture. Africans live within its cracks, dream of flight, and create a music of sorrow and transcendence. The city fascinates and beckons, and its trains connect black people to new growing things, new accents and sounds, the beginnings of a language in which English, the language of domination, is appropriated to express different orders of experience.

In many ways, Vera's emphasis on the space, perceptions, and sensibilities of a modern colonial world dramatizes what Bhabha has theorized about newness and cultural translation:

> The borderline work of culture demands an encounter with "newness" that is not part of the continuum of past and present. It creates a sense of the new as an insurgent act of cultural translation. Such art does not merely recall the past as social cause or aesthetic precedent; it renews the past, refiguring it as a contingent "in-between" space, that innovates and interrupts the performance of the present. (1994, 7)

For Vera, such a process of cultural translation begins as a drastic reorganization of women's traditional roles. The city's chaos and newness spawn a new breed of women who, uninhibited and forthright, challenge the established colonial and patriarchal orders. This is the world from which the protagonist, Phephelaphi, emerges as a woman who makes claims on time and space. Though Phephelaphi's personal quest dominates the novel's narrative, it is intertwined with the political and social history of the city and is not very different from the community's need to create a new identity and free itself from colonial limitations.

In constructing the narrative of *Butterfly Burning* around the individual and intertwined quests of women protagonists, Vera experiments with the possibilities of different and contrasting languages of culture. *Butterfly Burning* is narrativized on several levels as a communal quest. The community is constantly defined as a people pitched against a contrastingly hostile world. Men cutting grass, building city structures, or dancing are seen to be connected in their unified desires for space, voice, and agency.

Yet this communal quest represents only one layer, and there are layers of women's individual stories that enact Vera's awareness of the difference and specificity of female psychology. Her particular focus on women's narrative within the collective is an attempt to "give a language to the intrasubjective and corporeal experience of women left mute by culture in the past" (Kristeva 1986, 194). The narrative self-consciously states this specificity and focus from the very beginning, literally anticipating both the novel's ending and its moral underpinnings:

> [Phephelaphi] would be in flight like a bird, laden with the magnificent grace of her wings. She would be brimming with a lonely ecstasy gathered from all the corners of her mind. She would be whispering something which he could not hear, a message he would recall much later, when all his senses were finally free: he has moved from his own song into her astonishing melody. (Vera 1998, 29)

By implicating every space and character in the story of Phephelaphi and Fumbatha, Vera makes this story both the nucleus and the paradigm for exploring male-female cultural identification and identities. In this sense, Phephelaphi and Fumbatha become iconic figures whose relationship unravels the problematics of cultural representation and subjective identities. As the most masculinist figure in the novel and as the character most linked to the past of resistance, Fumbatha encapsulates the discourse of both patriarchy and liberation. But his friendship with Phephelaphi presents a path of possibility for the communication across genders that Aidoo envisions in *Our Sister Killjoy*.

Phephelaphi's background presents a view of struggle outside Fumbatha's experience: the struggle of women in their attempts to deal with motherhood, to find liberating identities and meanings beyond the false faces and identities that hide their wounds. It is a picture of women's lives that could transform the view of women's sexuality that has always characterized Fumbatha's relationships with the women of Makokoba township. At the same time, Fumbatha's own history of resistance and tragedy (which he never divulges to Phephelaphi) could provide a view of broader struggles to a young woman who has lived her life making individualistic claims on time, space, and existence as if these could be claimed at will.

But the possibilities suggested by their first meeting do not survive their claims on each other. Fumbatha sees Phephelaphi in conventionally feminized terms as a shelter, as one who will endorse his abandonment of a heritage of resistance and the making of a new dream. For Phephelaphi, Fumbatha is masculinized as an anchor, someone to hold onto in her efforts to attain freedom. While Phephelaphi's pursuit of individuality and agency leads her to abandon a vulnerable dependence, Fumbatha never recognizes the oppressiveness of making another individual an anchor for his dreams of freedom. Indeed, their entire relationship is fraught with contradictions and captures the city's untried realities and its distancing of memory.

In *Butterfly Burning*, contradictions are often presented as a contest of authority between the pedagogical and the performative. The yearnings and motivations that drive Phephelaphi's quest appear to lie outside the notions of womanhood and motherhood in her social world. That is why she looks for a new descriptive language that can define and inscribe her yearnings. Her awakening consciousness of her body as her personal possession and her heightened experience of her sexuality are part of a new language that questions the proprietary closeness and intolerable intimacy of her relationship with Fumbatha. In spite of her naive assumption that the hardened Deliwa, the "shebeen" queen and owner of the township's drinking parlor, possessed answers to her search for meaning, she is actually able to think through and refine her new perceptions as she reacts to cultural assumptions about the obligations of womanhood:

> It was about loving her own eyebrows before he had passed his fingers over them and showed her that she had a smile that was tucked down on the edges. . . . She wanted the time before time, before her legs felt empty without him in them. . . . She wanted the sense of belonging before that kind of belonging which rested on another's wondrous claim. (Vera 1998, 69)

In this sense, her quest involves framing a new way of being in a world that rejects women's subordination and marginality and claims their independent right to self-realization. Her question "How did a woman claim a piece of time and make it glitter?" (70) has no ready answers because the community's conception of womanhood appears to have no space for such a claim. Zandile, one of the older women of the city who is in fact Phephelaphi's biological mother, expresses the cultural consensus when she upbraids Phephelaphi for dreaming beyond what is achievable in a place such as Makokoba:

> What are you going to do in Makokoba without being a man? Do you not know that a woman only has a moment in which to live her whole life? In it she must choose what belongs to her and what does not. No one can verify her claim except time. Makokoba is unkind to women like you who pretend to be butterflies that can land on any blossom they choose. (110)

The entire crisis of identity that Phephelaphi faces as she struggles with pregnancy and the possibility of motherhood hinges on whether one can change this discourse and, in Kristeva's words, claim a multiple "women's time." For Kristeva, the challenge of women's multiple time involves a drastic project of channeling women's difference "into each and every element of the female whole, and, finally, [bringing] out the singularity of each woman, and beyond this, her multiplicities, her plural languages, beyond the horizon, beyond sight, beyond faith itself" (1986, 208).

Kristeva speaks in terms of a broader "antisacrificial" current that animates a new wave of feminism in contemporary Europe. Yet the general idea of women's multiple subjectivities and plural languages is consistent with the notion of agency theorized in Ogundipe-Leslie's work (1994) as critical transformations, a project that moves beyond revisionary engagements with male discourse to explore women's multifaceted social, psychic, and sexual identities. The value of Vera's *Butterfly Burning* is that its exploration of such multiple subjectivities also reveals the problematic nature of the personal in an African context. Redefining the symbolic order, as the novel demonstrates, is fraught with doubt, personal tragedy, and ultimate loneliness.

In *Butterfly Burning*, Vera rethinks this process of cultural identification through a determined and transgressive reframing of the language of culture to produce other meanings and other conceptions of the feminine. In her work, terms that signify the oppressive obligations of womanhood are decentered, displaced, or reframed to create new connotations. The obligations of fertility and motherhood are problematized in the counternarrative of abortion, narrativized not so much as a transgressive act but as one that dislodges cultural boundaries to free other feminine possibilities. Abortion offers an opportunity for Phephelaphi's emergence as an individual, freed to claim a piece of time: "The heart beating is hers, her arms, and she is she. She has emerged out of a cracked shell" (Vera 1998, 107). In the same way, her suicide and the manner in which she claims it indicate not an acceptance of defeat but a self-conscious act of control. She claims a right to die in her own storm and to rise into her own song in contradistinction to Fumbatha's view that woman's place in the national dream is nurturing and passive.

While Vera narrates Phephelaphi's independent acts sympathetically, she focuses on the tremendous difficulties of individual struggles for agency. Phephelaphi's abortion is performed in the bare and sparse landscape beyond the bushes of Makokoba, where the environment seems totally unreceptive. An act that is meant to "order" the disorder of pregnancy therefore appears to pull Phephelaphi into an untidy mess, and her quest seems to become a solitary and invalidated act. Yet Phephelaphi's total engagement with her self-inflicted pain is dramatized as a process toward insight and knowledge and suggests that only a woman's ability to claim agency and assert control over her body will lead to transformations in social and economic circumstances. By suggesting that Fumbatha will eventually rise into Phephelaphi's "song" when all his senses are finally freed, the narrative suggests that Phephelaphi's search for agency and the price she pays for that quest should in a broader sense symbolize the anticolonial struggle.

On another level, Phephelaphi's story is intertwined with the stories of a genealogy of women and their negotiations of culture. The strategy is Vera's way of placing women's condition at the center of the anticolonial struggle and combining gender and nationalist discourses. Phephelaphi's story is woven into the voices and histories of two other women characters. Zandile, for instance, presents a contrasting mode of negotiation in the world of the 1940s. As the most historically aware of the three women, she is also the figure most susceptible to compromising her creativity for necessity, the most willing to shoulder the burden of black pain and suffering, the most anxious to find her happiness through a relationship with a man. Deliwa, in spite of her alert eyes and hardened resilience, is as vulnerable as Zandile when it comes to the obligations of womanhood. Because the women are implicated in each other's histories, Phephelaphi's flight, however difficult, fraught, and "incomplete," speaks to all of them about the crucial importance of not just women's agency but the agency of all oppressed and marginalized people.

Extending the Possibilities of "Culture"

In *The Stone Virgins,* Vera's latest novel, the emphasis is on the meaning of culture and identity at different moments. Rather than narrating the history of past generations as the sum of an autonomous national culture, it presents different "contemporary" periods: colonial Bulawayo, rural Kezi, and postcolonial Bulawayo. The narrative is careful to separate its own fluid conception of history from the deterministic view that skews and destroys the mind of Sibaso, the disillusioned freedom fighter.

For the first time in a novel about war, Vera focuses simultaneously on both the public event and the private inner drama. Set in both the city of Bulawayo and rural Kezi, *The Stone Virgins* narrativizes two wars: the war against white settlers and the new Zimbabwean government's war against dissidents. Within these scenarios Vera weaves the story of Sibaso, a once ardent guerrilla fighter and now a dehumanized dissident who is driven to a dead end by an overpowering sense of disillusionment. His wanton and gratuitous beheading of Thenjiwe, a rural beauty, and his maiming of her sister Nonceba inspire the private story that parallels the public drama of the wars. For on another level the novel is also a love story centered on the love between the sisters and the different love relationships they experience with Cephas, a librarian from eastern Zimbabwe.

Two different perceptions present conflicting views of how histories and cultures construct identities. Sibaso's linear deterministic view sees his community as doomed by centuries of failures and betrayals. He sees his own progress from being an idealist of the struggle to its destroyed victim as one cycle in a continuum of political betrayals that dates back centuries. In his mind, the sacrifice of virgins several centuries ago is no different from the betrayals of the nationalist struggle and his own wanton killing and violation of Thenjiwe and Nonceba.

But the novel also suggests that cultures and identities are frequently contested and reorganized, particularly when there are changes in the structure of power. The novel enacts various moments of such contestations and reorganizations. Women war veterans dramatically reorient themselves differently from the community's cultural norms. Their distinctive experiences break the barriers of male and female roles and immediately create anxieties about possible gender transformations.

Vera presents us with two other situations in which time and context create different kinds of cultural identification and gender relations. The two different relationships Cephas Dube experiences with the sisters Thenjiwe and Nonceba are suggestive in considering new languages in relationships between men and women. In the case of Cephas and Thenjiwe, love, which grows out of the promise of independence, is influenced by the abundant hopes and possibilities this suggests. In contrast, the silent love and regard that grows slowly between

Cephas and the mutilated Nonceba evolves out of the collapse of the nation's imagined coherence and its unimaginably brutal self-destruction. It is therefore a different context that colors this relationship. Both Cephas and Nonceba work their way delicately and tentatively toward each other's feelings, allowing themselves space and freedom to exist as individuals. Vera dramatizes their relationship as a delicate creation, a translation and renewal of culture, rather than a continuum of past and present steeped in assumptions and established systems of meaning.

In *Butterfly Burning,* the dying Phephelaphi predicts that Fumbatha will one day rise into her astonishing melody when all his senses are finally free. While Fumbatha never gets this chance, in *The Stone Virgins* Cephas gropes toward such a possibility. He learns to appreciate not only the different melodies of the single theme of love but also the variegated and multiple nuances in women's personalities. The continuity of the deep feelings he has for the dead Thenjiwe and the living Nonceba illustrates both the incestuous desires he is afraid to admit to and the different needs and aspirations embodied in both sisters. For Vera, the two relationships are ways of thinking beyond fixed notions of culture, gender, and identity that define these categories within the totalities of the nation's ideology rather than in the fluid moments of the nation's becoming. And it is, of course, particularly significant that the male protagonist must make his way through the fluid, gender-conscious spaces of the nation's story.

Vera's work consistently critiques the construction of women within national cultures and the ideologies that stereotype them. As Eva Hunter has recently remarked, however, "She does not suggest for them the possibility of repositioning themselves or passing into other spaces in the country" (2000, 241). In *The Stone Virgins,* this possibility can be envisioned as part of the new language that creates the relationship between Cephas and Nonceba. In spite of visible and invisible scars, Nonceba can look forward to a new path, meet new people, build new friendships, discover qualities of her own, and find places to inhabit without Cephas. The wider implications of what Vera calls "the politics of geographical, historical and socio-economic positionality" (1995, 155) are also conveyed in the novel's attempt (through Sibaso's thoughts) to connect political betrayals in Zimbabwe to the image of a continent that has succumbed to a violent wind. Sibaso himself is too wrapped up in his self-inflicted ruin to explore the implications of his insights, yet his foreclosure marks the beginning of a new and extended context of exploration in Vera's work.

For a wider sense of the relationship between culture, gender, and the dynamics of the global system, we must turn to the work of Aidoo, and in particular to her pivotal work *Our Sister Killjoy.* It is in the dispersed contexts of this novel that we perceive the global forces that have shaped our modern African words. The cultural dilemmas, contradictions, and alienations explored in the local contexts of Aidoo's and Vera's works find their source in the global histories unearthed in the journey of the novel's protagonist, Sissie, a young and politicized Ghanaian woman whose journey to Europe makes up the narrative of *Our Sister Killjoy.*

While a heinous slavery supports the nineteenth-century modernity of the Akan coast in *Anowa,* in *Our Sister Killjoy* a cruel past and a bizarre present haunt the modern era that authorizes Sissie's visit to Europe. The bizarreness of the present is a result of the cataclysmic faults of the ages and the huge boulders thrown across the continent's pathway. It marks a new epoch of the dispersal of African people, a time when the whole continent stands in danger of becoming lost. What, Aidoo seems to ask, is the African's place within this global configuration? How can African cultures and identities be represented from within this wider location?

Bhabha has theorized this phenomenon of dispersal as the "demography of the new internationalism" where the very concepts of "homogenous national cultures, the consensual or contiguous transmission of historical traditions, or 'organic' ethnic communities . . . are in a profound process of redefinition" (1994, 5). Aidoo's novel writes against the grain of this celebrated migratory trend. It contests the notion of universality at the core of Enlightenment constructions of the autonomous subject and critiques assumptions about shared histories and destinies within a globalized world of possibility exemplified by Sissie's scholarship. In fact, Sissie makes a rejection of universalism the conceptual framework of her narrative. In rejecting universal truth, art, and literature, her narrative displaces the story of capitalist modernity and offers an Afrocentric and feminist narrative of the modern.

In the novel, therefore, exile is often a negative process of further slavery and self-diminishment. Sissie privileges an African memory and perspective, and this underlies her strategy of maintaining at all costs the survival of an "African self." It is an Afrocentric perspective, Kwaku Larbi Korang argues, "that is consistent with Mudimbe's argument elsewhere, for the need for the African to go from the situation in which he or she was perceived as a simple functional object to the freedom of thinking of himself or herself as the starting point of an absolute discourse" (1992, 53).

While such a perspective explains the history of European dominance and postcolonial self-diminishment, it may not be adequate for exploring new postcolonial identities in contemporary times. If we stress the relational nature of identity and difference and the productive tensions between them (Lionnet 1995, 5–6), we need more than the absolute discourse that Mudimbe proposes. Something of this possibility may be gleaned in the contradictory pulls of Sissie's account of her relationship with Marija, the German woman she encounters in her travels in Europe. Commentators are often so ready to link Sissie's viewpoint with the author's that they miss the nuances of Aidoo's characterization. It is in the conflicts, paradoxes, and contradictions of this relationship that we recognize the problematic nature of Sissie's strategy and conceptual frame. Sissie constructs Marija's identity from the perspective of her black-eyed squint and from her reading of German and European history, even though she admits that Marija may be different, too warm-natured for Bavaria. Similarly, Marija's own view of Sissie often filters through the assumptions of her history.

Yet Gay Wilentz is right when she observes that the one person who sees beyond Sissie's blackness is Marija, the unhappy housewife (1989, 163). Sissie self-consciously construes Marija's gift of plums as the seduction and appropriation of the West. On a basic everyday level, however, it is Marija who encourages Sissie's self-awareness and definition as an African, as a woman, and as a sexual being. It is within the space Marija provides that Sissie can embrace her own sensibilities as a woman and admit to anxieties about her body, about mother-hood, and about the loneliness of women within a gendered nationalist project. If, as Aidoo has remarked, Sissie responds to Europe through her memories of Africa, it is through her encounter with Marija that her African memories are made performative and given a contemporary relevance. Theoretically, this process of self-construction through other cultures can transform hegemonic systems by producing resistance and counterdiscourses. The process may transform the nature of the counterdiscourse itself. Sissie may see herself as asserting an uncontested African self, but it is in the gaps and inconsistencies of her narrative that the rigid dichotomies she sets up between Marija and herself and between Africa and Europe begin to crumble.

One level of the narrative therefore explores the possibilities of creating imaginative spaces within which power relations can be reorganized. It is here that another meaning of the universal may be explored, not in the sense of an Enlightenment ontology "with its hierarchical forms of rationality" (Bhabha 1994, 137) but in the sense that "the West and the rest share histories, modes of representation and of oppositionality, and that a study of such shared elements can only work against both provincialism and imperialism" (Lionnet 1995, 6).

The various contexts and negotiations of culture and identity that Aidoo and Vera explore provide important interventions into the discourse of culture in African thought and literature. They demonstrate that contrary to the suggestion that African nationalisms create a unified history of resistance, different and contending movements continually mediate and problematize their discourse. The flux of African women's agency throughout history places them in ambiguous and contradictory relations to nationalist ideology and the socio-symbolic order that constitutes women in specifically feminine and limiting ways. In seeking new representations of women's multiple, layered, and contradictory identities, Aidoo and Vera write distinctive trajectories of women's histories that probe totalizing conceptions of culture and normative gender values. Their narratives extend the meaning of culture and demonstrate that it is the gendered time within the redefined national space of women's narrative that yields innovative recreations of culture and identity.

Note

A version of this essay was originally published in *Feminist Africa* 2 (October 2003), available online at http://www.feministafrica.org/fa%202/2level.html.

References

Aidoo, Ama Ata. 1970. *The Dilemma of a Ghost and Anowa.* London: Longman.
——. 1977. *Our Sister Killjoy: Or Reflections from a Black-Eyed Squint.* London: Longman.
Bhabha, Homi. 1994. *The Location of Culture.* London: Routledge.
Cabral, Amilcar. 1980. "National Liberation and Culture." In *Unity and Struggle,* 139–154. Translated by M. Wolfers. London: Heinemann.
Davies, Carole Boyce. 1994. *Black Women, Writing and Identity: Migrations of the Subject.* London: Routledge.
Fanon, Frantz. 1965. "Algeria Unveiled." In *A Dying Colonialism,* 35–67. Translated by H. Chevalier. New York: Grove Press.
——. 1961/1967. *The Wretched of the Earth.* Translated by Constance Farrington. Harmondsworth: Penguin.
Hunter, Eva. 2000. "Zimbabwean Nationalism and Motherhood in Yvonne Vera's *Butterfly Burning.*" *African Studies* 59, no. 2: 229–243.
James, Adeola. 1990. *In Their Own Voices.* London: James Currey.
Korang, Kwaku Larbi. 1992. "Ama Ata Aidoo's Voyage Out: Mapping the Coordinates of Selfhood in *Our Sister Killjoy.*" *Kunapipi* 14, no. 3: 50–61.
Kristeva, Julia. 1986. "Women's Time." In *The Kristeva Reader,* edited by Toril Moi, 187–213. London: Blackwell.
Lionnet, Françoise. 1995. *Postcolonial Representations: Women, Literature, Identity.* Ithaca, N.Y.: Cornell University Press.
McClintock, Anne 1997. "'No Longer in a Future Heaven': Gender, Race and Nationalism." In *Dangerous Liaisons: Gender, Nation and Postcolonial Perspectives,* edited by A. Mufti and E. Shohat, 89–112. Minneapolis: University of Minnesota Press.
Ogundipe-Leslie, Molara. 1994. *Recreating Ourselves: African Women and Critical Transformations.* Trenton, N.J.: Africa World Press.
Scott, Joan Wallach. 1986. "Gender: A Useful Category of Historical Analysis." *American Historical Review* 91, no. 5: 1053–1075.
Vera, Yvonne. 1993. *Nehanda.* Harare: Baobab Books.
——. 1995. "The Prison of Colonial Space." Ph.D. Thesis, York University, Canada.
——. 1998. *Butterfly Burning.* Harare: Baobab Books.
——. 2002. *The Stone Virgins.* Harare: Weaver Press.
Wilentz, Gay. 1989. "The Politics of Exile: Ama Ata Aidoo's *Our Sister Killjoy.*" *Studies in Twentieth Century Literature* 15, no. 1: 159–173.
Young, Robert. 2001. *Postcolonialism: An Historical Introduction.* Oxford: Blackwell.

Part Four

Masculinity,
Misogyny,
and Seniority

13 Working with Gender: The Emergence of the "Male Breadwinner" in Colonial Southwestern Nigeria

Lisa A. Lindsay

As the title implies, this chapter is about the development of a male breadwinner ideal among wage earners in Yorùbáland, Nigeria.[1] At first glance, Nigeria seems an unlikely setting for any study of wage labor, since the vast majority of its economically active population has always been, and still is, engaged in non-wage activities. An International Labour Organization report of the mid-1950s listed Nigeria as the African colony least involved in a wage economy, with 3.6 percent of the able-bodied adult male population working for wages (as opposed, for example, to 7.4 percent in French West Africa, 38.0 percent in the Belgian Congo, and 27.3 percent in Kenya).[2] But even though Nigeria's colonial economy was based on the export of agricultural produce, wage labor was vitally important in creating and maintaining transport and communications infrastructure, as well as staffing mercantile firms and the state bureaucracy. In 1950, 13 percent (30,544 people) of the population of the capital of Lagos earned wages (Nigeria 1950, 83–84).

Moreover, southwestern Nigeria is a fascinating place to study masculinity and wage labor because of its particularly gendered history. As has been well documented, Yorùbá women have a long history of economic independence from men, typically based on careers in market trading. Married couples have historically not pooled their incomes, and in the past there was very little expectation that husbands would act as exclusive, or even primary, providers for wives and children (Fadipe 1940/1970, 88; Fapohunda 1988; Marris 1962, chapter 4; and Sudarkasa 1973). In the most radical treatment of Yorùbá gender history to date, Oyeronke Oyewumi (1997) has even argued that the unitary category of "woman" was not indigenous to southwestern Nigeria; the emergence of a notion of dependent wives was premised first on the colonial construction of Western gender categories in Nigeria. Wage labor in Nigeria was gendered as male from the start, since the colonial state hired only men (even for work that would have been quite familiar to women). Oyewumi argues that "the combination of male wage labor and migration produced a new social identity for females as dependents and appendages of men." Later, in a wonderful insight, she notes, "The symbolism of bread is particularly apt since both bread and the male as sole breadwinner are colonial infusions into Yorùbá culture" (151–152).

I do not dispute that the breadwinner ideal came to southwestern Nigeria as a result of colonialism. But I would like to complicate the story and bring in Nigerian working husbands and wives as active agents in the process, in a context in which the colonial state also operated with mixed motives. The creation of the male breadwinner image entailed two simultaneous moves: 1) to construe male earnings as supportive of wives and children; and 2) either to ignore women's income-earning or to define it as something other than remunerative work. As we will see, colonial officials, trade unionists, and individual male salary earners and their wives approached these two moves in complex and sometimes contradictory ways. The result was the construction of a male breadwinner image, but an ambiguous one. The ambiguities require that we see (Yorùbá) gender as flexible—which I think no one will dispute—and also, as Judith Butler (1990) originally argued, as performative. People "do gender," in a sense, by acting in particular ways for particular reasons, some of which have to do with existing gender ideologies but some of which can be improvisations for specific ends. These practices can then influence what people consider to be normative behavior for men and women.

Gender can be understood and explored in at least three different but overlapping ways: through discourse, through actions and practices, and through personal subjectivities.[3] Transformations in *discourse* about labor and gender in southwestern Nigeria were radical during the late colonial period. Wage earners increasingly defined themselves as financial providers for their wives and children, both at home in assertions of power and in union representations that called for a family wage and other social safety nets. Even employees' wives, themselves income earners, often referred to their husbands as breadwinners. As this suggests, gendered *practices* were more complex. While steadily employed wage earners provided increasing proportions of household resources, working wives remained crucial to domestic economies. The colonial state justified men's low wages by pointing to women's incomes even as they limited the ability of women to gain formal employment. And some activists assertively defended Nigerian women's access to wage employment in the face of official efforts to limit it. How can we account for the tensions between discourse and practice (not to mention subjectivity—a much more difficult issue that is barely dealt with in this chapter)? I argue that wage earners actively manipulated or *worked with* gender in relation to both their colonial employers and members of their households and families while government officials and Nigerian women worked with gender for their own ends.

Breadwinners versus the State

Yorùbá households do not have a tradition of pooling resources. During the economic depression of the 1930s and later, colonial officials and private employers referred to women's trade in order to justify the low wages paid to male employees. But beginning in the early 1940s, workers testified to cost of living commissions that women's income was marginal to family finances and that men should be considered primary providers. Nigerian trade unionists insisted on their family obligations in protests over cost of living increases during World War II. They particularly resented the government's payment of children's allowances to European officials (which were to compensate for the cost of maintaining children outside Nigeria) and argued that their obligations as husbands and fathers should be recognized with similar benefits. During the six-week general strike of 1945, Nigerian labor activists repeatedly argued that both family allowances and a major wage revision were necessary because "many of us have wives and children to support."[4] The government, however, insisted that African families were too different from European ones to justify entitlements and rejected the demand for family allowances for Africans.

Like trade unionists, individual workers based claims for jobs, wages, and benefits on their putative status as breadwinners for wives and children. In 1948, for instance, a group of port workers wrote to the executive engineer of the Apapa (Lagos) wharf requesting increased wages to help them deal with the high costs of "house rentage, food allowances, luxuries, and also family expenses generally. Bachelors play only a fair show on this subject, whilst married men are especially having the heavy burden to carry. . . . Our wives who are in a very delicate condition look on us every time to have p[ocket] money in case of emergency, or times to buy other stuffs of food, etc. This is in most cases particularly to pregnant women."[5] Many other examples make the same point: even though it was not always successful, discourse about male breadwinners represented a potentially useful strategy for trade unions and individual workers in their dealings with employers and the state.

Breadwinners Make Good Husbands

At the same time, my interviews with railway pensioners and a variety of other sources indicate that this was more than just discourse; wage and salary earners did to some extent see themselves as family providers.[6] From the early years of wage labor in southern Nigeria, the relatively small numbers of steady earners could be relied upon more frequently than farmers or the irregularly employed to provide for daily household needs as well as periodic expenses such as school fees. And as salaries and benefits improved throughout Nigeria during the 1950s and more workers made long careers as wage earners, steadily employed men seem to have become responsible for increasing portions of the household budget.[7]

Their financial potency, real or exaggerated, contributed to male wage earners' self-esteem and their sense of importance relative to women and kin. Divorce cases from the 1940s and 1950s show that women became exasperated with husbands who did not meet their material obligations, and lack of sufficient financial maintenance was the most frequent reason women gave for leaving their husbands.[8] In contrast, wage earners who brought home steady paychecks were often seen as good mates because they could be good providers. Discussing her reasons for marrying a railway clerk in the 1950s, one woman noted, "If anybody who works in the railway comes your way you would like to marry him. At that time, the railway paid very well . . . , so people loved them [the employees] and liked to mix with them."[9] According to the women's column of a popular newspaper in 1946, "A thrifty man stands a good chance of being a likeable husband" because he is able to "provide good meals, proper clothing and every comfort for his family" as well as draw on his savings "when ill health or accident occurs." The same columnist published a letter from a young woman who could not decide whether to marry a third class clerk. A Mr. Lotus Lily of the Nigerian Railway, Offa, responded that a steadily employed husband, even of the lowest salary grade, "promises you comfort and perhaps some occasional luxuries."[10]

This sense of steady earners' financial importance and masculine allure—described in the discourse of male breadwinners—nevertheless coexisted with the reality that women contributed income to their households. The 1950 Lagos census identified 76 percent of women as traders, and several surveys indicated that the wives of wage earners and salaried workers earned money through trade or other sources (Nigeria 1950, 17; Comhaire-Sylvain 1951, 169–187; Lindsay 1996). Yet Ibadan court cases from the 1930s on reveal that men and women often publicly asserted that husbands should be primary household providers even if in practice this was not the case. And the retired railway men I interviewed made it clear that they considered themselves financial heads of their households.[11]

Such men often were unaware of exactly how much money their wives earned and spent. In interviews, few railway pensioners were clear about their wives' earnings and generally dismissed them as insignificant. Interviewed women also hesitated to discuss their finances. Part of the reason was that personal money and income from trade are generally combined, making separate accounting difficult, but the most important motivation of the women seems to have been to keep their husbands ignorant of exactly how much they earned. That way, men's paychecks (or rather some agreed-upon portion of men's earnings) could be allocated for specified household needs. Women actively laid claim to part of their husbands' earnings, especially to pay for school fees and other expenses associated with raising children. Women lauded their spouses by referring to them as breadwinners even when they were earning incomes that their husbands did not acknowledge and when the men spent some of their income on their extended families.[12] Thus, women were also involved in the creation and dissemination of a discourse about male breadwinners.

Shortly after the 1945 general strike, a series of newspaper articles debated the extent to which wives should depend on husbands for support. A male letter-writer suggested that men's ability to channel money from their paychecks to their wives represented a crucial component of masculinity: "Let the woman hold the purse strings," he wrote, "and soon after the man will become a puppet of the woman."[13] As this suggests, the links between men's incomes and their relationships with women brought anxiety as well as pride. While men relished the power and prestige associated with contributing money to wives, girlfriends, and children, these factors diminished when women claimed men's paychecks as a matter of course. A joke from the mid-1950s went like this: "Said an employee to his employer, 'Do you think, sir, I might have a rise?' 'But I put a rise in your pay packet last week.' 'Oh, I'm very sorry sir, my wife never tells me anything.'"[14] In print, popular culture, and interviews, men often alleged that women were selfish, looking only for mates who could provide them with consistent maintenance as well as gifts. These representations may well be the mirror image of women's appropriation of the discourse about male providers, reflecting a mixture of pride over earning wages and the suspicion that perhaps being a "breadwinner" in some ways entailed a loss as well as an increase of autonomy and respect.

Women May Work, but They Are Not Breadwinners

The contradictions underlying the male provider ideal also come out in debates about female wage earners in the late colonial era. Wage labor in Nigeria was, from the start, gendered as male. Girls' education lagged behind education for boys, and the colonial government was extremely reluctant to hire women. But as the demand for workers skyrocketed during World War II, the government and some private employers looked to women as cheap labor, much as they did elsewhere. Male trade unionists opposed gender discrepancies in wages and benefits, in part on grounds of fairness and in part because they feared employers would replace male workers with lesser-paid women. The inaugural meeting of the Trades Union Congress (TUC) in 1944 included a discussion of discriminatory pay to female employees. The resulting letter to the government stated that the unequal treatment of women workers "definitely indicate[s] a tendency to cheapen and exploit labour."[15] Trade unionists had to tread carefully in defending women's paid employment, though, given that they were at the same time engaged in arguments with the government about family allowances and men's roles as household breadwinners.

Later that year, new government recommendations allowed the creation of more posts for women but limited their prospects for promotion and restricted their employment possibilities after marriage. Among other provisions, the government created a separate grade for women typists instead of integrating women into the standard clerical grade.[16] This move effectively removed female workers as a threat to male wages and jobs, and in that respect it may have been a response to union pressures. With the elimination of female workers as potential competition, the trade unions were then in a position to mount a vocal defense, on principle, of women's paid employment.

This does not mean that they were inclined to do so, however, and it was a woman who raised the issue within the TUC. At its December 1945 annual convention, Miss E. E. Duke, a representative of the Postal Workers Union, resolved "that in view of the relatively small number of women in the civil service, women must be employed in all government services, especially in the clerical sections." She argued that women's permanent jobs need not be given up at marriage and that women should be considered equally with regard to salary and promotions. Duke argued "that because African men were very poorly paid, and because some husbands find it difficult to maintain a comfortable living together with their wives, women, if employed after marriage, could help in the economic stand of their husbands, and thereby contribute more substantially to the comfort of the family." Trade union leader J. Marcus Osindero, fresh from the debate with the government over family allowances, argued to the contrary that "the woman's place is the home." After much debate, Duke's motion was tabled indefinitely.[17]

The matter remained public for months. Immediately after the vote, the influential *West African Pilot* editorialized that "the TUC lost a great opportunity to make history. . . . Nigerian workers cannot oppose racial discrimination and condone sexual discrimination."[18] Yet this position ignores the gendered implications of the recently concluded general strike: male workers had specifically argued that they were entitled to metropolitan-style benefits because they were men like European men; that is, they supported wives and children. In Nigeria in 1945, one way of opposing racial discrimination was to embrace a certain notion of masculinity that if not exactly condoning sexual discrimination certainly implied women's exclusion from the realm of formal employment. Moreover, some trade unionists may have favored the exclusion of poorly paid females from the labor force as a strategy to enforce generalized male breadwinner wages.

Government policy on the employment of women, which was formalized in 1948, forced all women to resign from permanent government posts when they married or became pregnant unless they were personally exempted.[19] As the notion of a male breadwinner became increasingly normative among steady earners and major employers, the assumption that women's wages were *not* necessary to support families entered government pronouncements. A 1954 Colonial Office report asserted that African women's employment "impedes educational advance and diverts maternal attention from the home and family needs." In addition, such work was regarded as insignificant: "While wives and families in West Africa do work, their earnings are thought to be less a necessity than a useful supplement to the income of the man."[20]

In some sense it seems ironic that an administration that continually insisted that the wives of male employees contributed to household budgets would also work to exclude women from formal employment. Through the postwar period, official statements about southern Nigerian women remained similar to those from the 1930s: "Where the wage economy is being established . . . the African wage-earner, although he may be earning sufficient, does not expect his salary to be used to maintain his wife—he still expects her to support herself as he does on the farm."[21] And even when they referred to women's financial earnings, officials in Nigeria dismissed trading as something other than real work. A 1944

246   *Lisa A. Lindsay*

report on social welfare lamented the limited political and economic opportunities for women and was unusual in recommending female industrial labor. But this report suggested that Nigerian women needed a means of earning independent incomes other than prostitution, as if that were their only profit-making occupation![22]

In the 1950s, some trade unionists vigorously defended women's access to wage-earning opportunities, although their motivations seem to have been mixed. On the railway, where only 37 out of over 33,000 employees were women in the mid-1950s,[23] male trade unionists made claims on behalf of their female colleagues. At the first conference of the Association of Nigerian Railway Civil Servants in 1949, motions addressed pay rates and maternity leave for female clerks, among other issues. Five years later, the same union considered a report that female railway employees were frequently terminated and replaced by men. The union's motion called such actions "retrograde" and advocated "a change of attitude on the part of the Management [to] encourage both the training and education of Nigerian girls as future mothers of the Nations."[24] As the Nigerian Railway was transformed into a parastatal corporation in the mid-1950s, trade unionists protested that new employment conditions were worse than the old. Included in their complaints was the charge that under the new contracts, married women employees would be dismissed or placed on temporary contracts and would lose their pensions. Such action, the union alleged in a press release, would "create social problems" by depriving women of the opportunity to earn decent incomes.[25]

The Corporation's conditions of service, which were finally published in 1957, did discriminate against female employees, as the union had feared they would. "No woman who is married . . . may be employed by the Corporation except in a temporary capacity on monthly terms," it stipulated. "Immediately on her becoming a married woman, . . . a woman officer shall resign or her services may be otherwise terminated."[26] Female employees in other establishments faced analogous conditions, which some unions continued to protest. In 1961, the Maritime Trade Union Federation resolved that female employees on permanent appointments should not be demoted to temporary grade upon marriage.[27] Through the 1960s, the public debate continued about women's access to wage employment.[28]

It seems an interesting contrast that trade unionists and others fought for fair wages and job security for women workers during the very era in which the notion of the male breadwinner was making its greatest gains. This is one more piece of evidence that points to the complexity and contingency of this particular aspect of working-class masculinity. It is also important to remember the extremely small numbers of Nigerian women actually working for wages, although those numbers continued to grow. In 1950, less than 2 percent of all paid employees in Nigeria were women (Afonja 1981). Although there were exceptions, women tended to be clustered in relatively low-paying jobs defined as female. Thus, male employees could defend women's employment without serious threats to their own jobs and wages. Indeed, this occupational structure allowed higher-paying "breadwinner" wages to be earmarked exclusively for men.

Finally, even though male unionists argued on behalf of female employees, individual men and trade unionists still talked about women's work as if it were insignificant, and they relegated women to the sidelines of the labor movement. As we have seen, male wage earners often did not acknowledge their wives' importance to household economies. A 1963 article on the woman's page of the *West African Pilot* took pains to remind readers that market women were in fact workers: "While others rage over women working or not working she [the market trader] goes about her business in her quiet way. . . . A career woman indeed!"[29] In 1960, the Maritime Trade Union Federation president called for organizing the female staff of the Ports Authority. Although he emphasized that they should be involved in general union activities, he directed that "[female employees] should be organised into a Special Auxiliary Unit responsible for the Social Programme of the Federation."[30]

Conclusion

I began this chapter by indicating the small proportions of Nigerians engaged in wage labor during the colonial period. As late as 1975, only 7.8 percent of the labor force worked for wages.[31] So it seems appropriate to point out that the notion of a male breadwinner who supports wives and children through steady wage employment has never comprised any "hegemonic masculinity" in southwestern Nigeria. Stephan Miescher and I have argued (as have other people) that the concept of "hegemonic masculinity" is not particularly useful anyway for colonial Africa, where so many ideologies mixed and mingled with varying degrees of power.[32] Still, if pressed, I would assert that the ideal of the "big man" who distributes resources and patronage through networks including but extending far beyond wives and children has been and remains the most dominant male aspiration in southwestern Nigeria.

In spite of that caveat, there is no question but that a male breadwinner model emerged in colonial Nigeria and that in some contexts it remains an ideal. For instance, after the financially troubled Nigerian Railway Corporation suspended the payment of salaries to current workers and pensions to retirees in 1993, a group of women identifying themselves as railwaymen's wives brought children and cooking pots to the Ministry of Transport, where they held a noisy and disruptive sit-down strike. The women eventually addressed the minister, demanding that the payments be reinstated on the grounds that they were used to support railwaymen's wives and children.[33] This is one of many protests in recent years that explicitly rested on the notion that women and children are financial dependents of wage earners.

How did such notions come to southwestern Nigeria? I have argued that attributing the emergence of the male breadwinner ideal to colonial impositions tells only part of the story. While the colonial state created the conditions under which nearly all wage jobs were filled by men, this did not mean that it turned men into the major providers for their households, especially since most people did not work for wages and women had access to their own incomes. In fact, until the 1950s administrators in Nigeria resisted male workers' claims for wages and benefits deemed suitable for family providers, and it was Nigerian men who first raised the male breadwinner ideal. For trade unionists and individual wage earners, the image of the male breadwinner was useful for making demands from the colonial state, even if that image sat uneasily with women's important economic activities. At home, steady wages and the breadwinner image had implications for men's marital relationships, household budgets, and self-esteem, even if those budgets were kept afloat through women's contributions. And in negotiations over household resources, women drew upon the fledgling male breadwinner norm to make their own claims to men's paychecks.

The ambiguity and contradictions within the male breadwinner ideal are particularly apparent in struggles over women's paid work. In the 1940s and beyond, government officials resisted the notion of Nigerian men as breadwinners (who could claim improved wages and benefits) by pointing to women's independent earnings and the support those earnings provided for their children. Yet they also restricted Nigerian women's access to formal sector jobs and defined market trading as something other than real employment. Women workers protested official restrictions on the grounds that they needed income to support themselves and their families. They received limited support from trade unions, even though the unions were of course composed of men who were married to market traders and other working women. In negotiations with the colonial state over men's wages and benefits, labor activists argued that women's contributions to household budgets were insignificant, thus participating themselves in the construction of market trading as a marginal occupation. For some trade unionists, these arguments affected their stance on women in formal employment, which they resisted as a threat to male breadwinner jobs. Yet other union leaders, as well as journalists and women's organizations, favored an improvement in women's employment conditions, arguing that national development depended on utilizing women's labor power.

Can we reconcile these different arguments and interpretations? I don't think so, nor do I think we should. Rather, it makes sense to think of gender not necessarily as something people *have* but as something people *do*. Butler (1990, 140) argues that gender is not "a stable identity or locus of agency from which various acts follow; rather, gender is an identity tenuously constituted in time, instituted in an exterior space through a stylized repetition of acts." Especially in a context such as colonial Africa—where gender was already quite malleable and a multiplicity of ideas about how different types of women and men should behave circulated with varying degrees of saliency—people could draw on gender ideologies not only to inform their sense of proper living but also for specific, material ends. How particular individuals *thought about* this in specific contexts is a different question and one that is much harder to get at (see Miescher, this volume). But the disjunctures as well as the overlaps between discourse and practice surrounding the male breadwinner norm in southwestern

Nigeria suggest not only that people shape their lives according to ideas about gender but that they shape gender in order to better their lives.

Notes

1. The material in this chapter appears in Lindsay (2003, chapter 4). I thank Catherine Cole and Stephan Miescher for inviting me to present it at the Santa Barbara conference and Luise White for earlier suggestions that I pay attention to Africans' consciousness of and manipulation of gender discourses.

2. All-Nigeria Trade Union Federation, "Paper on Need for Increasing Wage-Earning Employment in Nigeria," 1956, based on an unspecified International Labour Organization report. Nigerian Labor Archive (hereafter NLA), vol. 21, Schomburg Collection, New York Public Library.

3. This distinction is drawn out more fully in Lindsay and Miescher (2003).

4. Excerpt from speech entitled "Family Allowances," *The Nigerian Worker* 1, no. 7 (December 1944), 2. For more on the general strike and the unions' demands for family allowances, see Lindsay (1999).

5. Letter from "Painting Gang," Port Section, Marine Apapa to Executive Engineer, Port Section, Apapa Wharf, October 8, 1948, NLA, vol. 12.

6. In 1993–1994 I conducted a survey on career histories, domestic life, and household budgets among 167 retired railway men and fifty-three of their wives in Lagos and Ibadan. Most of the men are classified as "pensioners," meaning that they retired from pensionable appointments after fairly long careers. They were initially hired between 1930 and 1965. Focusing on this group allows me to draw some conclusions about what long-term salaried employment meant to people and families, but one should note that it does not yield much information about the casually employed or those low on the employment ladder. About thirty of the people surveyed later engaged in more open-ended interviews. I am grateful to Babajide Oyeneye, Olufunmilayo Carew, and Olusanya Ibitoye for their help with conducting and interpreting the surveys and interviews. For more information, see Lindsay (1996).

7. This point is developed more fully in Lindsay (1998).

8. Based on my examination of divorce records from Bere Native Court, Ibadan, located in the Obafemi Awolowo University Library, Ife. Also see Federation of Nigeria, *Annual Report of the Federal Social Welfare Department for the Year 1955–56* (Lagos: Government Printer, 1956), 10. For a later period, see "Wife Divorces Husband: 'Tired of Paying His Debts,'" *West African Pilot* (hereafter *WAP*), June 16, 1964.

9. Interview with Rebecca Uchefuna, February 21, 1994, Ibadan; interview with Raheem Balogun, head of the Lagos branch of the Railway Pensioners' Union, July 20, 1998, Lagos.

10. Miss Silva, "Husbands and Thrift," *WAP*, November 9, 1946; Miss Silva, "Marry the Third Class Clerk," *WAP*, April 15, 1946.

11. Examples include Ayi vs. Lawani, September 1930, Oke Are (Ibadan) Civil Record Book, vol. 21, 1693/30, 231–237; Moriamo vs. Raimi, June 1938, Bere (Ibadan) I Civil Record Book, vol. ? [torn cover], 529/38, 16–19; Foyeke vs. Obasawi, February 1942, Bere I Civil Record Book, vol. 23, 233/42, 125–126; S. A. Akinfanda vs. Sabititu, February

1950, Oke Are II Civil Record Book vol. 12, 33/50, 231–237, all located in the Obafemi Awolowo University Library, Ife.

12. Interview with Michael Odede, retired railway yard supervisor (formerly shunter), December 28, 1993, Ibadan. Also interviews with Bernard Aruna, December 28, 1993, Ibadan; S. O. Akintola, May 2, 1994, Ibadan; Florence Owolabi, January 7, 1994, Ibadan; and Sudarkasa (1973).

13. Miss Silva, "Men Should Not Submit Their Earnings," *WAP*, December 21, 1945.

14. *Sunday Times* (Lagos), February 14, 1954.

15. General Secretary, Trades Union Congress, to Chief Secretary to the Government, October 15, 1944, cited in Oluwide (1993, 277).

16. "Report by the Committee to Consider the Question of the Employment of Women in Government Service," November 1945, CSO 26/4322, National Archives, Ibadan (hereafter NAI), cited in Denzer (1989).

17. "Annual Convention of Nigerian TUC" and "Female Representative of Postal Workers Union Pleads for Her Sex at TUC Confab," *WAP*, December 18, 1945.

18. "Women Workers and Our Progress" (editorial), *WAP*, December 21, 1945.

19. Government Notice No. 297, extract from Nigerian Gazette, February 19, 1948, in unnumbered file on recruitment, Nigerian Railway Corporation (hereafter NRC) headquarters, Ebute Metta.

20. Colonial Labor Advisory Committee, "Report of the Sub-Committee on Wage Fixing and Family Responsibilities," n.d. [1953], CO 859/810, Public Record Office, London.

21. Minute by D. E. Faulkner, Social Welfare Officer, to Commissioner of the Colony, July 31, 1947, in ComCol 1/3236, NAI.

22. Alexander Patterson, "A Report to His Excellency the Governor of Nigeria on *Social Welfare in the Colony and Protectorate*," forwarded to the Resident, Oyo Province, July 26, 1944, in Oyo Provincial Administration file 1/4108, NAI.

23. "List of Women Employed by the Railway Corporation," n.d. [1956], General Manager (Staff) file (hereafter GMS) 302/15, vol. 2, NRC headquarters. Most of the twenty-two women worked in the accounts department.

24. "Report of the Proceedings of the Sixth Annual Delegates Conference of the Association of Railway Civil Servants at Zaria, June 7–10, 1954," GMS 28/6, NRC.

25. "Union Accuses Rail of Creating Social Problems," *Daily Service*, September 17, 1956; "Rail Unions Say NRC's Release Is Irresponsible," *WAP*, September 17, 1956; clippings in GMS 302/15, vol. 2, NRC.

26. Nigerian Railway Corporation, Standard Conditions of Service 1957: Officers, 12, NRC headquarters.

27. Motions/Resolutions for 5th Annual Conference of Nigerian Maritime Trades Union Federation, October 1961, in NLA, vol. 30.

28. See, for instance, "Opportunity" (opinion column), *Daily Times*, September 13, 1963, and "Career Woman," *WAP*, October 19, 1963.

29. "Career Woman," *WAP*, October 19, 1963.

30. O. A. Fagbenro Beyioku, President General, "Maritime Trades Union Federation General Policy, 1960/61," in NLA, vol. 28. For more on women's marginalization from trade unions, see Sokunbi, Jeminiwa, and Onaeko (1995).

31. Nigeria, *Third National Development Plan 1975–80*, 370, cited in Fashoyin (1980, 13).

32. The term was put forward most forcefully in Connell (1995). Critiques are in Lindsay and Miescher (2003) and Cornwall and Lindisfarne (1994).

33. Interview with Folasade Tade (railway pensioner and widow who took part in the protest), June 1, 1994, Lagos.

References

Afonja, Simi. 1981. "Changing Modes of Production and the Sexual Division of Labor among the Yoruba." *Signs* 7, no. 2: 299–313.

Butler, Judith. 1990. *Gender Trouble: Feminism and the Subversion of Identity.* New York: Routledge.

Comhaire-Sylvain, S. 1951. "Le travail des femmes a Lagos, Nigeria." *Zaire* 5: 169–187.

Connell, R. W. 1995. *Masculinities.* Berkeley: University of California Press.

Cornwall, Andrea, and Nancy Lindisfarne, eds. 1994. *Dislocating Masculinity: Comparative Ethnographies.* London: Routledge.

Denzer, LaRay. 1989. "Women in Government Service in Colonial Nigeria, 1862–1945." Boston University Working Papers in African Studies, no. 136.

Fadipe, N. A. 1940/1970. *The Sociology of the Yoruba,* edited by Francis Olu. Okediji and Oladejo O. Okediji. Ibadan: Ibadan University Press.

Fapohunda, Eleanor R. 1988. "The Non-Pooling Household: A Challenge to Theory." In *A Home Divided: Women and Income in the Third World,* edited by Daisy Dwyer and Judith Bruce. Stanford, Calif.: Stanford University Press.

Fashoyin, Tayo. 1980. *Industrial Relations in Nigeria (Development and Practice).* Ikeja: Longman, Nigeria.

Lindsay, Lisa A. 1996. "Putting the Family on Track: Gender and Domestic Life on the Colonial Nigerian Railway." Ph.D. diss., University of Michigan.

———. 1998. "'No Need . . . to Think of Home'? Masculinity Domestic Life on the Nigerian Railway, c. 1940–61." *Journal of African History* 39, no. 3: 439–466.

———. 1999. "Domesticity and Difference: Male Breadwinners, Working Women, and Colonial Citizenship in the 1945 Nigerian General Strike." *American Historical Review* 104, no. 3: 783–812.

———. 2003. *Working with Gender: Wage Labor and Social Change in Colonial Southwestern Nigeria.* Portsmouth, N.H.: Heinemann.

———, and Stephan F. Miescher, eds. 2003. *Men and Masculinities in Modern Africa.* Portsmouth, N.H.: Heinemann.

Marris, Peter. 1962. *Family and Social Change in an African City: A Study of Rehousing in Lagos.* Evanston, Ill.: Northwestern University Press.

Nigeria. Department of Statistics. 1951. *Population Census of Lagos, 1950.* Kaduna: Government Printer.

Oluwide, Baba. 1993. *Imoudu Biography, Part I: A Political History of Nigeria, 1939–1950.* Ibadan: Ororo Publishers.

Oyewumi, Oyeronke. 1997. *The Invention of Women: Making an African Sense of Western Gender Discourses.* Minneapolis: University of Minnesota Press.

Sokunbi, O., O. Jeminiwa, and F. B. Onaeko, eds. 1995. *Women and Trade Unionism in Nigeria.* Ibadan: NPS Educational Publishers Limited.

Sudarkasa, Niara. 1973. *Where Women Work: A Study of Yoruba Women in the Marketplace and in the Home.* Ann Arbor, Mich.: Museum of Anthropology.

14 Becoming an *Ɔpanyin:* Elders, Gender, and Masculinities in Ghana since the Nineteenth Century

Stephan F. Miescher

In many African societies, gender has a close relation to seniority. Having achieved the position of an elder, a man or woman embodies a different gender. This significance of elderhood exemplifies the flexibility and multiplicity of gender. Some scholars have taken the position that seniority supersedes gender in Africa. For example, Oyeronke Oyewumi (1997) has questioned the salience of gender as an analytical category among Yorùbá societies in Nigeria. She notes that the Yorùbá language, as other African languages, does not recognize gender as a grammatical marker. Declaring gender a Western import, she urges scholars to develop analytical concepts such as lineage, seniority, and motherhood that are more rooted in African contexts.[1] Oyewumi's intervention has generated much debate and some fellow Nigerians have offered critiques of her study in terms of Yorùbá culture. Bibi Bakare-Yusuf has questioned the importance ascribed to language, which supposedly reveals a cultural essence, without addressing the ways in which the meanings and usage of words change over time. Bakare-Yusuf notes the weakness in Oyewumi's argument of "privileging seniority as the only significant dimension of power" while overlooking how seniority discourse relates to practice. She argues that seniority is interwoven with other dimensions of power and that there is a productive tension between dominant ideas of elderhood and how individuals challenge and manipulate them in practice.[2]

This chapter explores ideas and practices of elderhood among members of a mission church in southern Ghana since the nineteenth century. Based on a collection of life histories and archival research, I show how a group of men creatively dealt with competing notions of masculinity, particularly senior masculinity, and how those notions are reflected in their subjectivity. Constituted out of collective experience and as a product of history, subjectivity is not static but multiple, gendered, and located in bodies, thus "a dynamic process during which individuals take up and change positions in discourse" (Mama 1995, 99).

In narrations about their lives, men created selves and acted as subjects.[3] I argue that in Ghana's Akan societies, seniority has been as crucial to the construction of identity as gender. Both men and women could become elders, but each had a different understanding of how they wield power. Here I focus on articulations of seniority, on the implications of becoming and being an ɔpanyin (elder) in the Akan area of Kwawu. How did people in Kwawu select, contest, and practice meanings of seniority in response to historical transformations? Elderhood, this chapter asserts, has remained a powerful ideal throughout the twentieth century. And yet responsibilities and expectations of elders changed over time.

Gendered Seniority and Masculinities

Africa's historians have emphasized the importance of age and seniority for the organization of gender relations.[4] In matrilineal Akan societies, men and women's gender positions change in the course of their lives. In precolonial Asante, "old age blurred the lines of gender politics" since men *and* women could occupy high offices (Akyeampong and Obeng 1995, 492). In a biographical portrait of Yaa Akyawaa Yikwan, Ivor Wilks (1993, 335) suggested that elite Asante women went through gendered stages: first as girls, then into young womanhood with puberty and nubility rites, then as childbearing women devoted to household and family, and finally as postmenopausal women. Women at this stage no longer posed a spiritual danger. They had become "ritual men" who, in special circumstances, occupied male stools, or chiefly offices (Akyeampong and Obeng 1995, 491).[5] These women embodied a form of "female masculinity," attaining social positions reserved for men. This is well documented in the case of Yaa Asantewaa, the Queenmother of Edweso, who led the war against British occupation of Asante in 1900–1901.[6] Colonial rule, however, led to a masculinization of the Asante political realm. Native Authority Ordinances not only formalized the system of indirect rule but also failed to recognize female elders and their courts. These colonial policies contributed to the "marginalization of women and commoners" (Allman and Tashjian 2000, 24; Manuh 1988).

In her pioneering history of female traders in Accra, Claire Robertson (1984) traced how age and gender intersected in access to economic resources. Prior to 1860, a "hierarchical corporate kin mode of production" ruled in southern Ghana, with senior men *and* women controlling the labor of juniors. From 1860 to 1952, a shift from the corporate kin mode to capitalist production reduced the power of male elders. While men dominated the increasingly important production of cash crops, the expansion of the trading system raised the status of women. During the period after self-rule that began in 1952, men and women became reintegrated "into a unitary social structure, but with a male dominated capitalist hierarchy in charge." For the most part, men profited because they regained political power and had more educational opportunities. Thus, gender, "rather than age, has become the primary social characteristic determining access to resources, indicating a major change in the nature of women's subordination."[7]

Beyond Robertson's materialist approach, historical research promises to reveal more about elders' gendered practices, about their self-presentations and subjectivity. Furthermore, it is not just seniority that matters. Rather, gender scholars must take into consideration changing ideas about masculinity. In Ghana, as elsewhere, most gender historians have concentrated on women (but see Akyeampong 1996). In order to understand more fully the complex dialectic between gender and historical transformations, scholars need to expand their focus: they must unpack the multiple constructions of masculinity, look at the diversity among men, and recognize men as gendered social actors too.[8]

In the Akan areas of southern Ghana, there were multiple and at times conflicting notions of masculinity during the colonial era. Institutions such as missionary societies and the colonial state introduced foreign ideas that challenged local ideals dominant in Akan societies, such as adult masculinity, defined by marriage, and senior masculinity and "big-man" status. The latter refers not only to men with disposable wealth but also to men who exhibited values such as generosity, the commitment to sharing one's riches. Senior masculinity implies less someone's age than the qualities embodied in the social position of ɔpanyin (Miescher 2005).

In the Akan-Twi language, the term ɔpanyin incorporates a broad semantic field. The leading dictionary distinguishes two groups of meaning: age ɔpanyin, "an old person, an adult," as opposed to a child; and status and achievements ɔpanyin, "a gentleman, respectable man, person of rank" (Christaller 1933, 375). The second definition relates to ɔpanyin as a figure of authority, either a chief or one who belongs to a chief's council of elders. Asking about the meaning of ɔpanyin triggered many responses in Kwawu. Rev. E. K. O. Asante, who was born in 1911, emphasized maturity and honor. He explained that ɔpanyin stems from the expression "wanyin, he or she has grown up" (1993b). An ɔpanyin's position is not permanent. People recognized as ɔpanyin must continue to prove their worthiness. Conduct, reputation, and the ability to speak well are considered decisive. People lose respect for misbehaving elders. Every occupant of a stool (the symbolic representation of a chiefly office) is ex officio an ɔpanyin. His or her misconduct reduces the office's honor and might lead to destoolment. Fatherhood is important in reaching both adult masculinity *and* senior masculinity. A man without children could not aspire to become a respected elder. Early in the twentieth century, Akan societies ridiculed married men who did not father children for being impotent. In Kwawu, there was a specific ritual to "out" an ɔkrawa (barren man). E. F. Opusuo (1994), born ca. 1923, narrated the story of an impotent man who was caught, publicly slapped, and decorated with food. The ɔkrawa was the antithesis of the ɔpanyin, a man who was not respected and honored but was despised and was the subject of gossip, mockery, and contempt.

In his work on aging in Kwawu, anthropologist Sjaak van der Geest (1998b) notes the fluidity of the transitions between the stages of life that followed adolescence: *aberantee* (young and approaching middle age), *ɔpanyin* (getting old), and *akwakora* (old man). The female equivalents are *ababawa*, *ɔbaa-panyin/ ɔpanyin*, and *aberewa*. He suggests that "*ɔpanyin* and *akwakora/aberewa* do not so much represent a chronological order—but a moral one, a difference in appreciation of old age" (454–456). In a discussion about proverbs, he lists an *ɔpanyin*'s virtues: wisdom, the ability to advise people, the ability to keep secrets, mutual respect with dependents, self-restraint, and honor. Van der Geest did not historicize the *ɔpanyin* ideal nor did he analyze it in terms of gender, though he noted that it was possible for a woman to become an *ɔpanyin*.

Although both men and women may become elders in Akan societies, they are expected to act differently. When Ɔkyeame Kwabena Asante (1994), born 1911, discussed the proverb "*Akokɔbere nim adekyee, nanso ɔhwe onini ano*—The hen is aware of the daybreak, but she watches the cock's beak (waits for the cock to announce it)," he elaborated on distinct gender roles. The proverb refers to a situation of a female elder acting as advisor in the chief's palace. Her input should be less public than that of her male colleagues. She should use her influence behind the scenes, playing the *aberewa* (old woman) who is consulted. Arhin Brempong (2000), writing about the *ɔhemaa* (queenmother), the most senior female chief, who is considered "wisdom personified," mentioned the same practice of male elders "going to consult *aberewa*." Arhin Brempong noted that as the *aberewa* of the town, the *ɔhemaa* was "the moral guardian of the females of the political community and a kind of moral censor: she examined adolescent girls before the main puberty rites which ushered them into adulthood and licensed their marriage" (106). Historically, as Pashington Obeng (2003) noted, women tended to supersede male elders only "during a moment of national crisis," such as the 1900 Asante uprising led by Yaa Asantewaa, "when the apparent malaise created a space for the power and status of senior masculinity—expressed in public military leadership—to be occupied by a woman" (200). While scholars of twentieth-century Asante have looked at the changing positions of female elders who as community leaders settled disputes, such as the *ahemaa* (queenmothers) who occupied political offices (Manuh 1988) or the so-called commodity queen mothers in the market (Clark 1994; Ebron this volume), male elders have received less attention. How have ideas about the *ɔpanyin* evolved under colonial rule? What were the experiences of those who sought to live up to expectations of senior masculinity in the past? The biographical portrait of John Yaw Atta, one of the first Basel Mission converts in Kwawu, offers a case study about becoming a male elder in the late nineteenth century.

The Afflictions of Ɔpanyin John Yaw Atta

In 1915, Ɔpanyin J. Y. Atta died after two decades of service as senior presbyter (church elder) of the Basel Mission congregation in Abetifi, Kwawu. After his death, the Abetifi pastor, Rev. D. E. Akwa, wrote an account of Atta's "life and death" for his superiors. Rev. Akwa followed the conventions of a conversion story, tracing Atta's development from a "heathen" youth to his success-ful integration into the congregation. Akwa's account is unusual among Basel Mission records; local pastors rarely produced reports about fellow converts that were this extensive.[9] Atta was born into the ruling matrilineage of Kwawu in 1854. Rev. Akwa described the trajectory of a young man of noble birth who became a prominent member of the Abetifi Christian congregation, achieving wealth and status while remaining trapped in his ties and obligations to his non-Christian relatives. Atta's remaking as a Christian man is reflected in his trans-formation from a member of the "royal family" who "dislik[ed] farm work" to "the most celebrated farmer in the whole district."[10] In 1876, Atta started work-ing as a "house-boy" for the Abetifi missionaries who had given him a loan to pay for court debts. As elsewhere across colonial Africa, the missionaries encour-aged their domestic servant to enter baptismal classes and divorce his three wives (see Hunt 1999). In 1878, he was baptized and became one of the first four Abetifi converts. He permanently moved to Christian Quarters, the sepa-rate settlement the Basel Mission had founded for its converts outside Abetifi. In the 1890s, Atta was elected to help the resident missionaries supervise the local congregation and became a presbyter.[11]

Rev. Akwa presented Atta as a "lover of civilization and improvements." Farming "became his favourite occupation at the middle age." As a royal, Atta used his connections to get a substantial piece of land for "Christians" and founded farm villages on it, launching the Kwawu cocoa industry.[12] Subse-quently, Atta owned an "extensive cocoa plantation," but, as Rev. Akwa noted, wealth "did not ruin his Christianity, as it has affected many other Christians." In 1907, Atta tried his luck with trading by selling cocoa to European mer-chants, who paid him with imported goods. This entrepreneurial spirit was for Rev. Akwa most evident in his ambition to construct "good roads . . . for trans-port" of cocoa and imports. He lobbied the colonial government to build a rail-way extension to Kwawu to facilitate shipping to and from the coast. Rev. Akwa emphasized his performance as senior presbyter. Atta participated in the state's "civil cases" as "excellent councilors [sic], witty juror, and faithful judge." The ɔmanhene (paramount chief) and mpanyinfoɔ (elders) did not settle major dis-putes without consulting him. Atta was known for his generosity: he paid debts for his relatives and served as "benefactor and kind hearted Christian to the Mission workers" stationed in Abetifi.[13] He became a respected ɔpanyin within the congregation *and* among chiefs, taking responsibility and sharing his wealth with both groups. Atta acted as a cultural broker, one of the "middle figures" who played a crucial role in the missionary project and other colonial encoun-ters (Hunt 1999; Peel 2000).

Yet Atta's biographer found his multiple commitments problematic and char-acterized them as "afflictions." Rev. Akwa suggested that Atta died a troubled man and that his skills in negotiating between different contexts were a sign of failure. In Akwa's perception, the world of Christian Quarters, created by mis-sionaries in collaboration with middle figures, was incommensurable with that of the *ahenfie* (chief's palace) in Abetifi's old town. These reflected opposing expectations of elders and competing forms of senior masculinity. Atta, although baptized, continued to acknowledge his status and obligations as a royal. According to Akwa, "he suffered too much about the affairs of his relatives," a reference to their financial and dynastic troubles. Whenever an emergency occurred, Atta was "the only man who [bore] the yoke." On his deathbed, he recalled spending over 600 pounds for "relatives and the improvement of the District" without receiving a word of thanks. Rev. Akwa recorded Atta exclaiming, "What pains me is that after my death, my relatives will say I did not leave them [anything]; but I dare say, I have spent all my income in paying their debts."[14] Rev. Akwa did not understand why Atta decided to assist during chieftaincy disputes and other crises, why he sought to fulfill the expectations of both his lineage and the mission.[15] Another affliction was based in gender expectations. Atta lacked a Christian marriage, the "true unity which is to exist between himself and family." This caused "the hardship" of his life and made him die "of broken heart." His wife was "not submissive, and not a good helper to the husband." His sons, who belonged to their mother's lineage, "disobeyed their father." Atta had confessed to the pastor that his children were not the "blessing to [his] marriage, but misery, or punishment from God." For Rev. Akwa, the lack of proper domestic arrangements was so damaging that Atta became vulnerable to other afflictions. A life closer to the missionary ideal of masculinity, one that included close conjugal bonds, would have enabled Atta to object to his relatives' numerous demands.[16]

These conflicting expectations culminated when Atta was elected to serve as *ɔmanhene* of Kwawu, "the most troublesome time of his life." In 1898, when a crowd carried him toward the *ahenfie* to be enstooled, he rejected the offer.[17] Still, at least in Rev. Akwa's account, Atta was tormented by the thought that he could not help his relatives by serving as *ɔmanhene* during a period of political instability. In 1905, the stool was again offered to him but he again refused.[18] The last time he was nominated, half a year before his death, the mission leadership in Abetifi informed him that "kingship is not a violation of God's commandments." He was encouraged "to rule as a Christian, resist all the stool temptations in his old age, and die as a Christian"; he was especially encouraged to "draw the heathens to the service of God." Atta confronted the kingmakers with a list of conditions, among them his insistence that he live in Christian Quarters and not marry any stool wives. He demanded that all "subjects" cease making libations and doing other rituals and instead attend church. The *Ɔkyeame,* speaking for the delegation, could not accept conditions that must have sounded outrageous. Although Atta was a devout Christian, a "modernizer," "generous," "plain speaking and truthful" who abstained "from all appearance of evil," he did not break away from his previous environment. Atta failed to embrace Christianity fully and live by its rules like the missionary version of senior masculinity. He was caught in the predicament of seeking to be a "good father," in the sense of an elder, "to both heathen[s], and Christians of Ɔkwawu country, outwardly and inwardly."[19]

In 1993, almost eighty years after J. Y. Atta's death, I had a conversation with

Ɔpanyin J. A. Wahyee, himself a former presbyter, about the Basel Mission's history in Abetifi. Wahyee, born in 1900, was full of memories and stories about Atta, who was his grandmother's twin brother.

> He had power in Kwawu! And so when the chiefs brought up something, which would go against the church, he went straight before them to tell them, "What you are doing is not good; you should stop." And they stopped, because he was an *ɔdehyeɛ* [member of ruling lineage] in Kwawu. (1993)

These days, Atta is celebrated as one of the founding heroes of the Presbyterian Church (successor of the Basel Mission) in Abetifi. People remember him as a model Christian with no word about the ambivalence so eloquently described by Rev. Akwa. Frequently, I heard the story about Atta refusing enstoolment as *ɔmanhene,* when he exclaimed, "My kingdom is not of this world" (Asante 1993c). Wahyee, in his version, emphasized how Atta acted like an *ɔpanyin.*

> He was held and was going to be enstooled. The Nkwatiahene [chief of neighboring town] was a very strong man; he lifted him on his shoulders and took him to the *ahenfie* to be enstooled. Seeing that they were really taking him there to be enstooled, he slapped him [the Nkwatiahene] and this one let him down. Later, he went to Nkwatia to kneel before him and apologized. . . . Further, he gave his niece to the Nkwatiahene to marry. The woman died recently, it is not even two months ago. So, that man [Atta] was really brave, *nebo yɛ duru* [literally, his chest was heavy]. (1993)

Using the expression *nebo yɛ duru,* a synonym of *ɔye barima* (he is a brave, valiant man), Wahyee referred to Atta's masculinity, emphasizing his reputation. Unlike Rev. Akwa, Wahyee thought that Atta succeeded in accommodating competing expectations as *ɔpanyin.* Atta conducted himself effectively in both settings, in Christian Quarters and among the *mpanyinfoɔ* at the *ahenfie.* This difference in interpretation is important. While Rev. Akwa saw the formation of multiple masculine identities among senior members of the Basel Mission congregation as problematic, this predicament had become normal for Wahyee two generations later, almost ordinary. Since the 1930s, members of the Presbyterian Church have gradually moved into the ranks of elders and stool-holders, especially in Abetifi.[20] Ɔpanyin Wahyee did not encounter the challenges his granduncle faced. How did a younger generation that was born in the early twentieth century experience the process of becoming and being an *ɔpanyin?*

Seeking Elderhood and Community Service

In his social history of alcohol in Ghana, Emmanuel Akyeampong (1996) argued that "the status of elderhood is the desired goal of all" (157). This was especially so for the first generation of male migrants to the coast, who anticipated temporary migration in the hope that urban wage labor would help achieve elderhood. The men and women I interviewed about migration addressed the following themes: preparation for returning home, community recognition, and the creation of a legacy. These reminiscences provide an entry into individual processes of becoming an *ɔpanyin* and reflect a catalogue of individual accomplishments. For those who worked outside Kwawu, returning to their hometown was a crucial transition in their lives. Phil Bartle (1978) suggested that for the Kwawu town of Obo, "at the final stage of the life cycle, the migrant return[ed] permanently to the hometown or satellite village and eventually live[d] off the produce of his investments: his children, his farm, his savings, his property" (408). This might happen early in life, or hometown stays could be interrupted by additional sojourns outside Kwawu. The preparations for the final homecoming—launching a cocoa farm, building a house, and providing children and relatives with education—related to the process of becoming an *ɔpanyin*.

Ɔpanyin Wahyee (1994), who traded beads across West Africa, returned to Abetifi in the early 1930s, when he took over his late brother's cocoa farms and focused on domestic responsibilities. Wahyee took care of many children, nephews and nieces for whom he paid school fees. This marked his transition to becoming an *ɔpanyin*. Back in Abetifi, Wahyee not only occupied a senior position within his matrilineage, but at the age of thirty-five he was also elected presbyter and was expected to support the local pastor "in the oversight of the Christian life in the congregation, especially the family life and the upbringing of children."[21] Wahyee organized "communal labor" to maintain and erect school buildings. He played an active part in settling marriage disputes and "enforced" church rules (Wahyee and Donkor 1994). The records of the Abetifi session, the congregation's governing body of presbyters, document Wahyee's influence. In 1963, he informed the session that Florence Adoma, who had been suspended for becoming a junior wife, knew well that her husband "had so many wives." The session decided to readmit her only if she ended the marriage.[22] Frequently Wahyee's intervention closed a case, a sign of his persuasive eloquence. If a congregation member challenged a presbyter, there were consequences. Yaw Opoku, who was "seriously sick in bed" and was seeking reacceptance, had to "render apology to Op. J. A. Wahyee whose authority and advice he had thwarted."[23] As a presbyter and cocoa farmer Wahyee stayed close to Abetifi. Whenever he was needed by the session or his lineage, he could reach his hometown within a day.[24] Because of his distinguished record of mediating cases, Wahyee's reputation as *ɔpanyin* grew beyond Abetifi's Christian Quarters. In the 1990s, when he was bound to his house as an *akwakora*, people still sought his advice. For Wahyee, elderhood had become permanent.

As salaried men, *akrakyefoɔ* (clerks, teachers, accountants) emerged as a new social category in the first half of the twentieth century in southern Ghana (Miescher 2003, 2005). Since they mainly worked outside their hometowns, their final return corresponded with retirement. If possible, they made preparations early in life, thereby initiating the process of becoming an *ɔpanyin*. Rev. Asante served as primary school head teacher in his hometown of Abetifi from 1937 to 1944. The outbreak of World War II provided Asante with the opportunity to prove himself as *ɔpanyin* by acting as a leader for the church: in late 1939, the colonial government decided to deport all German nationals, which included school supervisor Eugen Haegele and his wife, both of German nationality, who were arrested by the district commissioner accompanied by policemen. Because the pastor was on leave, Asante had "to take charge" (1993b). Although other Abetifi teachers and the presbyters were older and more experienced, the mantle of leadership fell on Asante's shoulders because of his qualification as a trained teacher-catechist. Presiding over Sunday services and looking after the Presbyterian schools, Asante became an ɔpanyin for the Abetifi congregation at the age of twenty-eight. Most presbyters had authority due to their advanced age and experience, qualities Asante lacked. Senior presbyter Joseph Okra, John Yaw Atta's successor, had served for more than twenty years. Asante's successful performance contributed to his admission to the Kumase theological seminary in 1945, leading to a distinguished career as a Presbyterian pastor that culminated in his status as a respected ɔpanyin.

While teaching in his hometown, Rev. Asante acquired land in a part of Christian Quarters that was then still "bush." Construction on a house began in 1943, and two years later some of Asante's maternal relatives moved in (1993b). By allowing his poorer relations to stay in the house, Rev. Asante acted as the generous ɔpanyin (1993c). In his career as a pastor, Asante was stationed outside Kwawu. Therefore, for several decades, his Abetifi house enhanced Asante's stature as ɔpanyin. It served as a reminder that he had provided shelter for his needy relatives and indicated his preparedness to return one day to take the position of elderhood within different hometown communities. For an ɔpanyin, male or female, the task of erecting a building that bears one's name fulfills several objectives. The building may house the ɔpanyin and his spouse and children and other family members. Moreover, serving as a mnemonic device, the building becomes a monument. It will remind the deceased's descendants of his (or her) former physical existence and offers a way to transcend death by creating an afterlife in the memories of others.[25]

In the 1990s, the social position of ɔpanyin still retained its importance in Kwawu. Most of the men and women I interviewed, who were born between 1900 and 1930, had permanently returned to their hometown to become resident elders. Following his retirement in 1980, Rev. Asante successfully balanced expectations from his matrilineage and the Presbyterian congregation. Although active in mediating lineage disputes, Asante declined to occupy a chiefly office. He helped enlarge and improve the "family house." He also assisted in training church workers and was instrumental in establishing the Abetifi vocational training school, which was funded by a German development grant. As a retired pastor, he did not want to "meddle in heathen affairs" and maintained a distance from rites involving veneration of ancestors or communication with Akan gods (1993a). Still, he was considered knowledgeable about Kwawu customs and history, and in old age he was frequently consulted about "traditions" (1993b). In 1994, when Kwawu chiefs celebrated the afahye festival after a hiatus of thirty years, Asante advised the occupant of his lineage stool about regalia and public appearances.[26] In this invention of tradition, a Presbyterian pastor assisted in building a bridge to the past and modifying the afahye to contemporary needs.

In 1937, Rev. Asante married Felicia Animaa. In contrast to common Akan practice, they shared a household and made a conscious effort to represent modern Christian family life, for example by devoting many resources to educating their ten children. They followed Presbyterian ideals of masculinity and femininity (Miescher 2005, chapter 5). Rev. Asante and his wife also exemplify the gendered differences among elders in the Presbyterian Church. Theologian Mercy Amba Oduyoye (1995) has critiqued the marginalization and subordination of women in African churches. In Ghana's Presbyterian Church, although women have been active at a grassroots level since the nineteenth century, forming the backbone of congregations, not until recently they have been admitted to ordination. Mrs. Asante has been a leader in the women's fellowship for decades, not just because of her marriage to a pastor but because of her own accomplishments, qualities, and reputation. After Rev. Asante's death in 1997, I conducted an interview with her. In reflecting about their marriage and church work, Mrs. Asante (2000) foregrounded her role as the pastor's wife who supported her husband, managed his household, and hosted his numerous guests. She allocated less time to discussion of her contribution as a female elder in the congregations where her husband had been stationed, especially the one at Abetifi since his retirement. Thus, to some extent the proverb "The hen is aware of the daybreak, but she watches the cock's beak" applies to Rev. and Mrs. Asante's different positions as elders in the Presbyterian Church. Although she was influential and had a considerable amount of authority, Mrs. Asante frequently stayed in the background and deferred to her husband for grand public statements. So far the public recognition granted by the Abetifi congregation also privileges Rev. Asante's service over that of his wife. In 2001, Abetifi's original Basel Mission chapel, which was built in 1875, was rededicated as the Rev. E. K. O. Asante Memorial Chapel.

Outside churches, modern politics have also intersected with ideas of elderhood in postcolonial Ghana. In 1984, E. F. Opusuo retired from his work as an education officer and returned to his hometown of Pepease. As an acting *abusuapanyin* (lineage head), he dealt with requests for support and organized funerals. He also chaired the local development committee that coordinated communal labor for weeding and building latrines. Pepease voters elected Opusuo to the Kwawu District Assembly, which was created by the PNDC (Provisional National Defense Council) government under J. J. Rawlings in 1988. District assemblies consisted of two-thirds elected and one-third appointed members. The central government appointed traditional rulers as well as nominees of churches, market women, farmers' associations, and benevolent societies.[27] Assembly members were predominately male and were "relatively well educated," drawn from "locally rooted community leaders" and activists (Crook 1994, 358). District assemblies, according to anthropologist Maxwell Owusu (1992), created a new democratic institution that provided more "effective 'people power' from local communities upward on a non-partisan basis." The assemblies constituted a system that built on "indigenous political traditions of local self-government that assume the existence of shared ethical and moral values" (391). Its members were expected to reflect virtues of accountability, service, and probity. The government-run *Ghanaian Times* editorialized:

> [The] most respected people in the village community owe their high public status and esteem to their service in the community. The most respected elder is not necessarily the one with a lot of money, a big house, a large well-educated family and so on. . . . But each owes his respect to definable services to the community. . . . In this communalist organization [the district assembly], the only reward an elder receives for his service to the community is the satisfaction of being among those whose counsel and planning lead to the progress of the community. (July 11, 1992, cited in Owusu 1992, 392)

District assemblies became a forum for *mpanyinfoɔ* to provide leadership within their local communities, not for the purpose of self-enrichment but to address their hometown needs. Although organizations such as the CDRs (Committees for the Defense of the Revolution) and the 31st December Women's Movement, run by the First Lady, were supposed to serve as watchdogs to prevent abuses of power by assembly members, Opusuo did not consider these organizations to be independent; instead, he saw them as partisan affiliates of the PNDC government (1993b). Still, in his efforts as an assembly member, he had to rely on the local CDR to gather support for projects such as cleaning the Pepease market and making improvements to the lorry station. In his assessment, Opusuo is close to that of historian Paul Nugent (1995), who noted the PNDC government's attempts to decentralize *and* broaden its support by reaching to "the most influential power brokers at the community level" (205).

Since the inauguration of the Fourth Republic in 1993, district assemblies have become more politicized, despite constitutional language that sought to retain nonpartisanship.[28] Opusuo (1993a), who was "not interested in party politics," refused to compete for a second term. In recognition of his service, the ɔmanhene of Kwawu presented him with a certificate. During the 1996 *afahye*, Opusuo's ɔpanyin status was again acknowledged. He wrote me in a letter:

> I was honoured by the Pepease Community on the 24th February for my ten years (1984–1994) of selfless, courageous, honest and dedicated leadership to the people of Pepease. I was given a beautiful wall clock as an award. I am now an advisor to the Pepease Town Council. (Pepease, March 20, 1996)

The leadership an *ɔpanyin* provides within his lineage and communities is a highly valued trait of senior masculinity that is alive and respected in Kwawu. Postcolonial state institutions such as district assemblies and the national Parliament offer venues beyond the immediate realm of the lineage for a man, and to a lesser degree for women, to prove worthiness as an *ɔpanyin* dedicated to service for the entire community.[29] Although these modern institutions are located outside the *ahenfie*, it remains up to the *ɔhene*, or on major occasions the *ɔmanhene*, to present awards of recognition within a "traditional area" on behalf of the people.

Conclusion

In Akan societies, becoming an adult man is the initial step in the process of reaching senior masculinity, the status of an elder. This intersection between age and gender has been neglected in most masculinity studies that draw on Australian, European, and North American material (Connell 1995; but see Gardiner 2002). Approaching gender from a generational perspective moves age as a social category to the foreground. Because generational masculinities (and femininities) matter, personhood and subjectivity are determined by the social position derived from a specific age.

In Kwawu during the twentieth century, the term *ɔpanyin* had different and at times ambiguous meanings. While an *ɔpanyin* has always been old in the sense of experience and maturity, he or she may be still young in years. Often the status of an *ɔpanyin* has been related to a social position, an office in the chief's court, election to the role of presbyter, or an election or appointment as a modern political official. All elders have been involved in dispute settlement in both formal and informal settings. *Mpanyinfoɔ* are expected to speak well and sensibly. The status of any *ɔpanyin* is never permanent. Elders who misbehave jeopardize respect and effectiveness even if they still carry a title. The social position of an *ɔpanyin* is not purely self-acquired but is the product of accomplishments and qualities acknowledged by a larger community. What constituted leadership skills, who qualified for the social position of an *ɔpanyin*, depended on specific historical contexts. In the case of senior presbyter J. Y. Atta, local tensions as well as competing notions of masculinities were articulated in conflicting opinions among different communities in the town of Abetifi about what the expectations and obligations of an *ɔpanyin* were. Looking at individual lives, the discussion has examined the processes of becoming an *ɔpanyin*. I argue that for migrants, the preparations and reasons for returning home correlated with invitations to accept lineage and community responsibilities suitable to an *ɔpanyin* and expectations that the migrating individual would accept such an invitation. Becoming an elder was not always a linear process; ideas about the *ɔpanyin*'s responsibilities and status were determined by historical contexts.

The social position of an *ɔpanyin* is not gender specific. Women have served as *mpanyinfoɔ* and *ahemaa* in the chief's palace or within their lineage and communities or, more recently, as elected officials. Yet in the course of the twentieth century, women's status has decreased. Social structures and local institutions that once guaranteed senior Akan women access to decision-making processes and resources have lost their relevance. Mission churches, which originated as patriarchal institutions, marginalized and subordinated women, leaving limited spaces for female leadership. But the story is more complicated, as the case of Mrs. Asante indicates. Female elders had a certain amount of power and influence, though it was more hidden and was frequently exercised in indirect ways.[30] More work is needed on how the experiences and recollections of female elders relate to and complicate the positions of male elders.

A historicization of a category such as *ɔpanyin* enhances our understanding of the Kwawu past as well as our understanding of larger units such as Ghana or West Africa. An exploration of the meanings and social position of *mpanyinfoɔ* and their subjectivity at specific moments leads to new answers to questions about the historical transformations of the twentieth century while they also enrich studies on gender in Africa and beyond.

Notes

1. For the argument that motherhood is a central category in African societies, see Oyewumi (2002) and the discussion of the online journal *Jenda,* which has promoted research on the meanings of motherhood, in "Production of Knowledge in the Digital Age" (this volume).

2. See Bakare-Yusuf (2004), quote cited in Pereira (2003, 8). Making a political argument, Patricia McFadden (2001, 61) has challenged Oyewumi's cultural claims: "When gender and women disappear from the conceptual landscape, then feminist resistance politics is also displaced, leaving [African women] without a political means of responding to patriarchal exclusion." Others have critiqued Oyewumi's use of linguistic and ethnographic evidence, most extensively Matory (2003, 425–431). Mugambi and Boris (both in this volume) raise questions about Oyewumi's assertion that the absence of a gendered language indicates the lack of a gender category.

3. For a discussion of this methodology, see my book *Making Men in Ghana* (Miescher 2005, 13–16); material about Kwawu in this chapter appears in chapter 6.

4. For the intersection of age, gender, and iron technology in African societies, see Herbert (1993); for gender and generational struggles in colonial Africa, see Mandala (1990) and McKittrick (2002).

5. Kwame Arhin (1983, 95) provides specific examples of women occupying male stools in the Akan states of Akyem Abuakwa and Dwaben; see Clark (1994, 94, 98).

6. Boahen (2003); see also Arhin Brempong (2000) and Obeng (2003). For the possibilities and limits of female masculinity in colonial Igboland, see Achebe (2003).

7. Robertson (1984, 13–17); for the gendered impact of the cocoa industry, see Allman and Tashjian (2000); for the feminization of the market, see Clark (1994).

8. See Morrell (1998, 2001); Lindsay and Miescher (2003); and Lindsay (this volume).

9. D. E. Akwa, "Report, Abetifi," August 12, 1916, Basel Mission Archive (hereafter BMA), D-3.7. For other conversion stories, see Wright (1993).

10. Akwa, "Report," 2.

11. Ibid., 5–6. Presbyters were elected by male congregation members who were at least twenty years old; for election procedures, qualifications, and presbyters' responsibilities, see *Ordnung für die Evangelischen Gemeinden der Basler Mission auf der Goldküste, revidiert 1902* (hereafter *Gemeindeordnung*), 11–14, BMA, D-9.1c, 13b.

12. Akwa, "Report," 18. For early-twentieth-century economic changes, see Garlick (1967).

13. Akwa, "Report," 10–12, 23. Rev. Akwa commented, "His advices, and decisions are like prophecy; whatever he utters, it comes to pass" (12–13). Atta's importance in state politics is well documented. The former ɔmanhene, Kwasi Diawuo, reported that Atta, who was his uncle, had helped negotiate his destoolment the previous year; Kwasi Diawuo to Governor, Mangoase, March 21, 1916, National Archives of Ghana (hereafter NAG), ADM, 11/1/1445.

14. Akwa, "Report," 14, 19–20.

15. There were many crises: for challenges by commoners in 1906, see Simensen (1975).

16. Akwa, "Report," 14–15. For Basel Mission marriage rules stressing a husband's obligation toward his wife and children at the expense of the matrilineage, see *Gemeindeordnung*, 26–36; see also Miescher (2005, chapter 5).

17. Akwa, "Report," 15–16. A traveling commissioner reported from Kwawu: "Ata was *the* man whom all of Kwahu would have preferred. He is the senior presbyter at the Mission station, one of the best natives I have, & in every way well suited to be King. But he would not consent." Traveling Commissioner H. M. Hull to Colonial Secretary, August 22, 1898, NAG, ADM, 11/1/1445.

18. For J. Y. Atta's nominations as ɔmanhene, see Edmond Perregaux, annual report, Abetifi, February 11, 1899, BMA, D-1.69, 133, and Otto Schimming, annual report, Abetifi, February, 1906, BMA, D-1.84b. See also District Officer F. Crowther to Secretary for Native Affairs (SNA), Abetifi, April 12, 1905, NAG, ADM, 11/1/1445.

19. Akwa, "Report," 16–18, 24.

20. In 1933, a member of the Presbyterian Church was enstooled as ɔmanhene Akuamoa Akyeampong; see Commissioner, Eastern Province to SNA, March 3, 1933, NAG, CSO, 21/22/11. His Christian faith caused problems; see Government Agent Mpraeso's confidential report to Government Agent Birim, April 2, 1953, NAG-K, ADM/KD, 29/6/1053.

21. The Presbyterian Church of the Gold Coast, *Regulations, Practice & Procedure*, revised 1929, 3, BMA, D-9.1c, 13c. See Wahyee (1993).

22. Session Minute Book, Abetifi Presbyterian Church, 12, November 4, 1963, Abetifi Presbyterian Church Archive.

23. Ibid., 93, December 26, 1967.

24. Wahyee, Donkor, and Addo (1994). Van der Geest (1998b, 462) learned that an ɔpanyin should no longer travel for business and stay elsewhere.

25. Throughout Abetifi and other Kwawu towns, older buildings are associated with deceased men and women; see van der Geest (1998a, 1998b).

26. E. K. O. Asante (1994). *Afahye* is the Kwawu version of the Akan *odwira* festival, when Kwawu subchiefs pay respect to the ɔmanhene in Abene; for *odwira* in precolonial Asante, see McCaskie (1995, 144–242).

27. Local Government Law (PNDC Law 207) of 1988; see Nugent (1995, 177).

28. According to the new constitution, a district assembly candidate "shall present himself to the electorate as an individual, and shall not use any symbol associated with any political party." Political parties "shall not endorse, sponsor, offer a platform to or in anyway campaign for or against a candidate seeking election to a District Assembly" (Republic of Ghana 1992, 153).

29. For a discussion of gender activism, women's movements, "wifeism," and wom-

en's organizations led by First Ladies that were mainly concerned about the needs of ruling regimes, see Manuh (this volume); for Nigeria, see Abdullah (1995 and this volume).

30. For the importance of indirection in Akan speech, see Yankah (1995).

References

Abdullah, Hussaina. 1995. "Wifeism and Activism: The Nigerian Women's Movement." In *The Challenge of Local Feminisms*, edited by Armita Basu, 209–225. Boulder, Colo.: Westview Press.

Achebe, Nwando. 2003. "'And She Became a Man': King Ahebi in the History of Enugu Ezike, Nsukka Division, 1880–1948." In *Men and Masculinities in Modern Africa*, edited by Lisa A. Lindsay and Stephan F. Miescher, 52–68. Portsmouth, N.H.: Heinemann.

Akyeampong, Emmanuel K. 1996. *Drink, Power, and Cultural Change: A Social History of Alcohol in Ghana, c. 1800 to Recent Times*. Portsmouth, N.H.: Heinemann.

——, and Pashington Obeng. 1995. "Spirituality, Gender and Power in Asante History." *International Journal of African Historical Studies* 28, no. 3: 481–508.

Allman, Jean, and Victoria Tashjian. 2000. *"I Will Not Eat Stone": A Women's History of Colonial Asante*. Portsmouth, N.H.: Heinemann.

Arhin, Kwame. 1983. "The Political and Military Roles of Akan Women." In *Female and Male in West Africa*, edited by Christine Oppong, 91–96. London: Allen and Unwin.

Arhin Brempong (Kwame Arhin). 2000. "The Role of Nana Yaa Asantewaa in the 1900 Asante War of Resistance." *Ghana Studies* 3: 97–110.

Asante, E. K. O. 1993a. Interview with the author. Abetifi, January 26.

——. 1993b. Interview with the author. May 18.

——. 1993c. Interview with the author. August 17.

——. 1994. Interview with the author. September 27.

Asante, Felicia. 2000. Interview with author and Pearl A. Ofosu. Abetifi, August 22.

Asante, Kwabena. 1994. Interview with the author and Kwame Fosu. Pepease, October 29.

Bakare-Yusuf, Bibi. 2004. "Yorubas Don't Do Gender: A Critical Review of Oyeronke Oyewumi's *The Invention of Women: Making an African Sense of Western Gender Discourses*." In *African Gender Scholarship: Concepts, Methodologies, and Paradigms*, edited by Signe Arnfred, 61–81. Dakar: CODESRIA.

Bartle, Philip. 1978. "Urban Migration and Rural Identity: An Ethnography of a Kwawu Community, Obo, Ghana." Ph.D. diss., University of Ghana.

Boahen, A. Adu. 2003. *Yaa Asantewaa and the Asante-British War of 1900–1*. Accra: Sub-Saharan Publishers.

Christaller, Johann Gottlieb. 1933. *A Dictionary of the Asante and Fante Language, Called Tschi (Twi)*. 2nd ed., revised and enlarged. Basel: Basel Evangelical Missionary Society.

Clark, Gracia. 1994. *Onions Are My Husband: Survival and Accumulation by West African Market Women*. Chicago: University of Chicago Press.

Connell, R. W. 1995. *Masculinities*. Berkeley: University of California Press.

Crook, Richard. 1994. "Four Years of the Ghana District Assemblies in Operation: Decentralization, Democratization, and Administrative Performance." *Public Administration and Development* 14: 339–364.

Gardiner, Judith Kegan. 2002. "Theorizing Age with Gender: Bly's Boys, Feminism, and Maturity Masculinity." In *Masculinity Studies and Feminist Theory*, edited by Judith K. Gardiner, 90–118. New York: Columbia University Press.

Garlick, Peter. 1967. "The Development of Kwahu Business Enterprise in Ghana since 1874—An Essay in Recent Oral Tradition." *Journal of African History* 8, no. 3: 463–480.

Herbert, Eugenia W. 1993. *Iron, Gender, and Power: Rituals of Transformation in African Societies*. Bloomington: Indiana University Press.

Hunt, Nancy Rose. 1999. *A Colonial Lexicon of Birth Ritual, Medicalization, and Mobility in the Congo*. Durham, N.C.: Duke University Press.

Lindsay, Lisa A., and Stephan F. Miescher, eds. 2003. *Men and Masculinities in Modern Africa*. Portsmouth, N.H.: Heinemann.

Mama, Amina. 1995. *Beyond the Masks: Race, Gender and Subjectivity*. London: Routledge.

Mandala, Elias C. 1990. *Work and Control in a Peasant Economy: A History of the Lower Tchiri Valley in Malawi, 1859–1960*. Madison: University of Wisconsin Press.

Manuh, Takyiwaa. 1988. "The Asantehemaa's Court and Its Jurisdiction over Women." *Research Review*, n.s., 4, no. 2: 50–66.

Matory, J. Lorand. 2003. "Gendered Agendas: The Secrets Scholars Keep about Yorùbá-Atlantic Religion." *Gender & History* 15, no. 3: 409–439.

McCaskie, T. C. 1995. *State and Society in Pre-Colonial Asante*. Cambridge: Cambridge University Press.

McFadden, Patricia. 2001. "Cultural Practices as Gendered Exclusion: Experiences from Southern Africa." In *Discussing Women's Empowerment*, edited by Brigitta Sevefjord and Berit Olsson, 58–72. Stockholm: SIDA.

McKittrick, Meredith. 2002. *To Dwell Secure: Generation, Christianity, Colonialism in Ovamboland*. Portsmouth, N.H.: Heinemann.

Miescher, Stephan F. 2003. "The Making of Presbyterian Teachers: Masculinity and Programs of Education in Colonial Ghana." In *Men and Masculinities in Modern Africa*, edited by Lisa A. Lindsay and Stephan F. Miescher, 89–108. Portsmouth, N.H.: Heinemann.

———. 2005. *Making Men in Ghana*. Bloomington: Indiana University Press.

Morrell, Robert, ed. 1998. Special issue on "Masculinities in Southern African Studies." *Journal of Southern African Studies* 24, no. 4.

———, ed. 2001. *Changing Men in Southern Africa*. London: Zed Books.

Nugent, Paul. 1995. *Big Men, Small Boys, and Politics in Ghana: Power, Ideology, and the Burden of History, 1982–1994*. London: Pinter.

Obeng, Pashington. 2003. "Gendered Nationalism: Forms of Masculinity in Modern Asante." In *Men and Masculinities in Modern Africa*, edited by Lisa A. Lindsay and Stephan F. Miescher, 192–208. Portsmouth, N.H.: Heinemann.

Oduyoye, Mercy Amba. 1995. *Daughters of Anowa: African Women and Patriarchy*. Maryknoll, N.Y.: Orbis Books.

Opusuo, E. F. 1993a. Interview with the author. Pepease, August 22.

———. 1993b. Interview with the author. September 28.

———. 1994. Interview with the author. August 27.

Owusu, Maxwell. 1992. "Democracy and Africa: A View from the Village." *Journal of Modern African Studies* 30, no. 3: 369–396.

Oyewumi, Oyeronke. 1997. *The Invention of Women: Making an African Sense of Western Gender Discourses.* Minneapolis: University of Minnesota Press.

———. 2002. "*Abiyamo*: Theorizing African Motherhood." *Jenda: A Journal of Culture and African Women Studies* 4, no. 1. Available online at http://www.jendajournal.com/jenda/issue4/oyewumi.html (accessed July 1, 2004).

Peel, J. D. Y. 2000. *Religious Encounter and the Making of the Yoruba.* Bloomington: Indiana University Press.

Pereira, Charmaine. 2003. "Locating Gender and Women's Studies in Nigeria: What Trajectories for the Future?" Revised version of paper presented at 10th General Assembly of CODESRIA, "Africa in the New Millennium," December 8–12, 2002, Kampala, Uganda. Available online at http://ww.gwsafrica.org/knowledge/pereira.html (accessed July 7, 2004).

Republic of Ghana. 1992. *Constitution of the Republic of Ghana, 1992.* Accra: Ghana Publishing Corporation.

Robertson, Claire. 1984. *Sharing the Same Bowl: A Socioeconomic History of Women and Class in Accra, Ghana.* Bloomington: Indiana University Press.

Simensen, Jarle. 1975. "The Asafo Movement of Kwahu, Ghana: A Mass Movement for Local Reform under Colonial Rule." *International Journal of African Historical Studies* 8, no. 3: 383–406.

van der Geest, Sjaak. 1998a. "*Yebisa Wo Fie:* Growing Old and Building a House in the Akan Culture of Ghana." *Journal of Cross-Cultural Gerontology* 13: 333–359.

———. 1998b. "Ɔpanyin: The Ideal of Elder in the Akan Culture of Ghana." *Canadian Journal of African Studies* 32, no. 3: 449–493.

Wahyee, J. A. 1993. Interview with the author and Joseph Kwakye. Abetifi, August 25.

———. 1994. Interview with the author and Joseph Kwakye. September 18.

———, and Kwadwo Donkor. 1994. Interview with the author and Joseph Kwakye. November 28.

Wahyee, J. A., Kwadwo Donkor, and E. V. Osei Addo. 1994. Interview with the author and Joseph Kwakye. Abetifi, October 31.

Wilks, Ivor. 1993. *Forests of Gold: Essays on the Akan and the Kingdom of Asante.* Athens: Ohio University Press.

Wright, Marcia. 1993. *Strategies of Slaves & Women: Life-Stories from East/Central Africa.* New York: L. Barber Press.

Yankah, Kwesi. 1995. *Speaking for the Chief: Ɔkyeame and the Politics of Akan Royal Oratory.* Bloomington: Indiana University Press.

15 "Give Her a Slap to Warm Her Up": Post-Gender Theory and Ghana's Popular Culture

Catherine M. Cole

Sexism in West African popular theatre is so ubiquitous that it "goes without saying" and has gone without extensive commentary in the growing literature on this topic.[1] *Africa After Gender?* provides an opportunity for further reflection on the dynamics of gender in West African popular culture, an arena that *because* of its popularity offers a unique window on social and cultural life.[2] Theatre is a particularly expressive form of popular culture, for performers are notorious for adapting their shows with great agility to current trends and local issues. Usually performed in African languages, popular theatre vividly represents how gender is enacted, expressed, and understood "on the ground," especially among the working class, who are the form's chief innovators and patrons.

Given the reliance of popular theatre on audience participation and the capacity to espouse contradictory meanings, it is difficult to locate precisely what this genre might be saying about *anything*, especially about a topic as complex as gender. Nevertheless, for this present book, which contemplates the slippery idea of an Africa that is somehow "after gender," I wish to explore how the concert party, Ghana's popular theatre, has depicted women, gender, and the difference between the two. What do we mean by "gender" in Africa? How does the western concept of gender relate to indigenous African knowledge systems and social categories? When and why did "gender" as a concept gain currency in Africa such that it is now a household word, as common in lorries and chop bars as it is in the houses of Parliament and the boardrooms of nongovernmental organizations? Gender's popularity in Africa may be explained in part because the term is simply more palatable than "women" or the even more incendiary term "feminism." One notes the distance between, on the one hand, the theoretical musings about a "post" gender question in recent scholarship (largely emanating from scholars residing in Europe and the United States) and, on the other hand, the lived realities of actual women on the ground in Africa. For while gender posits an inclusive, relational analysis that intersects with, but is not determined by, physical sex, those who *are* physically sexed as female in

Africa still have far less access than men do to material resources and political power. That discrepancy must not slip from view.

Helen Mugambi, in her essay in this volume, catalogues the many advancements and achievements women have made in contemporary Uganda. They have assumed prominent roles in Parliament, law courts, the university, and politics. Yet even with these formidable accomplishments, women are still frequently the victims of domestic violence. And the overall public perception is that such violence is condoned as justifiable behavior. Mugambi analyzes the case of Dr. Wandira Naigaga (Kazibwe), the country's vice president, who revealed that her husband, Charles Kazibwe, a prominent civil engineer, had beaten her. The public discourse surrounding this revelation exposed a high public tolerance of such acts, even when it is the vice president of the country who is being slapped. Mugambi asks, "If, in the midst of all these buoyant developments, there are people who think that it is frivolous for the Vice President of a country to object to being slapped 'only twice' by a man who thinks that he has the right to assault her because he is her husband, where exactly are we in the gender engagement process?" Mugambi's argument brings us back to the nitty-gritty realities of daily life and to the possibility that a discourse on gender that is liberatory, reflexive, critical, and uniformly applied to men and women is nascent—at best—in Africa.

In contrast to the very real slapping of a prominent female politician in Uganda, let us now consider a slap from the fictional realm of the concert party theatre genre from Ghana. At the beginning of the Jaguar Jokers' play *Onipa Hia Moa (People Need Help)*, Kofi Nyame Bekyere praises his wife Ama Comfort because she caters to his every need. When Kofi is hungry, she prepares food. When he wants her to sleep, she sleeps. When Kofi is feeling "happy in the house" and Ama comes near him, "I just look at her face, and give her a dirty slap. '*Chang!*' She will only say, '*Agee! Agyae ee!*' And then laugh it off" (Jaguar Jokers 1995a, 1995b, 6). The audience who witnessed this play in 1994 in the town of Teacher Mante responded loudly to this monologue, both shocked and amused by its brazenness. In a conspiratorial tone, Kofi addressed them:

> My dear married men here, listen to this piece of advice. If you marry a woman and you find that in the morning or afternoon she is feeling dull, you call her to come. Ask why she is feeling dull like that, and before she answers, you give her a slap to warm her up. She will only laugh it off, and there will be happiness in the house.[3]

Despite this dubious introduction, Kofi is unequivocally the play's sympathetic hero. His fond habit of slapping Ama is never brought up again. Rather it is Ama's disloyalty to Kofi that carries the play's moral freight.

Can we view Kofi's slap as an example of domestic violence? Definitions of domestic violence are, of course, subject to historical change and cultural interpretation. Historian Stephan Miescher asks whether in Ghana *all* slaps are considered violent or whether it is "necessary to draw blood in order to have a case"

(2003). Miescher's examination of the colonial archives of the Kwawu Native Tribunals justifies such fine distinctions: all slaps, it appears, are not considered equal under customary law. While it is difficult to discover the appropriate cultural terms in which to discuss Kofi's slap, American students to whom I have taught this play can speak of little else. "One surefire way to distance me from a theatrical piece," one student reported, "is to have a character proclaim that when he is feeling blue, all he has to do is hit his wife and he cheers up."

In addition to asking why West African plays were historically so overwhelmingly misogynist, a parallel and intersecting question that must be asked is why certain female characters dominated in specific time periods. Of all female roles in Ghana's concert party since its inception in the 1930s, three have enjoyed notable iconic status: the schoolgirl, the orphan, and the widow. These character types have been unblushingly copied over the decades by various concert party troupes vying for preeminence in a competitive field. What do they reveal about how gender has functioned in Ghana's popular culture? What can these characters tell us about the larger dynamics of gender identity as a means by which multiple forces in a society converge? In trying to come to grips with popular theatre's unfavorable treatment of women and its penchant for misogyny, we see in these evolving female roles a volatility of gender that is inherently a discourse about change and otherness. We also see the necessity for African gender scholarship that interrogates the rift between theories of how gender is constructed and the actual on-the-ground practices of how gender is performed and enacted.

Wicked Women Exposed

As a "blame-the-woman" play, *Onipa Hia Moa* represents a common strain of popular theatre not only in Ghana but throughout West Africa. During the course of the drama, all the prominent female characters are exposed as unreliable, greedy, even wicked.[4] Two women cause the play's dramatic crises: first the protagonist's aunt casts a spell on him and then his wife abandons him. Both women are motivated by resentment about money. And both are eventually exposed and ridiculed.

The crisis of *Onipa Hia Moa* arises when an aunt casts a spell on Kofi Nyame Bekyere. He becomes gravely ill. His wife initially attends to his physical needs, massaging him with herbal potions. But her friend Selena tempts her to run away. She asks: "Why waste your time on a man in this modern Ghana? . . . Let's go to Nigeria and have a good time!" (Jaguar Jokers 1995b, 42). Ama declines Selena's invitation, saying she is bound by duty and morality to stand by her man. Her rationale is severalfold: if she left her husband, this would bring shame on her parents and she would never receive blessings from above. Furthermore, her husband has been good to her (the slaps, it seems, do not warrant any mention here). Finally, if she left him now, how could she possibly return when he was restored to health? Selena responds that a man who has grown "lean like a kitten" will never recover. Though Ama again refuses, Selena's invitation lingers in her mind, gradually eroding her resolve. What most disturbs Ama is the profligate way Kofi has handed out money in the preceding scenes. Cedis have rolled off his fingertips. He has given a "dash" to his visiting parents, covered his brother's alcohol debt, bribed a policeman, and given a financial gift to an elder aunt. Yet what, Ama asks, is due to her? Kofi has not given her enough money nor has he provided a new cloth, as is his obligation. So she leaves him.[5] The rest of the play charts Kofi's demise, desperation, and eventual restoration to health through the unlikely assistance of his self-aggrandizing friend Opia.

The cause of Kofi's illness finally comes to light: a woman has cast a spell on him. The prayers of an evangelical Christian minister summon Kofi's aunt, Abba Kom. She appears on stage in a trance, balancing upon her head a witch's pot that contains a snake. She collapses on the floor and confesses not only to cursing Kofi and causing his sickness but also to casting spells on other male family members. In order to purge her wicked deeds, the pastor intones, "You woman sitting in front of me, damn your evil spirits, damn your witchcraft." These lines are gleefully repeated by Opia, and each time he does so, the audience howls in amusement. The laughter of spectators is part of Abba Kom's punishment, and thus comedy and audience participation become coercive instruments of the play's underlying misogyny.

When Kofi's wife Ama Comfort later returns from her travels and seeks forgiveness, she too is subjected to humiliation. Opia first tells her Kofi has died, and he gets the audience to conspire in this lie by having them tell Ama—in a half-dozen different languages—that Kofi is indeed dead. Opia next forces Ama to scurry around the stage picking up handkerchiefs wherever he drops them. Finally he tells her to wait while he pleads her case with Kofi. He returns with the final verdict, expressed with characteristic Akan euphemism, saying that Kofi has "stopped putting on Java prints, and he now wears Veritable Wax." In other words, he has parted with the old and inferior things and he now lives with new and superior ones. To put it bluntly, Opia tells her, "He has got a new wife" (69).

So a play that begins with a story about a woman being slapped by her husband for his pleasure resolves with a condemnation of female disloyalty and wickedness. The comedy of this particular play, as with so many popular dramas from West Africa, is delivered at women's expense. Scholar Karin Barber, in her study of cultural forms similar to the concert party among the Yorùbá of Nigeria, has taken us perhaps the furthest in understanding what misogyny in West African popular theatre might be about. As in Ghana, Yorùbá popular plays are conceived from a male point of view and a working-class male perspective at that. The plays' frequent iteration of a desire to put women in their place does not reflect, according to Barber, an affirmation of received traditions about appropriate gender roles. Rather the plays' misogyny is "more like a shrill cry of protest from the class of men who lose most by women's changing opportunities: an attempt not so much to preserve a valued traditional order as to put the brakes on social change at all costs" (1986, 23).

The modern urban sector of Nigeria's informal economy created new gender relationships. Whereas in precolonial societies the division of labor between men and women was clearly defined, in modern cities, men and women found themselves in direct competition with one another.[6] The audiences and artists involved in Yorùbá popular theater are predominantly working-class men, those of the entrepreneurial sector. Yorùbá popular plays reveal an escalating anxiety about what was perceived as women's privileged access to contracts and opportunities in a new economy. Barber notes that the frequency and intensity of misogynist themes increased over a 40-year period. Whereas plays of the 1950s were based more on folkloric themes and featured innocent, sympathetic heroines, by the 1970s and 1980s, after the influx of oil money into Nigeria and its concomitant social distortions, the "blame-the-woman" approach came to dominate Yorùbá plays. Can we see a similar transformation of gender typologies in Ghana, a neighboring country in West Africa?

Evolving Female Roles in Ghana's Concert Party

In the 1930s and 1940s, the sole female role in the concert party was the "schoolgirl," a westernized woman who was played by a male actor in drag. Newly married and childless, the schoolgirl dressed smartly in a frock and high heels and she could speak English fluently because she had been to school. She fascinated audiences, especially rural spectators, as a curiosity who enacted novel behaviors from *aburokyir,* from overseas. Yet within the dramatic action, the schoolgirl proved to be completely incompetent as a wife. She could not cook and would not clean. Furthermore, she was sexually suspect. E. T. Mensah's popular highlife song "School Girl" warns listeners to be wary of such women:

> Listen here, *skuul maame* [school girl] is no good, oh!
> Look, *skuul maame* is not good, oh! I tell you,
> If you go follow her, she no go follow you.
> I tell you, school girl is no good, oh. (Mensah 1990)

Early concert party narratives revolved around the woman's lover, who becomes accidentally trapped in her house and is then comically discovered by her husband. Sometimes the philanderer hides under the table, other times in a laundry basket or a cocoa sack. But wherever he hid, the play climaxed when he was discovered by the woman's husband. Plays generally concluded by heaping condemnation on the wife: she was depicted as innately duplicitous. First, she had two lovers, only one of which was her husband. Second, she was performing a gender identity from overseas, a fusion of western and Akan notions of womanhood. Third, the audience knows—either through common knowledge or through telltale physical details such as hand size or quality of voice—that the schoolgirl is not really a girl at all but a male actor in women's clothing. The schoolgirl was a kind of sexual, cultural, and gender infidel whose loyalties changed in mercurial fashion. She was, above all, untrustworthy. Not only did she have two lovers, she had two cultures. To which would she be faithful?

The schoolgirl was certainly not the only duplicitous character in early concert party plays. None of the stock characters were really what they seemed to be. The lady's husband was supposed to be rich and well educated, but we discover through the plays that he was in fact short on cash and had, at best, a feeble grasp of English. The houseboy, a servant from Liberia, was reputed to be dumb and illiterate. Yet the narratives invariably demonstrated not only that he was clever but that his values were more traditionally Akan than those of his locally born master or mistress. Unlike them, he was not trying to emulate European behaviors. However, of all the three stock roles in the early plays, the schoolgirl was the most *suspect* because she embodied cultural contradictions to a degree that far surpassed the other two.

The subsequent decades saw a profound evolution in female characters. The schoolgirl transformed from a figure that aroused curiosity and anxiety to one who could move audiences to tears, so transported were they by the pathos of the situations in which she found herself. Whereas formerly the schoolgirl was a cultural oddity and a curiosity, in the 1950s—on the cusp of independence—she became a more recognizable character. During that time, Kakaiku's theatre company developed a play called *Schoolgirl* about a young girl who was unable to complete her education.[7] Kakaiku's schoolgirl was literally a girl *in* school. By the 1950s, formal education was far more common than it had been in the 1930s, and many families went to extraordinary lengths to provide the requisite school fees and uniforms for their children (Foster 1965). They did so because they saw education as the road to economic advancement and social mobility for the entire family. In Kakaiku's *Schoolgirl*, a mother and father of modest means have scrimped to set aside money for their daughter to attend college. But the schoolgirl's friends entice her into another life of independent wage-earning and pleasure in the city. The play's central conflict reflects a generational disagreement about whether work or education is the greater good. The schoolgirl argues that the "ultimate aim in life is to work and earn money" (Koomson 1995). After much argument, she leaves her parents, goes to the city, and enjoys the "highlife." But she soon falls into a life of prostitution. The girl finally recognizes her error and returns home to ask forgiveness and take up her education again. But she is too late: her parents were forced to spend her college funds and the play ends tragically, as the girl laments the opportunities she has squandered.

On a certain level, this is yet another West African "blame-the-woman" play. The female character makes some bad decisions and must face the consequences. Yet Kakaiku's *Schoolgirl* is a departure from its misogynist predecessors. First, the schoolgirl is the sole protagonist and the narrative assumes that audiences will *care* about a girl's coming-of-age story. Second, though the play does cast judgment on the girl's misguided decisions, the audience is meant to sympathize with her. Finally, the play presumes that female children *should* be educated, a view that was not universally shared, for educating girls presented a whole host of complications to African families.

The schoolgirl's popularity diminished in the 1950s and 1960s, surpassed by other female characters. The first was the *egyankaba*, or "orphan." A young girl whose mother has died, the *egyankaba* is a kind of West African Cinderella. Because the orphan has lost her mother, she is unmoored from the maternal figure so key in the Akan matrilineal family structure. In the dramas of this period, the orphan suffers intolerable abuses as a servant in the home of some distant relative. What the schoolgirl and the orphan share in common is cultural and social dislocation. The schoolgirl's instability arises in part from the collision of traditional Akan gender norms and the performance of gender inculcated through Western education. Similarly, the orphan is dislocated from the *abusua,* the extended matrilineal family that is a precolonial social structure of profound legal and political significance. The *abusua* came under immense pressure in the twentieth century with the emergence of a cash economy and migrant labor. Further strains arose from changes in customary law that favored the inalienable rights of fathers, regardless of whether they fulfilled their family obligations, while the burden of social reproduction fell increasingly on the shoulders of women (Allman and Tashjian 2000). So when the *egyankaba* loses her mother in concert party plays, she is a person without a safety net, at the mercy of whatever distant relatives agree to take her in. The *egyankaba* must eat table scraps, work tirelessly at domestic chores, and endure the daily humiliations heaped upon her by a resentful stepmother and her children. Unlike the schoolgirl, she has no access to education. The orphan is in some ways the polar opposite of the schoolgirl, inasmuch as she has very little access to education and the upward social mobility that western culture and hedonistic pleasures that education were reputed to afford.

A third female archetype emerged in the late 1960s and 1970s: the "widow." Notable for her maturity and emotional depth, the widow is caught at the intersection of two distinct and conflicting legal systems: the traditional Akan matrilineal society and the patrilineal structures inherited from Britain. In a typical concert party story, the widow and her children are unceremoniously tossed from their home and disenfranchised from the father's wealth. While the deceased's nephew receives and "chops" the entire inheritance, the widow and her children are left in penury, despite the fact that they have been instrumental in earning the husband's and father's wealth during his lifetime. The concert party widow stands at the intersection of customary law and colonial law, getting the worst of both worlds, claimed by neither and left with little recourse in the de facto practices of a postcolonial (dis)order.

The death of a male head of household that is the centerpiece of Kwame Anthony Appiah's book *In My Father's House* (1992) offers only a hint of the social strife caused by the ubiquitous inheritance disputes that bedevil postcolonial Ghana.[8] The confusion over inheritance involves the messy imbrication of British law, which favored the patriarchal nuclear family, with customary Akan law, which took the extended matriclan as the fundamental defining unit. The descriptor "legal pluralism" gives a misleadingly tidy impression of the quagmire postcolonial law faces throughout Africa. Having two or more legal systems coexisting within the same social order makes the death of any relative an occasion for high drama. What is "legal" or "traditional" is not at all clear. An

Akan proverb states that the matriclan is like a forest: if you are outside, it is dense; if you are inside, you see that each tree has its own position (Appiah 1992, 192). While each tree in the matrilineal forest may have a discrete position, concert party plays about widows remind us that the trees in the matriclan's forest, like those in *Macbeth*, are constantly on the move; every position is open to negotiation and contestation.

Real Women/New Gender Roles

The widow emerged as a significant character in Ghanaian theatre only in the postcolonial period, and her introduction can be linked directly to a period when real women entered the concert party entertainment profession. The increasing complexity and sympathy of female characters in the postcolonial years can be tied, in part, to women's entrance into this entertainment field. For behind the story of gender in concert party plays is another story, one about how women gained access to the means of theatrical production. During the years 1927 to 1957, all female roles were played by men in drag. Social mores dictated that "if you are a girl and you go to the stage, people will say you are a prostitute or a harlot" (Kwame Mbia Hammond 1993). The woman credited with being the first to appear on professional stages was Margaret Quainoo. When I interviewed her, she reported the difficulties she faced:

> Sometimes when I appeared on stage, audiences remarked they had never before seen a woman actor, so they jeered at me. But the more they jeered, the more I performed with zeal. . . . The people would say "Useless, yes! You are a hopeless person who has left her mother and taken to acting." Because of this, I sometimes remained indoors after the show for fear people would attack me. I was the first and only woman permanently performing in a concert party. (1995)

During the colonial and early postcolonial years, women were rarely members of theatre companies (which collectively authored plays), and they were likewise excluded from leadership or producing capacities. So it is not surprising that Ghana's popular theatre provided such a limited range of representations of females during this period. But that began to change in the 1960s with the emergence of a government-sponsored concert troupe, the Workers Brigade Concert Party. It was in that troupe that Margaret Quainoo and her compatriot actress Esi Kom got their start. This vanguard of women was followed by others, including Kakaiku's daughter Adom Oppong. However, women remained marginal to popular theatre until one formidable woman arrived on the scene: Efua Sutherland, or "Auntie Efua," as she was known. Playwright and founder of the troupe Kusum Agoromba, Efua Sutherland mentored many promising actresses into the profession, including the talented Adeline Ama Buabeng (Sutherland-Addy 2002). Kusum Agoromba created several Akan-language concert plays that featured strong, complex female roles. *Hena Bedi M'ade?* (*Who Will Be My Heir?*) is one such play. Its novel dramatic structure, complex treatment of gender issues, and diversity of female characters are testaments to the influence of real women in creating it, including that of Sutherland and the many fine actresses who performed in this piece.

Recently *Hena Bedi M'ade?* was adapted as a Ghana Film—that is, a narrative feature video (Ampah 1998a).[9] The play has been kept alive in Kusum Agoromba's repertoire for over twenty years. Originally commissioned by a bank in the 1970s, *Hena Bedi M'ade?* reflects a time when there was a public campaign to encourage people to write wills. (Banks, after all, had a vested interest in avoiding inheritance disputes.) Stylistically *Hena Bedi M'ade?* represents an amalgamation of the early concert party style, like that practiced by the Jaguar Jokers, and a newer form more evocative of theatrical realism. The narrative is distinctive for the diversity of its women's roles and for its structure, which derives from the West African dilemma tale. At the end, the story is left unresolved and the audience must debate the final outcome.

What emerges from *Hena Bedi M'ade?* is a glimpse into the lived experience of legal pluralism and the ways in which uncertainty about the law offers males in positions of power ample opportunity to manipulate so-called tradition to their advantage. As in earlier concert parties, women in this play get the short end of the stick. Yet they also demonstrate remarkable agency. *Hena Bedi M'ade?* features industrious and resourceful women who work within the system—however opaque and shifting that system may be—to secure a place for themselves in the postcolonial order. The play begins when the lead character Asamoa, who sells tickets at a lorry station, learns that his uncle has just died. He exclaims, "Ha, ha, the news is ripe as a pepper!" Surprised by his enthusiasm, the messenger asks, "Why should you laugh when someone is dead?" Asamoa replies, "I am the next in command. I'm going to inherit my uncle." According to matrilineal custom, when a man dies, his wealth belongs not to his wife and children but rather to the matriclan, specifically to his nephew. Asamoa happily takes up his new post and as he occupies his uncle's house, evicts the man's wife and children and pours libation to the ancestors:

> O Almighty Kwame [god of the sky], as for you, you don't drink, but we show it to you to bless it for us. This is your drink. Asase Afua[10] [goddess of the Earth], this is your drink. What is today? This is a great day for me. Elders, you made it a tradition for the nephew to inherit. Blessed unto you, this is your drink. I am the one who inherited my uncle Ampofo. Owing to this, I have moved and taken over all the property. Ancestors, I was selected, after a careful process. . . . Owing to tradition, I am made to replace an elder. You take a drink from me. All those who wished me Asamoa to be roaming at the lorry station as a bookman, all those who wished me ill: it's over for them. (Ampah 1998b, 4)

Asamoa's libation repeatedly stresses that inheritance is a matter of tradition, a customary practice devised by previous generations and blessed by the gods. His position, he asserts, is unassailable. This libation sounds an overarching theme of the video. *Hena Bedi M'ade?* asks What exactly is meant by "tradition"? When a character invokes tradition as justification for his actions, other characters challenge: "Whose tradition is that? Has it changed?" suggesting that supposedly unchanging tradition is in far more flux than many will admit (107).

Once Asamoa has poured libation, he continues to drink, liberally. Former lovers, friends, and the spokesperson for the local chief come to visit. Having heard of Asamoa's good fortune, they wish to claim their "share" of both his wealth and his alcohol. While no one questions Asamoa's entitlement to his inheritance, some do question his treatment of the deceased's wife, Maame Abena. Death has "done her wrong," for Asamoa has evicted her and her children from the house "as if they were chickens" (21). Abena laments, "In this world, if you marry a man, and you labor with him, and you are not given your share before he dies, then you have worked in vain" (30). Legally, a widow can lay claim to her husband's wealth if she can prove that she was instrumental in earning his wealth through her labor. While Ama asserts her rights, Asamoa and his male cohorts defend their ill treatment of widows, saying that these women have it easy. "In some places, when your husband dies, broken bottles are used to shave your head bald. After shaving it, they use pepper. The pepper is poured on the woman's head and she alone carries her husband's corpse to the cemetery" (15). This custom, he claims, is to make sure the wife knows that it was her fault that her husband died.[11]

The schoolgirl archetype makes a brief appearance in this story. Maame Abena's daughter has won a scholarship to go overseas. She and her mother approach Asamoa for assistance, but he rebuffs them. He says that they should sell what little land they have and that he will buy it from them. So incensed are the wife and children at the thought of selling their property to their despicable uncle that the girl decides to turn down her scholarship and stay and farm with her family instead. Her decision to stay and work rather than go to school echoes the decision Kakaiku's schoolgirl made several decades before. Yet the outcome in *Hena Bedi M'ade?* is far more favorable. Through their industry and hard work on the farm, Maame Abena and her children become very wealthy. Meanwhile, Asamoa experiences a sudden reversal. He sells his land and before he is able to invest the money, thieves (who are, in fact, his friends in disguise) steal his entire inheritance. He is left so poor that he packs his bags and plans to go to Accra to be a "kaya," a porter in the market—the most menial of jobs.

There are more plot complications in *Hena Bedi M'ade*, too elaborate to detail here. The struggle and debate over Asamoa's inheritance continues throughout the entire narrative and never finds resolution. The final scene takes place in a chief's court, a battle with all the principal figures in which they debate both petty and substantive issues, all of which stem from confusion over inheritance. Some characters advise that in the future such cases should be handled differently: one person advocates that a wife should inherit everything, as is done in Europe. Others say that wives should be entitled to half of the estate and that the matriclan should receive the other half. Still others propose splitting inheritance into thirds between the wife, the children, and the *abusua*. The chief says he cannot resolve the matter and that it is for the community assembled to discuss among themselves and come back another day to deliberate.[12] And so the play does not end so much as dwindle away as one by one the chiefs, elders, plaintiffs, and defendants leave the scene. Asamoa is the last to go, and he vociferously defends his right as the nephew to take everything. The audience hoots at Asamoa in disapproval, "Hoo!" Asamoa threatens to sue the audience or fine them a sheep because their disrespectful behavior violates "tradition."

This lack of narrative closure makes *Hena Bedi M'ade?* a significant departure from its concert party predecessors, which always ended with summations and advice. Such conclusions guaranteed for the audience that no matter how frivolous and incoherent the preceding action had been, the drama had at heart been "educative." Yet *Hena Bedi M'ade?* ends not with aphorisms but with a question mark. Both in its title and structure, the story asks Who will inherit me? Given the unresolved state of the case at the end of the play, the ultimate resolution is anyone's guess.

Conclusion

The three iconic figures from Ghana's popular culture that I have analyzed here—the schoolgirl, the orphan, and the widow—reflect a changing discourse on gender over a 55-year period. Each figure served as a lightening rod for historically specific cultural preoccupations. The schoolgirl of the 1930s and 1940s was the only available female role at that time, and she embodied the conflation of cultural anxieties about formal education, cultural fraternization with "western" ideas, and sexual infidelity. The schoolgirl was captivating, for she had unusual speech, foreign manners, and imported clothing. Yet she was not to be trusted.

The emergence of the female orphan, or motherless child, as a protagonist in the 1950s can be tied to the obligation of mothers during this time period to shoulder an increasing load of childrearing responsibilities (Allman and Tashjian 2000). Finally, in the widow character, who emerged in the 1970s and continues to have great relevance today, we see how women are disenfranchised by the confusion between customary and statutory law. The lack of clarity produced by legal pluralism provides occasions ripe for exploitation, and women are particularly disadvantaged by the confusion.[13]

Unlike the popular theatre in Nigeria studied by Karin Barber, Ghana's concert party narratives and character types became more hospitable to women over time, and shows portrayed females in an increasingly sympathetic light. The presence of actual women in the creation and production of plays was central to making this cultural form more inclusive of a range of female gender roles. The Jaguar Jokers' play *Onipa Hia Moa* from the 1960s is a classic example of a "blame-the-woman" play. The dramatic crises is caused by the aunt who casts a spell on her nephew, and the action is further propelled when the man's wife abandons him so that she can go have "fun" in Nigeria. *Hena Bedi M'ade?* from the 1970s portrays women more favorably. Indeed, we might ask whether this play becomes, conversely, a "blame-the-man" play. Asamoa and Okyeame do indeed behave despicably. They are depicted as self-centered men who are comfortable manipulating so-called tradition for their personal gain at the expense of others. But there are other men in the play who behave quite honorably, including the widow's brother and son, who stand by her and help her work on the farm. Rather than heap blame on any one category of person—by gender, class, or ethnicity—*Hena Bedi M'ade?* depicts the way certain individuals in power exploit confusion over inheritance for their personal aggrandizement. The venal and selfish motives of Asamoa and Okyeame are a source of comedy in the play, but the narrative also casts their behavior in a critical light.

Hena Bedi M'ade? dramatizes how gender as an aspect of personhood is inextricably linked with other identities. For instance, the play shows the profound significance of marital status (widowhood) and reproductive status. A widow is a different category of person, and all widows are not the same, for they are divided by whether or not they have had offspring. In a poignant scene between Maame Abena and another widow, Asi Wɛnɛn, they discuss how the latter's fortunes are far worse than Abena's, for without children, she has almost no claim at all to the property she and her husband earned during his lifetime (29–31). As Oyeronke Oyewumi argues, our analysis of gender in Africa must be attentive to the unique shadings and gradations of identity that arise from local circumstances (1997). Ghana's more recent popular plays provide a glimpse of how this layering of identity infuses and informs daily interactions.

Is there an Africa that is "after" gender? Some, such as Oyeronke Oyewumi, argue that gender is a discourse imported from Europe and that in Africa other categories such as reproductive status and seniority carry far more weight. Other scholars, such as Stephan Miescher, argue that even if gender is an imported idea, it has been part of African countries now for over a century. Gender has become indigenized, and scholarship must examine how gender has been incorporated into colonial and postcolonial society. Still others, such as Helen Mugambi, argue that in using the term "gender," which is more inclusive and relational than "women," we must not lose sight of the status of women in Africa and of the realities they face on the ground. Just as the chief's court was unable to make a final ruling at the end of *Hena Bedi M'ade?*, so too the question of what Africa will be "after gender" is open for public deliberation, and the question must be deliberated by the audience.

Notes

1. See Barber (2000); Barber, Collins, and Ricard (1997); Cole (2001).

2. For more on the significance of popular culture, see Barber (1997) and Newell (2000).

3. Recorded on video in 1995, this performance of *Onipa Hia Moa* is included (in abridged form) in the documentary *Stageshakers! Ghana's Concert Party Theatre* (Braun 2001).

4. On "wicked" women in Africa, see Hodgson and McCurdy (2001).

5. As historians Jean Allman and Victoria Tashjian have argued, a greater monetization of domestic relationships is one of the most profound impacts colonialism had on Asante women (2000, 85–132).

6. For more on gender relations and Nigerian labor, see Lisa Lindsay's contribution to this volume. See also Cornwall (2003).

7. It appears that there is no extant script of this production, either published or in manuscript form.

8. See Allman and Tashjian (2000); Manuh (1997); Miescher (1997); Vallenga (1986).

9. For background on Ghana's video industry, see Aveh (2000); Sharfstein (1995); Sutherland-Addy (2000).

10. Though typically Akan libations honor "Asase Yaa," the goddess of the earth, fictional representations such as the concert party sometimes use false names within dramatized spiritual practices. So here the earth goddess is called "Asase Afua," perhaps to keep the libation from having true spiritual efficacy.

11. See the amendment to the Criminal Code (Act 29 of 1960), which prohibits cruel and inhumane treatment of widows.

12. Stephan Miescher (1997, 2005) notes that the first suggestion of a wife (and children) inheriting everything was the legal norm introduced in the original Marriage Ordinance of 1884, which applied to a small minority of educated Christian persons along the Coast. The second suggestion resembles the revised Marriage Ordinance of 1909, which stipulated that two-thirds of the deceased man's property should go to his wife and children and one-third to the *abusua*. The third suggestion of dividing the man's estate into thirds between wife, children, and *abusua* was the practice that had been advocated by the Presbyterian church since 1929.

13. See PNDC Law 111, the Interstate Succession Law, which provides definite shares for both surviving spouses and children and the natal family.

References

Allman, Jean, and Victoria Tashjian. 2000. *"I Will Not Eat Stone": A Women's History of Colonial Asante.* Portsmouth, N.H.: Heinemann.

Ampah, Kwamena. 1998a. *Hena Bedi M'ade? (Who Will Inherit Me?).* Developed and adapted by Kusum Agoromba. Video by Nathan Kwame Braun. Translated by Jacob Amponsah and Henry Bekoe. Distributor pending.

———. 1998b. *Hena Bedi M'ade? (Who Will Inherit Me?).* Developed and adapted by Kusum Agoromba. Translated by Jacob Amponsah and Henry Bekoe. Unpublished manuscript.

Appiah, Kwame Anthony. 1992. *In My Father's House: Africa in the Philosophy of Culture.* New York: Oxford University Press.

Aveh, Africanus. 2000. "Ghanaian Video Films of the 1990s: An Annotated Select Filmography." In *FonTomFrom: Contemporary Ghanaian Literature, Theater and Film,* edited by Kofi Anyidoho and James Gibbs, 283–300. Special issue of *Matutu: Journal for African Culture and Society,* no. 20–21.

Barber, Karin. 1986. "Radical Conservatism in Yorùbá Popular Plays." In *Drama and*

Theatre in Africa, 5–32. Bayreuth African Studies Series 7. Bayreuth, Germany: Bayreuth African Studies Series.

———. 2000. *The Generation of Plays: Yoruba Popular Life in Theater.* Bloomington: Indiana University Press.

———, ed. 1997. *Readings in African Popular Culture.* Bloomington: Indiana University Press.

Barber, Karin, John Collins, and Alain Ricard, eds. 1997. *West African Popular Theatre.* Bloomington: Indiana University Press.

Braun, Nathan Kwame. 2001. *Stage-Shakers! Ghana's Concert Party Theatre.* Video. Bloomington: Indiana University Press.

Cole, Catherine M. 2001. *Ghana's Concert Party Theatre.* Bloomington: Indiana University Press.

Cornwall, Andrea. 2003. "'To Be a Man Is More Than a Day's Work': Shifting Ideals of Masculinity in Ado-Odo, Southwestern Nigeria." In *Men and Masculinities in Modern Africa,* edited by Lisa A. Lindsay and Stephan F. Miescher, 231–248. Portsmouth, N.H.: Heinemann.

Foster, Philip. 1965. *Education and Social Change in Ghana.* Chicago: University of Chicago Press.

Hammond, Kwame Mbia. 1993. Interview with author. Videotaped by Nathan Kwame Braun. Adoagyiri, August 9.

Hodgson, Dorothy, and Sheryl A. McCurdy, eds. 2001. *"Wicked" Women and the Reconfiguration of Gender in Africa.* Portsmouth, N.H.: Heinemann.

Jaguar Jokers. 1995a. *Onipa Hia Mmoa (People Need Help).* Performed in Teacher Mante, July 15. Videotaped by Catherine M. Cole and Nathan Kwame Braun.

———. 1995b. *Onipa Hia Mmoa (People Need Help).* Translated by O. N. Adu-Gyamfi. Unpublished manuscript based on performance in Teacher Mante, July 15.

Koomson, Samuel Kwame. 1995. Interview with author and K. Acquaah Hammond. Translated by Charlotte Akyeampong. Videotaped by Nathan Kwame Braun. Tarkwa, April 23.

Manuh, Takyiwaa. 1997. "Wives, Children, and Intestate Succession in Ghana." In *African Feminism: The Politics of Survival in Sub-Saharan Africa,* edited by Gwendolyn Mikell, 77–95. Philadelphia: University of Philadelphia Press.

Mensah, E. T., and the Tempos. 1990. "School Girl." From the compact disc *Giants of Danceband Highlife.* Afrodesia/Original Music.

Miescher, Stephan. 1997. "Of Documents and Litigants: Disputes on Inheritance in Abetifi—A Town of Colonial Ghana." *Journal of Legal Pluralism and Unofficial Law* 39: 81–119.

———. 2003. Personal correspondence. September 14.

———. 2005. Personal correspondence. June 20.

Newell, Stephanie. 2000. *Ghanaian Popular Fiction: "Thrilling Discoveries in Conjugal Life" & Other Tales.* Athens: Ohio University Press.

Oyewumi, Oyeronke. 1997. *The Invention of Women: Making an African Sense of Western Gender Discourses.* Minneapolis: University of Minnesota Press.

Quainoo, Margaret. 1995. Interview with author and K. Acquaah Hammond. Videotaped by Nathan Kwame Braun. Accra, July 15.

Sharfstein, Daniel J. 1995. "Move Over 'Forest Gump'; In Ghana, It's 'Sugar Daddy.'" *New York Times,* April 23, H:13, 23.

Sutherland-Addy, Esi. 2000. "The Ghanaian Feature Video Phenomenon: Thematic

Concerns and Aesthetic Resources." In *FonTomFrom: Contemporary Ghanaian Literature, Theater and Film,* edited by Kofi Anyidoho and James Gibbs, 265–277. Special issue of *Matutu: Journal for African Culture and Society,* no. 20–21.

———. 2002. "Drama in Her Life: Interview with Adeline Ama Buabeng." In *African Theatre: Women,* edited by Martin Banham, James Gibbs, Femi Osofisan, and Jane Plastow, 66–82. Bloomington: Indiana University Press.

Vallenga, Dorothy Dee. 1986. "The Widow among the Matrilineal Akan of Southern Ghana." In *Widows in African Societies,* edited by Betty Potash, 220–240. Stanford, Calif.: Stanford University Press.

16 The "Post-Gender" Question in African Studies

Helen Nabasuta Mugambi

A group of girls were returning from collecting firewood when the girl in front accidentally hit her toe on a tree stump in the middle of the road. She warned the others and moved on. Despite the warning, the last girl in line accidentally hit her toe on the stump and tried to uproot it. She gave up when the stump started to bleed. Later, the girls returned to the spot. They found that the stump had grown into a Iimu ready to take vengeance. One by one, the girls gave him the beads he demanded and sang their way past him. But when the last girl sang and gave him two beads, the Iimu only kept asking the same question: "Why did you pull me out?" The girl gave him more and more beads. When she surrendered her last bead, the Iimu seized her and devoured her.

Adapted from John S. Mbiti, *Akamba Stories*

The construction of gender goes on as busily today as it did in the earlier times, say, the Victorian era. And it goes on not only where one might expect it to—in the media, the private and public schools, the courts, the family, nuclear or extended or single-parented—in short, in what Louis Althusser has called the "ideological state apparati." The construction of gender also goes on, if less obviously, in the academy, in the intellectual community, in avant-garde artistic practices and radical theories, even, and indeed especially, in feminism.

Teresa de Lauretis, *Technologies of Gender*

Through life-cycle socialization, popular culture, or academic theorization, gender formation and propagation continues as it did in ancient African folklore. Hence, the idea of "Africa after gender?" is tantalizing. It invites dialogue from scholarship that foregrounds gender as dynamic and always in flux. It is also problematized by Teresa de Lauretis's (1987) argument that the theorization of gender, no matter how radical, is an aspect of gender construction. In other words, scholars involved in gender debates are effectively constructing gender regardless of their stance toward its continuing centrality.

It may be tempting to think of a time when gender in Africa will fade away, enabling people to live without apprehension about the lingering impact of sociosexually assigned roles and spaces. However, contemplating an "after gender" phase for African scholarship unleashes a cascade of questions. What, for instance, are the theoretical, political, and activist implications of the "after gender" proposition? Given the nature of some of Africa's twentieth- and twenty-first-century pressing problems, which include how men and women experience gendered identities during the (re)formation of postcolonial nations, famine, the AIDS pandemic, global economic structures, and internal/external migrations, has scholarship exhausted the exploration of gender? Has scholarship fully explored what transpires when these problems are rendered more complex by class, religious beliefs, ethnicities, socioeconomic hierarchies, and mass militarization of women in postcolonial Africa? Have scholars paid meaningful attention to the implications of the scarcity of female names among the African heads of state and their deputies or to gender-based domestic abuse in ordinary households? Do researchers have enough data about postcolonial African masculinities and about how current national postcolonial power structures affect indigenous systems of gender? How, then, would declaring an "after gender" phase affect emerging scholarship posited on the multiplicity of gender identities? These are only a few of the questions that justify an interdisciplinary survey of issues surrounding this topic.

The present dialogue on "Africa after gender?" comes at an opportune time, when gender debates are multivoiced and varied. Although some critics engage the substance of gender (i.e., the everyday negotiation of gendered identities), others highlight the relationship (as I do) between everyday gendered identities and gender epistemologies. Obioma Nnaemeka's Women in Africa and the African Diaspora (WAAD) conference series as well as her creative insights on gender (2003) powerfully exemplify scholarship that increasingly engages the complexities in current gender scholarship. Feminist scholar Olabisi Aina states that "different feminist priorities are created by African social structures" (1998, 67); while Zulu Sofola believes that gender hierarchization is a Western construct. Using Yorùbá cosmology to illustrate her point, Sofola highlights the egalitarianism of the traditional creation myth in which man and woman were made equal and in counterpoint to each other (1998, 54).[1] Scholars such as Nkiru Nzegwu also challenge the applicability to the Yorùbá of what she and other scholars, most notably Oyeronke Oyewumi (1997), consider a Western-based categorization of gender. Nzegwu (2001) paraphrases an argument by Oyewumi that "the Yorùbá 'do' seniority, not gender" (115). Representing another point of view, Olabisi Aina (1998) addresses the subordinate position of African women, who she maintains are silent in the battle for feminism (67). In contrast to Sofola, and like many other scholars, Aina highlights women's disempowerment and a need for mobilization and liberation. Thus, discussions of gender (in general) or feminism (in particular) encompass a plethora of voices speaking from a myriad of cultural contexts that reflect the diversity of the continent. This chapter addresses issues in scholarship in contexts where gender continues to manifest itself as a powerful indigenous and dynamic epistemological category complicated by many of the questions stated above.

It would be pretentious to lay claim to comprehensive insights into the status of gender studies in the academy or to provide an intellectual assessment of the current issues in women's lives at various political and socioeconomic levels across the continent. To avoid a totalizing approach, I will simply draw attention to some of the approaches for rethinking gender in African studies and by implication interrogate the "Africa after gender?" idea.

My overall goal is to stimulate a serious examination of the current epistemological status of gender in African studies. I focus on places where people's everyday lives are affected by indigenous gendered social structures and highlight scholarship that seeks to uncover and engage both men's and women's voices at the grassroots and academic levels. My specific goals are twofold. First, I wish to examine the theoretical implications of the "after gender" stance in the context of the dynamic nature of gender and to propose that this dynamism makes it problematic to contemplate an "after gender" phase in African studies. Second, I will present examples that shed light on gender as lived experience in Africa to argue that the ongoing gender equity battles, by their nature, will continue even when a certain level of gender fairness is achieved. The discussion should reveal that if metagender (the academic engagement with or the theorizing of gender) becomes disengaged from gender as lived experience and from current gender contestations, it will render itself extraneous to the future of the African continent.

On the theoretical plane, I would like to briefly address the concepts of "gender" and "after" as presented in "Africa after gender?" Although the meanings of these labels appear to be obvious, they cannot be taken for granted in an assessment of gender as a useful analytical category. The call for contributions to this volume encouraged scholars to "explore sites of local knowledge production in Africa where indigenous categories are formulated, contested, and renegotiated in a dialectic response to historical transformations."[2] The implicit acknowledgment of ongoing dialectical formations of indigenous categories justifies probing the implications of "after" as a concept in order to ground the theoretical significance of the present discussion.

"After" is an Anglicization of the more familiar but contested "post" concept that has dominated humanities discourse for decades. Debates centered on the meaning of this concept still rage in Western scholarship as well as in postcolonial literary studies. Grounding our discussion of "after gender" with critiques of the "post" in "postcolonial" will help avoid the pitfalls that have plagued the use of the prefix in theorizing African experience. Carole Boyce Davies (1994) presents an excellent assessment of the "post" in the concept of postcoloniality and illustrates how postcoloniality is a premature totalizing formulation that fails to take into account current realities.[3] In elaborating her argument, Davies quotes Ama Ata Aidoo, who characterizes the application of the concept "postcolonial" to Africa as a "a most pernicious fiction, a cover-up of a dangerous period in our people's lives" (1991, 82–83). Such statements point toward parallel critiques that can be levied if the usage of "post" in relationship to gender in African scholarship remains unproblematized.

Contemporary Postcolonial Theory (Mongia 1996) presents multiple instances of interrogating "post." Kwame Anthony Appiah (1996) questions whether the "post" in postmodernism is the "post" in postcolonial (55). Appiah's framework significantly places the "after" into existing theorizations of Africa, thereby questioning demarcated patterns of analysis. Ruth Frankenberg and Lata Mani (1996) analyze the implications of "post" as they highlight the difference between post–civil rights and postcolonial (348–349). Their analysis suggests that "post" may not necessarily signal an "after" or periodization but can rather "mark spaces of ongoing contestation" (349).

Ania Loomba (1998) summarizes the debate: "It has been suggested that it is more helpful to think of postcolonialism, not just as literary theory coming after colonialism and signaling its demise, but more flexibly as the contestation of colonial domination and the legacies of colonialism" (12). Within such discourses of the "post" concept, one only needs to substitute "gender" for "colonialism" to generate identical arguments. For instance, "after" can be read as a call for ongoing theorizing about gender that does not preclude venturing into other analytical categories.

Nevertheless, the question remains whether we can unproblematically use the "after" in relationship to gender: although colonialism is dateable, gender is not. We can specify the year when the European scramble to control African territory occurred and when colonial powers declared protectorates over Africa. We know the day and date that each African nation declared its independence. Can we do the same for gender? Did gender happen or was it always present, constructed from within the cultures from the beginning, always evolving and embodied within some founding myths and folk narratives? The often-cited Gikuyu example is a classic example: at the beginning of time . . . women were the heads of households in Gikuyu land. It is believed that they tyrannically reigned over men till men revolted and "genderfully" overthrew them by simultaneously making all of them pregnant and then revolting at the point when the women were too heavy with child to fight. Since then, patriarchy has reigned in that land. This old story of gender conflict complicates and enriches our understanding of recent gender wars in Kenya, many of which have taken place in the heart of Gikuyu land and the surrounding areas. Women have demonstrated against their men who are incapacitated by alcohol, a social problem caused by high unemployment set in motion by postcolonial forces. In a recent example, a news report by Philip Ngunjiri (1998) on such occurrences reports how 300 women demonstrated in a Kikuyu town against the destruction of their men by illicit liquor and forced the police to take action:

> The women who came from Gikambura, 26 km west of the capital Nairobi, demanded the banning of the sale of alcohol, traditionally made from sorghum, yeast and sugar. During the demonstration, the women carried banners reading:

'Our husbands and sons are married to Sorghum,' 'Root the devil,' 'They can't perform in any way, any more.' (Ngunjiri 1998)

Such examples point to the dynamic nature of gender and serve to highlight the impossibility of an "after gender" phase in Africa and African scholarship. Moreover, they suggest that gender is continually (re)formulated by, and should be understood in relation to, fluid postcolonial conditions.

Gender in Africa cannot be frozen in time. As a socially constructed mark of identity, it is particularly vulnerable to transformation when socioeconomic forces are intensified by internal migrations, militarization, and cultural globalization. Such forces serve to intensify gender's fluidity as a mark of identity. Stuart Hall's (1996) elucidation of the complex nature of identity is an invaluable resource if applied to the periodization of gender. Hall states that "instead of thinking of identity as an already accomplished fact . . . we should think, instead, of identity as a 'production,' which is never complete always in process, and always constituted within, not outside, representation" (110). If, like other identities, gender is always in process, the theorizing of gender will necessarily remain in process.

I am not proposing the continued study of gender at the expense of less-explored categories. Rather, I propose that scholarship should simultaneously engage all categories of analysis and delve even deeper into gender and its intersections with other categories. Visualizing this proposition will illustrate my point. The explicit periodization in "after gender" presents a linear view of this category. We would be better served if we reconceptualized African studies in a circular configuration, plotting gender and other categories of analysis on the circumference of this circle. Such a configuration will alleviate the problematic temporality implicated in the "before" and "after" linearity. Moreover, points of intersection between and among categories can easily be plotted, because all points on the circle would be simultaneously visible and equidistant from the central reference point. Any undertheorized categories would be rendered visible; hierarchizing among categories will be minimized. Furthermore, the cyclical implication of the configuration offers tantalizing possibilities of moving forward (along the circle) as a process of a possible return to any one category of analysis, again minimizing the idea of a linear "after."

Avoiding the temptation to periodize gender is especially relevant today. As the questions raised above suggest, the epistemological status of gender is at a critical historical moment, given the political and sociopolitical turmoil in many parts of the continent. Numerous dimensions of gender have yet to be explored as they exist in expressive, popular, and material culture or in the sociopolitical institutions that govern everyday life. It is important to reiterate that excursions into gender theorization are at different stages within the various African studies disciplines, which necessarily affects perceptions of the "after gender" issue. Masculinity, in particular, remains a barely tapped area in current scholarship. Although Suzette Heald (1999), Robert Morrell (2001), and Lisa A. Lindsay and Stephan F. Miescher (2003) have published groundbreaking works on the subject, unfortunately they are part of a minuscule number of texts in masculinity scholarship.

To fully grapple with the "after gender" issue, it is vital to start with individual disciplines. I will briefly comment on the status of the epistemological status of gender in literary studies. If the study of gender has achieved maturity in other disciplines, it is obvious that gender theorizing is still in its infancy in areas such as African literature, orature, and popular culture. For instance, it is only in the past few years that scholarship has moved from the descriptive first stages of identifying images and representations of women in literature to actually theorizing those representations. Even though a number of recent texts have seriously examined women authors' texts, Chikwenye Okonjo Ogunyemi (1995) reports that as late as 1986 she received only a limited response when, as co-editor of a special issue of *Research in African Literatures,* she called for papers on writings by African women. Over fifteen years later, Tuzyline Jita Allan and I received equally scant responses to our call for papers that examine masculinities in African literature and film. Commenting on the state of scholarship, Ogunyemi remarks:

> Up until now, there has been a dearth of theoretical and critical material on African women's literature. Two of the five books devoted entirely to African women writers that have appeared were authored by men: Lloyd W. Brown's (1981) *Women Writers in Black Africa* gallantly tackles controversial feminist issues from the viewpoint of the male feminist, while Oladele Taiwo's (1984) *Female Novelists of Modern Africa* glosses over them. The third book, *Ngambika: Studies of Women in African Literature,* a collection of essays edited by Carole Boyce Davies and Anne Adams Graves (1986), illuminates as it seeks to carry out the double burden of theorizing and examining women's images in men's and women's writings. (Ogunyemi 1995, 2)

Many studies on gender have been published since this period, including Ogundipe-Leslie's *Recreating Ourselves: African Women and Critical Transformations* (1994), Davies's *Black Women, Writing, and Identity: Migrations of the Subject* (1994), Stratton's *Contemporary African Literature and the Politics of Gender* (1994), Allan's *Womanist and Feminist Aesthetics: A Comparative Review* (1995), Ogunyemi's *African Wo/man Palava: The Nigerian Novel by Women* (1995), Nnaemeka's *The Politics of (M)Othering: Womanhood, Identity, and Resistance in African Literature* (1997), Kolowale's *Womanism and African Consciousness* (1997), and Nfah-Abbenyi's *Gender in African Women's Writing: Identity, Sexuality and Difference* (1997). Because most articles and books on gender include a history or review of texts or ideas on gender, it would be redundant to reproduce yet another review in order to reinforce my point about the need for further scholarship on gender. However, I will draw attention to Chikwenye Okonjo Ogunyemi's (1995) introduction to *African Wo/Man Palava* and Kenneth W. Harrow's (1998) reviews of the state of literary gender studies because of their mutually enlightening and divergent emphases. Among other issues, Ogunyemi stresses the significance to the political process (and hence to the ongoing construction of gender) of the issues raised by women's fiction. Harrow's comprehensive review provides the most in-depth presentation of the history of the study of women's issues in African literature. He assesses developments and gaps in recent critical writings in the field. After evaluating the critical scholarship in both Anglophone and Francophone literatures, he concludes that for the most part, "the critical voices most in evidence from the time of Ngambika on, have found it to their advantage to deploy Western feminist formulations in their attempt to forge an independent position for African feminist criticism" (187). This conclusion reflects the dual position of the African/Africanist feminist voices—or feminist writers—who recognize the similarities in the global female condition while addressing the specificity of a unique cultural milieu. It is significant that Harrow does not highlight the importance of original vernacular theories presented by scholars such as Ogunyemi. This omission demonstrates how scholars who have produced original works that theorize gender from within and have used indigenous or African language-based concepts, such as *uhamili* (Nfah-Abbenyi 1997), *umoja* (Kolowale 1997), and *kwenu* (Ogunyemi 1995), have yet to receive adequate critical attention.

Ogunyemi's proposal of "a vernacular theory as a background to understanding twenty-eight novels by eight established Nigerian women writers" illustrates this point. She describes the contribution of women's fiction as follows: "In writing the hitherto unwritten, in voicing the hitherto unspoken and unspeakable, the women writers have, wittingly or unwittingly, fashioned a political agenda. The different strata of governmental authority in Nigeria, the Nigerian people themselves, and the international readership are willed to address issues of oppression raised in the texts, which also grapple with controversies in contemporary culture traced to their traditional roots" (1995, 3). Ogunyemi links the fictional world created by female writers to the real world, thus connecting the construction of gender in both. Her discussion also reinforces the relationships across disciplines in the ongoing transformations of gender as she proposes indigenous ways of looking at gender dynamics. As evident from her stated aim in that text, her main contribution is her delving into an indigenous theory in order to theorize gender. She aims to establish a theory under the rubric of vernacularism in which womanist theory is obviously implicated. She writes, "I will explore woman's space to (dis)cover women in an attempt to explain their place in the household and in the public; hypothesize the nature of women's vernacular discourses; and then analyze the texts generated from this burgeoning but indeterminate background, thereby returning women from obligatory exile to legitimize their position in our parents' house" (Ogunyemi 1995, 8). The omission of such original approaches to gender from Harrow's comprehensive review reflects the need for a redefinition of "cutting edge" literary theory to include indigenous concepts such as *palava, kwenu, uhamili,* and *umoja* as applied to works by and about women. Overall, within the academic arena, focused scholarship that takes into account the continuous (re)construction of both masculine and feminine gender identities will greatly help in situating gender alongside other analytical categories.

On the sociopolitical landscape in Africa, "gender" has become a code word signaling the institutionalized attention to women's search for cultural and economic agency in the postcolonial male-centered world. In many cases, "gender" is synonymous with "female" and the creation of women's development projects. In Uganda, for instance, internal local pressures from militarized women in the 1980s, among other factors, led to the formation of a Ministry of Gender, Labor, and Social Services, an important force in the transformation of gender relationships across the nation. The impact of such developments on public and private lives has yet to be adequately theorized. Are militarized women and socioeconomically independent women giving birth to a feminist state? How do we account for the celebratory spirit in Dr. Sylvia Tamale's (2001) report on Ugandan women's 2001 election victories?

> Despite very serious and fundamental flaws in the recently concluded election exercise, the women's movement in Uganda has good reason to celebrate. Uganda as a nation should celebrate one more brick in the rebuilding of our fledgling democracy. Women have gained both quantitatively and qualitatively in the seventh parliament. Out of nearly 40 women who competed for the county seats, 11 have trounced their opponents. This is no mean feat if you compare it with the 8 who won similar seats in the last parliament. The new figure pushes Uganda further up the list of African countries with the highest number of women in a national assembly from fifth position to fourth. Female representation in South Africa and Mozambique stands at 30 percent, while that of Namibia is 25 percent. We have surpassed Eritrea whose representation currently stands at 22 percent.

Rwanda's 2003 Parliament has the highest percentage of women members in Africa. According to the United Nations Development Program (2003), "Women won 45 percent of seats in the September elections, including 39 out of 80 seats in Parliament and six out of 20 seats in the Senate. Only the Swedish legislature matches this proportion." These numbers—and the changes they reflect—suggest the question Can the processes that led to women's political involvement on this scale be theorized with reference to the 1994 genocide in Rwanda and women's roles in the country since then? These numbers indicate the need to devote even more energy to interrogating the issue of gender in Africa.

In discussing the "after gender issue," it is also prudent to distinguish between the phenomenon and the discourse. The realities of "being or doing" the "differences of being either female, feminine, woman or male, masculine, man" (Coates 1998, 295–296), the socially assigned sequestered private spaces and public roles we encounter in our daily lives, are not to be confounded with metagender. There should, therefore, be concurrent dialogues, one on gender and the other on metagender, particularly in view of the "after gender" issue. As de Lauretis (1987) has observed: "The need for feminist theory to continue its radical critique of dominant discourses on gender . . . is all the more pressing since the word post-feminism has been spoken, and not in vain" (25).

Although gender is ever-changing, particularly in the postcolonial world, and although scholars like d'Almeida (1994) have contributed to "Destroying the

Emptiness of Silence" by theorizing women's postcolonial fiction and declaring the end to women's silencing, the void to be filled should be based on explorations of the multiple African systems of thought. The void is caused mainly by the scarcity of women's precolonial voices. Little research has been done to unearth indigenous voices in precolonial texts that would provide a wider spectrum and a firmer foundation for theory in contemporary scholarship. The scarcity of indigenous critical theories on gender is partly due to the unavailability of past histories and primary texts created by African men and women on the continent, and, until recently, the suppression of their formation. Nevertheless, the preponderance of forays into gender or feminist issues across the continent *is* an indication of the need to focus on gender.

The prevalence of women's conferences, "women's" groups, and "women's" initiatives speaks to the impressive range of women's issues. Initiatives such as Women Writing Africa (WWA), whose goal is to unearth women's scholarship and creative expression on the African continent, and the WAAD conference series exemplify only two of the approaches to gender scholarship (see Nnaemeka 1998). On a global scale, the fact that hundreds of African women traveled to China in 1995 to attend the UN's Fourth World Conference on Women in Beijing speaks to the ongoing prevalence of gender-focused fora, particularly as they pertain to women's issues and feminism. Discussions in the above scenarios have consistently highlighted the omission of women's voices at the grassroots within both pre- and postcolonial histories. The WWA project of the Feminist Press, in particular, exemplifies the crucial steps in the process of remedying this omission. One of the project's objectives is to document lost, unknown, or underappreciated creative productions of Africa's women.

The greatest challenge of an Africa "after gender" for many women, particularly those in patricentric societies, is at the basic level of engagement with gender: the harsh realities of living with socially imposed, assumed, and presumed differences of female and male. These range all the way from language, custom, and social organizations to beliefs and attitudes. Faced with these realities, one must have a very long line of vision to even begin to imagine an Africa "after gender." It happens that I wrote the initial drafts of this chapter at my base in the United States. However, as I lived in Uganda during the revision stages, interacting with scholars and chatting with grassroots members of communities about gender issues, I became even more intent on emphasizing the need to scrutinize women's and men's lived experiences against theoretical approaches that define the terms of gender discourse. It might be relatively easy for scholars to speak objectively and dispassionately about gender despite battles for equity, choice, and subjectivity. But these battles are different from the battles of the grassroots African woman who happens not to be protected by indigenous structures or by political and economic status. For a woman in this situation, the gender battle is almost literally a matter of life and death. We were all relieved at Amina Lawal's last-minute rescue from the stoning pit in northern Nigeria in 2004. But the dreadful questions linger in every concerned person's mind: Why was such a trial considered rational? Why, in such prolonged proceedings, was the culpability of the man responsible for her pregnancy, and hence "adultery," never regarded as a major issue? For Lawal and all she symbolizes, the battle is not about mainstreaming gender but about recognizing gender as a formidable force in women's lives. Are we in the "after gender" or in the "pre-gender" phase?

I do not want to venture into the embattled zone of "female genital mutilation," but the reality of gender is further illuminated by the debates raging over this practice. These practices are still found in geographic regions as disparate as northern Ghana and southern Africa. In 2003, the International Planned Parenthood Federation reported what had been Ghanaian national news: the impending imprisonment of an elderly northern woman for mutilating three young girls. This was the first case in Ghana (where the practice is relatively uncommon) where a woman was imprisoned for such an act. Though female circumcision is more often perceived as a by-product of a male hegemonic society striving to repress all aspects of female sexuality, it is even more strongly rooted in gender discourse. In many societies where the practice is upheld, a woman who has not been circumcised is not considered marriageable. The even more telling underlying sentiment is that she is not considered a woman. Thus, the rite of passage is not merely another step in the development into womanhood but is an indoctrination into a "gender."

This ideological indoctrination holds true for the male circumcision widely practiced in several parts of eastern and southern Africa. It is common knowledge that in most cases, traditional initiation takes the form of an elaborate ceremony in which boys are sequestered for many days and made to undergo hardships that will transform them into men. It is also common knowledge that the traditional initiation culminates in the circumcision of the boys without the use of anesthesia—and in some cases with a blunt knife. Though some such operations have been known to result in death or in "organ amputation" following gangrene infection, the desire to undergo the ceremony is still strong (Africa Online 2001). A widely held belief among circumcising societies is that circumcision is one of a few remaining measures to test masculinity (strength, endurance, tenacity). In short, an uncircumcised man is not a man, in much the same way as an unmarriable woman (in circumcising cultures, a woman who has not been circumcised) is not a woman (see Thomas 2003). The existence of such categories and, even more important, their construction out of a defined set of perceived characteristics bears noticing. For not only does it tell us that the qualifications for masculinity and femininity become problematic within contemporary frameworks and require urgent theorization but also that in many cases, a difficult gender discourse exists, whether or not academics choose to engage it.

In few cases is the persistence of gender discourse—and the attendant gender hierarchy that it breeds—as well illuminated as in a case in which the police had to be called upon to protect a community of Kikuyu women in Kiambu Kenya after male followers of a fanatical sect identified as "Mungiki" had threatened, through a series of raids, to perform forcible circumcisions on all the women

(Murimi and Ogutu 2002). Such occurrences are strong commentaries on the nature of gendered categories in the grassroots context.

It is important for this discussion to note that the absence of a term for "gender" or the lack of precise etymological constructions for "gender" within African languages does not preclude the presence of gendered hierarchies within a culture. For example, Augustine Bukenya explains that in Kiswahili debates are still raging about the most suitable term for gender among a host of recent suggestions, including "*umenke*," "*uana*," or the Arab-derived "*ujinsia*."[4] It would be too easy to deny the existence of gender within the Kiswahili culture or to even profess an evolution to "post-gender" based on the lack of precise terminology for it. But basing an argument on that factor alone could yield misleading conclusions. In everyday speech, in Luganda, my mother(!) tongue, only a man can marry (*okuwasa*), whereas a woman can only be married (*okufumbirwa*). Among the Baganda, as in many other kneeling cultures, women are "expected" (i.e., obliged) to kneel when they greet or talk to men and older women. That said, a man would never kneel to a woman. Such examples diminish the temptation to conclude that the absence of gendered vocabulary for a concept implies the absence of gendered practices. Ama Ata Aidoo (1993) presents the now famous answer for us in her novel *Changes*. The absence of an expression for marital rape does not mean that Esi, the novel's heroine, was not a victim of rape by her husband. Similarly, the absence of gendered pronouns in Luganda (the words for "he" and "she" are identical) does not mean that the ethnic group is egalitarian in the ways men and women are treated. Patriarchal and hierarchical institutions, many of which are not too kind to women, exist despite the lack of gendered pronouns.

The pervasiveness of gender hierarchies and the complex real and psychological discourses of gendered identities in patriarchal societies and postcolonial institutions throughout the continent suggest that it would be utopian to conceive of an Africa "after gender." In a recent newspaper article, Ugandan president Yoweri Museveni was reported as contemplating putting a ban on male circumcision due to its high death and infection rates. He was quoted as saying "If necessary, we can stop circumcision. I do not care about losing votes" (Etengu 2003). Bravado aside, this quote underscores a fact that may be less familiar: the conflict between maintaining gendered traditional practices and discarding them is a delicate political process. It entails walking a fine line between facilitating the longevity of the continent's unique cultural traits and becoming a parody of Western ideals and "civilization" to the detriment of any kind of cultural salience. More important, it underscores the extra caution required in dealing with deeply steeped traditional practices, most of which have their roots in a gendered discourse.

The delicacy necessary to navigate this traditional gender discourse and its attendant roles was illustrated when Nelson Mandela visited Uganda in the late 1990s and the vice president, Dr. Speciosa Wandira Naigaga (Kazibwe),[5] knelt when talking to him at a public function. This caused an uproar among the Ugandan public, where, encouragingly, the gender equity lobby is strong.

Dr. Naigaga brushed the criticisms aside by observing that the posture she takes when addressing anyone is her business and no one else's. The point, however, is that prescribed "appropriateness" is still problematic in African gender relations. Public opinion on the salience of these traditional gender practices is often contradictory. The roots of this are traditional "gendered" practices that are pervasive, despite changing relationships between men and women.

Customs such as "bridewealth," even when explained away as gifts to parents or tokens of appreciation (e.g., 20 cows and 50 goats), which effectively link women with commodification, survive almost intact in many African societies. I am aware that many African professional women defend bridewealth as a positive and desirable tradition. The complicating issue here is that if the level of a woman's Western education determines how much bridewealth she fetches, then it is difficult to keep commodification out of the equation, let alone the assignment of value based on imported Western educational systems. This is a different debate, but it also demonstrates how historical forces affect gender valuation.

Within African homes, as elsewhere in the world, domestic violence remains an ongoing problem. Michael Koening (2003) interviewed 5,109 women and 3,881 men living in Rakai district (Uganda), the initial epicenter of the AIDS epidemic. Koening's team found that about one in three women "experiences verbal or physical threats from their partners" and that 50 percent of them "receive physical injuries as a result" (54–56). Even though it is questionable whether those ratios apply to the rest of this multicultural nation, the most revealing point the study makes is in the following conclusion: "A total of 70 percent of male respondents and 90 percent of female respondents viewed beating of a female partner as justifiable in one or more circumstances." The top three reasons cited for being assaulted were "neglecting household chores, disobeying a husband or elders, and refusal to have sex." Only 5 percent of women said they had "physically threatened or assaulted their male partners during the previous year" (56–57). Thinking of such statistics and listening to news on African radio broadcasts, one realizes the distance between the worlds of grassroots men and women and the "Africa after gender" intellectual contemplations. But these issues are not limited to grassroots individuals. The syndrome cuts across the social spectrum.

In 2002, Ms. Agnes Ndetei, a member of the Kenyan Parliament, revealed that her husband had regularly beaten her.[6] Was this an anomaly? Unfortunately, no. At about the same time, Ugandans were horrified when Dr. Speciosa Wandira Naigaga (Kazibwe), the country's first female vice president, went public with the revelation that she had been a victim of violence from her husband, Charles Kazibwe, a prominent civil engineer. The debates that followed took many forms. A few people congratulated Dr. Naigaga for her frankness and hailed her confession as significant inspiration to the numerous victims of domestic violence to speak out. Many others, however, criticized her, saying that a "decent" woman and a "dutiful" wife should never disclose the secrets of her household ("*eby'omunju tibittottolwa*" in Luganda). But the most revealing comment about perceptions of gender in this case probably belongs to Mr. Kazibwe. Interviewed about Dr. Naigaga's claims, he admitted that he had assaulted her but by way of self-defense added, "I only slapped her twice." Just in case one should dismiss Mr. Kazibwe's remarks as a solitary mode of thinking, one is referred to the criticism of Dr. Naigaga that continued when she filed for divorce over what the critics regarded as "frivolous" reasons. Clearly, privileged class or status do not necessarily exempt women from gender oppression. Although Dr. Speciosa Naigaga represents the more powerful women of Africa, she has still been a victim of spousal abuse in a country that is lauded for its progressive approach to gender equity, especially over the past two decades. Dr. Naigaga was vice president of Uganda for nearly ten years, until she resigned in mid-2003.

The increasing number of women in powerful postcolonial political positions calls for specific gender studies on the impact of such developments. In Uganda, Dr. Naigaga is not a lone exception in the Ugandan cabinet, Parliament, and public life in general. She is one of a formidable force of high-achieving women, like Miria Matembe (a lawyer and former minister), Winnie Byanyima (a flight engineer and eminent parliamentarian), Justice Julia Sebutinde (of the Uganda High Court), and Margaret Sekaggya (chair of the National Human Rights Commission), most of whom are household names among well-informed Ugandans. Ugandan leaders have, since 1986, pursued a consistently vigorous policy of affirmative action in the area of gender equity, largely owing to the demands of Ugandan women, who participated actively in the protracted armed liberation struggle that rid the country of a tyrannical dictatorship. The policy has yielded fruit, and the country has, as mentioned, one of the highest percentages of female representation in Parliament in Africa—about 30 percent. The 1995 Constitution stipulates that, apart from directly elected constituency representatives, who may be either female or male, each district must have a woman representative in Parliament who is elected by a college of women voters. There are also special women representatives on every elected body, down to the village level. Though not stipulated in the Constitution, the appointment of women to senior ministerial posts—Energy, Justice and Constitutional Affairs, and Defense—is a regular and expected practice of the current Ugandan administration. This is also true of other areas such as the judiciary. One of the challenges for scholars is to usefully examine the implications of such developments on a continental scale.

In higher education, affirmative action, such as the awarding of an automatic one-and-a-half points to every female candidate for admission to the public universities (to compensate for the toll of domestic chores on female students' study time at the elementary and high school levels), has led to an almost equal ratio of females to males in several of these institutions.[7] Makerere University, Uganda's oldest and most prestigious university, houses a dynamic Women and Gender Studies Department, which successfully hosted the Quinquennial International Women's Studies Conference in 2002 and is very active in promoting gender scholarship by both men and women.

These are no mean achievements in a country beset by all sorts of growth problems and ranked among the poorest in the world. But the point is that if, in the midst of all these buoyant developments, there are people who think that it is frivolous for the vice president of a country to object to being slapped "only twice" by a man who thinks that he has the right to assault her because he is her husband, where are we in the gender engagement process? There are so many debates and actions to be undertaken that it is sometimes bewildering to determine where to begin. A possible starting point may be ending the fallacy, held by as many women as men, that gender is just about women and that empowering women will automatically set things right. Or one might start with the skeptics of affirmative action, who think that such action is patronizing and degrading and perpetuates inferiority complexes. Recently, the Minister of Gender, Labor, and Social Services, who is a member of Parliament in Uganda, infuriated her fellow parliamentary female members and other advocates of affirmative action when she declared in Parliament that she considered herself superior to the women's parliamentary representatives because she, unlike them, had been elected in "competition with men." If a Minister for Gender reasons that her worth and identity are to be measured in terms of "competition with men," are we near, let alone beyond or "after," the gender discourse?

To conclude, I would like to return to my opening proposition to plot all categories of analysis in African studies, including gender, on a circular configuration. Not only will this conceptualization mitigate the problematic temporality implicated in the "before" and "after," it will also alleviate the temptation to shift theoretical attention away from any category at the expense of another. It should offer a much-needed theoretical framework capable of encompassing all types of scholarship, even those eons away in the "pre-gender" discourse and struggle. I would suggest that even if individual scholars are able to move into an "after gender" space in their own work, failing to stay connected to the rest of us still thinking about gender and its implications is a serious business. The prospect reminds me of the girls in the Akamba story quoted at the beginning of this chapter. Those isolated scholars might be doing little more than deserting those in the battle against the stump, which can, and does, sometimes turn into a devouring monster.

Notes

1. See the full discussion in Nnaemeka (1998).

2. Original conference proposal, "Africa After Gender? An Exploration of New Epistemologies for African Studies," circulated in 2000.

3. Davies (1994) engages this issue in chapter 4, "From Post-Coloniality to Uprizing Textualities."

4. Author's interview with Augustine Bukenya, member of the Women Writing

Project and Senior Lecturer, Makerere University, Kampala, July 10, 2003. My thanks to Austin Bukenya for his input, especially the interviews he granted me to discuss local current gender issues in Uganda and Kenya.

5. After Dr. Naigaga filed for divorce from Mr. Charles Kazibwe in 2003, she dropped the name "Kazibwe."

6. Augustine Bukenya interview, July 10, 2003.

7. Ibid.

References

Africa Online. 2001. "SA Circumcision Initiate Loses Penis." *Africa Online*, December. Available online at http://www.africaonline.com/site/Articles/ (accessed November 10, 2004).

Aidoo, Ama Ata. 1991. "The Captious Topic, Gender Politics." In *Critical Fictions*, edited by Philomenia Mariani. Seattle, Wash.: Bay Press.

———. 1993. *Changes*. New York: Feminist Press.

Aina, Olabisi. 1998. "African Women at the Grassroots: The Silent Partners of the Women's Movement." In *Sisterhood, Feminisms and Power*, edited by O. Nnaemeka, 65–88. Trenton, N.J.: Africa World Press.

Allan, Tuzyline J. 1995. *Womanist and Feminist Aesthetics: A Comparative Review*. Athens: Ohio University Press.

Appiah, Kwame Anthony. 1996. "Is the Post in Postmodernism the Post in Postcolonial?" In *Contemporary Postcolonial Theory*, edited by P. Mongia, 55–71. New York: St. Martin's Press.

Brown, Lloyd W. 1981. *Women Writers in Black Africa*. Westport, Conn.: Greenwood Press.

Coates, Jennifer. 1998. " 'Thank god I'm a woman:' The Construction of Differing Femininities." In *The Feminist Critique of Language*, edited by D. Cameron, 295–320. New York: Routledge.

d'Almeida, Irene A. 1994. *Francophone African Women Writers: Destroying the Emptiness of Silence*. Gainesville: University Press of Florida.

Davies, Carol Boyce. 1994. *Black Women, Writing, and Identity: Migrations of the Subject*. London: Routledge.

———, and Anne A. Graves. 1986. *Ngambika: Studies of Women in African Literature*. Trenton, N.J.: African World Press.

De Lauretis, Teresa. 1987. *Technologies of Gender*. Bloomington: Indiana University Press.

Etengu, Nathan. 2003. "Museveni Threatens to Ban Circumcision." *New Vision* (Kampala, Uganda), October 14.

Frankenberg, Ruth, and Lata Mani. 1996. "Crosscurrents, Crosstalk: Race, 'Postcoloniality,' and the Politics of Location." In *Contemporary Postcolonial Theory*, edited by P. Mongia, 347–364. New York: St. Martin's Press, 1996.

Hall, Stuart. 1996. "Cultural Identity and Diaspora." In *Contemporary Postcolonial Theory*, edited by P. Mongia, 110–121. New York: St. Martin's Press.

Harrow, Kenneth W. 1998. " 'I'm not a Western feminist but . . .'—A Review of Recent

Critical Writings on African Women's Literature." *Research in African Literatures* 29, no. 4: 171–190.

Heald, Suzette. 1999. *Manhood and Morality: Sex, Violence and Ritual in Gisu Society.* London: Routledge.

International Planned Parenthood Federation. 2003. "Ghana: Female Genital Mutilation—Woman Jailed for Five Years." *IPPF News,* September. Available online at http://www.ippfnet.ippf.org/pub/IPPF_News/News_Details.asp?ID=2943 (accessed November 10, 2004).

Koening, Michael et al. 2003. "Domestic Violence in Rural Uganda: Evidence from a Community-Based Study." *Bulletin of the World Health Organization* 81:53–60.

Kolowale, Mary E. M. 1997. *Womanism and African Consciousness.* Trenton, N.J.: Africa World Press.

Lindsay, Lisa A., and Stephan F. Miescher, eds. 2003. *Men and Masculinities in Modern Africa.* Portsmouth, N.H.: Heinemann.

Loomba, Ania. 1998. *Colonialism/Postcolonialism.* London: Routledge.

Mbiti, John S. 1984. *Akamba Stories.* Nairobi: Oxford University Press.

Mongia, Padmini, ed. 1996. *Contemporary Postcolonial Theory.* New York: Arnold.

Morrell, Robert, ed. 2001. *Changing Men in Southern Africa.* London: Zed Books.

Murimi, Joseph, and Evelyn Ogutu. 2002. "Police Tell Mungiki: We're Ready for You." *East African Standard,* July 7.

Nfah-Abbenyi, Juliana M. 1997. *Gender in African Women's Writing: Identity, Sexuality and Difference.* Bloomington: Indiana University Press.

Ngunjiri, Philip. 1998. "Devil in a Bottle." Inter Press Service, June 28. Available online at http://www.oneworld.org/news/world/health.html (accessed November 12, 2004).

Nnaemeka, Obioma. 2003. "Nego-Feminism: Theorizing, Practicing, and Pruning Africa's Way." *Signs: Journal of Women in Culture and Society* 29, no. 2: 357–385.

———, ed. 1997. *The Politics of (M)Othering: Womanhood, Identity, and Resistance in African Literature.* London: Routledge.

———, ed. 1998. *Sisterhood, Feminisms and Power: From Africa and the Diaspora.* Trenton, N.J.: Africa World Press.

Nzegwu, Nkiru. 2001. "The Politics of Gender in African Studies in the North." In *Women in African Studies Scholarly Publishing,* edited by C. R. Veney and P. Zeleza, 111–146. Trenton, N.J.: Africa World Press.

Ogundipe-Leslie, Molara. 1994. *Recreating Ourselves: African Women and Critical Transformations.* Trenton, N.J.: African World Press.

Ogunyemi, Chikwenye Okonjo. 1995. *African Wo/man Palava: The Nigerian Novel by Women.* Chicago: University of Chicago Press.

Oyewumi, Oyeronke. 1997. *The Invention of Women: Making an African Sense of Western Gender Discourses.* Minneapolis: University of Minnesota Press.

Sofola, 'Zulu. 1998. "Feminism and African Womanhood." In *Sisterhood, Feminisms, and Power,* edited by O. Nnaemeka, 51–64. Trenton, N.J.: Africa World Press.

Stratton, Florence. 1994. *Contemporary African Literature and the Politics of Gender.* London: Routledge.

Taiwo, Oladele. 1984. *Female Novelists of Modern Africa.* New York: St. Martin's Press.

Tamale, Sylvia. 2001. "Bravo Women MPs: From 18 to 24%." *The Daily Monitor* (Kampala), June 30.

Thomas, Lynn M. 2003. *Politics of the Womb: Women, Reproduction, and the State in Kenya.* Berkeley: University of California Press.

United Nations Development Program. 2003. "Rwanda's Women Legislators, Nearly Matching Men in Numbers, Lead the World." *UNDP Newsfront,* November 17. Available online at http://www.undp.org/dpa/frontpagearchive/2003/ November/17nov03/index.html (accessed November 20, 2004).

The Production of Gendered Knowledge in the Digital Age

In the past decade, the Internet has revolutionized the availability of information and the dissemination of knowledge throughout the world, especially in Africa (Everett 2002, forthcoming). In every major town across the continent, cybercafés have opened, and most universities are equipped with computers connected to the Internet. In many ways, electronic transmission of information has leveled the playing field and provided equal access to previously excluded constituencies. However, as Aghi Bahi's (2004) study about Abidjan, Côte d'Ivoire has shown, Internet access in itself remains a gendered experience; 70 percent of the customers in cybercafés are men.

African gender activists have creatively used the Internet for community building and information sharing. In Uganda, several organizations have developed information and communications technologies (ICT) to address issues of gender equity. The Women of Uganda Network (WOUGNET), founded in 2000, advocates ICT programs that are gender sensitive, taking into account women's specific needs. This includes opportunities for training and establishing access points (cybercafés) led by women. A high priority is the creation of software in local languages and a program interface accessible to illiterate users. WOUGNET, supported by allied groups, has trained coaches to pass on ICT skills to rural and urban women. One workshop showed women entrepreneurs how ICT use can strengthen their businesses: the program featured an introduction to computers, training in Internet and e-mail basic skills, and training in product marketing. Another workshop addressed the potential of ICT use for improving women's health, such as distributing care information and HIV/AIDS prevention education. The Uganda office of Isis-WICCE (Isis-Women's International Cross-Cultural Exchange) has incorporated ICT to document women's experiences in situations of armed conflict, which have ravaged parts of the country for thirty years. Difficulties of ICT use remain, especially in rural areas. Women's poverty and illiteracy make it difficult for them to pay for and access ICT services. Many ICT programs do not deal with women's most pressing economic needs, such as access to credit and income-earning opportunities.[1]

The African Women's Development and Communications Network, FEMNET, operates as a network that links African women and their groups together through the production and dissemination of information through e-mail and the Internet (see http://www.femnet.or.ke). Through the use of ICT, FEMNET has been able to play a leadership role in the organization of international and African regional conferences. From the Beijing conference of 1995 though the Beijing + 5 and Beijing + 10 conferences, FEMNET has been a focal point around which African women have accessed information to guide their participation in preparatory meetings at the regional level and in the main meetings in Beijing and New York. FEMNET's leadership role in the African caucus has helped translate views and opinions into concrete decision-making positions. FEMNET played a lead role in organizing African women to contribute discussions about ICT from a gender perspective during the organization of the World Information Society (WIS).

African women are also using ICT to gain visibility through networks such as Dimitra, an information-sharing and -dissemination project that brings rural women's organizations in the agricultural sector together through its Web site (see http://www.fao.org/Dimitra/new_index.jsp).

Organizations such as ABANTU for development, an African-centered and gender-oriented NGO with regional offices in East and West Africa, has also trained grassroots women's groups in the use of ICT, especially in terms of how to access information from the Internet and communicate through e-mail. ABANTU has also drawn attention to the gender gaps in ICT policies in West Africa.

In South Africa, the African Gender Institute (AGI), established at the University of Cape Town in 1996, has become the most prominent site for coordination, stimulation, and dissemination of feminist research and teaching in gender studies across Africa. In 2001, the AGI launched the Gender and Women's Studies for Africa's Transformation Project (GWS Africa Project), which features several ICT initiatives: online discussion groups, a Web site, and electronic distribution of feminist research and teaching resources.[2] Given the expense and difficulty of acquiring books and journals in Africa, electronic dissemination is proving to be a cost-effective alternative. The online journal *Feminist Africa* (see http://www.feministafrica.org) has become the AGI's most important outreach instrument and a vehicle for engaging with the contested gender politics of postcolonial Africa. Amina Mama (2002) notes that this activist journal speaks to the "heightened salience of gender in African political and intellectual landscapes." *Feminist Africa* advocates women's liberation to counteract Africa's continued poverty, militarism, outbreaks of civil conflicts, the "triumphalist rhetoric of globalization, [and] the re-marginalization of women in the new African Union"—all "deeply gendered phenomena that demand incisive analysis and response" (1). The first issue focused on engendering African institutions of higher learning. Women are underrepresented at African universities as students and faculty (only about 6 percent of universities in the Association of African Universities are led by women), and they also face widespread misogyny in the form of institutional discrimination, sexual harassment, and sexual violence. Many African women, including university students and professionals in the workplace, "accept this discrimination as 'normal'" and do little to change it.[3]

In an important article, Charmaine Pereira (2002) outlined the space for feminist scholarship on Africa that should invigorate progressive research. Feminism is not just a struggle to overcome male dominance and fight for women's equality. Rather, it is as much about "transforming what goes on in the minds and hearts of women and men as it is about realizing rights and justice" (3). Pereira points to the need to expand the concept of gender beyond the identity "woman." Feminist work needs to link men's male violence to constructions of masculinity and explore the histories and socioeconomic conditions that have shaped "the development of men's gendered subjectivities" (5). *Feminist Africa* has entered controversial topics like the silence around sexuality in scholarly African writing or the conservative understanding of African culture deployed by researchers operating within a development framework. In the second issue on "Changing Cultures," Sylvia Tamale reports on the resilience of homophobia in Uganda (2003 and this volume).[4] Others unpack "naturalized discourses of 'culture'" that serve to perpetuate women's obedience (Lewis 2003) and show how African novelists Ama Ata Aidoo and Yvonne Vera have challenged male-centered inventions of the nation, thereby envisioning new ideas about community and identity (Wilson-Tagoe 2003 and this volume).

Online publishing about gender and African women has also been generated from outside the continent. In 2001, a group of Nigerian women, transnational scholars based in the United States, launched *Jenda: A Journal of Culture and African Women Studies* (http://www.jendajournal.com/). Co-editors Nkiru Nzegwu, Mojubaolu Okome, and Oyeronke Oyewumi did their undergraduate studies in Nigeria and received doctorates from universities in North America. They represent different disciplines: Nzegwu is a philosopher and art historian, Oyewumi a sociologist, and Okome a political scientist. The name *Jenda* refers to an approximation of how "gender" is pronounced in West African Pidgin English. *Jenda* occupies an oppositional space in the U.S. academy, though with a clear intellectual and political program. Its founders were disillusioned by the publication practices of established Africanist and feminist scholarly journals, which were controlled by non-African gatekeepers. *Jenda* provides a forum for African women to write about their own experience and develop their own theories and thereby offer a counterdiscourse to academic "Americocentrism," particularly the domination of "white women as scholars of Africa" (Nzegwu 2001a, 13; 2003). As a peer-reviewed journal, *Jenda* aims to reach a global audience and initiate new channels of scholarly exchange. Although it operates with no outside funding and little institutional support, *Jenda* has been a success: tens of thousands have visited its Web site. The editors receive e-mail correspondence from across the English-speaking world. Oyewumi (2004) recalls an Indian reader praising *Jenda* as a way for Asians "to talk directly to African women without any Western mediators." Unlike the contributors of *Feminist Africa,* those of *Jenda* are critical of, or at least ambivalent about, embracing a feminist language. The editors have problematized Western concepts such as gender, patriarchy, and the social category "woman" when applied to African contexts. Instead, they have called for a theorization of African concepts. For example in the Òyó Yorùbá society, seniority and relative age are more relevant than sex and gender (Oyewumi 1997, 2002). Others have advocated African epistemologies, such as the Igbo's dual-sex system and the Nnobi flexible gender system (Nzegwu 2001b; Amadiume 1987).

One theoretical intervention promotes research about the meanings of motherhood. *Jenda* published papers presented at the 2003 conference on "Images of 'Motherhood': African and Nordic Perspectives," convened by Signe Arnfred in Senegal. With the exception of Nancy Chodorow (1978), most Western feminists have had little to say about mothers and mothering; they preferred to concentrate on labor, sexuality, and representation. Some African scholars have begun to theorize the centrality of motherhood practices in African societies. Amadiume (1997) proposed the "motherhood paradigm" that foregrounds the interrelations between the male-focused ancestral house and the women-focused matricentric unit (21). This model "de-centers the male subject, moving the focus not to a *female* subject, but to a social relationship" (Arnfred 2003, 9). The issue is less about mothering as a "physical act" than about the "social position and importance given to motherhood, the *meaning* of motherhood" (Arnfred 2002, 15).[5] African feminists have critiqued this celebratory motherhood paradigm for overlooking regimes of power that determine reproductive choices. Bibi Bakare-Yusuf (2003) emphasized the "danger of venerating maternity while failing to investigate the meaning of paternity," since a patriarchal construction of maternity tends to valorize fatherhood. Instead she called for a "genealogical investigation" that explores power relations, representational regimes, and religious, political, and ideological structures that have shaped the discourses and experiences of maternity and paternity in Africa, historically and in the present (5).

The controversy over motherhood is just one example of the vibrant and multifaceted debates that animate current studies of gender in Africa. This empirically rich and theoretically informed discourse is transpiring in "real time," enabled and disseminated by online publications that follow close on the heels of conferences. These online journals promote a circulation of ideas across the continent and the globe. *Feminist Africa* and *Jenda* represent and are critical participants in the growth of Anglophone Africanist gender studies. The field has demonstrated a remarkable ability to harness the power of new technologies in order to "move the center" of research to Africa. It has also successfully cultivated the connection between activism and scholarship by producing scholarship that is as relevant to university-based researchers as it is to bureaucrats and political organizers. While the online circulation of ideas is promising, there are some concerns about the longevity of this knowledge, as Web sites are far more fluid and ephemeral than printed books and journals. In an effort to bring some of this exciting online research into the more permanent domain of print culture, several essays are reprinted in this volume.

Notes

1. At the second Afro-GEEKS conference, UC Santa Barbara, May 19–21, 2005, Milton Aineruhanga of WOUGNET and Ruth Ojimbo Ochieng of Isis-WICCE presented their activities. See http://www.wougnet.org and http://www.isis.or.ug.

2. Boswell (2003). For the GWS project, see http://www.gwsafrica.org.

3. Rathgeber (2003, 8); see also Bennett (2002), Kasente (2002), and Prah (2002).

4. According to the Ugandan penal code, homosexuality is illegal and carries a maximum sentence of life imprisonment. After Sylvia Tamale, a human rights activist and legal scholar at Makerere University, spoke in support of including sexual orientation in proposed nondiscrimination legislation in February 2003, she received vicious attacks from numerous writers in the Ugandan daily, *New Vision*. See AGI, "News Alert! Sylvia Tamale Attacked for Supporting Non-Discrimination on Basis of Sexual Orientation," available online at http://www.gwsafrica.org/news/tamale2.htm (accessed July 2, 2004). Excerpts are reprinted in this volume.

5. The conference explored the wife-mother distinction and different conditions for motherhood and mothering in various contexts. For the Òyó Yorùbá society, see Oyewumi (2003); for black and white communities in South Africa, see Magwaza (2003); for African migrants in France, see Rassiguier (2003). Motherhood in white South African communities, as in Europe, is individualized; in black communities co-mothering is frequently the norm.

References

Amadiume, Ifi. 1987. *Male Daughters, Female Husbands: Gender and Sex in an African Society.* London: Zed Books.
———. 1997. *Reinventing Africa: Matriarchy, Religion and Culture.* London: Zed Books.
Arnfred, Signe. 2002. "Simone de Beauvoir in Africa: 'Women=The Second Sex?' Issues of African Feminist Thought." *Jenda: A Journal of Culture and African Women Studies* 2, no. 1. Available online at http://www.jendajournal.com/vol2.1/arnfred.html (accessed July 1, 2004)
———. 2003. "Images of 'Motherhood': African and Nordic Perspectives." *Jenda: A Journal of Culture and African Women Studies* 4, no. 1. Available online at http://www.jendajournal.com/issue4/arnfred.html (accessed July 1, 2004).

Bahi, Aghi. 2004. "Internet Use and Logics of Social Adaptation of Youth in Abidjan Cybercafés." *CODESRIA Bulletin* 1–2: 67–71.

Bakare-Yusuf, Bibi. 2003. "Beyond Determinism: The Phenomenology of African Female Existence." *Feminist Africa* 2. Available online at http://www.feministafrica.org/fa%202/02-2003/bibi.html (accessed July 2, 2004).

Bennett, Jane. 2002. "Exploration of a 'Gap': Strategising Gender Equity in African Universities." *Feminist Africa* 1. Available online at http://www.feministafrica.org/fa%201/01-2002/jane.html (accessed July 2, 2004).

Boswell, Barbara. 2003. "Locating Gender and Women's Studies Teaching and Research at African Universities: Survey Results." African Gender Institute, University of Cape Town. Available online at http://www.gwsafrica.org/directory/index.html (accessed July 2, 2004).

Chodorow, Nancy. 1978. *The Reproduction of Mothering: Psychoanalysis and the Sociology of Gender.* Berkeley: University of California Press.

Everett, Anna. 2002. "The Revolution Will Be Digitized: Afrocentricity and the Digital Public Sphere." *Social Text* 71: 125–146.

———. Forthcoming. *Digital Diaspora: A Race for Cyberspace.* Albany: State University of New York Press.

Kasente, Deborah. 2002. "Institutionalising Gender Equality in African Universities: Women's and Gender Studies at Makerere University." *Feminist Africa* 1. Available online at http://www.feministafrica.org/fa%201/01-2002/kasente.html (accessed July 12, 2004).

Lewis, Desiree. 2003. "Editorial." *Feminist Africa* 2. Available online at http://www.feministafrica.org/fa%202/2level.html (accessed June 30, 2004).

Magwaza, Thenjiwe. 2003. "Perceptions and Experiences of Motherhood: A Study of Black and White Mothers of Durban, South Africa." *Jenda: A Journal of Culture and African Women Studies* 4, no. 1. Available online at http://www.jendajournal.com/issue4/magwaza.html (accessed July 7, 2004).

Mama, Amina. 2002. "Editorial." *Feminist Africa* 1. Available online at http://www.feministafrica.org/fa%201/01-2002/editorial.html (accessed June 30, 2004).

Nzegwu, Nkiru. 2001a. "Globalization and the JendaJournal." *Jenda: A Journal of Culture and African Women Studies* 1, no. 1. Available online at http://www.jendajournal.com/vol1.1/nzegwu1.html (accessed July 1, 2004).

———. 2001b. "Gender Equality in a Dual-Sex System: The Case of Onitsha." *Jenda: A Journal of Culture and African Women Studies* 1, no. 1. Available online at http://www.jendajournal.com/vol1.1/nzegwu.html (accessed July1, 2004).

———. 2003. "O Africa: Gender Imperialism in Academia." In *African Women and Feminism,* edited by Oyeronke Oyewumi, 99–157. Trenton, N.J.: Africa World Press.

Oyewumi, Oyeronke. 1997. *The Invention of Women: Making an African Sense of Western Gender Discourses.* Minneapolis: University of Minnesota Press.

———. 2002. "Conceptualizing Gender: The Eurocentric Foundations of Feminist Concepts and the Challenge of African Epistemologies." *Jenda: A Journal of Culture and African Women Studies* 2, no. 1. Available online at http://www.jendajournal.com/vol2.1/oyewumi.html (accessed July 1, 2004).

———. 2003. "*Abiyamo:* Theorizing African Motherhood." *Jenda: A Journal of*

Culture and African Women Studies 4, no.1. Available online at
http://www.jendajournal.com/issue4/oyewumi.html (accessed
July 1, 2004).
————. 2004. Phone conversation with Stephan F. Miescher, July 12.
Pereira, Charmaine. 2002. "Between Knowing and Imagining: What Space for Femi-
nism in Scholarship on Africa?" *Feminist Africa* 1. Available online at
http://www.feministafrica.org/fa%201/01-2002/pereira.html (accessed
June 30, 2004).
Prah, Mansah. 2002. "Gender Issues in Ghanaian Tertiary Institutions: Women
Academics and Administrators at Cape Coast University." *Ghana Studies*
5: 83–122.
Rassiguier, Catherine. 2003. "Troubling Mothers: Immigrant Women from Africa in
France." *Jenda: A Journal of Culture and African Women Studies* 4, no. 1. Avail-
able online at http://www.jendajournal.com/issue4/raissiguier.html (accessed
July 7, 2004).
Rathgeber, E. 2003. "Women in Universities and University-Educated Women: The
Current Situation in Africa." In *African Higher Education: An International
Reference Handbook,* edited by Damtew Teferra and Philip G. Altbach, 82–92.
Bloomington: Indiana University Press.
Tamale, Sylvia. 2003. "Out of the Closet: Unveiling Sexuality Discourses in Uganda."
Feminist Africa 2. Available online at http://www.feministafrica.org/fa%202/
02-2003/sp-tamale.html (accessed June 30, 2004).
Wilson-Tagoe, Nana. 2003. "Representing Culture and Identity: African Women
Writers and National Cultures." *Feminist Africa* 2. Available online at
http://www.feministafrica.org/fa%202/02-2003/nana.html (accessed July 7,
2004).

Resources for Further Reading

Review Essays

Harrow, Kenneth W. 1998. "'I'm not a Western feminist but . . .': A Review of Recent Critical Writings on African Women's Literature." *Research in African Literatures* 29, no. 4: 171–190.

Hunt, Nancy Rose. 1989. "Placing African Women's History and Locating Gender." *Social History* 14, no. 3: 359–379.

———. 1996. "Introduction." Special issue on "Gendered Colonialism in African History." *Gender & History* 8, no. 3: 323–337.

Lewis, Desiree. 2002. "African Feminist Studies: 1980–2002: A Review Essay for the African Gender Institute's 'Strengthening Gender and Women's Studies for Africa's Social Transformation' Project.'" African Gender Institute, University of Cape Town. Available online at http://www.gwsafrica.org/knowledge/index.html (accessed July 2, 2004).

Mama, Amina. 1996. *Women's Studies and Studies of Women in Africa during the 1990s.* Working Paper Series 5/96. Dakar: CODESRIA.

Potash, Betty. 1989. "Gender Relations in Sub-Saharan Africa." In *Gender and Anthropology,* edited by Sandra Morgan, 189–227. Washington, D.C.: American Anthropological Association.

Robertson, Claire. 1987. "Developing Economic Awareness: Changing Perspectives in Studies of African Women, 1976–1985." *Feminist Studies* 13, no. 1: 97–135.

Strobel, Margaret. 1982. "African Women: Review Essay." *Signs* 8, no. 1: 109–131.

Edited Collections

Allman, Jean, Susan Geiger, and Nakanyike Musisi, eds. 2002. *Women in African Colonial Histories.* Bloomington: Indiana University Press.

Arnfred, Signe et al., eds. 2004. *African Gender Scholarship: Concepts, Methodologies, and Paradigms.* Dakar: CODESRIA.

Cornwall, Andrea, ed. 2005. *Readings in Gender in Africa.* Bloomington: Indiana University Press.

Grosz-Ngate, Maria, and Omari H. Kokole, eds. 1997. *Gendered Encounters: Challenging Cultural Boundaries and Social Hierarchies in Africa.* New York: Routledge.

Hafkin, Nancy, and Edna Bay, eds. 1976. *Women in Africa: Studies in Social and Economic Change.* Stanford, Calif.: Stanford University Press.

Hansen, Karen Tranberg, ed. 1992. *African Encounters with Domesticity.* New Brunswick, N.J.: Rutgers University Press.

Hay, Margaret Jean, and Sharon Stichter, eds. 1995. *African Women South of the Sahara.* 2nd ed. London: Longman.

Hay, Margaret Jean, and Marcia Wright, eds. 1982. *African Women and the Law: Historical Perspectives.* Boston University Papers on Africa No. 7. Boston: African Studies Center, Boston University.

Hodgson, Dorothy L., and Sheryl A. McCurdy, eds. 2001. *"Wicked" Women and the Reconfiguration of Gender in Africa*. Portsmouth, N.H.: Heinemann.

Imam, Ayesha M., Amina Mama, and Fatou Sow, eds. 1997. *Engendering African Social Sciences*. Dakar: CODESRIA.

Kaplan, Flora S., ed. 1997. *Queens, Queen Mothers, Priestesses, and Power: Case Studies in African Gender*. New York: New York Academy of Social Sciences.

Lindsay, Lisa A., and Stephan F. Miescher, eds. 2003. *Men and Masculinities in Modern Africa*. Portsmouth, N.H.: Heinemann.

Mikell, Gwendolyn, ed. 1997. *African Feminisms: The Politics of Survival in Sub-Saharan Africa*. Philadelphia: University of Pennsylvania Press.

Morrell, Robert, ed. 1998. Special issue on "Masculinities in Southern African Studies." *Journal of Southern African Studies* 24, no. 4.

———. 2001. *Changing Men in Southern Africa*. London: Zed Books.

Murray, Stephen O., and Will Roscoe, eds. 1998. *Boy-Wives and Female Husbands: Studies of African Homosexualities*. New York: St. Martin's Press.

Nnaemeka, Obioma, ed. 1997. *The Politics of (M)Othering: Womanhood, Identity, and Resistance in African Literature*. London: Routledge.

———. 1998. *Sisterhood, Feminisms, and Power: From Africa to the Diaspora*. Trenton, N.J.: Africa World Press.

Ouzgane, Lahoucine, and Robert Morrell, eds. 2005. *African Masculinities: Men in Africa from the Late Nineteenth Century to the Present*. New York: Palgrave.

Oyewumi, Oyeronke, ed. 2003. *African Women and Feminism: Reflecting on the Politics of Sisterhood*. Trenton, N.J.: Africa World Press.

———. 2005. *African Gender Studies: A Reader*. New York: Palgrave.

Parpart, Jane L., and Gloria A. Nikoi, eds. 1989. *Women and Development in Africa: Comparative Perspectives*. Lanham, Md.: University Press of America.

Parpart, Jane L., and Kathleen A. Staudt, eds. 1989. *Women and the State in Africa*. Boulder, Colo.: Lynne Rienner.

Parpart, Jane L., and Sharon Stichter, eds. 1988. *Patriarchy and Class: African Women in the Home and the Workforce*. Boulder, Colo.: Westview Press.

Robertson, Claire, and Iris Berger, eds. 1986. *Women and Class in Africa*. New York: Africana Publishing Co.

Robertson, Claire, and Martin A. Klein, eds. 1983. *Women and Slavery in Africa*. Madison: University of Wisconsin Press.

Sheldon, Kathleen, ed. 1996. *Courtyards, Markets, Cities, and Streets: Urban Women in Africa*. Boulder, Colo.: Westview Press.

Works of Synthesis and Theory

Amadiume, Ifi. 1987. *Male Daughters, Female Husbands: Gender and Sex in an African Society*. London: Zed Books.

Berger, Iris, and E. Francis White. 1999. *Women in Sub-Saharan Africa: Restoring Women to History*. Bloomington: Indiana University Press.

Coquery-Vidrovitch, Catherine. 1997. *African Women: A Modern History*. Translated by Beth Raps. Boulder, Colo.: Westview Press.

Nfah-Abbenyi, Juliana M. 1997. *Gender in African Women's Writing: Identity, Sexuality, and Difference*. Bloomington: Indiana University Press.

Ogundipe-Leslie, Molara. 1994. *Recreating Ourselves: African Women & Critical Transformations*. Trenton, N.J.: Africa World Press.

Oyewumi, Oyeronke. 1997. *The Invention of Women: Making an African Sense of Western Gender Discourses.* Minneapolis: University of Minnesota Press.

Sheldon, Kathleen. 2005. *Historical Dictionary of Women in Sub-Saharan Africa.* Lanham, Md.: Scarecrow Press.

Contributors

Hussaina J. Abdullah is an independent scholar who has researched extensively on women's politics, labor, and employment relations in Nigeria.

Nwando Achebe is Associate Professor of African History at Michigan State University. She is the author of *Farmers, Traders, Warriors, and Kings: Female Power and Authority in Northern Igboland, 1900–1960* (2005) and has published on research methods, Igbo women and gender, and indigenous "slave" systems.

Susan Z. Andrade is Associate Professor in the Department of English at the University of Pittsburgh. She is co-editor of *Atlantic Cross-Currents/Transatlantiques* (2001) and author of *The Nation Writ Small: African Fictions and Feminisms, 1958–1988* (forthcoming).

Eileen Boris is the Hull Professor of Women's Studies at the University of California, Santa Barbara, and Director of the Center for Research on Women and Social Justice. She has published extensively on the racialized gendered state and is the author of *Home to Work: Motherhood and the Politics of Industrial Homework* (1994), which won the 1995 Philip Taft Prize in Labor History; *Homeworkers in Global Perspective: Invisible No More* (1996); and *Major Problems in the History of American Workers* (2nd ed., 2002).

Catherine M. Cole is Associate Director of the Interdisciplinary Humanities Center and Associate Professor of Dramatic Art, University of California, Santa Barbara. She is the author of *Ghana's Concert Party Theatre* (Indiana University Press, 2001), and co-creator of the dance theatre production *Five Foot Feat*, which toured North America in 2004.

Paulla A. Ebron is Associate Professor of Cultural and Social Anthropology at Stanford University. She is the author of *Performing Africa* (2002).

Eileen Julien is Professor of French, Comparative Literature, and African Studies at Indiana University. She is the author of "The Extroverted African Novel," published as "Il romanzo africano: un genere 'estroverso'" in *Il romanzo* (2003); and "Reading 'Orality' in French Language Novels from Sub-Saharan Africa," in *Francophone Postcolonial Studies: A Critical Introduction* (2003).

Lisa A. Lindsay is Associate Professor of History at the University of North Carolina at Chapel Hill. She is the author of *Working with Gender: Wage Labor* *and Social Change in Southwestern Nigeria* (2003) and co-editor (with Stephan F. Miescher) of *Men and Masculinities in Modern Africa* (2003).

Adrienne MacIain is a Ph.D. candidate in Dramatic Arts at the University of California, Santa Barbara. She was first introduced to West African theatre as a Fulbright Scholar studying and performing in Côte d'Ivoire, Burkina Faso, and Senegal.

Takyiwaa Manuh is a scholar-activist with training in law and anthropology. Currently she is Professor of African Studies at the University of Ghana, Legon, and serves as Director of the Institute of African Studies. Recipient of numerous awards, she has published widely about law, migration, transnationalism, and gender in Ghana, Africa, and the African diaspora.

Stephan F. Miescher is Associate Professor of History at the University of California, Santa Barbara. He is the author of *Making Men in Ghana* (Indiana University Press, 2005). He has co-edited (with Lisa A. Lindsay) *Men and Masculinities in Modern Africa* (2003) and (with Luise White and David William Cohen) *African Words, African Voices: Critical Practices in Oral History* (Indiana University Press, 2001).

Helen Nabasuta Mugambi is Associate Professor in the Department of English, Comparative Literature, and Linguistics at California State University, Fullerton. She has published on gender, song, and performance.

Bianca A. Murillo is a Ph.D. candidate in the History Department at the University of California, Santa Barbara. Her research focuses on the development of consumer culture in twentieth-century Ghana. Her dissertation explores the role of household commodities in shaping new ideas about the home, marriage, and the gendered division of labor in relation to global capitalism and national debates about modernization and progress.

Gay W. Seidman is Professor of Sociology at the University of Wisconsin-Madison. Her articles on the emergence of feminist claims during the process of democratization in South Africa have appeared in *Signs, Gender & Society,* and *Feminist Studies.* An extended version of "Institutional Dilemmas" that focused on gender in post-apartheid South Africa was published in a special issue of *Feminist Studies* (September 2004) that focused on post-apartheid South Africa.

Sylvia Tamale is Associate Professor and Dean of Law at Makerere University in Uganda. Her research interests include gender and politics, gender and sexuality, Third World women and the law, feminist legal theory and method, and the ideology of race and class. She has published widely on these topics, and has published a groundbreaking book *When Hens Begin to Crow: Gender & Parliamentary Politics in Uganda* (1999).

Bridget Teboh is Assistant Professor of History at the University of Massachusetts, Dartmouth. She is currently completing a monograph entitled *Women and Change in the Cameroon Grassfields: A Social and Economic History of Moghamoland c. 1889–1960.*

Lynn M. Thomas is Associate Professor of History and Adjunct Professor of Women Studies at the University of Washington, Seattle. She is the author of *Politics of the Womb: Women, Reproduction, and the State in Kenya* (2003).

Nana Wilson-Tagoe teaches African and Caribbean literature at the School of Oriental and African Studies, University of London. She has published *Historical Thought and Literary Representation in West Indian Literature* (1998) and is co-editor of *National Healths: Gender Sexuality and Health in a Cross-Cultural Context* (2004). She has a forthcoming book on Ghanaian writer Ama Ata Aidoo.

Index

AAWORD. *See* Association of African Women for Research and Development

ABANTU for Development, 304

Achebe, Chinua, 86–87, 205

activism, gender: Ghanaian, 131–135; representations v. actual, 6–7, 85–101; sexuality issues inclusion in, 5, 17–28, 159, 198, 200–201; teaching and research links to, 137–139. *See also* enactments, gender; gender work, Ghanaian

activism, Ghanaian: GVSSN, 132, 133–134; NETRIGHT, 132, 133; NGO gender work and, 131–135; Sisters' Keepers, 132, 133; violence coalition, 132, 134; Women's Manifesto coalition, 132, 134–135

Adéjobí, Oyin, 108, 111–115, 119

Adoma, Florence, 260

Affiliation Act (Kenya), 55

affirmative action: educational, 297; political, 11, 298

Africa Today, 206

African Gender Institute (AGI), 128, 143, 304

African gender studies: biological v. social identities in, 192–195; celebratory suppositions regarding, 7, 88, 93–95, 101n4; dialogues on field-based, 63–77; engagement with gender's role in, 293–294; gender hierarchies' relation to, 18–19, 22, 286, 294–296; postcolonialist gender perception and, 48–49, 57, 109, 153, 193–194, 205, 241–242; gender performance's relation to, 6–7, 8, 9, 85–92, 89, 171–187, 191–201, 205–219, 220n10, 223–237; gendered power expressions and, 197–200, 201; global feminist theory's relation to, 1–3, 7–8, 9, 11–12, 74–77, 141–144, 171–187, 191–201, 286–287; information resources for, 304–305, 309–311; language relevance in, 75–77, 295; motherhood's relevance to, 253, 305; multicategory identity analysis within, 85, 96, 100, 195–197, 281, 289, 298; political equity and, 297–298; "post-gender" phase of, 3, 285–298; public sphere participation's relation to, 85–101, 181–184; publishing issues regarding, 74–77; rebellion-based, 93–96; representation v. mobilization issues and,

30–45; sexuality addressed in, 2, 5, 17–28, 159, 194, 198, 200–201; sociopolitical landscape and, 292–293; theory-empirical work balance in, 143–144, 293, 306; transdisciplinary approach to, 3–4, 68, 108–109, 121. *See also* dialogue, gender study; feminism; institutions, feminist; knowledge dissemination; performance, gender; "post-gender" concept; public sphere

African National Congress (ANC), 32, 40

African Platform for Action. *See* Beijing (African) Platform for Action

African Wo/Man Palava: The Nigerian Novel by Women (Ogunyemi), 290

African Women's Development and Communications Network, 303

age: gender ideologies' association to, 180, 181, 183–184, 187, 253–265; identity's relation to, 10, 196–197, 253–265; *jali* women's socialization and, 180; market women's socialization and, 181, 183–184. *See also* elderhood

Agence France-Presse, 99

AGI. *See* African Gender Institute

Agonglo, King, 71

Agyeman-Rawlings, Nana Konadu, 130

Ahimbisibwe, Fortunate, 26

Aidoo, Ama Ata, 1, 9, 225, 304; *Anowa* by, 226–229, 236; *Changes* by, 295; literary commentary and, 207; *Our Sister Killjoy* by, 228, 231, 235–237; "post" concept and, 287

AIDS. *See* HIV/AIDS

Aina, Olabisi, 286

Akamba Stories (Mbiti), 285, 298

Akwa, D. E., 256–259

Akyeampong, Emmanuel, 259

Alamo, Christine Agnes, 24

"Algeria Unveiled" (Fanon), 224

Allan, Tuzyline Jita, 290

Allman, Jean, 200

Althusser, Louis, 175, 285

Amadiume, Ifi, 50, 153; kinship and, 196–197; motherhood paradigm and, 305; traditional gender roles theories by, 48–49, 109, 193, 205

ANC. *See* African National Congress

CLP. *See* Community Life Project

CNN, 99

The Coalition on the Women's Manifesto for Ghana, 132, 134–135

CODESRIA. *See* Council for the Development of Social Science Research in Africa

Cohen, Barney, 52

colonialism: African literature influenced by, 9, 86–87, 90, 209–213; domesticity inculcated through, 10, 66, 198–199, 241–250, 254–255; elderhood transformations due to, 254; gender perception post-, 48–49, 57, 109, 153, 193–194, 205, 241–242; literary reflections on, 86–87, 90, 209–213; marriage perceptions post-, 111, 122n4; power expression's relation to, 197–200; procreation's relation to, 48–58; public sphere's influence by, 85–86; wage labor development through, 241–250. *See also* wage labor, gendered

Community Life Project (CLP) (Nigeria), 158–159

Contemporary African Literature and the Politics of Gender (Stratton), 290

Contemporary Postcolonial Theory (Mongia), 288

Convention on the Elimination of all Forms of Discrimination against Women (CEDAW), 130, 151, 155

Cornwall, Andrea, 111, 113, 116

Council for the Development of Social Science Research in Africa (CODESRIA), 127–128, 206

Country Women's Association of Nigeria (COWAN), 153, 159–160

COWAN. *See* Country Women's Association of Nigeria

Cross of Gold (Ngcobo), 87

culture: *Anowa*'s representation of, 227–229; *Butterfly Burning*'s representation of, 229–234; dominant narratives regarding, 223–224; extension of, 234–237; fluidity of, 223, 253, 254, 289; Ghanaian theatre's popular, 10–11, 270–281; language of, 228, 230–233, 234–235; *Lániyonu*'s reflection of, 119–121; literary representations of, 113, 119–120, 223–237; *Our Sister Killjoy*'s representation of, 235–237; performativity's relation to, 224–225, 242; *Scarlet Song*'s portrayal of, 214–215, 219; *Stone Virgins*' representation of, 234–235; Yorùbá theater reflections of, 113, 119–120, 273–274. *See also* ethnography; literature, African; theatre, Ghanaian; theatre, Nigerian

Culture and Society (Williams), 95

d'Almeida, Irene A., 292

Dangarembga, Tsitsi, 89

Davies, Carole Boyce, 228, 287, 290

Davis, Natalie Zemon, 96

de Beauvoir, Simone, 175

de Lauretis, Teresa, 285, 292

Death and the King's Horseman (Soyinka), 9, 215; acts of, 209–210; gender-based nationalism within, 208–213, 219; masculinity representations in, 210, 212–213, 219

Decade for Women (UN), 8, 127, 150

dialogue, gender study: African historian-related, 65–68; African identity–based, 63–65; Igbo field research, 69–74, 77; Moghamo field research, 68–69, 76, 77; writing and publishing, 72–77

Dimitra project, 304

domestic sphere: colonialism's influence on, 10, 66, 198–199, 241–250, 254–255; nationalism's relation to, 85, 88–90; public sphere's relation to, 85, 88–90; wage labor structure and, 241–250. *See also* wage labor, gendered

domestic violence, 297; legislation regarding, 132, 134; Rwandan genocide and, 11; statistics on, 296; theatrical portrayal of, 271–272

Domestic Violence Bill (Ghana), 134

Doran, D'arcy, 99–100

Duke, E. E., 245

economic empowerment, 159–161

Ecweru, Musa, 26–27

education: affirmative action in, 297; female v. male, 88, 245; gender studies in higher, 128–129, 145n9; gender transformations through, 5, 6; misogyny in, 304; pregnancy's relation to, 52–58; prostitution's relation to, 54–58; research and activism's link to, 137–139

Efuru (Nwapa), 89

Ekwensi, Cyprian, 87

elderhood: community service's tie to, 259–264; district assembly forums for, 262–263; female authority in, 254, 256, 264–265; gender's relation to seniority and, 10, 253–265; masculinity constructions tied to, 253–259, 263–264; migration's relation to, 259–260; *ɔpanyin*'s connection to, 255–256; stages leading to, 254, 255–256

Electoral Reform Network (Nigeria), 164

Emecheta, Buchi, 89

enactments, gender: *Anowa*, 226, 227–229; *Butterfly Burning*, 226, 229–234, 235; ChevronTexaco case study on, 97–101; *Death and the King's Horseman*, 208–213,

215, 219; ethnographic interview representations of, 8, 178–181; film, 173–174, 181–
184; literary representations of, 6–7, 8, 9,
85–92, 96–97, 205–219, 220n10, 223–237;
nationalism explored through literary, 9, 85–
92, 96–97, 205–219, 223–237; *Our Sister Killjoy,* 235–237; political, 6–7, 85–86, 91–101;
public sphere, 6–7, 85–86, 92–100, 181–184;
Scarlet Song, 213–219; *The Stone Virgins,*
234–235. *See also* activism, gender; nationalism; performance, gender
L'Enfant noir (Laye), 86
Engendering African Social Sciences, 127
Epprecht, Marc, 198
Equal Opportunities Commission (Uganda),
5; homosexuality addressed by, 17, 21–28
ethnicity: feminist representations and, 1–2,
36–37, 45, 45n5; identity's relation to, 45,
85, 96, 100, 195, 196–197; *Scarlet Song's*
portrayal of, 214–215, 219; social changes'
relation to, 86, 97–101
ethnography: developmental theory genre of,
171–173, 184–187; film genre of, 173–174,
181–184; interview genre of, 8, 178–181;
performance and performativity in, 174–177
L'Ex-père de la nation (Fall), 87

Fall, Aminata Sow, 87
Fanon, Frantz, 9, 76, 86, 223–225, 229
*Farmers, Traders, Warriors and Kings: Female
Power and Authority in Northern Igboland*
(Nwando Achebe), 73
Faye, Safi, 172–174, 177
Feldman-Savelsberg, Pamela, 52
Female Novelists of Modern Africa (Taiwo), 290
feminism: African v. global theory on, 1–3, 7–
8, 9, 11–12, 74–77, 141–144, 171–187, 191–
201, 286–287; antisacrificial current in, 232;
celebratory suppositions within, 7, 88, 93–
95, 101n4; ethnicity's relation to, 1–2, 36–
37, 45, 45n5; ideological interpretation of,
1–2, 11, 37–40, 41–44; mobilization issues
within, 40–45, 286; mono-sex v. dual-sex
system of, 195, 304; representation v. mobilization issue within, 30–45. *See also* institutions, feminist; theory, feminist
Feminist Africa, 143, 304–306
"Femme noire" (Senghor), 215
FEMNET, 303–304
femocrats, 32
FIDA-Ghana, 132
films, ethnographic, 173–174, 181–184
Financial Times, 99

Fourth World Conference on Women (Bei-
jing), 144, 151, 162, 293
Frank and Candy organization, 21
Frankenberg, Ruth, 288
Fraser, Nancy, 86, 90–92, 96, 100
Freedom and Roam Uganda organization, 21

GADA. *See* Gender and Development Action
GALA. *See* Gays and Lesbians Alliance
Gambia, 178–181, 184–186
Gay Uganda organization, 21
Gays and Lesbians Alliance (GALA)
(Uganda), 18, 20–21
gender: age status's relation to, 180, 181, 183–
184, 187, 253–265; class status's relation to,
179–180, 181–182, 183, 187; *Death and the
King's Horseman's* representations of, 208–
213, 219; enactments, actual of, 6–7, 8, 91–
101, 173–174, 178–184, 191–201; enactments, literary of, 6–7, 8, 9, 85–92, 205–219,
220n10, 223–237; fluidity of, 223–224, 253,
254, 289, 291; Ghanaian theater representations of, 10–11, 270–281; hierarchies
within, 18–19, 22, 286, 294–296; identity
intersectionality and, 85, 96, 100, 195–197,
281, 289, 298; institutionalization of African, 127–131; nationalism enactments' relation to, 6–7, 9, 85–101, 205–219, 223–237;
power expression's relation to, 197–200,
201; public sphere's relation to, 85–86, 90–
91; *Scarlet Song's* representations of, 213–
219; seniority's relation to, 10, 253–265;
sexuality's relation to, 18–19, 22, 194, 200–
201; social transformation's influence on,
5–6, 289; social v. biological aspects of,
192–195; Yorùbá theater representations
of, 7, 108–121, 122n4, 123n18, 253. *See also*
age; enactments, gender; gender studies;
literature, African; nationalism; theatre,
Ghanaian; theatre, Nigerian
Gender and Development Action (GADA)
(Nigeria), 160, 161–162
Gender and Women's Studies for Africa's
Transformation Project (GWS Africa Project), 128, 304
*Gender in African Women's Writing: Identity,
Sexuality and Difference* (Nfah-Abbenyi),
290
gender studies: celebratory suppositions in, 7,
88, 93–95, 101n4; global variations in, 1–3,
7–8, 9, 11–12, 74–77, 141–144, 171–187,
191–201, 286–287; multi-category identity
analysis within, 85, 96, 100, 195–197, 281,

289, 298; "post" concept in evolution of, 3, 285–298; sexuality inclusion in, 2, 5, 17–28, 159, 194, 198, 200–201; theory-empirical work balance in, 143–144, 293, 306; transdisciplinary approach to, 3–4, 68, 108–109, 121. *See also* African gender studies; feminism

Gender Studies and Human Rights Documentation Centre, 132

Gender Trouble (Butler), 175

Gender Views (Nigeria), 157

Gender Violence Survivors' Support Network (GVSSN) (Ghana), 132, 133–134

gender work, Ghanaian, 125; activism and, 131–135; autonomy for, 136; gender concept's relation to, 136–137; gender institutionalization and, 127–131; motivations for, 136–137; survey regarding, 135–144; teaching's link to activism and, 137–139; theory's place within, 139–144; women's v. men's participation in, 126. *See also* survey, gender work (Ghana); theory, feminist

The Generation of Plays (Barber), 110–111, 118, 119

genital cutting: circumcision, 196, 294; clitoridectomy, 51, 52, 74, 164, 165, 199, 294

Ghana: activism within, 131–135; affirmative action taken in, 129; *Anowa* setting in, 227–229, 236; class division's influence on, 7–8; economic history of, 254–255; elderhood practices in, 253–265; gender institutionalization within, 129–131; gender performance studies in, 172, 181–184; gender survey in, 135–144; gender work within, 125–144; literary gender representations in, 226–229, 235–237; *Our Sister Killjoy* setting in, 235–237; theatrical gender representations in, 10–11, 270–281; university gender studies in, 128–129. *See also* activism, Ghanaian; elderhood; gender work, Ghanaian; theatre, Ghanaian

Ghana Association for the Welfare of Women, 132

Ghana Poverty Reduction Strategy, 133

Ghanaian Times, 263

Gikandi, Simon, 87

Gilbert, Sandra M., 95

Giles-Vernick, Tamara, 198

Global Pan-African Movement, 25

The Graduate (Ogot), 90

Graves, Anne Adams, 290

Gray, Leslie, 194

The Guardian, 100

Gubar, Susan, 95

GVSSN. *See* Gender Violence Survivors' Support Network

GWS Africa Project. *See* Gender and Women's Studies for Africa's Transformation Project

Habermas, Jürgen, 85–86, 90–92

Haegele, Eugen, 261

Halberstam, Judith, 193

Hall, Stuart, 289

Harlow, Barbara, 87

Harrow, Kenneth W., 290–291

Hausa society, 66

Heald, Suzette, 289

Hena Bedi M'ade? (Who Will Be My Heir?), 277; identity intersectionality in, 281; inheritance theme in, 278–280, 281

Herbert, Eugenia W., 193–194

Hill, Christopher, 96

HIV/AIDS, 286; activism regarding, 128; Nigeria and, 159; prevention education on, 303; prostitution's relation to, 54–55; South Africa and, 39, 41, 44; Uganda and, 22, 26

Hobsbawm, Eric, 96

Hodgson, Dorothy L., 196, 199

homosexuality: historical occurrences of, 17–18; South African discourse on, 198; Ugandan discourse on, 5, 17–28, 28n1

Hove, Chenjerai, 89

How to Do Things with Words (Austin), 176

human rights: BAOBAB for, 154–155; Nigerian NGOs' themes on, 153–157; WLDC for, 156–157; women's justice program on, 155–156

Hunt, Nancy Rose, 48, 50, 66; feminist historiography by, 93–96, 97; power expressions and, 198

Hunter, Eva, 235

Hunter, Mark, 54

Hutchful, Ebo, 128

ICTs. *See* information and communications technologies

identity: age's relation to, 10, 196–197, 253–265; *Anowa*'s representation of, 227–229; biological v. social formation of, 192–195; *Butterfly Burning*'s representation of, 229–234; Christianity's role in shaping of, 71, 256–259, 260–262, 264–265; class and, 7–8, 85–86, 90–91, 96, 100, 179–180, 181–182, 183, 187, 196–197; dialogue on African, 63–65; dialogue on African researcher's, 65–68; dominant narratives regarding, 223–224;

in, 113, 119–120, 223–237; *Death and the King's Horseman* in, 9, 208–213, 215, 219; dominant narratives in, 223–224; female v. male, 87–90, 207–208; gender performance within, 6–7, 8, 9, 85–92, 205–219, 220n10, 223–237; gender's role in shaping of, 205–219; language and narrative expectations in, 225, 295; masculinity portrayals in, 212–213, 225–229, 234–235; nationalism discourse in, 6–7, 85–92, 96–97; nationalism enactments in, 9, 85–92, 96–97, 205–219, 223–237; novel's history in, 86; periodization of, 207; *Scarlet Song* in, 9, 89, 208–209, 213–219, 220n10; women's political participation in, 6–7, 85–92; worldview monopolies within, 74–77. *See also* culture; identity

Lonsdale, John, 54

Loomba, Ania, 288

Loti, Pierre, 218

Lovedu society, 195

Luswata, Mark, 25

Maasai society, 196, 199

The Madwoman in the Attic (Gilbert and Gubar), 95

Mafabi, David, 25

Magazu, Bariya, 163

Magona, Sindiwe, 50

"Makerere Don Defends Gays," 17; public commentary on, 22–28

Makerere University, Uganda, 128, 297

Mama, Amina, 127, 304

Mandela, Nelson, 30, 295

Mandinka *jalis* (praise singers), 178–181

Mani, Lata, 288

Maritime Trade Union Federation (Nigeria), 247–248

market women: domestic role of, 182–183; public role of, 181–182, 183–184

marriage: performance's relation to, 182–183; polygamy issues in, 38–39; postcolonialist perceptions of, 111, 122n4; pregnancy's relation to, 51–52, 56; wage labor ideals in, 243–245, 249; woman-to-woman, 194, 197; Yorùbá theater depiction of, 109–113, 122n4. *See also* pregnancies, schoolgirl

Marxism, 48, 88, 94, 95

masculinity, 2, 113; *Anowa* representation of, 227–229; *Death and the King's Horseman's* representations of, 210, 212–213, 219; elderhood and seniority's relation to, 253–259, 263–264; fatherhood's tie to, 255; female, 193, 254; literary portrayals of, 212–213,

225–229, 234–235; multiple constructions of, 253, 255, 256–259, 262; nationalism representations through, 208, 210, 212–213, 215, 217, 219; power expression's relation to, 197–200, 201; Presbyterian ideals of, 262; *Scarlet Song* representations of, 215, 217, 219; scholarship on, 289–290; sexual difference's tie to, 192–195; South African studies on, 36; *The Stone Virgins'* representation of, 234–235; violence's link to, 304; wage labor's tie to, 10, 241–248

Matembe, Miria, 297

Mbiti, John S., 285

Mbuti society, 195

McClintock, Anne, 224

Mensah, E. T., 274

Meru society, 51–52, 56

Mikell, Gwendolyn, 49, 50

Milne, Claudia, 181

Ministry of Gender, Labor, and Social Services (Uganda), 292

Ministry of Women's and Children's Affairs (Ghana), 131

misogyny: domestic violence and, 11, 132, 134, 271–272, 296; educational, 304; theatrical representations of, 10–11, 271–274, 280

Mkandawire, Thandika, 128

Mmaa Nkomo (television program), 135

Modern Girl Research Group (U.S.), 50

Moghamo society, 78n8; field research on, 65, 68–69, 76, 77

Mohanty, Chandra, 95

Mongia, Padmini, 288

Moore, Gerald, 86

Morrell, Robert, 289

Mother to Mother (Magona), 50

motherhood, 253, 305

Mpiemu society, 198

Mpondo society, 195

Mtintso, Thenjiwe, 34

Mukasa, Sarah, 26

Museveni, Yoweri, 23, 295

Musisi, Nakanyinke, 66

Mwanga, King, 19

Mwangi, Meja, 50

Mwenda, Andrew, 24–25

Naigaga, Wandira, 271, 295–296

Nairobi Forward-looking Strategies, 130, 151

Nandi society, 52

National Coalition on Domestic Violence Legislation (Ghana), 132, 134

National Coalition on Violence Against Women (Nigeria), 163

National Council on Women and Development (NCWD) (Ghana), 130, 131–132
National Policy on Women (Nigeria), 164
nationalism: *Anowa*'s representation of, 227–229; *Butterfly Burning*'s representation of, 229–234; *Death and the King's Horseman*'s representations of, 208–213, 219; discourse, literary on, 6–7, 85–92, 96–97; domestic sphere's relation to, 85, 88–90; dominant narratives regarding, 223–224; enactments, actual of, 6–7, 91–101; enactments, literary of, 9, 85–92, 96–97, 205–219, 223–237; feminine representations of, 208, 210–213, 215–219; masculine representations of, 208, 210, 212–213, 215, 217, 219; *Our Sister Killjoy*'s representation of, 235–237; performativity's relation to, 224–225; public sphere's relation to, 85–101; rebellion studies and, 93–96, 102n10; *Scarlet Song*'s representations of, 208–209, 215–219; *Stone Virgins*' representation of, 234–235; women writers' portrayal of, 9, 85–92, 96–97, 208–209, 215–219, 220n10, 225–237. *See also* enactments, gender; public sphere
NCWD. *See* National Council on Women and Development (Ghana)
Ndetei, Agnes, 296
Nehanda (Vera), 226
Nervous Conditions (Dangarembga), 89
NETRIGHT. *See* Network for Women's Rights (Ghana)
Network for Women's Rights (NETRIGHT) (Ghana), 132, 133
New Vision commentaries, 22–28
Nfah-Abbenyi, Juliana M., 290
Ngambika: Studies of Women in African Literature (Davies and Graves), 290
Ngcobo, Lauretta, 87
NGOs. *See* nongovernmental organizations
Ngunjiri, Philip, 288
Nicholson, Linda, 192
Nigeria: Biafran War in, 7, 68, 120; Chevron-Texaco protest in, 97–101, 103n19; class division's influence on, 7–8; Igbo Women's War in, 92–93, 97; male breadwinner ideal in, 241–250; marriage perceptions in, 111–113, 122n4; masculinity perceptions in, 10, 113; political climate in, 150; university gender studies in, 128; post-1990 women's organizations in, 150–166; Yorùbá popular theater in, 7, 108–121, 122n4, 123n18, 253, 273–274. *See also* Nigerian organizations, women's; Yorùbá popular theater (Nigeria)

Nigerian National Archives, 67–68
Nigerian organizations, women's, 166; challenges to, 165; economic empowerment theme in, 159–161; international influence on, 150–152; 1990s era, 152–153; political empowerment theme in, 161–165; reproductive health and rights theme in, 157–159; women's human rights theme in, 153–157
Njambi, Wairmu Ngaruiya, 194
Nnaemeka, Obioma, 1, 286, 290
nongovernmental organizations (NGOs): activism influenced by, 7–8; economic empowerment-based, 159–161; evolution of African, 131, 132; gender study influenced by, 2, 4; Ghanaian gender work by, 131–135; human rights–based, 153–157; Nigerian, 150, 153–166; political empowerment-based, 161–165; reproductive health–based, 157–159; survey perspectives from members of, 136–137, 138–139
Nugent, Paul, 263
Nwapa, Flora, 89
Nzegwu, Nkiru, 195, 286, 305

Obayi, Lady, 71
Obbo, Christine, 208
Obeng, Pashington, 256
O'Brien, William E., 194
Odúnjo, J. F., 112
Oduyoye, Mercy Amba, 262
Ogoni Nine, 99
Ogot, Grace, 89–90
Ògúndíjo, Báyò, 109
Ogundipe-Leslie, Molara, 200, 224–225, 232, 290
Ogunleye, Bisi, 161
Ogunyemi, Chikwenye Okonjo, 290, 291
Okome, Mojubaolu, 305
Okra, Joseph, 261
Olakunle, George, 213
Olukoshi, Adebayo, 128
100 Women Working Group (Nigeria), 160–161
Onipa Hia Moa (People Need Help), 271–273, 280
Opoku, Yaw, 260
Oppong, Adom, 277
Opusuo, E. F., 255, 262–263
Oread Daily, 99
Osindero, J. Marcus, 246
Our Sister Killjoy (Aidoo), 228, 231, 235–237
Owusu, Maxwell, 262
Oyewumi, Oyeronke, 50, 305; gender inven-

tion theories by, 48–49, 57, 109, 193–194, 205, 241–242, 286; identity contexts and, 253, 281; kinship perspectives of, 196
Oyono, Ferdinand, 86

The Palm-Wine Drinkard (Tutuola), 87
ɔpanyin (elder): expectations of, 254, 256–259, 261, 264; meaning of, 255; permanence of, 255; process of becoming, 259–264; signifying factors of, 197
Pare tax riots (Tanzania), 92
Le pauvre Christ de Bomba (Beti), 86
People of the City (Ekwensi), 87
Pereira, Charmaine, 128, 304
performance, gender, 171; audience's role in relation to, 172–173; biological v. social identity and, 192–195; ethnographic texts' relation to, 184–187; film observation of, 173–174, 181–184; identity intersectionality's relation to, 195–197; interviews as observations of, 8, 178–181; literary observations of, 6–7, 8, 9, 85–92, 205–219, 220n10, 223–237; performativity v., 174–177; power expression's relation to, 197–200, 201; real v. constructed, 173–174; theories interpreting, 174–175. *See also* enactments, gender
performativity, 224–225, 242; performance v., 174–177; researchers' relation to, 186
Piliso-Seroke, Joyce, 34
PNDC. *See* Provisional National Defense Council (Ghana)
A Political Agenda for Nigerian Women, 162
politics: empowerment challenges in, 165; empowerment of Nigerian women in, 161–165; impact of women in, 297–298; national agenda strategies regarding, 162–164; NGO themes on, 161–165; women's enacted participation in, 6–7, 85–86, 91–101, 297–298; women's literary participation in, 6–7, 85–92
Politics of the Womb: Women, Reproduction, and the State in Kenya (Thomas), 49
The Politics of (M)Othering: Womanhood, Identity, and Resistance in African Literature (Nnaemeka), 290
Postal Workers Union (Nigeria), 245
"post-gender" concept, 3, 285–286; debate on meaning of, 287–288; domestic violence's relation to, 296–297; gender engagements' relation to, 293–294; gender hierarchies and, 294–296; ongoing gender study v., 289–293; political equity and, 297–298
pregnancies, schoolgirl, 5, 6; colonialism's rela-

tion to, 50–58; fiancée pregnancies and, 56; initiation rituals' relation to, 51–53; laws regarding, 55, 59n22; prostitution and, 54–56; repercussions of, 50, 51
Presbyterian Church, 259–262
procreation: colonialism's relation to ideologies of, 48–58; gender study occlusion of, 48–49; Igbo women's manipulation of, 73–74; schoolgirl, 5, 6, 50–58, 59n22. *See also* pregnancies, schoolgirl; reproductive rights
The Promised Land (Ogot), 89
prostitution: defining aspects of, 54–56; HIV/AIDS relation to, 54–55; schoolgirl pregnancies' relation to, 54–56; sexuality's relation to, 41; South African discourse on, 41–42, 45n5
Protection of Women's Rights in Religious, Customary and Statutory Laws (Nigeria), 164
Provisional National Defense Council (PNDC) (Ghana), 130, 145n14, 262
PRP group (Nigeria), 152
public sphere: bourgeois aspects of, 97; class's relation to, 85–86, 90–91; domestic sphere's relation to, 85, 88–90; gender enactments within, 6–7, 85–86, 92–100, 181–184; market women's relation to, 181–184; nationalism's relation to, 85–101; rebellion studies and, 93–96; subaltern counterpublics within, 86, 90–91, 96, 100, 102n10; women's rioting contributions in, 85–86, 91–101; women's writing contributions in, 85–92, 96–97
Puja, Grace Khwaya, 55

Quainoo, Margaret, 277
queer theory, 193–194, 200
Quinquennial International Women's Studies Conference, 297

race. *See* ethnicity
Radhakrishnan, R., 207, 210
Rawlings, J. J., 262
Recreating Ourselves: African Women and Critical Transformations (Ogundipe-Leslie), 290
Representation of the People Act (Ghana), 129
reproductive rights: Nigeria NGOs for, 157–159; sexuality addressed in, 159; STDs and, 158, 159. *See also* procreation
Research in African Literatures, 290
Resistance Literature (Harlow), 87
resources, gender study: edited collection, 309–310; online, 304–305; review essay, 309; synthesis and theory, 310–311

teaching. *See* education

Technologies of Gender (de Lauretis), 285

Thawite, John, 27

theatre, Ghanaian: cultural reflections in, 273–274; domestic violence representations in, 271–272; female representations in, 272, 274–277; gender representations in, 10–11, 270–281; *Hena Bedi M'ade?* play in, 277–280, 281; male portrayal of females in, 274, 277; misogyny in, 271–274; *Onipa Hia Moa*, 271–273, 280; orphan girl archetype in, 275–276, 280; period-specific gender roles in, 272; schoolgirl archetype in, 274–276, 280; *Schoolgirl* play in, 275; widow archetype in, 276–277, 280; women's leadership of, 277–278

theatre, Nigerian: cultural reflections in, 113, 119–120, 273–274; gender representations in, 7, 108–121, 122n4, 123n18, 253; *Kúyè* play in, 108, 111, 112–115, 116, 118; *Lániyonu* play in, 7, 109, 112, 116–121, 123n18; misogyny in, 10–11, 273–274, 280; opening glees in, 110–112; *The Road to Riches* play in, 109, 111, 112, 115–116, 118; stigmas associated with, 122n4; Yorùbá, 7, 108–121, 122n4, 123n18, 253, 273–274

theory, feminist: African studies' relation to global, 1–3, 7–8, 9, 11–12, 74–77, 141–144, 171–187, 191–201, 286–287; empirical work balanced with, 143–144, 293, 306; ethnography's relation to, 171–173, 184–187; gender work survey regarding, 135, 139–144; Ghana gender work's use of, 135, 139–141; "post-gender" concept and, 287–288; publications on, 310–311. *See also* African gender studies; feminism; gender studies

theory, queer, 193–194, 200

Things Fall Apart (Chinua Achebe), 86–87

31st December Women's Movement, 130, 131–132, 263

Thompson, E. P., 95–96

trade unions, 242, 243; women's marginalization by, 245–248, 249; women's representation by, 247–248, 249

Trades Union Congress, 132, 245

Tsikata, Edzodzinam, 130

Tswana society, 52

Tungar, Safiya Hussani, 163

Tutuola, Amos, 87

Uganda, 271; affirmative action policies within, 11; gender development agencies in, 292; homosexual rights in, 5, 17–28, 28n1; political gender equity in, 297; sexuality laws in, 19, 21, 22, 27, 28n1; women's movement in, 21–22, 134

Uganda Human Rights Commission, 25

Ugbabe, Ahebi, 194

"Under Western Eyes" (Mohanty), 95

United Nations: Decade for Women by, 8, 127, 150; gender-based activism influenced by, 7–8, 129, 150–151, 165

United Nations Development Program, 292

Universal Declaration of Human Rights, 155

University of Buea, Cameroon, 128

University of Cape Town, South Africa, 128

University of Ghana, 129

University of Zambia, 128

Vaid, Sudesh, 207

van der Geest, Sjaak, 255–256

Vera, Yvonne, 9, 225, 227, 304; *Butterfly Burning* by, 226, 229–234, 235; *Nehanda* by, 226; *The Stone Virgins* by, 234–235

Vidal, John, 100

Une vie de boy (Oyono), 86

"Violence Against Women" (BAOBAB), 154

WAAD. *See* Women in Africa and the African Diaspora

wage labor, gendered: discourse v. practice of, 242, 249–250; female earnings marginalization and, 244, 245–248, 249; government policy regarding, 246; marital ideals associated with, 243–245, 249; masculinity's relation to, 10, 241–248; state-based arguments regarding, 243–244, 249; trade unions' relation to, 242–243, 245–248, 249

Wahyee, J. A., 259

Walakira, Geoffrey, 23

West African Pilot, 246, 248

White, Luise, 54, 200

WHON. *See* Women's Health Organisation of Nigeria

WID. *See* women in development

Wiegman, Robyn, 192

Wilentz, Gay, 236

Wilks, Ivor, 254

Williams, Raymond, 95

WIN. *See* Women in Nigeria

WJP. *See* Women's Justice Program (Nigeria)

WLDC. *See* Women, Law and Development Centre (Nigeria)

Womanifesto (Nigeria), 164

Womanism and African Consciousness (Kolowale), 290